THE LAST PRUSSIAN

A Biography of Field Marshal Gerd von Rundstedt
1875-1953

General Field Marshal Gerd von Rundstedt.

THE
LAST PRUSSIAN

A Biography of
Field Marshal Gerd von Rundstedt
1875-1953

CHARLES MESSENGER

BRASSEY'S (UK)

(Member of the Maxwell Macmillan Pergamon Publishing Corporation)

LONDON · OXFORD · WASHINGTON · NEW YORK · BEIJING
FRANKFURT · SÃO PAULO · SYDNEY · TOKYO · TORONTO

First edition 1991

UK editorial offices: Brassey's, 50 Fetter Lane, London EC4A 1AA

orders: Brassey's, Headington Hill Hall, Oxford OX3 0BW

USA editorial offices: Brassey's, 8000 Westpark Drive, First Floor, McLean, Virginia 22102

orders: Macmillan, Front and Brown Streets, Riverside, New Jersey 08075

Distributed in North America to booksellers and wholesalers by the Macmillan Publishing Company, N.Y., N.Y.

Library of Congress Cataloging-in-Publication Data
Messenger, Charles, 1941-
The last Prussian: a biography of Field Marshal Gerd von Rundstedt, 1875–1953/Charles Messenger.—1st ed.
p. cm.
Includes bibliographical references and index.
1. Rundstedt, Gerd von,––1875–1953. 2. World War, 1939–1945––
Germany. 3. Germany––Armed Forces––History––20th century.
4. Marshals––Germany––Biography. 5. Germany––Armed Forces––
Biography. I. Title.
DD247.R8M47   1991
940.54′1343′092––dc20 [B]   90-27026

British Library Cataloguing in Publication Data
Messenger, Charles 1941–
The last Prussian: a biography of Field Marshal Gerd von Rundstedt 1875–1953.
1. World war 1 & 2. Military operations
I. Title
940.40943

ISBN 0-08-036707-0

Printed in Great Britain by B.P.C.C. Wheatons Ltd, Exeter

Contents

LIST OF PLATES		vi
LIST OF MAPS		ix
CHRONOLOGY		x
Introduction		xiii
1.	Early Life	1
2.	The First World War	21
3.	The Weimar Years	39
4.	Enter Hitler	59
5.	Poland	81
6.	Assault in the West	96
7.	Invasion Talk	123
8.	Russia 1941	139
9.	Return to France	158
10.	Normandy and the Bomb Plot	185
11.	Recalled Once More	203
12.	The Last Battles	218
13.	Prisoner of War	232
14.	War Criminal	258
15.	The Twilight Years	292
16.	The Reckoning	307
APPENDIX ONE THE VON RUNDSTEDT FAMILY TREE		322
APPENDIX TWO DECORATIONS AWARDED TO GERD VON RUNDSTEDT		323
SOURCE NOTES		325
SELECT BIBLIOGRAPHY		351
INDEX		355

LIST OF PLATES

(Unless otherwise indicated, all are from the von Rundstedt Archive)

(Frontispiece) General Field Marshal Gerd von Rundstedt

1. The young Gerd with his father and brothers Joachim and Udo
2. The Cadets – Udo, Gerd, Joachim and Eberhard at Oranienstein
3. Lieutenant and Regimental Adjutant
4. Gerd and Bila on their wedding day
5. Hans Gerd and Bila, Kassel 1911 *(Barbara Papanastassiou)*
6. German artillery passing through Brussels, August 1914 *(IWM)*
7. The Narew battlefield, July 1915 *(IWM)*
8. General von Beseler with Graf Slepycki *(IWM)*
9. Eastern Front 1918 – Russian and German troops fraternising
10. A cavalryman at heart – umpiring manoeuvres, Bavaria, 1926
11. Reviewing the 2nd Cavalry Division, Breslau, 1929
12. Gerd, Bila and Hans Gerd, Berlin, Spring 1932
13. Von Rundstedt, von Hammerstein-Equord and von Hindenburg, 1933
14. Von Rundstedt, von Fritsch and von Kluge, 1935
15. Raeder, von Blomberg, Hitler, Goering and von Rundstedt on Hitler's 47th birthday
16. With Hitler during the *Gruppenkommando 2* autumn manoeuvres 1936
17. Grim-faced, von Rundstedt takes the salute at Breslau, 28 September 1938
18. Poland, September 1939 – German infantry on the march *(IWM)*
19. Polish prisoners after the reduction of the Kutno pocket *(IWM)*
20. Polish Jews being questioned by an SS officer, 5 September 1939
21. France, May 1940 – elements of Rommel's 7th Panzer Division
22. The Dunkirk pocket – British and French prisoners, 27 May 1940 *(IWM)*
23. Preparations for SEALION *(IWM)*

24. Visiting the 18th Infantry Regiment, Winter 1940–41
25. Russia – a Rumanian artillery unit crosses the River Pruth, September 1941 (*IWM*)
26. Autumn rains in the Ukraine (*IWM*)
27. Russia – the first snows. Vehicles waiting to cross the Dnieper by ferry (*IWM*)
28. German troops fight their way into Rostov-on-Don, November 1941 (*IWM*)
29. Dieppe, August 1942 (*IWM*)
30. Von Rundstedt visits Seyss-Inquart, Reichs Commissioner for the Netherlands, July 1943
31. Inspecting the Atlantic defences in the La Rochelle area, August 1943
32. Von Rundstedt in April 1944
33. Tea with Guderian at St Germain, 1 May 1944
34. A visit to Marshal Pétain
35. Von Rundstedt and Blumentritt say farewell to Rommel. La Roche Guyon
36. Von Rundstedt with General Vercellino, Toulon, early 1944
37. Von Rundstedt with von Sodenstern, commanding Nineteenth Army, in southern France
38. Sepp Dietrich points out his dispositions to C-in-C West
39. The beginning of the end – Allied troops coming ashore, Normandy, 6 June 1944 (*IWM*)
40. September 1944 – von Rundstedt with Hans Gerd and Blumentritt on reassuming as C-in-C West
41. Planning conference for the Ardennes counter-offensive
42. Speer visits von Rundstedt on the eve of WATCH ON THE RHINE
43. The last flourish in the West fails (*IWM*)
44. February 1945, von Rundstedt with Schlemm, commander First Parachute Army
45. German prisoners at Remagen Bridge, March 1945 (*IWM*)
46. Hans Gerd and Gerd with Major General Frank W Milburn, commander XXI US Corps, shortly after their capture
47. Wiesbaden, June 1945
48. Arrival at Island Farm Camp, January 1946 (*Dr Tom Jefferson*)
49. At Bridgend railway station on return from Nuremburg, August 1946 (*Philip Davies*)
50. At Nordstadt Hospital, Hannover, after the Field Marshal's release in 1949

51. Von Rundstedt's grandsons, Gerd and Eberhard, with his ceremonial baton on the day of his death
52. The Last Salute. Hannover-Stöcken, 28 February 1953

SYMBOLS

The formation symbols shown below have been used in this book. Where special symbols have been needed, these are shown in the Key to the appropriate map.

German formations   Division

Allied formations   Infantry

Army Group   Armoured

Soviet Front   Panzer Grenadier

Army   Parachute

LIST OF MAPS

MAP 1. Imperial German Corps Boundaries up until November
        1918.   23

MAP 2. Battle of the Marne.   29

MAP 3. The Eastern Front 1915–1917.   35

MAP 4. Wehrkreis Boundaries 1921–1935.   45

MAP 5. Wehrkreis Boundaries 1939.   74

MAP 6. Poland, 17 September 1939.   88/89

MAP 7. The Drive to the Channel, May 1940.   114

MAP 8. Russia, 1941.   142

MAP 9. German Dispositions in the West, 6 June 1944.   187

MAP 10. The West, September–December 1944.   220

Gerd von Rundstedt Chronology

12 December 1875	Born, Aschersleben
1 April 1888	Entered junior cadet college at Oranienstein
Spring 1890	Entered higher cadet college at Lichterfelde
22 March 1892	Appointed *Portepee Fähnrich* in 83rd Infantry Regiment, Kassel
17 June 1893	Commissioned Lieutenant, 83rd Infantry Regiment
1 October 1896	Adjutant, 3rd Battalion 83rd Infantry Regiment, Arolsen
1 October 1900	Adjutant, 83rd Infantry Regiment, Kassel
1 October 1901	Promoted Senior Lieutenant (*Oberleutnant*)
22 January 1902	Married Luise (Bila) von Goetz
21 January 1903	Hans Gerd born
1 October 1903	Student *Kriegsakademie*, Berlin
1 April 1907	Attached *Grosse Generalstab*, Berlin
24 March 1909	Promoted Captain on the *Grosse Generalstab*
1 October 1910	HQ XI Corps, Kassel
1 October 1912	Company commander 171st Infantry Regiment, Colmar
30 July 1914	Chief of Operations (1a), HQ 22nd Reserve Division, Western Front
Autumn 1914	Fell sick
28 November 1914	Promoted Major
1 December 1914	Military Government, Antwerp
1 April 1915	Chief of Staff, 86th Infantry Division, Eastern Front
July 1915	Fell sick

5 September 1915	Chief of Administration and Logistics (1b), Military Government, Warsaw
1 November 1916	Chief of Operations HQ XXV Reserve Corps, Eastern Front
1 October 1917	Chief of Staff HQ LIII Corps, Eastern Front
1 August 1918	Chief of Staff XV Corps, Western Front
December 1918	*Grosse Generalstab*
1 October 1919	HQ *Wehrkreis V*, Stuttgart
1 May 1920	Chief of Staff HQ 3rd Cavalry Division, Weimar
1 October 1920	Promoted Lieutenant Colonel
1 March 1923	Promoted Colonel
1 October 1923	Chief of Staff *Wehrkreis II* and HQ 2nd Infantry Division, Stettin
1 May 1925	Commander 18th Infantry Regiment, Paderborn
1 October 1926	Chief of Staff *Gruppenkommando 2*, Kassel
1 November 1927	Promoted Major General
1 October 1928	Commander 2nd Cavalry Division, Breslau
1 March 1929	Promoted Lieutenant General
1 February 1932	Commander *Wehrkreis III*, Berlin
1 October 1932	Promoted General of Infantry and Commander-in-Chief *Gruppenkommando 1*, Berlin
1 March 1938	Promoted Colonel General
1 November 1938	Retired and appointed Colonel 18th Infantry Regiment
May 1939	Appointed to head *Arbeitstab von Rundstedt*
23 August 1939	Commander-in-Chief Army Group South, Eastern Front
1 October 1939	Commander-in-Chief East
25 October 1939	Commander-in-Chief Army Group A, Western Front
19 July 1940	Promoted General Field Marshal
1 October 1940	Commander-in-Chief West
10 June 1941	Commander-in-Chief Army Group South, Eastern Front
5 December 1941	*Führer-Reserve* OKH
15 March 1942	Commander-in-Chief West and Army Group D

2 July 1944	*Führer-Reserve* OKH
5 September 1944	Commander-in-Chief West
9 March 1945	*Führer-Reserve* OKH
1 May 1945	Captured, Bad Tölz
10 July 1945	To England
15 May–	
19 August 1946	Nuremberg
12 January 1948	Death of Hans Gerd
23 July 1948	To Germany
29 August 1948	Formally declared a war criminal and discharged from the Wehrmacht
1 January 1949	Formally presented with detailed war crimes charges
5 May 1949	Declared medically unfit to plead and released from captivity
4 October 1952	Death of Bila
24 February 1953	Died, Hannover

Introduction

If there was one man who appeared to personify the traditional Prussian image, it was General Field Marshal Gerd von Rundstedt. During the Second World War, the Western Allies widely regarded him as the most outstanding of the German generals, while those Germans who strove to remove Hitler and all he stood for, but did not know von Rundstedt well, looked to him to provide the lead in any military action which might be taken against the régime. They viewed him as the personification of all that was good about the Prussian Junker class, but never forgave him for not taking an active part in resistance to Hitler, an attitude which exists in Germany to this day.

It is, however, surprising that no one has examined von Rundstedt in any depth until now. True, there have been two biographies of him. One was by his erstwhile Chief of Staff, Günther Blumentritt, but this, as will be seen, was written for a particular purpose, and begged more questions than it answered. The second, by that distinguished military historian John Keegan, was a slim volume, part of a large paperback series on the Second World War, which allowed the author neither the time nor the scope to explore his subject in any depth. Von Rundstedt, too, has had numerous entries, ranging from a few lines to complete chapters, in various biographical dictionaries and essay collections. Some have been grossly inaccurate, relying largely on Allied wartime propaganda for their facts, but the general verdict has been that he was an enigmatic character and it has been left at that.

As with my earlier biography of Sepp Dietrich, *Hitler's Gladiator*, this has not been an easy biography to write. Von Rundstedt kept no diary and wrote no autobiography. Nevertheless, the discovery of some of his letters to his wife and of the majority of the annual efficiency reports made on him have gone some way towards helping to establish his inner character. Even so, typical of his class, he was never one to reveal his innermost thoughts willingly and it has often only been possible to surmise the rationale behind some of his actions. What, however, has made this study especially rewarding for me has been the opportunity to examine events which were often comparatively well known from a fresh perspective. In some cases, this has caused me to alter my views on them. In order to get the significance of Gerd von Rundstedt's life story and military career into perspective, I have perforce had to set it against the broad canvas of the whole course of German history since the turn of the century, with special emphasis being placed upon the tempestuous years of the Hitler era. Across the face of that canvas, von Rundstedt's own contribution runs like a thread (more visible at some times than at others) through the coarser weave of his country's story.

As is inevitable with a book like this, it could not have been written without the help of numerous individuals and institutions. With regard to the latter, I would like to express my sincere thanks to the assistance given by the follow-ing – Berlin Document Centre; Bundesarchiv, Koblenz; *Bundesarchiv–Militärarchiv*, Freiburg am Breisgau; *Deutsche Adelsarchiv*, Marburg; *Deutsche Dienstelle* (WASt), Berlin; Imperial War Museum, London (Departments of Documents, Printed Books and Photographs); Liddell Hart Centre for Military Archives, King's College, London; *Institut für Zeitgeschichte*, Munich; The London Library; National Archives, Washington DC (Military Archives and Textual Reference Divisions); Public Record Office, London; Wandsworth Public Library, London (Battersea and West Hill branches).

In terms of individuals, my most grateful thanks go to the following: Antony Beevor, Klaus Benseler, Tom Bower, Stephen W Bumball, Miss R Campbell (Librarian, St Antony's College, Oxford), Peter Calvacoressi, Lieutenant Colonel Charles Clements MC, Elizabeth Crookenden, Philip J Davies, the Editors of the *Eastern Daily Press*, *Glamorgan Gazette* and *Westmorland Gazette* for publishing my letters, Jean Feather, R M Forrester (Honorary Secretary The Ambleside Oral History Group), Helmut Guetler, Professor Nigel Hamilton, P J Holt-Wilson, Joseph Hutchinson, J Iorweth Davies (Assistant Director of Education, Mid Glamorgan County Council), Dr Tom Jefferson, Colonel Vincent M Lockhart USAR (Retd), Charles A Lusby Sr, David Littlejohn, my elder daughter Emma Messenger, R A Nightingale, the late 'Bunny' Pantcheff, Jonathan Prickett of The History Bookshop, London, Ernie Ridgway, Professor Doktor Jürgen Rohwer of the *Bibliothek für Zeitgeschichte*, Stuttgart, Ian Sayer, The Rt Hon Lord Shawcross GBE PC, Matthew Barry Sullivan, Professor Telford

Taylor, Elgiva Thomas, Olive Wilson, and Professor Earl F Ziemke.

I would, however, like to single out Lothar Schaefer for special mention. As with *Hitler's Gladiator*, Lothar was of invaluable help, both in translation of German documents and in research at various German archives. He also acted as a most perceptive sounding board for my ideas and theories.

Finally, very special thanks are due to three of Field Marshal von Rundstedt's grandchildren. Barbara Papanastassiou answered numerous questions by letter, while Oberstleutnant Gerd von Rundstedt and his wife Catharina, in the company of his brother Eberhard, warmly entertained my wife and myself at their house. The brothers not only told me much about their grandfather, but also allowed me to inspect his archive and copied numerous documents and photographs for me. All three grandchildren have enabled me to put much flesh on the bones of my subject and without their help it would have been immeasurably more difficult, if not impossible, to probe the depths of the Field Marshal's character. It remains for me to sincerely hope that they will not feel that their generosity towards me was misplaced.

London, 1990   CHARLES MESSENGER

I
Early Life

THE NAME Rundstedt is derived from the German for 'round town' or fortress. The family that bears it has traditionally been part of the *Uradel*, the *ancienne noblesse* of the Prussian aristocracy, membership of which requires documentary evidence that the family's lineage stretches back to at least the year 1350. A Berengarus de Ronstede is recorded as early as 1109, and a century later his descendant Rudolphus de Ronstede was alive.[1] Berengarus was Grand Steward to the Bishop of Halberstadt, which lies north-east of the Harz Mountains, and it was in this region that the family largely settled. One branch acquired an estate near Stendal, just west of the River Elbe and some seventy miles west of Berlin, in 1331. Gerd von Rundstedt's side of the family was descended from Rudolphus. By the end of the 16th century, it had established itself in two estates, Badingen and Schönfeld, near Helmstedt, midway between Brunswick and Magdeburg. During the Cold War years after 1945, Helmstedt became well known as one of the few official crossing points over the Inner German Border, but the von Rundstedt estates themselves lay just inside East Germany and so were lost to the family in 1945.

Apart from managing their estates, the von Rundstedts, like their fellow members of the nobility, also pursued the military profession, serving both in the armies of the German states and as mercenaries. Thus, a Hans von Rundstedt reached high rank in the service of William of Orange during his wars against the Spanish in the 16th century. Two hundred years later, a Joachim von Rundstedt was with the Hessians in the English service in Scotland at the time of the rising of the Young Pretender, more popularly known as Bonnie Prince Charlie. The Hessians, though, took no part in the fighting. On the direct line of descent to Gerd von Rundstedt was Gebhard von Rundstedt, who served in the Swedish Army. The Swedish monarch to whom he offered his sword was Gustavus Adolphus, the Lion of the North, and one of the great military captains of history. That he should have done so was because German states were being ravaged at that time by the Thirty Years War. The von Rundstedts, coming as they did from the Mark of Brandenburg, one of the centres of the Reformation, were, and still are, devout Lutherans and their religion was under grave threat from the forces of the Counter-Reformation. Gustavus, a champion of Protestantism, was seen as the one hope for the German Protestants and many flocked to his colours, taking part in his famous victories. Gebhard himself survived the war, dying in 1651.

Brandenburg itself was ruled by the Hohenzollern family whose head was the Elector. The Thirty Years War left the state drained, but not for long. In 1654, Charles X ascended the Swedish throne and, determined to emulate his cousin, embarked on wars of aggression against Denmark and Poland. He overran both countries, but died before he could consolidate his gains. The Elector of Brandenburg, however, gave his support to the Poles in return for the Duchy of Prussia and proved to be the only real winner when peace treaties were signed in 1660. Forty years later the Swedes tried again, this time under Charles XII, but after some spectacular victories he met his match at Poltava in 1709, during an attempt to invade and overcome Russia. Brandenburg, whose army was beginning to gain a reputation, acquired more territory as a result, this time Swedish Pomerania. In the meantime, in 1701, Frederick I, Elector of Brandenburg, sought and was granted the permission of the Holy Roman Emperor, to whom all German states owed allegiance, to title himself King of Prussia. His accession was to create a new force in Europe and one in which the von Rundstedt family would become deeply entwined.

The man who was indirectly to shape and influence Gerd von Rundstedt more than anyone or anything else was Frederick II, otherwise known as Frederick the Great, who came to the Prussian throne in 1740 and was to rule his country with an iron hand until 1786. For the first 23 years of his reign, he was almost entirely at war, usually against superior odds. That Prussia survived and was on the winning side was largely due to him and to the army which he shaped. Yet, to build such an army required sacrifices. In order to obtain support for it, Frederick, as his father had done before him, looked to the aristocracy for complete commitment and to provide the backbone of the officer corps. In return, he gave his officers status above all other estates in the hierarchy. Gerd's great, great grandfather, August, was born in 1731 and probably served at the tail end of the War of the Austrian

Succession and in the Seven Years War. That both he and his eldest son had Friedrich among their forenames, and their wives, likewise, Friederice, was in itself a demonstration of the total loyalty which the King of Prussia received in return for the privileges that he was prepared to grant.

During the Napoleonic era, Prussia was beaten to her knees at Jena-Auerstadt in October 1806 and Napoleon entered Berlin in triumph. A few Prussian officers refused to acknowledge the humiliating terms which Napoleon forced on their country, even though Prussia did not join the Confederation of German States, which he created. One of these was Gerd's great grandfather, Joachim, a Lieutenant Colonel in the 10th Gendarmes Regiment (Cuirassiers). He and other like-minded officers created a resistance movement which was to bear much fruit when a resurgent Prussia took to the field again against Napoleon in 1813.

Von Rundstedt's grandfather Eberhard also served in the Royal Prussian Army, probably as a cavalryman, and retired as a Major. He, though, was the youngest of four children and had two brothers. The eldest died whilst still a boy and the next brother, Werner Rudolf Otto, inherited the family estates. Eberhard's branch of the family now became the cadet line. He, in turn, also produced four children, of which again the youngest, Gerd Arnold Konrad, was the future Field Marshal's father. He, too, had two elder brothers and all three became Hussars, while their two first cousins were Dragoons. They all served in the Franco-Prussian War, in which the second brother was killed. In 1874 the young Hussar married Adelheid Eleanore Fischer. In this he went outside the normal custom of the von Rundstedts, which was to marry their own kind, the Prussian aristocracy. The Fischers were of Huguenot descent and it may well have been this blood that gave Gerd his natural affinity for France and the French.

Gerd von Rundstedt himself was born on 12 December 1875 at Aschersleben, a small but ancient town 35 miles north of Halle and on the eastern edge of the Harz Mountains. He was christened Karl Rudolf Gerd, but was always called by his third forename. Gerd was not to remain an only child for long. During the next three and a half years Adelheid bore three more sons, Udo, Eberhard and Joachim. By the time Joachim was born, Adelheid was still only 22 years old, but exhausted and a semi-invalid. To assist her in looking after the boys, she employed an English nanny, a fact which helped to give Gerd and his brothers a grounding in the language. His brother Udo later wrote that Gerd showed an early talent for music and drawing; the latter skill was something which would be of considerable help in bearing the strain of captivity in Britain after the Second World War. He also blossomed into a very good mimic, with a marked ability for imitating German dialects and foreign languages.[2]

Gerd's father was now transferred to the 13th Hussars, who were stationed at Mainz, and it was here that Gerd first went to school. Udo recalled that he, Gerd and Eberhard first met a member of the House of Hohenzollern in the military swimming pool at Mainz. The Crown Prince Frederick, who was visiting the city in order to inspect troops, romped with them, but none of the boys realised who their older playmate was. One of their schoolmates was an English boy, Douglas Harrington, which would have increased the boys'grasp of English and English ways. In 1886, the boys' father was posted again, this time to the staff of the 22nd Infantry Division, whose headquarters was then at Frankfurt-am-Main, and Gerd attended the local Gymnasium (high school).

Given the long military tradition of the von Rundstedt family, it was virtually pre-ordained that Gerd and his brothers should enter the Royal Prussian Army. There were two ways of doing this if a commission was the goal. The more popular method was for a youth, once he had completed his studies at the Gymnasium, to apply to a regiment to become *Fahnenjunker* or aspirant officer. This entailed serving in the ranks for six months while he did his basic training. He was, however, accommodated separately from the ordinary rank and file. If considered by the commanding officer to have the right potential he would attend *Kriegsschule* (War School) for six months in order to train as an officer and, provided that he passed the final exams, he returned to his regiment as a *Fähnrich* (officer cadet) for a further period of probation before eventually being granted his commission. The other method, favoured by the not so well off upper classes, which, of course, included the von Rundstedts, was through cadet college. The attraction of this method, for the parents at least, was that the fees were very low. Admission could be as young as ten years old and a boy began by attending one of the twelve or so junior colleges scattered around the country. For their final two years, which equated to the last two years at Gymnasium, the cadets moved to Grosse Lichterfelde in Berlin. Like the *Fähnenjunker*, they then had to apply to a regiment and, if accepted, also served six months in the ranks of their chosen regiment. They were termed *Portepee Fähnrich* (cadet officer, *Portepee* being the term used for the officer's sword knot) which gave them a slightly higher status, in view of their previous military training, and they were very quickly equated to non-commissioned officers. Like the *Fähnenjunker*, they also had to attend *Kriegsschule* and then returned to their regiments as *Seconde Leutnant*, which was not a fully commissioned rank in the old German Army. When they were finally commissioned they received seniority over the *Fähnenjunker*. The drawback of this long training, the backbone of which was the traditional strict Prussian discipline, was that it tended to produce officers with a narrow and rigid outlook. As the eminent German siege specialist, and later von Rundstedt's superior as Governor of Warsaw, General von Beseler remarked to the British World War 1 official military historian Brigadier General Sir James Edmonds, the system was 'numbing' and produced officers who were 'faithful to duty, but stupid (*Pflichttreu aber Dumm*)'.[3] This was perhaps somewhat sweeping and certainly did not apply to the cream of the Royal Prussian Army, but it did have a ring of truth when measured against the average regimental officer.

On 1 April 1888, with his brother Udo, the youthful von Rundstedt entered the junior cadet college at Oranienstein, situated at Diez, east of Koblenz and today a Bundeswehr divisional headquarters. Here, in spite of the discipline and initial homesickness, he continued to display his natural liveliness and his talent on the stage. While acting the part of Varus in the von Kleist play *Hermannsschlacht* (Hermann's Battle), which commemorated the defeat of the Romans by the German of that name in AD 9, Gerd suffered a serious wound to the head from his fellow cadet playing Hermann, who had been provided with a Japanese *Samurai* sword by his doting father. Two years later, both brothers went on to Lichterfelde, where again Gerd's high spirits were much admired by his fellows. His brother recalled that:

'Supervision at the college was inadequate. It was difficult for the instructors to hold a thousand cadets together. Disciplinary relations were completely reversed in the case of some of these instructors. Gerd was not the last to play such pranks. One day, when an instructor dawdled at the door, addressing him with the familiar *Du*, he [Gerd] called out to him: "Now, are you coming in or going out?" As a punishment, the instructor, a Dr Reich, entered the offender's name in the class-book thus: "Rundstedt, *lebhaft*" (cheeky, keen). When the book was laid before the military superintendent, a captain, he took this entry for praise, and Gerd got special leave to Berlin! On Sunday, leave began after Church service. Gerd once contrived to get off earlier on the grounds that he wanted to go riding in the woods with his grandmother, although, actually, the old lady was ill in hospital.'

The cadets of Lichterfelde were in a privileged position, taking part in the parades of the Guards, and going on manoeuvres with them. This close connection with the Kaiser's household troops often enabled the cadets to see the Kaiser himself, which would have done much to inspire them. Equally memorable during Gerd's time at Lichterfelde were two parades for the great von Moltke the Elder, mastermind of Prussia's victory over France in 1870. On his 90th birthday, the cadets presented arms to him in front of the buildings of the *Grosse Generalstab*. A year later, they lined the route of his funeral procession.[4]

Gerd wanted to follow the von Rundstedt cavalry tradition, but the family's limited finances would not allow this. Instead he tried for the field artillery, probably because it was also mounted, but there were too many candidates for the number of places available and he was unsuccessful. Perhaps it was because he was not sufficiently competent in mathematics and science when compared with some of the other applicants. Thus, he was left with the infantry and joined the Regiment von Wittich (3rd Hessian), but more commonly known in the Royal Prussian Army as the 83rd Infantry Regiment, at Kassel for his six months as a *Portepee Fähnrich* on 22 March 1892. Since the regiment was part of 22nd Infantry Division, Gerd's father would have known it well and was probably instrumental in getting Gerd appointed to it. Kassel, which was to become Gerd's home town for over fifty years, was the capital of the state of Hessen-Nassau at that time and had a population of 100,000 inhabitants. During his initial period with the 83rd Infantry Gerd was allowed to take his meals in the officers' mess and also roomed apart from the rank and file. He was to find himself put very much under the microscope, not just by his commanding officer, but by all the officers in the regiment, who had to decide if he was of suitable character and had the qualitities to become one of them. If he was disappointed at not becoming an artilleryman, Gerd clearly did not show it and entered the *Kriegsschule* at Hannover in autumn 1892 for the penultimate state of his long officer training. After six months, and having passed the necessary exams, he returned to the Regiment as a *Seconde Leutnant*. He was now subjected to even closer examination by the officers of the regiment. They particularly watched a cadet officer's behaviour in the mess, even to the extent of getting him drunk to see if he did so like a gentleman. Finally, the officers voted on whether to elect him to be one of them. In Gerd's case, the election was in his favour. On 17 June 1893, he reached the end of the long road and was commissioned *Leutnant* in the 83rd Infantry Regiment. Udo and Joachim followed Gerd into the infantry, joining the 163rd and 80th Infantry Regiments respectively. Eberhard, however, succeeded in becoming an artilleryman in the 27th Field Artillery Regiment, but resigned his commission after a few years.

The army that Gerd and his brothers joined was still riding very much on the crest of the wave of its victory over France over 20 years earlier. It must be remembered that although Bismarck had unified it under Prussia, Germany was still a collection of states, enjoying varying degrees of autonomy. All save three had placed their armies under Prussian control, the last, Brunswick, in 1886. Of the three exceptions, Saxony and Württemberg had their own war ministries, but were even so under overall Prussian control, although Saxony maintained her own officer corps and promotion was within the Royal Saxon Army. The same applied to the third, Bavaria, which enjoyed even greater independence. However, like all the other states, her army was equipped and organised on Prussian lines and was subordinated to Berlin in time of war.

The German armies were conscript, with every male being liable to serve three years with the colours and four years with the active reserve, before passing on to further service with the *Landsturm*, which equated to a home defence force. In 1893, the year that von Rundstedt was commissioned, there was a radical reorganisation. For a start, service with the colours was reduced to two years, except for mounted arms. A man was registered with the *Landsturm* on his 17th birthday, but was not called upon to join the standing army until he was 20. Even so, the constitution laid down that only one per cent of the population could be active soldiers at any one time. Hence not all German males, by any means, actually donned uniform. The Army was thus able to select its recruits and preferred to take them from rural areas rather than the growing industrial cities, since there was a danger that the latter would have been imbued with socialist ideas. The fact that the population of Germany was growing rapidly (from 41 million in 1871 to 65 million by 1910) and increasing tension in Europe meant that Gerd was joining an expanding army.

The Prussian Army still occupied a very privileged position, one that it had maintained since the era of Frederick the Great 150 years earlier. This was primarily reflected in the officer corps. From Frederick's time it had been cocooned and nurtured as a body which was answerable only to the Kaiser, and totally isolated from the civil community. As General Hahnke, Chief of the Military Cabinet in the 1890s, said: 'The army must remain an insulated body into which no one dare peer with critical eyes.'[5] When the young Kaiser Wilhelm II succeeded his short-reigned father (the von Rundstedt boys' erstwhile playmate in the baths at Mainz) in 1888, he did so determined that Germany should have 'her place in the sun'. To bring this about, he was prepared to pander to Britain, making maximum use of the fact that he was Queen Victoria's grandson, but was unconcerned that this heightened Russian suspicions. France would, of course, never warm to Germany until she had regained the lost provinces of Alsace and Lorraine. Her enmity and growing Russian coldness meant that the possibility of war on two fronts became increasingly real. This danger was not lessened by the fall of Bismarck, who had striven so hard to maintain the balance of power in Europe. Wilhelm, recognising that a strong army was essential if he was to achieve his ends and deter his neighbours, encouraged every move to expand it.

The officer corps itself was kept bound to the Kaiser through privilege, as it had been for the past 200 years. While pay was low, even compared to British officers, whose financial rewards from their country were hardly generous, the social standing of the German officer was higher. Even a reserve commission was much valued and sought after by politicians among others, besides being a means of making a rich marriage match. Just as significant was the fact that the German officer was so insulated from civilian life that he could not be brought before a civil court. The reason for this was the Prussian Code of Honour.

It is important to understand this code because it was to exert a significant influence on von Rundstedt's life. One cannot do better for a description of the Prussian concept of honour than to quote from an 1874 order by Wilhelm II's grandfather:

> 'I therefore look to the whole corps of officers of My Army to make honour their finest jewel in future as they have always done hitherto. To keep its honour pure and spotless must be the sacred duty of the whole Estate and of every member of it. If that duty is fulfilled, then every other duty incumbent on an officer will be fully and conscientiously performed. True honour cannot exist without faithfulness unto death, without invincible courage, firm determination, self-denying obedience, simple truthfulness and strict discretion, nor without self-sacrifice in the fulfilment of what may seem but trivial tasks. Honour requires, too, that an officer's outward bearing shall reflect his conscious pride in being a member of the Estate to which the defence of Throne and Fatherland has been entrusted. An officer should endeavour to keep no company but that in which high standards are cherished; and least of all in public places should he forget that he will be looked upon not merely as a man of education but as one who represents the honour and highest obligations of his Estate. He should keep aloof from all dealings that may reflect upon the good name of

the individual or of the fellowship to which he belongs; especially from all excess, from drunkenness and gambling, from contracting any obligation that may lead to even the slightest appearance of dishonest conduct, from speculative dealings on the Stock Exchange, from taking part in any commercial enterprises whose aims are not unimpeachable or whose reputation is not of the highest. Never should he lightly pledge his word of honour.

As luxury and good living become widespread in other walks of life, the more it is an officer's serious duty never to forget that it is not in his possession that he gained, or will preserve, the highly honoured place that he occupies in the State and society. It is not simply that his military value may be reduced if he lives in comfort; the pursuit of riches and good living involves the danger that the very foundations on which the officers' Estate is built may be brought to total ruination.

The more attention the corps of officers pays to cultivating the genuine comradeship and a true *esprit de corps*, the easier will it be to prevent excess of any kind, bring comrades back if they stray from the right path, and avoid senseless quarrels and unworthy wrangling.'

The Kaiser then went on to exhort his officers never to display 'lack of respect' or 'arrogance' to the 'other Estates', because all must have confidence in the officer corps.[6] Honour, however, served to keep the Army isolated from the 'other Estates'. The traditional Prussian argument was that only someone who bore arms could be considered a man of honour. Since the Army was the only sector of society entitled to bear arms only army officers had honour. Encapsulated within the Prussian definition of honour was the edict that a man of honour could not be tried in a court of law by someone who lacked it. This was the justification for army officers being immune from civil justice. If an officer did commit some crime, he had to come before a military Court of Honour. If found guilty, and the crime was sufficiently serious, he could be ordered to resign his commission. By so doing, he lost his honour and hence could be tried by the civil authorities. This concept of honour was to be carried on throughout the First World War, the Reichswehr and the Wehrmacht, and was to have particular consequences for Gerd in 1944. Furthermore, coming as he did from a family with many generations of soldiers, the Code of Honour would have been imbued in him virtually from birth and was to exert a deep influence on him throughout his life.

Gerd quickly settled into the life of an officer in Kassel and made an early favourable impression. Colonel von Mayer, commanding the 83rd Infantry Regiment, in his first annual report on him, noted that Gerd was 'well attuned physically and mentally, shows great diligence to duty and promises to become quite a useful officer. He is well educated, has good manners and is well regarded by his comrades.'[7] This indicates a more serious von Rundstedt than the cadet, and a 'putting away of childish things' in order conscientously to pursue a military career. Two years later, Freiherr von Thoma, who had taken over command of the Regiment, reported on him on much the same lines, confirming his diligence and noting his 'modest and tactful demeanour'. He also drew attention to Gerd's skill as a horseman and remarked in conclusion that Gerd's finances were 'in order'.[8] The finances of their young officers was always a matter of concern for commanding officers, as in most armies, especially because of the danger that they might get into the clutches of money-lenders. A more serious consideration was that young officers finding themselves in this predicament made themselves vulnerable to the attention of the espionage agencies of foreign powers. Indeed, the Germans themselves were using this technique on French officers. Consequently, each regiment had an officers' assistance fund from which loans could be made; the Russian Army had a similar system.[9]

Von Rundstedt's promise received its first reward in October 1896 when he was made adjutant of the 3rd Battalion of his regiment, a post he was to hold for the next three years. His battalion was detached from the rest of the regiment and stationed at Arolsen, some 20 miles west of Kassel. This was a small town of less than 3,000 inhabitants and the capital of the small principality of Waldeck. Von Rundstedt came to know the young Prince well since he was a frequent visitor to the mess. Furthermore, Gerd attended a number of balls and other functions at the small Court. At one of these he met Wilhelmina, the teenage Queen of the Netherlands, whom he much admired.[10] It was probably as a result of his friendship with the Prince that Gerd was awarded the Waldeck Merit Cross 4th Class. In spite of these social *divertissements*, Gerd continued to take his chosen career very seriously. He now wanted to attend the *Kriegsakademie* (War Academy) in Berlin, the Royal Prussian Army's Staff College and the passport to promotion to the higher ranks of the Army. The main hurdle to this was a very rigorous entrance examination. Candidates for admission had to have a minimum of three years' service, be unlikely to be promoted captain within five years of entry, be in good health, and have their private affairs in order. The examination itself was competitive and only some 130 candidates were successful each year. It consisted of papers on theoretical and applied tactics, artillery and small arms, fortification, topography and plan drawing, a selected period of history, geography and a choice of either French or mathematics. Its object was to 'ascertain whether the candidate possesses that degree of general education and knowledge which is requisite in order to be able to profit from the lectures at the *Kriegsakademie*. Besides this the examination must show whether the candidates possess powers of judgement which give promise of increase and development.'[11] This entailed much preparation and most officers resorted to crammers. It is probable that von Rundstedt relinquished his adjutancy in order to study for the exam, which he sat in March 1899. Apart from writing the papers, he also had to submit to his army corps chief of staff a written autobiography, stressing his intellectual development and how he had prepared himself for his examinations to become an officer. He also had to state whether he wished to study mathematical sciences or languages at the *Kriegsakademie*. Gerd almost certainly opted for the latter and took the French paper. In addition, his commanding officer had to attach a corroborative report on the degree of assistance which he had received in preparing for the *Kriegsakademie* exam. Finally, the commanding officer had to submit a report to cover the candidate's practical military aptitude, his intellect, health, conduct and character, and personal finances. An indication of what Gerd's commanding officer, now Colonel von Hennigs, wrote is given in his annual report for 1899:

> 'He is an especially able, useful, sound and well suited officer, full of diligence and enthusiasm. He filled the post of battalion adjutant very well. . . . Very pleasant, he combines good manners with modest and tactful behaviour. He is suited for regimental adjutant and promotion.'[12]

Gerd's hard work and his commanding officer's recommendation were successful and he passed the exam at the first sitting. He was, however, still a junior Lieutenant and not senior enough to gain immediate entry to the *Kriegsakademie*.

At the beginning of October 1900, however, von Hennigs did make Gerd his regimental adjutant, a move which he clearly had no cause to regret. In his report on him for 1901 he especially noted that Gerd's 'good military eye, his opinions and skill in matters on and off duty, together with his great reliability and popularity, make him a very good regimental adjutant'. It was also clear from this report that Gerd was working hard to prepare himself intellectually for the *Kriegsakademie*.[13] On 1 October, he was finally promoted to Senior Lieutenant (*Oberleutnant*). By this time, Gerd's mind was not dwelling on military matters alone for he was in love. She was a local girl, from Kassel itself, and the daughter of a retired major. Gerd and Luise von Goetz became officially engaged in May 1901 and were married on 22 January 1902. A year later, on 21 January 1903, their union was to be blessed with the birth of their only son and child, Hans Gerd. Bila, as she was always known, was tall, slim and elegant. Like Gerd, she was modest in character and rather shy, something which she concealed behind a mask of coolness. She also had a very strict moral code.[14] Bila and Gerd were to enjoy fifty years of married life together and would remain very close until the end. There is no doubt that it was a true love match, as Gerd's letters to his wife reveal, and he would draw great strength from it.

In the autumn of 1903 Gerd was at last posted as a student to the *Kriegsakademie* in Berlin. Before he did so, he spent the summer on attachment to the headquarters of XI Corps, of which his regiment formed part, for a staff ride and other exercises. Once again he impressed and his regimental commander was moved to recommend him for prefential promotion, writing that 'he is one of those officers who can surely expect later to be employed in the higher positions of the Army'. This was endorsed by his brigade commander, who also considered him suitable for the Imperial Guard. General von Heringen, his divisional commander, while agreeing that Gerd justified 'good hopes for the future', was not prepared to support the recommendation for accelerated promotion on the grounds that Gerd had only held his present rank for little more than a year.[15]

The course at the *Kriegsakademie* was to last three years.[16] The Regulations laid down its aim as 'the initiation of a limited number of qualified officers of all arms into the higher branches of the military science, so as to deepen and widen their military knowledge, and to clear and sharpen their military judgement'. The students were to also try to 'penetrate more deeply into such branches of general science as are useful in the Army, and to attain fluency in the oral and written employment of certain modern languages'. The established strength of the student body was some 400 Senior Lieutenants, divided into three classes. In practice, the actual number of students was considerably less than this. They were only attached to the *Kriegsakademie* for a year at a time, remaining on the strengths of their regiments, and of the 130 students who arrived for the first year only some 20 per cent would complete the full three years, so rigorous and searching was the course. The students in the first and second years received 25 hours of formal instruction each week. This was based on lectures, oral and written work. The core subjects were Tactics, Military History, Fortification, Military Law and History. In addition, the students either opted to study science (Mathematics, Physics, Physical Geography) or General Geography and a language. On offer were French, Russian and Polish, but English had recently been added, and the selection was indicative of the countries whom Germany regarded as her most likely potential enemies. Von Rundstedt chose the language option and by the end of this time at the *Kriegsakademie* had qualified as a French interpreter, something he was to find especially useful 40 years later. During the second year, Artillery, Communications, Topography and Survey, Plan Drawing and Military Hygiene were introduced, and those who had chosen the science option studied Mathematics and Chemistry, the others continuing to study their chosen language. In the third year, the hours of instruction were reduced to 21 and, apart from Tactics and Military History, the only two subjects studied throughout by everyone, Staff Duties, Siege Warfare, Maritime Warfare, State Administration, Public and International Law were covered. Mandatory projects done at home were not encouraged during the first two years, although there was nothing to stop the keen student producing voluntary ones. In addition to the classroom instruction a number of visits were made to arms factories, technical institutions, manoeuvre areas around Berlin, and the fortifications of Spandau and Küstrin (on the Oder).

The instructional staff were a mixture of officers and civilians. What was significant was that almost all the former held important staff posts and taught part-time. Likewise, the majority of the civilian instructors were professors at the University of Berlin. The students were very carefully monitored throughout the course. Indeed, Brigadier General Sir James Edmonds, who visited the *Kriegsakademie* on a number of occasions during the period noted that:

'The special feature of the institution was the very thorough investigation of the character, talents, and attainments of the students. They were always under the microscope. The Commandant told me that he had a report on every student from every instructor every quarter, and that the students had to report what use they made of their spare time. A record was kept of every piece of work, essay, and problem that each man did. At the end of three years, as General von Manteuffel told me, there was very little he did not know about his students.'[17]

At the end of each year of formal instruction, in June, the students had to sit examinations. Their results and reports were then reviewed to decide whether they should be readmitted for the next year. The year itself ended with the students of the first year being attached to an arm other than their own. In von Rundstedt's case, as an infantryman, he was attached to an artillery regiment within his own corps, 11th Field Artillery Regiment, which was part of von Rundstedt's own division, 22nd Infantry. At the end of his second year, after carrying out a three week survey exercise, Gerd was attached to a cavalry regiment, the 5th Dragoon Regiment, also part of the 22nd Infantry Division. This he clearly enjoyed and the regimental commander noted that he quickly adapted to cavalry ways and became an excellent patrol commander. All with whom he served were impressed by his enthusiasm and brain and at the end of 1905 his corps commander, General of Infantry Linde, wrote: 'With his demonstrable achievements in every post and his whole personality, Oberlt v. Rundstedt justifies the certain belief of employment in the higher posts of the Army in the future. I recommend his preferential promotion.'[18]

Gerd impressed throughout his time at the *Kriegsakademie* and his final report from there described him as,

> 'An outstandingly able officer with a serious outlook on life, determined in his demeanour, with a firm character and very good manners. Outstandingly able in tactical matters, very sound and reasoned in opinion and judgement, quick and positive in decision and orders, he is well suited for the General Staff.'[19]

Once again, he was recommended for accelerated promotion by his regimental, brigade and divisional commanders, but his training as a staff officer was not yet completed. After a brief return to his regiment, he then had to do an attachment to the General Staff as a test of his practical abilities. This attachment could either be to the *Grosse Generalstab* (Great General Staff) in Berlin or to the *Truppengeneralstab* (Troops General Staff), usually at the headquarters of an army corps. For Gerd it was to be Berlin once more and an opportunity to experience at first-hand the centre of the German military web.

In April 1907, when von Rundstedt joined it, the *Grosse Generalstab* was headed by the Quartermaster General, who equated to the Army Chief of Staff, and at that time was Count Helmuth von Moltke the Younger, nephew of the man who had masterminded Prussia's victory over France in 1870 and who himself, as we shall see, would tinker with the Schlieffen Plan in 1914 in such a way as to ensure its failure. He had a staff of just over one hundred officers organised into sections as follows:

Section 1 – Russian (including the Balkans), Far East.
Section 2 – Deployment and mobilisation.

Section 3 – France and the West.

Section 4 – Foreign armies (with Section 7 as a sub-section).

Section 5 – Training and *Kriegsakademie* (with Section 8 as a sub-section).

Section 6 – Manoeuvres.

Section 9 – Austria.

Two other sections covered military history and map-making.[20] It has not been possible to establish which section von Rundstedt joined, but given his fluency in French and English, it is possible that he joined Section 3. The usual length of this attachment was one year, but for some reason, possibly because he was still considered too junior, von Rundstedt did two years before being promoted Captain on the General Staff and thus entitled to wear its carmine striped trousers and silver collar tabs. There were two main promotions each year, in spring and autumn, and von Rundstedt was promoted with a large number of other Senior Lieutenants on 24 March 1909.[21]

During his time on the *Grosse Generalstab* Gerd would have almost certainly been privy to the General Staff's plans for war. As we have seen, the greatest fear at this time was the war on two fronts – something which became a very real possibility after the formation of a military alliance between France and Russia in 1892, whereby each agreed to attack Germany if the other was attacked by either Germany, Austro-Hungary or Italy, the members of the Triple Alliance. The German Chief of Staff at the time was Count Alfred von Schlieffen, who had been appointed to this post the previous year. The plans bequeathed to him by his predecessors, von Moltke and Count von Waldersee, called for a defensive war against France and a decisive battle against the Russian Army, after which the forces in the West, which would have probably been forced into an initial withdrawal, would then turn and fight the French. This concept smacked of protracted war to the more aggressively minded von Schlieffen, something which would put severe strains on Germany's economy. It was far better, he argued, to emulate Frederick the Great and look for quick, decisive victories. Since the Russian mobilisation machine was that much more unwieldy and slower than that of France, it made sense for Germany to strike west first. A small force of some ten divisions was to guard East Prussia against the Russian threat, while the bulk of the German armies quickly deployed to the West. A massive offensive would then be mounted which was designed to envelop the Frencharmies. To do this, von Schlieffen intended to defend with comparatively weak forces in Alsace-Lorraine and to use these as a pivot for the bulk of the German armies to execute a vast wheel, taking in the whole of Belgium, without regard to her neutrality, and the southern tip of Holland, with whom he hoped that freedom of passage could be negotiated. The two extreme right hand armies were to be the strongest and would pass west of Paris and then swing south-east in order to carry out the envelopment. In order to guard their ever extending lines of communication, von Schlieffen planned, the situation permitting, to switch forces from the left wing and also to deploy six reserve divisions to follow in the path of the right wing armies. Crucial to the plan was the efficient and speedy deployment of the armies and this was dependent on the German railways. It is thus understandable why Section 2 of the *Grosse Generalstab*, sometimes called the Railway Section, should be considered the most important. Von Schlieffen came to recognise that there were flaws in the plan, especially the assumption that the Dutch would allow German troops to pass through their territory and that perhaps there was a danger of underestimating the French defensive capability. While he refused to accept criticism from others, he continue to polish the plan until his death in 1913. His successor, the nephew of the great von Moltke and Gerd's chief, became mesmerised by the threat of a French attack in Alsace-Lorraine and could not accept von Schlieffen's contention that a loss of territory here would not count for much once the wheel had really got going. He also blanched at the concept of using Dutch territory. Consequently, the right wing armies had less room in which to operate and von Moltke gradually reinforced the left wing at the expense of the right. What neither fully appreciated, however, were the problems of keeping the right wing resupplied once it had moved beyond the comprehensive network of the German railway system. What von Rundstedt thought of this at the time is not known, but in later years he would hold strong views. By then he would be speaking not just from hindsight, but also from his own personal experience in what culminated in the Battle of the Marne.

He served for a year as a fully-fledged member of the *Grosse Generalstab* and continued to shine. His section chief, Lieutenant Colonel Brozi, wrote of his capacity for hard work and 'energetic and independent personality' combined with his tact and modesty. Significantly, von Rundstedt carried out a staff ride with XVIII Corps, whose Chief of Staff, Colonel Ilse, praised his 'outstanding eye for country' and the fact that he was 'militarily educated above his age' and recommended him for the *Truppengeneralstab*. Von Moltke himself endorsed all that had been written on this 'excellent officer'.[22] This recommendation was duly taken up and, on 1 October 1910, Gerd was posted to the staff of XI Corps. This meant a return to Kassel, which would have pleased both him and his wife. His talents were also being recognised not just in the annual reports written on him, but also by a growing number of decorations awarded to him (see Appendix 1).

The staff of an army corps was responsible for mobilisation, manoeuvres and firing practice and, once again, Gerd tackled his duties with his accustomed enthusiasm and capacity for hard work. The fact that he was back with his parent army corps helped in that he knew the formations and regiments and many of the key personalities. It was, however, considered important that staff officers did return to regimental duty from time to time and in September 1912 von Rundstedt was appointed to command No 6 Company of the 2nd Upper Alsatian (171st) Infantry Regiment at Colmar on the west bank of the Rhine between Strasbourg and Mulhouse.

Colmar was one of the so-called frontier garrisons. These had a notorious reputation because of their isolation and claustrophobic atmosphere. A great furore had been created some years earlier by the publication of a novel, *Life in a Garrison Town*, written by a serving officer, Lieutenant Oswald Fritz Bilse,[23] which revealed exactly what life in the garrison of Forbach, west of Saarbrücken, was supposed to be like. The picture he portrayed was one of indolence among the officers, marital infidelity and injustice to inferiors. Perhaps worst, at least in the eyes of the authorities, was the corruption of the Code of Honour. In one incident an officer was forced to fight a duel with one of his fellows who had run off with his wife, even though the victim had become fed up with her infidelities and wished to have no more to do with her. If the officer had not fought he would have shown himself to be dishonourable and would have been arraigned before a Court of Honour. Bilse himself was court-martialled at Metz in November 1903 for publishing his book without permission. In his defence he stated:

'I entered the Army, for I felt that to be my vocation, and in the beginning I was quite happy. Later, when I was transferred to Lorraine, I recognised the great difference between life in the frontier garrison towns and the other garrisons of the empire. I observed evils and abuses which took away all my illusions. These I noticed especially in my garrison of Forbach. There have been innumerable complaints about the condition of the frontier towns, and so I thought that another voice raised in protest would do no harm.'[24]

Questions were asked in the Reichstag and the Minister of War admitted that there was much truth in what the book said, but this did not prevent Bilse being sentenced to six months' imprisonment and all copies of the book being destroyed. Unfortunately, he had fallen into the error of drawing his fictional characters too close to his real-life brother officers. Von Rundstedt would have doubtless known of this saga when he was at the *Kriegsakademie*. Indeed, he may even have known Bilse, who was stationed at Kassel before being posted to Forbach. If he hoped that conditions had improved during the past few years, he was to be disappointed.

At root was the fact that Alsace and Lorraine were occupied territories. Their people might be German-speaking, but their hearts were with France; not for nothing had the first singing of the *Marseillaise* taken place in Strasbourg. In the years since 1870, the German civil administration had worked hard to give the province a degree of self-autonomy, but the German Army continued to see itself as an occupation force whose purpose was to ensure that the province was thoroughly Germanised, viewing every easing of restrictions as playing into the hands of the French. The fact that the ratio of soldiers to civilians in Alsace-Lorraine was four times higher than anywhere else in the German Empire did not help and increasing enmity had developed between the two, thereby aggravating the isolation of the garrisons. A series of incidents came to a head in 1913. In Colmar itself an attempt was made by HQ XV Corps to remove the Mayor on the grounds that he was a spy. He had been visiting his wife in hospital in Paris when he could have put her in just as good a hospital in Germany. But this was a minor event compared with what became known as the Zabern Affair.

On 28 October 1913, Lieutenant Freiherr von Forstner and Sgt Höflich of the 99th Infantry Regiment, which, like von Rundstedt's regiment, was in XV Corps, although in the other division, were lecturing recruits on local civil-military relations at the Regiment's barracks in Zabern. Turning to one of the recruits, who had been charged with knifing a local, von Forstner assured him that he would reward him with money if he knifed another Alsatian and the Sergeant supported him. A few days later the local press got hold of the story and printed it, demanding that the officer and NCO be punished. The regimental commander refused, saying that they were merely referring to rowdy elements, and was supported in this by HQ XV Corps. Demonstrations followed in the town and the corps commander, in an effort to cool things down, ordered the regimental commander to confine von Fostner to his rooms and to place the NCO under close arrest. Colonel Reuter, the regimental commander, who had fallen out with the chief local civil official, the *Kreisdirektor*, now asked for sick leave. When a removal van was seen outside his quarters, the local people assumed that he had been removed from his command. In the meantime, von Forstner, who seems to have been a very arrogant young man, made further inflammatory remarks to his soldiers, which also reached the ears of the press. The matter now came to the attention of the Kaiser, whose military advisers told him that not to reinstate Reuter would mean loss of face. Reuter therefore returned to his command, secure in the thought that he had the Kaiser's personal backing, and began a witch hunt among both the Alsatian soldiers in his regiment and the local populace over the press leaks. The climax came on 28 November, when Reuter's troops arrested 28 civilians and, totally illegally, had them up before a military court. Alsatian deputies now asked questions in the Reichstag and a day long debate followed, at the end of which the government suffered a severe defeat. It was thus decided to move 99th Regiment to a manoeuvre area in order to allow matters to quieten down and to court-martial those directly involved. Some soldiers were given short terms of military imprisonment, but Reuter, von Forstner, who had seriously injured a lame civilian who had allegedly laughed at him, and another officer were eventually acquitted, although posted to other regiments. Indeed the Kaiser even rewarded Reuter with the Order of the Red Eagle 3rd Class. The affair rumbled on, with the 99th finally returning to an icy homecoming in Zabern in April 1914. That same month it was laid down that Alsatian conscripts were no longer to be allowed to do their military service in their homeland, but would be posted to other parts of the Reich. The net result was that military-civil enmity increased not just in the region but between France and Germany as well.

History does not record what von Rundstedt thought of all this. The atmosphere cannot have made life particularly pleasurable when compared to that in Kassel. Judging from his character, it is likely that he went through one of his introverted periods, concentrating on his company and family. The former, especially, would have kept him busy. Every 1 October, the year's new recruits joined and during the autumn and winter underwent their basic training in drill and weapon training. The spring and summer would then be devoted to field training, beginning with group/section and platoon drills and culminating with formation manoeuvres. The time-expired men were then discharged. September was taken up with supervising the annual two weeks' training of the first-line reservists and then the year began again. Under this system, if war came it should ideally do so in the late summer, when all those serving with the colours were fully trained. This, of course, is what happened in 1914. Certainly, in the eyes of his peers, Gerd made a success of his company, as he had his previous posts. His commanding officer noted how well trained No 6 Company was and also its good spirit. His divisional commander, Freiherr von Matter, wrote that von Rundstedt maintained his company in 'highest discipline and order' (*Zucht und Ordnung*, a very Prussian expression) and both he and the corps commander recommended Gerd for further general staff employment.[25] It was thus inevitable, and Gerd probably knew it, that, however hard he had worked during the past year to make No 6 Company ready for war in all respects, he was not destined to lead it in battle. His training and expertise as a staff officer were too valuable, especially since mobilisation was about to double the size of the German Army. Thus, at the end of July 1914, he was ordered to hand over his company to another officer and to return to the staff.

2

The First World War

On 30 July 1914, Captain von Rundstedt joined the staff of 22nd Reserve Infantry Division as the 1a (Chief of Operations). This division formed part of IV Reserve Corps and was commanded by Lieutenant General von Riemann. IV Reserve Corps itself was to be part of Alexander von Kluck's First Army, which also included II, III, IV Corps and III Reserve Corps. The German armies were only formed on mobilisation, although their headquarters were in place in peacetime as inspections. These, however, did not necessarily have responsibility for the same corps as they would command in wartime. Thus, First Army set up its headquarters at Stettin, while Inspection No 1 had its peacetime headquarters at Danzig, and von Kluck drew one standing corps (II) from Inspection No 8 based in Berlin and III Corps from Inspection No 4 based at Munich, which also controlled the three first line Bavarian corps, and IV Corps from Inspection No 6 based at Stuttgart. In terms of the peacetime areas of responsibility of the three corps, II Corps covered Pomerania, III Corps Brandenburg and IV Corps Prussian Saxony. The two Reserve corps in First Army drew their men from the same area as the standing corps, but not necessarily those of the same title number. Thus von Rundstedt's corps, IV Reserve, formed in both IV and XI Corps areas of responsibility. His own division drew on the latter, which, of course, von Rundstedt knew well from his days as a subaltern in 83rd Infantry Regiment and his staff tour with HQ XI Corps. 22nd Reserve Division's two infantry brigades, 43rd and 44th Reserve, each consisted of two regiments each of three battalions. Both regiments in 44th Reserve Brigade were reserve formations of 22nd Infantry division, while the two 43rd Reserve Brigade regiments represented units in 22nd Infantry Division's sister division, 38th, in the first line XI Corps. The reservists who made up the rank and file of 22nd Reserve Division were not more than five years away from their two years' conscripted duty with the colours. This meant that the men of von Rundstedt's division were in the 21–26 age bracket. The officers and senior NCOs were older and some would have been known to von Rundstedt, the main reason why he would have received this posting.

Von Kluck's First Army was to play the key role in the invasion of Belgium and France, being the right flanking formation and the one that would have to march the furthest in the great von Schlieffen 'wheel', as modified by von Moltke. Crucial, of course, to the German plan was the quick deployment of the armies to the frontiers, both East and West. This had been the main problem on which the *Grosse Generalstab* in Berlin had been working for the past decade, and the reason why its Railway Section was considered the most prestigious. That it had done its planning well, was demonstrated during the next two weeks as the troop trains rolled endlessly to the West and East. First Army began its move from its mobilisation areas to the Belgian frontier on 7 August. Six days later, and fully assembled, its advance to the first main objective, the River Meuse, began. By this time, IX Corps had also been placed under von Kluck's command and his army advanced on three routes, II, III and IV Corps leading, and the other three corps following. IV Reserve Corps marched behind IV Corps. Each route was controlled by a general, but the most difficult challenge was the fact that all three routes passed through Aix-la-Chapelle (Aachen). Nevertheless, some 200,000 men successfully negotiated the town in little more than 24 hours, an impressive demonstration of the precision of the German staff work. The depth corps followed a day's march behind the leading ones, with IV Reserve Corps initially on the centre route, which took it through Tongres. Once through St Trond, it switched to the left-hand route until west of Tirlemont, when it returned to the centre route, arriving at Louvain on 21 August. Von Rundstedt's corps next entered the Belgian capital, which had been evacuated by the withdrawing Belgian Army two days earlier. During this time, IV Reserve Corps had been the Army reserve and so it was hardly surprising that it should be ordered to detach two battalions and then the whole of 43rd Reserve Brigade to temporarily garrison Brussels until they could be relieved. It was a loss that von Riemann would come to sorely miss in the days to come. At the time, though, there was no chance to ponder the implications of this. The remainder of the corps had no time to enjoy the delights of occupying the enemy's capital, but now began to swing south-west towards what most believed to be their ultimate objective, Paris.

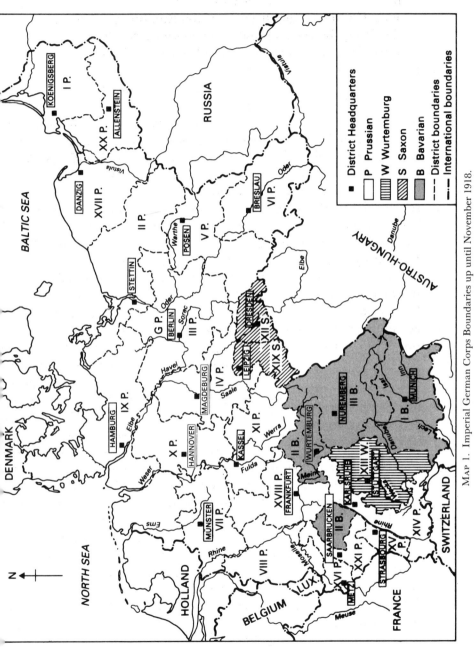

MAP 1. Imperial German Corps Boundaries up until November 1918.

The drama being played out during those hot August days was on a vast canvas and only at the very top, at theatre command level, was there a reasonable picture of exactly what was happening. Even then, the further the armies advanced, the more difficult it became to accurately gauge the situation. As one moved down through the command levels, so did the area of the canvas which could be seen with any clarity become smaller. Thus von Rundstedt, besides conducting the operational affairs of his own division, would have had a good idea of how his sister division, 7th Reserve, was faring and a reasonable idea of what the other corps in First Army were doing, but otherwise his information would have been sketchy at best. He would have probably known that First Army was conforming to the movements of the right-hand corps of Second Army, von Kluck's immediate left-hand neighbour, but he would have had only very vague news of the fierce fighting that had been taking place further south. This was the Battle of the Frontiers, which saw the French put their Plan XVII into action against the German armies in Alsace and Lorraine, only to be bloodily repulsed. In the meantime, for First Army there were problems and frustrations.

Having secured Brussels, von Kluck's task was to cover Antwerp and guard the right flank of the German wheel against the Belgian Army and British Expeditionary Force (BEF). He therefore decided to advance south-west, keeping west of Mauberge, but maintaining contact with the right-hand corps of Second Army on his immediate left. Von Bülow, commanding the Second Army, saw matters rather differently and believed that von Kluck should conform much more closely to his movements than the latter wished to do. Von Kluck complained, but it was to no avail. The German High Command, von Moltke's *Oberste Heeresleitung* (OHL), placed him under von Bülow's temporary command in order to rein him in and ensure that he fulfilled his primary role of guarding Second Army's right flank. Von Kluck thus found himself advancing south and not south-west. The upshot of this came on the 23rd. While the German Second Army engaged the French Fifth Army across the Sambre, von Kluck came up against the British Expeditionary Force (BEF) positioned along the Mons-Condée Canal. This marked the first significant engagement that First Army had had in the campaign this far. Von Kluck attacked with four corps in line and they were bloodily repulsed by the British infantry, who were trained to fire fifteen aimed shots per minute. IV Reserve Corps, and hence von Rundstedt's division, was not, however, involved and was still a long way north, marching on the road from Brussels to Hal when the battle opened. By evening the British were still firm in their positions, but Lanrezac, commanding the French Fifth Army on their right, had not been so successful and the Germans were across the Sambre in several places. Accordingly, he began to withdraw and the BEF was forced to conform; otherwise it would have been cut off.

Now began the great retreat as the British and French fell back towards the Aisne and then the Marne. Von Kluck pursued the BEF while von Bülow followed the French Fifth Army. On the 25th, the British fought a fierce rearguard action at Landrecies and on the following day Smith-Dorrien's II Corps turned on its pursuers at Le Cateau before resuming its march south-west. It was here that IV Reserve Corps began to take a more active part in the campaign. Von Kluck ordered it to get round the left flank of Smith-Dorrien's position. While 7th Reserve Division, assisted by elements of von der Marwitz's Cavalry Corps, attacked the British 4th Division and forced it to give some ground before a temporary stalemate ensued, von Rundstedt's division, still less one of its two brigades, tried to work its way round the British flank, but ran up against and was held by a French Territorial division. Sordet's French Cavalry Corps then enabled both British and French to break contact and withdraw in the evening.

Exhaustion increased by the day both for pursued and pursuer. Walter Bloem, a company commander in III Corps:

> 'For three whole weeks, ever since we detrained at Elsdorf on August 10th, we had had not a single rest-day, nor even a suggestion of one. Day after day onwards without ceasing. . . . And how the men's feet suffered! From time to time we had to examine them; and it was no pleasure to look at the inflamed heels, soles, and toes of my wretched young lads, whole patches of skin rubbed off to the raw flesh. Many a morning we company commanders would ride up to the battalion commander: "Major, could you explain to the higher command the need for a rest-day? The men literally can go on no further and if we were asked to stand and fight any day now we could not be responsible for their conduct under present conditions . . ."'[1]

The march had to be continued, though, especially since von Kluck now believed that he was in a position to cut the BEF from its base, which he mistakenly thought was Calais. Consequently, his orders for the 27th specified a change of direction. First Army would now advance south-west in order to cut the British lines of communications and its next task would be to force crossings over the Somme. He was supported in this by OHL, which released him from von Bülow's command. Thus, as the BEF, covered by French cavalry and a group of French Territorial divisions (Groupe d'Amade), continued to withdraw southwards, First Army, with four corps in line (reading west-to-east II, IV Reserve, IV, III), pressed forward. On the 28th, they reached the Somme, but not before two divisions from Groupe d'Amade had surprised some of von der Marwitz's cavalry in their billets. It took part of II Corps and the whole of IV Reserve Corps to drive them off. The result of this was that II Corps reached the river opposite the crossings allocated to IV Reserve Corps, which now found itself following in the former's wake. In the meantime, on orders of the French commander-in-chief, Joffre, Lanrezac had halted on the River Oise and was preparing to launch a counter-stroke into the flank of the German First and Second Armies. This took place on the following day, the 29th. A series of uncoordinated actions resulted in a stalemate. Simultaneously with the Battle of Guise, as this action was called, First Army crossed the Somme. Von Kluck himself considered that his priority now was the French rather than the British and he wanted to find their flank in order to drive them away from Paris. OHL saw the situation slightly differently. They believed that there was a danger that the Allies would concentrate fresh forces on the Aisne or lower Seine and their orders to First Army on the evening of the 28th had been to 'march west of the Oise towards the lower Seine. It must be prepared to co-operate in the fighting of the Second Army. It will also be responsible for the protection of the right flank of the Armies, and will take steps to prevent any new enemy concentration in its zone of operations.'[2] Von Kluck interpreted this as meaning that he was expected to continue to advance south-west for the time being, but was to be prepared to swing south. As it happened, fresh forces, in the shape of Maunoury's newly formed Sixth Army, were gathering south of Amiens and First Army was now advancing towards them. Von Rundstedt's corps, however, had now been deployed on the open flank, to guard both it and the Army's communications. It entered Albert on the evening of the 29th, after a day of skirmishing with elements of Groupe d'Amade.

On 30 August, Lanzerac, on orders from Joffre, began to withdraw from the Oise. Von Bülow asked von Kluck for assistance in exploiting this success and, that evening, First Army was ordered to wheel to the south-east in order to catch Lanrezac in the flank. This fitted perfectly with von Kluck's own view of the situation. Besides, although he was aware of French forces south of Amiens, he did not consider them of much significance. Hence First Army began to swing across the front of

Maunoury's French Sixth Army in a path which would take it well to the east of Paris. To guard his right flank, von Kluck detailed just IV Reserve Corps, which had entered Amiens that day, but then fell further and further behind as the other corps headed and crossed the Oise. On 1 September, the German First Army came up against the BEF rearguards once more and von Kluck again saw the chance to annihilate the British. Hence he ordered his corps south once more, but the British were too quick for him and continued back towards the Marne. On the following evening, von Moltke, who had now moved OHL from Koblenz, where it had been situated since the beginning of the campaign, to Luxembourg, issued fresh orders by wireless. Von Kluck was now to 'follow in echelon behind Second Army and to be responsible for the flank protection of the Armies'.[3] This revealed how out of touch von Moltke was with the situation at the Front, for First Army was a day's march ahead of Second Army and for von Kluck to carry out the OHL order would mean that he would have to halt for two days. If he did this, the object of driving the enemy away from Paris could not be achieved and it would allow the Allies a valuable breathing space. On the other hand, the task of protection of an ever longer flank was weakening his combat power and he was desperate for the return of 22nd Reserve Division's other brigade, as well as for additional reinforcements. He therefore resolved to continue his advance without halting, leaving IV Reserve Corps to continue to cover any possible threat from the Paris direction, a threat, which, unknown to von Kluck, was about to become reality. For, recognising the increasing vulnerability of the German First Army, the French Sixth Army was preparing to strike.

On 3 September von Kluck sent von Moltke a telegram stating that he had crossed the Marne and that at least part of the enemy in front of him was becoming totally disorganised. It was not, however, until the following evening that von Moltke saw this message and when he did he was aghast. Not only was First Army's right flank now vulnerable, but that of Second Army as well. The time had come to switch the main effort to the centre. First and Second Armies were now to face west to guard against any thrust from Paris, while the other armies broke through in the Verdun area and then swung westwards. As he made this decision so Sixth Army was beginning to advance towards IV Reserve Corps.

The morning of the 5th found IV Reserve Corps advancing on two parallel routes towards the Marne, the only one of von Kluck's corps yet to cross the river. 7th Reserve Division, with some cavalry, was on the right and 22nd Reserve Division, still with just one infantry brigade, on the left. Unknown to von Gronau, the corps commander, the leading division of the French Sixth Army was at that moment advancing from the west towards him. At 1000 hours von Gronau ordered his troops to halt, much welcomed since they had been on the march since the early hours, and they set about preparing for a meal. At the same time von Gronau's cavalry began to bring in reports of French activity in the west. As they did so, the leading French regiment halted for its midday meal in a village less than three miles west of the Germans. Between the two lay a piece of high ground. This von Gronau decided he must occupy and immediately sent 7th Reserve Division to do this. The French regimental commander also thought that he should at least send patrols up on to this high ground, but he was too late. The Germans beat him to it and began to shell his regiment. Both sides had missed their meal and the Battle of the Marne had begun.

The French now tried to drive von Gronau off the high ground, but succeeded only in the north, and were then driven off again by a counter-attack. Von Rundstedt's division had already been committed and the fighting continued until darkness fell. It was to be some hours, however, before von Kluck knew that IV Reserve Corps was heavily engaged. In the meantime, the remainder of his corps continued south and crossed Le Grand Morin over 15 miles to the south of von Gronau's position. True, he had received the OHL change of plan at 0700 hours, but dismissed it, considering that von Moltke was making too much of the Paris threat and was out of touch with the real situation. In the evening, though, as reports from von Gronau began to trickle through with urgent requests for reinforcements to be sent to him, the situation suddenly appeared very different. 'We find ourselves facing a grave crisis', as von Kluck's chief of staff commented.[4] This was reinforced by Lieutenant Colonel Hentsch, who arrived that evening at von Kluck's headquarters from Luxembourg to amplify von Moltke's new orders. For the first time the army commander was made aware of the fact that everywhere along the front the French resistance had hardened and that he was now out on a limb. Accordingly, he halted his advance south and ordered II Corps to retrace its steps in order to assist von Gronau. The other corps, too, were to prepare to fall back to the Marne.

During the night, von Gronau, who, like his adversaries, had suffered significant casualties, withdrew to the east. His reason was that his present position was too vulnerable to an outflanking movement and hence he pulled his troops back to the next ridge to the east, the Multien plateau which stood with its back to the Ourq.

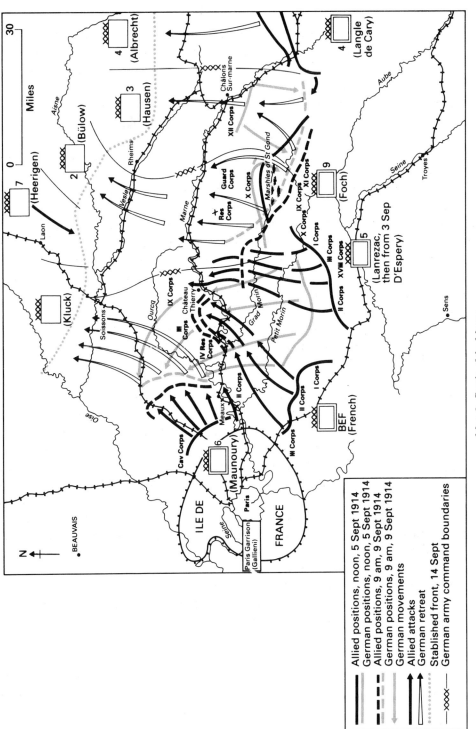

MAP 2. Battle of the Marne.

Allied positions, noon, 5 Sept 1914
German positions, noon, 5 Sept 1914
Allied positions, 9 am, 9 Sept 1914
German positions, 9 am, 9 Sept 1914
German movements
Allied attacks
German retreat
Stablished front, 14 Sept
German army command boundaries

Maunoury's men occupied the ground surrended by IV Reserve
Corps and by mid-morning on the 6th the French were pushing against
von Gronau's new line. Once again, the fighting was heavy, but von
Gronau's men, cheered by the knowledge that II Corps was on its way,
held their ground. One concern was that the British were involved in
the attack, the khaki uniforms of the Moroccans in the French Sixth
Army being confused with those of the BEF. Von Kluck was alarmed
enough by this mistaken report to order IV Corps to move back that
night to lend its weight on the Ourcq. Next day, the fighting grew even
more in intensity. By now the Germans knew, thanks to a captured
French order, that the Allies were mounting a general offensive, and
this was confirmed when the French Fifth and Seventh Armies began to
pressure von Kluck's remaining corps in the south (III, XI) and the
German Second Army. Maunoury, now reinforced with additional
elements sent to him by taxi from Paris, continued to batter his head
against the Ourcq position, which still held. IV Reserve Corps continued to bear the brunt of this, but the situation was becoming
desperate. In von Gronau's words, his men had now been fighting for
three days against 'an obviously superior enemy . . . without reserves,
under a burning sun throughout the day, without water and without
provision'. Behind the front line, chaos was growing, as regimental
supply columns 'roamed about in search of their units, the wounded
flowed back towards the rear and eventually filled the churches . . . at
cross-roads staff officers were detaining deserters . . . many were rov-
ing about looking for food.' Permeating all was 'the acrid smell of
smoke', to which was added 'the stench of dead horses'.[5] Von Rundstedt's divisional commander, von Reimann, was severely wounded
during this time, which left him running the division. However, his
calm leadership apparently proved an 'inspiration' to all.[6] Von Kluck
now felt forced to withdraw his two remaining corps in the south, which
he had temporarily given over to von Bülow, and these began to
withdraw on the 7th, leaving Second Army's flank in the air much to
von Bülow's chagrin. The bulk were directed to withdraw north and
then swing round and attack Maunoury on his left flank, but Bloem's
division was directed to relieve the hard pressed IV Reserve Corps.
Bloem's own regiment was detailed to relieve von Rundstedt's division,
or more precisely the remains of its one brigade:

> 'As darkness drew on, the roar of battle suddenly ceased, after a final mad
> burst of firing, a usual custom apparently, and soon afterwards we were
> ordered forward to relieve the remnants of the 44th Reserve Brigade, the
> 32nd and 82nd Regiments, in the front line. We marched on across the

hollow, then up the hill into the village, which was now gradually crumbling away and burning into a heap of rubble. Dead men lay in the road, shadowy forms passed by our equally shadowy forms, voices asked: "What regiment? Where are you going?" A captain, wandering aimlessly and alone, spoke to me: his speech was confused, and the light of my torch showed a haggard face with the restless shifting eyes of a madman: "I once had a company. I'm all that's left of it." On all sides was the tramping of troops, the clatter of horses, the rattle of guns on the march, and the shouting or moaning of human beings.'[7]

The arrival of Bloem's division frustrated Maunoury's attempt to outflank the Ourcq position from the south, although the Germans did surrender some ground. Likewise, Maunoury had been denied success in the north by the arrival of von Kluck's other forces from the south. He was therefore ordered to cease attacking and go on to the defensive while the BEF struck von Kluck from the south.

During this same day, 8 September, von Moltke had despatched Hentsch on a lightning tour of the armies. Moving from east to west, he found that Fifth, Fourth and Third Armies were reasonably satisfied with the situation. He arrived at von Bülow's headquarters late that night and the Second Army commander immediately made plain to him his concern over the gap that had appeared between him and von Kluck. Next morning Hentsch had a further discussion with von Bülow's chief of staff and chief of operations. It was clear that von Kluck, engaged as he was with the French Sixth Army, could do nothing to close the gap and the only answer was for Second Army to withdraw back across the Marne. This was especially urgent since British cavalry had crossed the river in von Kluck's sector at dawn and the Fifth French Army was also on the move. Hentsch then got into his motor car to travel to von Kluck's headquarters at Mareuil. He arrived here at midday to find that von Kluck had launched an attack with his IX Corps against Maunoury's left, but had also, in the face of the BEF threat, ordered his centre and left to wheel so that they faced south. At the same time, news came from Second Army that their withdrawal had begun. Now Hentsch had been told by von Moltke that if he found that one of the right-hand armies was withdrawing the other was to conform. Second Army was to pull back to the line of the River Vesle, a tributary of the Aisne, and First Army to the line of the Veskle and Aisne as far west as Soissons. In this way the gap would be closed. Accordingly, with von Bülow now in retreat, Hentsch told von Kluck that he was to pull back to the line Soissons–Fismes. Von Kluck therefore stopped the IX Corps attack and gave the necessary orders.

By the end of 11 September First Army was back across the Aisne, with von Rundstedt's division in the right centre of the line, around Fontenoy. Pressure from the French Fifth Army and the BEF had, however, combined to prevent von Kluck from extending as far east as Fismes and had also forced von Bülow north-east, where he had taken up a position along the River Vesle in the Reims area. All that covered the 30 mile gap was a thin screen of cavalry and other elements equating to one division. It was as well that the British and French were as exhausted as their enemy and were unable to exploit this. Even so, Maunoury's Sixth Army did try to get round von Kluck's right flank. However, although he managed to cross the Aisne, the German defences on the heights above the river proved too strong. In the meantime, von Moltke managed to plug the gap between von Kluck and von Bülow, first with a Reserve corps, which had been beseiging Mauberge, and then with Seventh Army, which he brought round from Alsace.

There now began that period known as the Race to the Sea, as the German armies tried to exploit the open Allied left flank. First Army's role in this was, however, small and purely defensive. This was a shallow hook to the Noyon area during the second half of September in order to frustrate further efforts by Maunoury to outflank the position on the Aisne. Trench warfare now set in.

Von Rundstedt's personal view of the campaign was that it failed because the strong right flank demanded by von Schlieffen had been fatally weakened. He also considered that von Moltke had not commanded with sufficient firmness and that his headquarters was too far to the rear to be able to influence events. He also condemned von Kluck for his obstinacy and asserted that it was he alone who had created the crisis on the Marne.[8] Since his division had come the closest of any to Paris he had some cause to feel strongly about the matter.

Von Rundstedt's own efforts did not go unrecognised. It was probably at this time that he was awarded the Iron Cross 1st Class. On 28 November 1914 he was also promoted to Major. A few weeks earlier, he had fallen sick with a lung infection, probably caused by the intense strain of the past two months, and was forced to relinquish his post.[9] By the beginning of December, however, he had recovered sufficiently to return to duty. He was posted to the Military Government in Antwerp, probably because the doctors considered that to expose him to the rigours of a more active appointment would undermine his health once more.

Von Rundstedt remained at Antwerp throughout the winter and on 1 April 1915 was appointed chief of staff to the 86th Infantry Division.

This was a newly raised formation, with one infantry brigade of three regiments and a field artillery regiment of three battalions, the units being found from existing divisions, which were also reduced to this lower establishment. This was sent to the Eastern Front to join von Gallwitz's costly offensive to the River Narew which took place in July 1915.

At the beginning of 1915, the Central Powers had launched two offensives with the ultimate aim of trapping the Russian armies by double envelopment. In the south, the Austrians, supported by the Germans, had attacked in the Carpathians and initially made good progress before being flung back in March by Russian reinforcements made available through their capture of the fortress of Przemysl which they had been besieging. In the north, von Hindenburg, with two armies, had attacked from the Masurian Lakes and destroyed the Russian Tenth Army, only to be brought to a halt by the appearance of a fresh Russian army. After some debate, it was decided that a fresh offensive be launched in Galicia. This opened on 2 May and reaped spectacular results. By the end of the month Przemysl had been recaptured and the Russians driven back over 100 miles. Lemberg then fell and by mid July the Austro-Hungarian and German forces were closing up to the River Bug. This left a significant Russian salient around Warsaw and, in order to pinch this out and trap the Russian forces within it, the Germans launched a subsidiary attack from the north on 13 July. This was to involved Gerd's division. On the 24th the Narew was crossed, but then the Russians began to counter-attack and prevented any immediate further German advance. A German soldier on the Narew described what the fighting was like in a letter home:

'We were certainly not in an enviable position. Behind us was the Narew, cutting off any communication with the rear. Ammunition was running short. All the time there were shouts: "Careful on the left! Careful on the right! Strong enemy column gathering on the left. Enemy column on the right," and so on. . . . Our rags were at last beginning to get dry, but on the second evening it started raining again. And how it poured! The rain lasted the whole night. I was sitting against the back of the trench, wet to the skin, when suddenly I heard loud cheering and trumpet sounds on the left . . . on the left flank two Russian brigades launched an attack against one of our battalions. Next day I felt pretty awful. My rags were wet again, with sand clinging to them. I was cold and hungry, for apart from the few bites which each of us had brought with him there was nothing to eat. And nothing to drink, only the water of the Narew, in which dead bodies were floating about. The sight of so many dead behind our trench, and the groans of the wounded, were not exactly encouraging, either.'[10]

In the midst of this Gerd's health broke down once more and he was evacuated sick with both lung and heart trouble,[11] probably brought about by the combination of weather and strain. His divisional commander, General von Wernitz, was clearly sorry to see him go and praised his clear judgement and willingness to work. Significantly, though, von Gallwitz added the rider that Gerd had to develop a 'more lively' character, an indication that his health was troubling him for some time before he actually reported sick.[12]

While Gerd was away recovering, the Russians eventually decided to withdraw from the Warsaw salient and fell back to a line which left virtually the whole of Poland in German hands. Warsaw was entered on 5 August and a military government set up under General von Beseler. It was to this that Gerd was now posted on 5 September. While it would have made sense to give him the post of Chief of Operations (1a), in view of his experience, this was already filled by an officer junior to him. He therefore had to make do with the 1b position which gave him responsibility for administration and logistics. While this may not have been wholly to his taste, he must have realised that the experience would have been good for his long term development as a staff officer and also that it would have done him little good to have returned to a combat formation before he was fully recovered. Indeed, it may well be that while at Antwerp he had agitated for such a job and been given it before he was fully fit and hence the second breakdown in his health. As it was, he impressed both von Beseler and his chief of staff. The latter noted in particular his clear judgement and enthusiasm for his work. These qualities were echoed by von Beseler, who also commented on his sincerity and humour – an indication that Gerd had overcome the depression that had plagued him during summer 1915.[13]

Von Beseler gave Gerd a strong recommendation for the post of chief of staff to an army corps. On 1 November 1916 he was appointed as 1a to HQ XXV Reserve Corps in the Carpathians, but within days of his arrival the chief of staff departed on leave for a month, leaving Gerd in charge. Apparently, the corps commander was not popular with the staff and since he had praised von Rundstedt before his arrival, the staff feared that Gerd would be like the general and were cool towards him at first. A few evenings later, however, one young officer said to him: 'Really, Major, you are quite nice!', and the ice was broken.[14]

During the summer the Central Powers had been on the defensive on the Eastern Front and had had to fight hard to contain Brusilov's

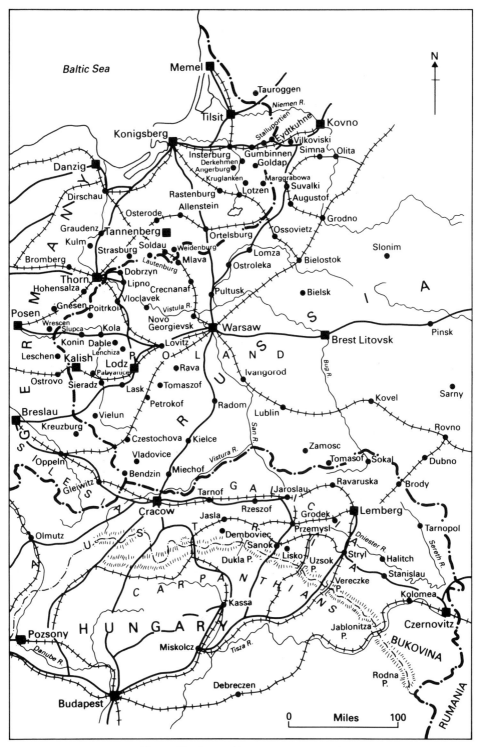

Map 3. The Eastern Front 1915–1917.

offensive, which made spectacular gains from the Pripet marshes in the North to the Rumanian border in the South before it began to run out of momentum. Then, at the end of August, Rumania declared war on the Central Powers. A month later Austro-German forces invaded her and the Russians were forced to deploy increasing numbers of troops in a vain effort to prop up their new ally. In order to try and divert his enemies, Brusilov mounted a number of diversionary attacks elsewhere along the front. Von Rundstedt had to cope with one of these at the end of November and received high praise for his efforts from Freiherr von Richthofen, his corps commander, for his performance, as well as another strong recommendation for the post of corps chief of staff.[15] He was, however, to remain as 1a to XXV Reserve Corps until autumn 1917. As such he took part in the repulsion of Kerensky's ill-fated July 1917 offensive astride the Dniester, the last gasp of the old Russian Army, as part of Graf von Bothmer's *Südarmee*, which was a mixed Austro-German formation, but which also included two Turkish divisions and it was their presence which brought about the award to von Rundstedt of the Turkish Iron Crescent. When the Central Powers' counter-offensive began on 19 July von Rundstedt again distinguished himself and his efforts were rewarded when on 1 October he was appointed Chief of Staff of LIII Corps. This was part of Army Detachment D, which was commanded by the King of Saxony, and was located in the northern part of the Eastern Front.

The hostilities on the Eastern Front were now virtually at an end. On 7 November 1917 the Bolsheviks seized power in Petrograd and then announced their intention to bring Russia's part in the war to an end. Negotiations were opened with Germany and these eventually led to the Treaty of Brest-Litovsk, which was signed on 3 March 1918. The terms were swingeing, with the Russians renouncing all rights to Poland, Courland and Lithuania and agreeing to evacuate Finland, Estonia and Livonia, as well as recognising Ukraine's right to independence. The path of negotiation was by no means smooth, however, and in February the Germans reopened hostilities and pushed forward eastwards into the Ukraine and elsewhere. During this renewed burst of fighting, von Rundstedt added further to his reputation. On 3 March, the day the Treaty was signed, his commander, General Siebourg, recommended him for Prussia's highest decoration, the Pour Le Mérite. He praised Gerd's 'sound judgement and pertinent grasp of the situation' which 'led to the daringly executed raids' which brought the Germans up to Lake Peipus, which lies today on the Estonian-Russian border, and brought about 'outstanding successes consequent in the enormous bounty of liberated territories which were overrun'. The citation also cited Gerd's performance during the July 1917 fighting.[16] The Chief of Staff of Army Detachment D, in another report written two weeks later, also wrote that he 'proved himself in an excellent way in the execution of the attack' through his 'quick grasp of the situation and his energy'. Colonel von Kleist, the King of Saxony's aide, endorsed this, recalling that in Galicia in summer 1917 he was 'an outstandingly able 1a with my neighbouring corps' and that Gerd was 'an outstanding personality'.[17] After Brest-Litovsk, however, Gerd's duties were mainly concerned with the policing of the newly seized territories and there is no doubt that his experience at Antwerp and Warsaw was now put to good use. As Siebourg later wrote: 'During the occupation and administration of the conquered territories, Major v. Rundstedt displayed a good organisational talent and impact in economic, police and political respects.'[18] In spite of all this high praise, Gerd did not receive the Pour Le Mérite, possibly, one suspects, because the citation, as it stood, was not strongly enough written up and indicated that his performance was little more than would be expected of an experienced member of the *Grosse Generalstab*.

If the Germans, by spring 1918, appeared victorious in the East, it was to be a different matter on the Western Front. During the period March–July 1918 they launched no less than five desperate attacks on the Allies with a view to gaining a decisive victory. The first three made significant inroads into the Allied defences, but did not break them. Finally, after the failure of the final drive against the French Fourth and Fifth Armies in the Reims area in mid-July, Ludendorff was forced to recognise that he had shot his bolt. The initiative passed to the Allies and, within weeks, they had begun to attack. It was now that von Rundstedt returned to the Western Front, assuming the appointment of Chief of Staff of XV Corps, the same corps in which he had served as a company commander just before the war, in von Bothmer's Nineteenth Army on 1 August 1918. A week later the British attacked with tanks at Amiens in what Ludendorff later called 'the Black Day of the German Army'. It was the beginning of the end.

These last few months were probably the most frustrating that von Rundstedt suffered during the whole of the First World War. Nineteenth Army was in Alsace and, in spite of careful preparation, it would not face any major Allied attack. All it could do as a helpless bystander was watch the remorseless progress of the Allied armies to the north. Yet, von Rundstedt seems to have been an inspiration to all with whom he served. The Chief of Staff of Nineteenth Army, Colonel von Hemmler, wrote of him:

> 'He is as a chief should be: clear thinking, balanced, positive in decision and judgement, remarkably practical and trained in an excellent way for General Staff duty. He stands out in any situation, even the most difficult, and he does not shy away from problems. He is a shining ideal for the whole staff, which he has led with all his powers to a most excellent performance. A complete man, of distinguished mien, of as fine a nobility in his beliefs and way of thinking, as you could wish for in this period of deepest misery.'

This was endorsed by von Bothmer, who described him as 'a wholly excellent staff officer and aimiable comrade'.[19] This 'time of misery' for the prewar regular officers of the German armies, especially those of the *Grosse Generalstab*, was just that. Not only were the Allied attacks unceasingly successful, but as the autumn wore on, so the cracks in the infrastructure of Germany itself grew wider. Then, at the end of October, came the mutiny of the Grand Fleet at Kiel. Simultaneously came the setting up of Soldiers' Councils in more and more units in the West. It must have seemed to Gerd, with his recent experience in the East, that the tide of Bolshevism had broken through the shield of German forces and was now engulfing the whole of Germany. The abdication of the Kaiser on 9 November would have served to confirm this, as well as knocking away, at one blow, the foundation stone on which Gerd and his brother officers based their *modus vivendi* of Duty, Loyalty and Honour. Yet, whatever he thought, he kept to himself and still strove to maintain order amid the growing chaos. This was so much so that, a month after the guns had finally ceased firing in the West, his corps commander cited him yet again for the Pour Le Mérite.

> 'It was mainly due to him alone that an effective defence was established despite enormous obstructions and difficulties and that the planned enemy attacks were not executed. I consider Major v. Rundstedt's merits during the war as that high and important for the Army and Fatherland . . . It would be regretted to the highest degree if the events of 9 November and the sad end of the war would rob Major v. Rundstedt of his hard earned decoration. It would also be an injustice of the greatest kind if awards, which were earned during the long war, were extinguished at one blow.'[20]

Sadly for von Rundstedt, this is exactly what had happened. The old régime was dead and Germans, both military and civilian, faced an uncertain future.

3
The Weimar Years

AFTER THE Armistice, Gerd's corps withdrew back across the Rhine with the rest of German forces in France and Belgium. It was a very dispiriting time, especially with the unrest that was sweeping the troops. The influence of the Soldiers' Councils over Friedrich Ebert's Majority Socialist government in Berlin, and unrest in Bavaria, where an independent republic was set up, bore all the hallmarks of the Russian Revolution. The only comfort that Gerd could take at this troubled and doom-laden time was that he and all his brothers had survived the war (although Udo had lost an eye) and that he would be reunited with his wife and son.

The pre-1914 XV Corps area was, of course, Alsace, but there was no question of it returning here in 1918 and it is not certain where the corps headquarters did eventually come to rest. Once across the German border, the old Army quickly disintegrated amid the anarchy of defeat and it is probable that the corps headquarters was quickly disbanded.

On 11 December 1918, troops lately returned from the Western Front paraded under General Arnold von Lequis in Berlin. It was to be the last flourish of the Royal Prussian Army. In some ways they appeared not as a defeated army, but one that had triumphed. The officers wore all their decorations and many of the soldiers bore crowns of oakleaves, as did their heavy weapons. This impression was reinforced by Ebert, who addressed the parading troops at the Brandenburg Gate: 'I salute you, you whom no enemy has defeated on the battlefields.'[1] On the other hand, they did not bear the old Imperial banners. Instead, they carried simple brown flags. The unsmiling expressions on the soldiers' faces did not display any feeling of victory, and the modest crowds of bystanders were muted in their applause. Some, especially members of the People's Naval Division, were merely sullen. For the next two days, nine divisions' worth of soldiers trooped through Berlin. From there they went to their depots and were disbanded.

Ebert, pressured as he was by left wing and liberal elements in the government, felt forced to remove the army's teeth and, apart from von Lequis's troops would not allow it back into Berlin. Instead, he formed a citizens' militia to counter the increasing provocations of the mutinous bands of sailors and soldiers in the Prussian capital. The Supreme Command (OHL) under von Hindenburg and Groener came to rest at Wilhelmshöhe outside Kassel, but pledged its support to Ebert. He, however, was now forced to pass on demands by the workers' and soldiers' councils for the 'demilitarisation' of the army. This included the removal of all rank insignia, election of officers by their soldiers, and the eventual disbandment of the army in favour of a nationwide citizens' militia (*Volkswehr*). Von Hindenburg and Groener could not possibly accept these terms. In the meantime, with anarchy growing in Berlin and elsewhere, some officers called for volunteers from among the few still loyal soldiers. These became the early *Freikorps* and it was on them alone that the Supreme Command came to rely in its efforts to prevent Germany being swamped by red revolution.

According to the *Militärarchiv* at Freiburg, Gerd was posted to the *Grosse Generalstab* in December 1918.[2] It is probable that he was actually assigned to the OHL, which would have suited him, bearing in mind its location. It is also possible that Groener may have summoned Gerd in person, since, having been chief of staff to the army of occupation in Russia, he probably knew him. No evidence survives of what Gerd felt or how he reacted to the chaos of those last weeks of 1918 and first of 1919. It would have been in his character that, whatever his private feelings, he maintained his loyalty to von Hindenburg and hence to Ebert.

In January some of the embryo *Freikorps* were allowed into Berlin, thanks largely to Ebert's defence minister, Gustav Noske, and began to clean out the Spartacists, as the left wing revolutionaries called themselves. Berlin was cleared of them within a week. Other *Freikorps* moved to deal with similar uprisings in Northern Germany, while others still were battling with Polish irregulars determined to grab as much territory from Germany as possible in order to present the Allied peacemakers in Paris with a *fait accompli* with regard to Poland's borders. In order to insulate himself from further unrest which might take place in the capital, Ebert then moved the seat of government to Weimar, 150 miles south-west of Berlin, and held elections for the National Assembly. These returned his Majority Socialists as the largest party and gave him a firm mandate to remain in office.

Ebert could now devote attention to drawing up a charter for the German Armed Forces of the future within the democratic republic that Germany now was. Much of this was done in consultation, but not without much debate with the Supreme Headquarters, which had now moved to Kolberg in Pomerania in order to be closer to the fighting on Germany's eastern borders. The result was the Law on the Provisional Reichswehr, which came into force at the beginning of March 1919. This restored badges of rank, albeit new designs from those of the old army, but officers would no longer be permitted to wear their epaulettes, which angered some. There would be no conscription, but six to nine years' voluntary engagements, and soldiers were to be entitled to vote. Saluting was upheld and units would elect soldiers' councils, although these would merely concern themselves with welfare. In the meantime further left wing revolts were put down by the *Freikorps*, culminating in the overthrow of the month-old revolutionary government of Bavaria in May. By this time, they and the elements of the standing army numbered some 400,000 men. All were to be organised into brigades, one to each of the 25 corps areas of the pre-1914 German armies. In the midst of this reorganisation a bombshell struck.

On 7 May, the Allies presented Germany with the terms to which she must accede if she was to achieve formal peace with her late enemies. Among the surrenders of territory, those parts given to the newly independent state of Poland were especially resented by many Prussian officers. Not only would East Prussia now be isolated from the remainder of Germany by the Polish Corridor, but a significant portion of industrially rich Silesia was to be handed over to the Poles. The Army itself was to be reduced, after a transitionary period, to 100,000 men on long-term engagements, with strictly limited armaments – no tanks, no guns above 105 mm calibre, no aircraft. In addition, the *Grosse Generalstab* was to be disbanded. Worse, apart from crippling reparation payments, Germany had to acknowledge that she had started the war and to hand over anyone whom the Allies suspected of having committed war crimes. These demands became known as the 'paragraphs of shame'. A movement led by Colonel Walther Reinhardt, then the Prussian War Minister, but later to be Gerd's chief, advocated acceptance of the terms in the West, but not in the East, arguing that before the Poles were properly organised the Army could snatch back at least some of the about-to-be-lost regions. They also demanded that the 'paragraphs of shame' be removed. The terms were debated at a meeting of senior army officers held at Weimar on 19 June. The majority followed Groener, who argued that Germany was militarily and economically ill-equipped to resist the Allies should they decide to implement the terms by force. The Government felt the same and on 28 June the Treaty of Versailles was signed. This must have been hard for Gerd, but he would undoubtedly have followed Groener's line. Others, however, would continue to harbour a canker of resentment, although this was removed to some extent when the Allies later agreed that Germany could try her own war criminals and the Weimar Government permitted the reintroduction of the officer's epaulette.

Versailles laid down that the Provisional Reichswehr must be reduced to 200,000 men by 1 October 1919, and that the 100,000 man Army was to come into being by 31 March 1920. It was to consist of, and this was strictly laid down by the Treaty, seven infantry and three cavalry divisions, with no more than two higher formation headquarters. To accommodate this, two *Gruppenkommando* (Group Commands) were to be created, and each infantry divisional headquarters would also command a geographic military district (*Wehrkreis*). At the top of the command pyramid a *Heeresleitung* (Army Leadership) was created, which, together with the *Marineleitung* (Navy Leadership), was directly subordinated to Noske as defence minister. After Versailles had been signed, von Hindenburg and Groener felt themselves duty bound to resign and appointed as to head the *Heeresleitung* was none other than Reinhardt. Under him was the *Truppenamt* (Troop Office), which substituted for the *Grosse Generalstab* and would, in fact, act as a camouflage for it. To run this, General Hans von Seeckt was appointed, a man who was to have almost complete control on the shaping of the truncated German Army during its formative years.

On 1 October 1919, the new Provisional Reichswehr came into being. A ceiling of 4,000 officers had been imposed on it and this inevitably meant that many had to be retired. Among them were Udo and Joachim, Gerd's brothers, who retired with ranks of Major and Colonel respectively. Both went to live in Ratzeburg near Kiel, where their now widowed mother resided. Eberhard, having held a reserve commission during the war, had already been demobilised. Gerd himself had received another strong recommendation in April, from his former corps commander in France, that he should be retained.[3] Indeed, with his proven experience as a high class staff officer, he was exactly the material which von Seeckt was seeking in order to create the right foundations for the Army of the future. Accordingly, on 1 October 1919 Gerd was appointed to the staff of *Wehrkreis* V, based at Stuttgart. This, though, proved to be merely a transitional appointment while the second phase of the drastic manpower reduction was carried out, an operation which was to cause severe ructions and threaten the whole fabric of the infant republic.

The spark that lit the flame of what came to be known as the Kapp Putsch was the status of two Freikorps naval brigades, Ehrhardt and von Loewenfeld. Reinhardt and von Seeckt feared the independence of some of the Freikorps (not all of whom, by any means, had been properly assimilated into the Provisional Reichswehr) and wanted to use the mandatory strength reductions to disband them. The Inter-Allied Military Control Commission, responsible for seeing that the Versailles military clauses were honoured, insisted that these two brigades should be considered part of the German Navy, now to be reduced to 15,000 men. An obstacle stood in the way of this, General Walter Freiherr von Lüttwitz, who headed *Gruppenkommando* 1 in Berlin. The brigades were at the time under his command and, not only did he not want to lose them, but he also vehemently resisted any reductions in strength, doing his best to thwart all orders to this effect. The order to disband the two brigades was promulgated on 29 February 1920, but on the following day von Lüttwitz told the Ehrhardt Brigade that he would not allow this to happen. Ten days later, probably in an attempt to calm the situation, Noske ordered that the brigades should be transferred to the Navy. Von Lüttwitz's reaction was to go and see Ebert. He not only demanded that the brigades remain under his command, but that Reinhardt should be sacked and fresh national elections called. He was supported in this by Dr Walther Kapp, a right wing politician. Noske then relieved von Lüttwitz of his command, but he refused to go. At the same time, Noske was made aware that a mutiny was brewing. However, attempts to arrest some of the ringleaders failed. On 12 March, the Ehrhardt Brigade, which was based at Döberitz, just outside Berlin, announced its intention to march to Berlin and the garrison at Potsdam sided with it. Reinhardt was prepared to meet force with force, but many officers in Berlin, notably von Seeckt, who offered his resignation, were not prepared to see soldiers fire on soldiers. The Government therefore decided to leave Berlin for Dresden and ordered the troops there to remain in their barracks, thus enabling the Ehrhardt Brigade and its supporters to enter the capital unopposed.

The effects of the events in Berlin split the Reichswehr down the middle. The eastern *Wehrkreise*, which were under *Gruppenkommando* 1, generally indicated their support for von Lüttwitz. In the west of the country it was different. Significantly, Gerd's commander in *Wehrkreis* V, General Walter von Bergmann, immediately declared in favour of the government.[4] He would have undoubtedly consulted his staff and Gerd probably said to him, as he did before the International Military Tribunal at Nuremberg in 1946 when questioned about the Putsch: 'It is a very ancient Prussian tradition that an officer does not concern himself with politics.'[5] The other two *Gruppenkommando 2 Wehrkreise* commanders, at Münster and Munich, preferred to await developments and took a neutral stance. Kapp tried to set up a government, but the immediate reaction to this was a General Strike. On 17 March, realising that he did not have popular support, Kapp fled, leaving von Lüttwitz to pick up the pieces. The Putsch was over. Von Rundstedt's verdict on it was: 'Kapp was a failure and a very stupid one at that, a very stupid putsch which could never succeed.'[6]

In the aftermath of the Kapp Putsch, Noske resigned, having lost much support from the electorate. Reinhardt stepped down as chief of the Heeresleitung, feeling that he could no longer remain in post when so few officers had supported his preparedness to use force to crush the rebels. He was replaced by von Seeckt. In the words of Joachim von Stülpnagel, who was to work closely with von Seeckt: 'He entered office with the clear intention of forming an army, loyal to the constitution, well disciplined, faithful to the Prussian tradition, and devoted to himself.'[7] He moved quickly to achieve this, making the two group commanders directly subordinate to him instead of to the defence minister, as they had previously been, and placing all the various army departments in Berlin firmly under his control. Within a year, he had banned soldiers from taking part in any political activity and managed to create a situation where the Army was, in his words, 'the first instrument of the power of the Reich'.[8] Nevertheless, he kept it at arm's length from the Weimar Republic. Even though von Seeckt was cold and distant in character, his policy coincided with the beliefs of von Rundstedt and many others and they came to regard him rather than the President as the figurehead of the state.

In May 1920, von Rundstedt was made Chief of Staff of 3rd Cavalry Division, which had its headquarters at Weimar. Having been unable to join the cavalry as a young man, this was a posting which must have given him much pleasure. It was also a step up the rung of the career ladder and a sign that he continued to be highly regarded by his peers. This was reinforced, when, on 1 October 1920, he and four other majors were promoted to Lieutenant Colonel. His fellow promotees were Werner von Blomberg, Fedor von Bock, Kurt Freiherr von Hammerstein-Equord and Wilhelm von Leeb. All were to reach high rank and make their mark on the German Army during the next twenty

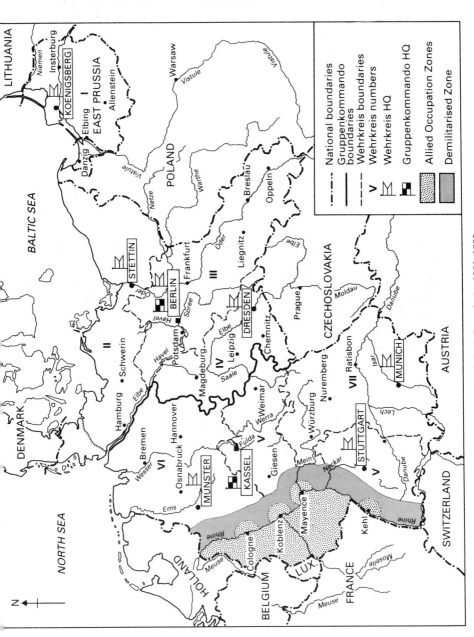

MAP 4. Wehrkreis Boundaries 1921–1935.

years. Von Seeckt was not merely grappling with the present, but was also looking to the future and wanted to groom selected officers whom he could trust to maintain the Army in the character in which he was shaping it.

Gerd shone as a cavalry chief of staff. His commander, General Elzborn, reporting on him in November 1921, wrote that he 'could not wish for better'. In spite of not being a cavalryman, von Rundstedt had 'fully grasped the essence of cavalry training'. Elzborn also drew attention to Gerd's 'organisational talent, which became obvious during the war'. He also commented on the 'unusual respect' and simpatico which he enjoyed with both his contemporaries and subordinates. The report also made mention of the 'spartan simplicity' of Gerd's life style.[9] During the winter of 1921–22, the divisional commander personally ran an equitation course, which Gerd attended and 'prepared his horse in a model way'. Significantly, too, his commander paid tribute to Gerd's emphasis during exercises on all arms cooperation and the use of radio.[10] This certainly indicated a man whose mind was not set in the past and who was prepared to apply modern technology. On the other hand, 'W E Hart', the supposed pseudonym for an officer who was believed to have served in the Reichswehr before fleeing from Germany in the 1930s, claimed that von Rundstedt spent the years 1920–23 writing an in-depth analysis of Germany's defeat in the late war. Other historians have echoed this.[11] When asked about this by Basil Liddell Hart at the beginning of 1946, von Rundstedt categorically denied it, saying, at another point in the interview, 'I can hardly write my own name!'[12] Furthermore, if he had written such a report one would have expected it to have been mentioned in the confidential reports on him over this period.

Likewise, W E Hart accused von Rundstedt of being personally responsible for putting down the 1923 Communist uprising in Thuringia with great ruthlessness and subsequently organising an election there in such a way as to ensure that deputies to the Reichstag were untainted by Socialism and would act to protect the interests of the Reichsheer.[13] The facts, however, do not support this. Von Rundstedt, who had been promoted Colonel on 1 March 1923, ahead of those who had been promoted Lieutenant Colonel with him, took up a new appointment on 1 October that year, as Chief of Staff of *Wehrkreis* II and 2nd Infantry Division in Pomerania. He was not, in fact, very happy about this since he had been promised command of a cavalry regiment. This, however, had been changed because growing unrest in Munich, created by Hitler and his National Socialists, had unsettled the staff of

Wehrkreis VII there and it was decided that von Leeb, who was a Bavarian, should be sent there and that von Rundstedt was to take his place in Stettin.[14] In any event, the Army was not called in to deal with the left-inspired Thuringian unrest until October, by which time von Rundstedt was already in his new post. Before he did so, he received another glowing report from his divisional commander. He described Gerd as a 'successful racehorse jockey and daring cross-country rider', who rode his horse with 'youthful exuberance'. He was especially complimentary on the way that Gerd handled his subordinates – 'he gave them the maximum possible independence but nevertheless guided them with a firm hand'. Furthermore, 'with his noble, honest character, his endless work for the wellbeing of the command, and his friendliness, he enjoys an extraordinary popularity everywhere'.[15]

Versailles had severely weakened Germany's eastern borders. Not only was East Prussia now an island separated by the Polish Corridor from the remainder of Germany, but the loss of the province of Posen, now called Poznan by the Poles, left a large Polish salient in German territory pointing ominously towards Berlin. The Poznan salient also made Silesia much more vulnerable and this was further aggravated by the new state of Czechoslovakia in the south. Polish attempts to grab Upper Silesia in 1921 and the fact that Poland's standing army was 250,000 strong gave von Seeckt great cause for concern. In consequence, half the strength of the Reichsheer was allocated to defence of the East. The sensible, purely military, solution for deploying these comparatively meagre forces would have been to have kept them concentrated in order to provide an effective defence of the key areas, especially Berlin. Politically, though, this was not so satisfactory. Germans living close to the Eastern borders were understandably nervous about the Poles and it was seen as important to reassure them. Also, the presence of German forces in every area, however thinly spread, would at least be some form of deterrent to what was seen as Polish adventurism. Hence von Seeckt dispersed his forces. One division was based in East Prussia, a cavalry division in Silesia, and a further infantry and a cavalry division in the Berlin area. Von Rundstedt's division, 2nd Infantry, which had its headquarters at Stettin, was responsible for Pomerania. This was not seen to be as severely threatened as the other areas. Even so, it had its problems. While its main task was to prevent an enemy thrust on Stettin itself, the division also had the Baltic coast to look after. The snag here was that Versailles did not permit any fresh fortifications to be constructed. These, in themselves, would have been a force multiplier, but, as it was, half the division had to cover the coast. The creation of realistic defence plans for the region must therefore have been a worthy challenge for von Rundstedt and one that he eagerly grasped in a way that impressed both his superiors and subordinates. Heinz Guderian, the future leading light of the Panzer force, was also serving in 2nd Division at this time and later wrote: 'He already convinced through the clarity of his thoughts and the self-confidence with which he put them across'.[16]

Gerd was to remain for only some 18 months at Stettin. On 1 May 1925, he was appointed to command 18th Infantry Regiment at Paderborn. W E Hart wrote that he had been given this command because he had been too overtly political in his attitude while in Stettin and it was thought better if he cooled his heels for a while.[17] Von Rundstedt himself said that he asked for a regiment because he felt that he had been on the staff for too long.[18] This was certainly so, and it made sense for him to prove himself as a regimental commander if he was to reach the highest ranks of the Army. Contrary to Hart's further accusation that he cared little for his regiment, he quickly displayed the wholehearted commitment with which he had approached all his previous jobs. His divisional commander heaped high praise on him after he had been in command for six months and noted especially his relationship with the young 'for whose activities he has warm sympathy and understanding'. This was endorsed by General Wilhelm Reinhardt, now commanding *Gruppenkommando* 2: 'He has a firm grip of the reins of command of the regiment and promises to command it well.'[19]

Again, von Rundstedt was not destined to enjoy his command for long. The *Truppenamt* were grooming him hard for higher things and on 1 October 1926 he was placed on the next logical rung of the ladder, Chief of Staff of *Gruppenkommando* 2. Clearly, Reinhardt had something to do with this, since it was for him that von Rundstedt was to work. Although he would have been sad to leave his regiment, the prospect of a return to Kassel must have pleased both Bila and himself. Reinhardt had no cause to regret his choice. Within six weeks of von Rundstedt taking up his post, he was writing that he promised well as chief of staff and, an indication that Reinhardt personally liked him, a year later: '. . . he is a witty, intelligent entertainer within a familiar circle.' Indeed, he was by now 'an excellent chief of staff' who promised to become 'an able commander of our highest formations'.[20] In that same year of 1927, though, he had a bad riding accident, which resulted in a fractured hip joint and a permanent reminder in the form of a scar on his lower left cheek.[21] Compensation for this came towards the end of the year when on 1 November he was promoted Major General.

His riding accident does not, however, seen to have curtailed von Rundstedt's equestrian activities. He had not given up the ambition to command a cavalry formation, even if circumstances had prevented him from commanding a cavalry regiment, and Reinhardt pushed his candidacy for a cavalry division. This was rewarded when he was appointed to command 2nd Cavalry Division, with headquarters in Breslau, with effect from 1 October 1928. By now von Seeckt had been retired and his place taken by General Wilhelm Heye. Von Seeckt had done much to give the Army back its self respect and to provide it with the basis for becoming an effective modern army once the shackles of Versailles could be thrown off. Indeed, one of the major planks in his policy was the setting up of secret but close military ties with Russia, whereby, in return for technical advice for their own arms industry, the Russians provided the facilities for secret German arms factories to be set up and for selected German officers to be given training in the weapons denied to the Reichswehr by the Allies. He had, however, increasingly pursued his own foreign policy line and the Army had become what Philipp Schiedemann, a Social Democrat politician and 1919 Chancellor, called 'a state within a state'.[22] It was clearly not a situation that the government could endure and eventually they managed to get rid of von Seeckt in October 1926 on the grounds that he had allowed the eldest son of the Crown Prince Wilhelm to take part in manoeuvres in uniform. Von Seeckt was not, however, as missed by the Army as he might have been. For a start, Heye was his own selection to succeed him. More important, in May 1925 von Hindenburg had been made President of the German Republic. In terms of prestige he far outshone von Seeckt and gave the Army not merely a military figurehead, but a Head of State up to whom it could look with pride. Germany's overall position had also improved. 1923 had been the worst year since the anarchy of 1919–20. Galloping inflation, Hitler's attempted putsch in Munich, unrest in Thuringia, the Ruhr and other areas had all combined to reveal the weaknesses of Weimar Republic. Allied realisation, through the 1924 Dawes Plan, that Germany could not pay the reparations at the rate demanded, and agreement in 1926 that she should be invited to join the League of Nations, helped to restore her self respect.

Von Rundstedt took up his new command in Silesia at an interesting time. Wilhelm Groener had taken over as Defence Minister in early 1928, having pursued a political career after retiring from the Army in 1919. While von Seeckt had been a great believer in mobility as the only means by which the small Reichswehr had any chance of defending

Germany's borders, he was somewhat conservative in his thinking when it came to the means of achieving this mobility. He considered that motorisation rather than mechanisation was the way forward, believing that it would be many years before the tank, regardless of its prohibition in Germany, was technically developed enough to become a decisive weapon. He also retained faith in the horse and even rejected a proposal that the German cavalryman give up his lance in order to increase his firepower.[23] Groener, on the other hand, was convinced that the shape of land warfare in the future would be dominated by the tank. He made this plain in an article on the development of war which he wrote late in 1928. Nevertheless, he did agree with von Seeckt that the cavalry was still an important arm, but it needed to be brought up to date: 'We need "modern Hussars", which I picture as a sort of machine gun corps.' Even so, the degree to which the cavalry should be motorised was something which would not become clear until 'the next decade'.[24] It would have been most surprising if von Rundstedt, as the commander of a cavalry division, did not read this. While he would have been reassured by Groener's continued belief in cavalry, he was not convinced by the potential dominance of the tank thesis, although he was prepared to listen to those who were. Guderian recalled meeting him on a training area in 1931:

> 'He wanted to inspect cavalry soldiers while I was occupied with the first trials of motorised troops. He condemned my endeavours because he did not want to believe in their implementation. But when I said, in an attempt to defend myself, "What else is a cavalry division today but an enormous baggage train with insufficient escort?" he became very serious and replied: "Perhaps you are right".'[25]

Guderian and von Rundstedt were fellow believers in the value of radio in modern war; indeed, von Rundstedt, when he was chief of staff of 3rd Cavalry Division, might well have drawn on Guderian's firsthand World War I experience in this field. But the tank was something which von Rundstedt not only saw as a threat to his beloved horse, but more seriously as upsetting the combined arms balance if used in the way that Guderian and others were advocating. Yet Guderian clearly felt an affinity to a man who was very much his senior, in that he was able to speak so frankly to him and it says much for von Rundstedt that he recognised that there were two sides to the coin.

Of more immediate relevance to von Rundstedt's new command was Groener's policy of dealing with the Polish threat. He was opposed to von Seeckt's 'penny packeting' of the forces allocated to guard

Germany's Eastern borders. While this might have reassured the local civilian population it made little military sense since the units based on the border would be quickly overrun. He therefore withdrew them and, to a degree, concentrated them to the rear. Thus, von Rundstedt's five regiments, which had formerly occupied no less than 15 garrisons were, at the time he arrived in Breslau, being reduced to 11. Groener also believed that fortifications would help the defence of the Eastern borders. In this he followed von Seeckt's view, and also agreed with him that, while in themselves they would not be decisive, they would help to deter the Poles, especially since their artillery was in a poor state. Hence, one of von Rundstedt's responsibilities was to create fortifications in the frontier districts of Silesia. This had to be done with discretion in order not to openly infringe the Versailles terms and, initially, the defences consisted merely of a skeleton lay-out of infantry weapon positions. Allied to this was the forming of covert border units to man them. Local responsibility for these and defence construction rested with District Leaders (*Kreisleiter*), appointed after screening by local landowners and industrialists. Von Rundstedt himself liaised with the *Oberpräsident* of Breslau and Oppeln, who headed the local government of Silesia, while, at a lower level, command posts in the garrison towns oversaw the defences and occasionally held map exercises. Inevitably, perhaps, the border units attracted several National Socialist members. Eventually, this became a very real problem when they declared in 1932, that they would only serve with fellow Nazis.[26]

Von Rundstedt continued to be highly thought of and this was reflected in his promotion to Lieutenant General on 1 March 1929. His cup was thus full at this time, or at least nearly so. There was, however, one aspect which caused him personal difficulties and created what was probably the only rift that he and Bila had during their otherwise long and happy marriage. In July 1930, Bila, Gerd and possibly Hans Gerd as well, spent a holiday, probably in Switzerland. It should be said here, that von Runstedt, like many of his kind, was not a great traveller and that Switzerland was the only foreign country which he visited in peacetime, apart from one official visit to England (see Page 68). At the end of the holiday, von Rundstedt went directly to rejoin his division on the Altergrabow manoeuvre area in East Prussia, where it was to carry out work-up exercises for the Reichswehr autumn manoeuvres, the largest to be held since the end of the war. Unhappily, the holiday itself was not as successful as it might have been, as von Runstedt indicated in a letter to Bila, written shortly after his arrival at Altergrabow.[27] He had noticed that Bila had been lost in deep thought and had cried all night, and knew what the reason was. He had struck up a friendship with a woman very much younger than himself. They both met in person and regularly exchanged letters. He refers to her as 'E.K.' and indicated that she lived in 'BL' (he always abbreviated place names in his letters), which he promised he would not visit while he was at Altergrabow. 'BL' itself probably refers to Berlin, where the headquarters of *Wehrkreis* III, von Rundstedt's superior headquarters, was situated. Von Rundstedt assured his wife that he was not in love with 'E.K.' and denied that the relationship reflected any diminishing of the love he had for Bila. He was, on the other hand, not prepared to give up writing letters to 'E.K.' and reassured Bila that 'there can be no lack of faithfulness or dallying because of a liking for "young girls"'. It is most unlikely that there was a sexual aspect to the relationship and 'E.K.' may possibly have reflected the daughter that von Rundstedt never had, besides reflecting the liking for young people that had been indicated in the reports on him when he commanded the 18th Infantry Regiment. He signed the letter 'Your faithful Gerd' and he seems to have maintained this form of ending his letters to Bila for the rest of their life together – certainly the letters that survive indicate this.

The 1930 autumn manoeuvres took place in the area of Bad Kissingen, north of Schweinfurt. For the first time, all the Reichswehr divisions were involved. The setting was an attack by a large Red force (France) across the Rhine followed by a withdrawal by the inferior Blue (German) forces into the centre of Germany. All the foreign military attachés, apart from the Belgian, French and Polish, were invited to attend and were most impressed by the professionalism of the troops and the degree of modernisation of the equipment, especially in terms of motorisation. A report in the Berlin newspaper *Tempo* especially noted significant changes in the cavalry, which had now finally given up its lances:

> 'There exists no parade formation proper in the modern cavalry. But a parade is nowadays one of the few occasions where one can really ride. In lieu of the line of lances of former times straight as a chalk line, one now sees a pace of riding past the reviewing stand which takes the breath away. In about twenty minutes, six cavalry regiments and two horse artilliery battalions have dashed past, and the parade is over.'[28]

Also taking part in the manoeuvres was the 3rd (Prussian) Motor Transport Battalion. Commanded by Heinz Guderian, this had a company of dummy tanks and one of dummy anti-tank guns, as well as real armoured cars and a motor-cycle company.

At the beginning of 1932, von Rundstedt received further promotion. He was appointed to command *Wehrkreis* III and formally assumed his new post on 1 February, handing over 2nd Cavalry Division to Ewald von Kleist. He was now based in Berlin and controlled not only his former command, but also 1st Cavalry Division (headquarters Frankfurt-am-Oder) and 3rd Infantry Division (Berlin). The last-named controlled the Berlin garrison and meant that von Rundstedt could not help but become involved in the political battles then raging.

He arrived just in time for the presidential elections. Held in March, the first ballot gave von Hindenburg victory, with just under 50 per cent of the vote, but the runner up was Adolf Hitler with 30 per cent. Because von Hindenburg had not secured the necessary outright majority there was a re-run the following month. This time, with the Nationalist Colonel Dusterberg having dropped out, it was a three-cornered fight. Von Hindenburg was successful, but Hitler significantly increased his vote, while the communist Ernst Thälmann was a poor third. This marked an enormous leap forward for the Nazis from the 1928 Reichstag elections, when they had only secured 12 out of 491 seats. Much of the reason for this was Germany's economic situation, which had been gravely affected by the 1929 Wall Street Crash – unemployment would reach six million by the beginning of 1932. The centrist parties believed that retrenchment was the only answer, but the Socialists would have none of it. In despair, the Chancellor, Hermann Müller, resigned in March 1930. In his place von Hindenburg had apponted Heinrich Brüning, a man on the right of the centre parties, promising him emergency powers if he could not obtain Reichstag support for his policies. These he quickly needed for the Reichstag refused to back his austerity measures and hence he dissolved it, ruling by presidential decree. His efforts to restore Germany's economic fortunes were by and large a failure and he began to lose the support of the middle classes. In consequence von Hindenburg dismissed him in May 1932.

Brüning's successor was Franz von Papen, a former member of the *Grosse Generalstab* and a right wing Roman Catholic. His selection was by no means unilateral; von Hindenburg had been heavily influenced by General Kurt von Schleicher, the *eminence grise* of the last Weimar years. Having been commissioned into von Hindenburg's old regiment, von Schleicher had served at the Supreme Headquarters during 1914–18 and was well known to the President. Groener had appointed him to head the *Ministeramt*, which he had created to act as a bridge between himself and the Reichswehr, so as to penetrate the insulation with which von Seeckt had covered it. Von Schleicher believed that the Reichswehr should be the supreme force in Germany and saw von Papen as an ideal tool to achieve this. Von Schleicher himself now took over as Minister of Defence, and the addition of Konstantin Freiherr von Neurath as Foreign Minister and Count Schwerin von Krosigk as Finance Minister, gave the von Papen administration such a Junker character that it quickly became known as the 'barons cabinet'.

What von Rundstedt thought of all this is not recorded, although he did comment to Liddell Hart in a postwar interview that, even though he knew von Schleicher well, they were not friends because von Schleicher was not especially interested in military matters. He accepted, though, that von Schleicher was politically clever.[29] On the other hand, Blumentritt asserted that von Schleicher and von Rundstedt were on 'good terms'.[30] Given his antecedents, von Rundstedt would have probably supported von Papen in preference to Brüning, but it is most unlikely that he would have worn his political convictions on his sleeve and would have tried to concentrate solely on the organisation and training of the troops under his command. Berlin, too, benefited him domestically. Hans Gerd had gone against the family tradition and had become an academic. This does not seem to have disappointed his father, who thought that he would have been a 'lousy soldier'.[31] By now Hans Gerd had successfully achieved a doctorate and was an archivist at the University of Berlin, which meant that he could and did live at home, which would have delighted his parents.

In 1934 a book was published in Britain entitled *The Berlin Diaries*. The editor was Dr Helmut Klotz, a German emigré who had recently settled in Paris. The sub-title was 'The private journals of a General in the German War Ministry revealing the secrete intrigue and political barratry of 1932–33'. As to who the General was is a mystery. At the time it was thought that it might be von Schleicher himself, who was murdered, together with his wife, during the Night of the Long Knives, or his successor in the *Ministeramt*, General Ferdinand von Bredow, another victim of 30 June 1934. Klotz, while he accepted that he had had close contact with von Schleicher up to mid-February 1932, denied that either was the author.[32] Klotz's Foreword and Introduction give the impression that the diary entries might have been compiled from an amalgam of individuals, but it is possible that they may have been the work of the Commander-in-Chief of the time, Kurt Freiherr von Hammerstein-Equord. Junior, in terms of length of service and age, to von Rundstedt, it will be remembered that they had been promoted Lieutenant Colonel on the same day in 1920. Von Hammerstein-

Equord's father-in-law was the ill-fated von Lüttwitz of Kapp fame, but his son-in-law refused to side with him and became a protegée of both Groener and von Schleicher. He had succeeded Heye in 1930 and was convinced that the Reichswehr should drop its policy of isolation and establish links with the mass of the German population. As a result, some sectors of the defence ministry viewed him as a 'red general', and could use the fact that his three daughters were communists to support their case.[33] In fact, he was equally opposed to the Left and the Right and abhorred Hitler – his reluctance to support him would eventually bring about his dismissal in February 1934. Because it cannot be proved that he was the author of the Diary, or even the leading light in its compilation, the author(s) will be referred to as 'General X'. This is important, because during summer 1932, von Rundstedt's name flits across its pages.

Von Schleicher believed that the only way to tame Hitler and his followers was to allow them a share of the government. One of the first olive branches that he and von Papen offered the Nazis was to lift the ban on the SA, Hitler's political shock troops, a ban which had been imposed by Brüning in April 1932, because of the SA's violent activities. Hitler, however, expected more than this. He wanted the SA to become more involved with the Reichswehr, especially with regard to military training. General X recalled meeting Hitler at the house of a Berlin financier on 11 June. Hitler proposed that SA officers should attend military manoeuvres. General X was vehemently opposed to this – 'I have little inclination to throw the Army open to a gang of fellows like Captain Roehm [SA Chief of Staff]' – but could not very well say this to Hitler. 'General Rundstedt relieved me from my disagreeable embarrassment. Rundstedt's opinion of the "Leader" is exactly the same as my own. The two of them don't seem to be exactly the best of friends!'[34] It is hardly surprising that von Rundstedt thought little of Hitler, but what is interesting is that he told Liddell Hart after the war that he did not meet Hitler until after he had been installed as Chancellor at the end of January 1933.[35] Given, however, von Rundstedt's position in Berlin, it would have been most surprising if he had not come across Hitler during 1932. A month later, though, von Rundstedt was drawn further into the political arena. On 12 July von Papen gave a dinner at the *Herren Klub*, the most prestigious of Berlin's gentlemen's clubs. Present at it were General X, von Schleicher, von Hammerstein-Equord, von Blomberg, von Seeckt and, among others, von Rundstedt. The object was to ensure that the Reichswehr gave von Papen full support for a plan which he had to remove the Prussian State Government.

The Prussian Government itself had been Social Democrat since 1923 and had increasingly become a thorn in the flesh for both Brüning and von Papen. The final straw was the Government's refusal to lift the ban on paramilitary organisations, which placed von Papen in an invidious position. He also wanted to woo the Nationalist vote away from Hitler and believed that this could be achieved through the forcible dissolution of the Prussian Government, using the 'catch all' Article 48 of the Weimar Constitution. This was particularly urgent since Reichstag elections were to be held at the end of July. According to General X, von Papen's plan met with stunned silence on the part of the Generals, except for von Schleicher, who warned of the danger of civil war, but was overridden. After the dinner General X walked a short distance with von Rundstedt. 'Unlike myself, he is filled with admiration for the plan and for Papen. The whole business seems strange to me. I have a feeling that things have already gone farther than Papen admits, and that von Rundstedt himself knows more than he considers it expedient to say.'[36] This was probably so, for von Rundstedt was to be the instrument for removing the Prussian Government and had been briefed before the dinner took place. Thus, on 14 July he requested the use, if need be, of cavalry units in *Wehrkreis* II and was told that he could contact those in Pomerania and Mecklenburg, but could not use them without permission of the defence ministry.[37] While he planned to secure all strategic points in Berlin, in case of both civil unrest and resistance by the Prussian Police, von Rundstedt intended to employ the principle of minimum force when it actually came to arresting the Prussian ministers.

On July 1932, von Papen informed the Prussian Cabinet that he had been appointed *Reichskommissar* of Prussia by President von Hindenburg, who was using Article 48. Von Papen declared a state of emergency. The *Ministerpräsident*, Otto Braun, and his interior minister, Karl Severing, refused to be cowed by this and declared that force would be required to remove them from office. Von Rundstedt sent a lieutenant and 12 soldiers from the 9th Infantry Regiment to remove them and, with this symbolic gesture of force, Braun and Severing and others stepped down.[38] Von Rundstedt himself was appointed Holder of Plenipotentiary Powers for the Region of Greater Berlin and Brandenburg Province, but, although the operation had gone like clockwork and there had been no violence, he did not enjoy his new political status. The next day he visited General X 'imploring me to try to get his provisional commission withdrawn again as soon as possible'.[39] Von Schleicher, too, was unhappy and purposely distanced himself from the affair. By the 25th, however, apparently aware of von Rundstedt's feelings on the matter, he was agitating for martial law to be lifted.[40] Von Papen duly acceded to this on the following day, and, as General X noted, von Rundstedt was 'at peace again'.[41]

As it happened, the removal of the Prussian Government gained von Papen nothing. In the elections held on 31 July, Hitler achieved a narrow overall majority in the Reichstag and was now in a position to demand that the reins of power be handed over to him. Von Papen tried to compromise, but Hitler would have none of it, and the Reichstag was dissolved. The events of July 1932 had also done little for the Army. It had forced it into the political arena and, while officers like von Rundstedt wanted strong government, they did not want to be seen as the tool used to enforce it.

It was therefore probably with much relief that von Rundstedt could turn his attention to the main autumn manoeuvres, which took place in the Küstrin – Frankfurt-am-Oder area. He commanded Blue forces, consisting of 3rd Infantry Division, while Fedor von Bock, with 1st and 2nd Cavalry Divisions, was the Red Commander. The aims were to trial new cavalry and infantry organisations, which reflected a very much higher degree of motorisation than heretofore, and to practise river crossings. The scenario painted was of a Red attack out of the Poznan salient. Blue had to prevent Red crossing the Oder. In the event, von Bock did succeed in making crossings, but then came under threat from Blue's reserves. Among the guests at the manoeuvres was Mikhail Tuchachevsky, the Russian Chief of Staff, then developing the concept of Deep Battle,[42] who would have been especially interested in the use by both sides of bypassing and threatening flanks, as well as the rapidity of movement. Indeed some cavalry units covered as much as 100 kilometres per day for three days without any noticeable strain. While von Hammerstein-Equord was not impressed by the handling of the river crossings, which were delayed by 'many hours', he was especially pleased with the motorised units: 'The dash of the newly formed motorised units, even though the tactical conception was sometimes wrong, is deserving of commendation.'[43] Here lay the foundations of *Blitzkrieg*.

Once again, von Rundstedt's reputation shone. On 1 October 1932 he was promoted General of Infantry and given command of *Gruppenkommando* I. This meant that he would remain in Berlin with responsibility for the three Eastern *Wehrkreise*, with four infantry and two cavalry divisions.

Shortly after he took over his new command, and at the beginning of November 1932, further Reichstag elections were held. Although

Hitler's National Socialists lost seats – a reflection of a slightly improved enonomic situation and the German withdrawal from the Disarmament Conference until she was allowed equality in armaments – von Papen failed to gain support. He then offered his resignation to von Hindenburg, but also proposed that martial law should be implemented and that he should rule by decree until a more authoritarian constitution could be drawn up. Von Schleicher schemed against him, however, and told von Hindenburg that the Reichswehr would not support this. He also believed that he could wean some of those on the left of the Nazi Party away from Hitler and, with support from the Centre and Socialist parties, form a progressive socialist administration within the existing constitution. Consequently, he was appointed Chancellor on 2 December in von Papen's place. The Weimar Republic was about to breathe its last gasp.

4
Enter Hitler

VON SCHLEICHER's hopes of forming a broad-based government were quickly dashed. Neither the left wing of the National Socialists, nor the centrist and socialist parties were prepared to work with him and he was forced to ask von Hindenburg for the right to rule by decree as von Papen had tried to do before him. The President, having turned down von Papen's request for this, was not prepared to grant the same to von Schleicher. Hence, by now totally isolated, the latter resigned on 28 January 1933. In the meantime, von Papen had opened negotiations with Hitler, believing that with his support he could gain his revenge on von Schleicher and control Hitler by placing Nationalists in his cabinet. Consequently, the two were able to inform von Hindenburg that they had the necessary support in the Reichstag to form a government. Accordingly, on 30 January von Hindenburg appointed Hitler as Chancellor. The Weimar Republic was dead and the Third Reich was born.

Hitler's first cabinet significantly contained just two National Socialists – Interior Minister Wilhelm Frick and Hermann Goering, who was Minister Without Portfolio. Von Papen, as Vice-Chancellor, therefore believed that he could control Hitler and regain the reins of power for himself. Hitler, however, called for fresh Reichstag elections for 5 March. In so doing, he took full advantage of the mysterious circumstances of the destruction of the Reichstag by fire on the night of 27 February, responsibility for which he immediately laid at the door of the Communists. This enabled him to persuade von Hindenburg that there was a danger of a communist uprising. The President therefore issued a decree severely restricting civil and political liberties. Thus, even though the National Socialists did not gain an overall majority and were forced to continue their alliance with von Papen's Nationalists, Hitler now had the means to consolidate his hold on government and by the end of summer 1933 had forced the dissolution of all parties except the National Socialists.

One important ally Hitler had at this time was General Werner von Blomberg, the Minister of Defence, who had been appointed to 29 January 1933 amid fear that von Schleicher might try to use the Army to subvert von Hindenburg's position. Von Blomberg, whom Berliners, with their very individual brand of humour, nicknamed 'Rubber Lion',[1] had first met Hitler in 1931 when he was commanding *Wehrkreis* I in East Prussia and had quickly succumbed to his influence. Determined that Hitler should have the support of the generals, he organised a dinner for him on 2 February at von Hammerstein-Equord's house, just three days after he had been made Chancellor. Von Rundstedt was present and recalled that Hitler made a speech, but was very ill at ease.[2] Von Rundstedt himself had little time for von Blomberg, probably because he did not understand him. As he was later to tell the court at Nuremberg: 'He always remained a bit distant. He seemed to live in a different sphere. He was a pupil of the Steiner school of theosophy and no one really liked him.'[3] Von Blomberg's slavish support for Hitler was also difficult for von Rundstedt to accept. On the other hand, in von Rundstedt's eyes Hitler had obtained power legally, and unpalatable though his policies might be, it was not in the Army's gift to oppose them. Fabian von Schlabrendorff, a brilliant young lawyer, who was deeply involved in the opposition to Hitler and even used his honeymoon as cover to visit Churchill in England in order to warn him of Hitler's designs on Czechoslovakia, recalled a conversation that he had with von Rundstedt some months after Hitler had come to power: 'He had a reputation of being a non-Nazi. Our talk revealed that he was quite ready to use strong words against the Nazis, but he was equally determined to take no action against them.'[4] Furthermore, von Rundstedt was probably, like many others of his ilk, somewhat reassured by Hitler's determination, which he voiced at the 2 February dinner, to create a strong army once more and his assurance, given a week later to members of the defence ministry, that the Army would never again be used to subdue internal conflict since Hitler had 'other means at his disposal'.[5]

Von Rundstedt's superior, the Army chief von Hammerstein-Equord, thought highly of him, describing him as an 'excellent Commander-in-Chief'.[6] Unlike von Rundstedt, who was prepared to endure the new régime, von Hammerstein-Equord, did his best to dissuade von Hindenburg from giving Hitler his backing. It was, however, to no avail since von Hindenburg distrusted von

Hammerstein-Equord as being a von Schleicher man. Worse, von Blomberg had imported his own chief of staff, Walther von Reichenau, into the Defence Ministry. Von Reichenau was also an officer of National Socialist sympathies, as much if not more so than von Blomberg, and the two conspired to bypass von Hammerstein-Equord, often dealing directly with the branches of the Army Office. Von Rundstedt himself was scathing about von Reichenau, describing him as a 'right roughneck (*Rakauke*) who used to run around half naked when taking physical exercise'.[7] He also strongly disapproved of the fact that von Reichenau and von Blomberg both wore the Nazi party badge in uniform. Increasingly isolated, it became clear that von Hammerstein-Equord's days were numbered and eventually, on 1 February 1934, he was dismissed. Both Hitler and von Blomberg pressed von Hindenburg to appoint von Reichenau in his place, but the President refused and nominated Werner Freiherr von Fritsch instead. It has been asserted that von Rundstedt and others voiced their objections to von Reichenau being appointed on the grounds of his comparative youth and lack of command experience and it is possible that von Hindenburg took note of this.[8] Blumentritt also stated that von Rundstedt offered his resignation at the time that von Hammerstein-Equord was retired, but was told by both von Hindenburg and von Schleicher that he must stay on.[9] As it was, von Fritsch was much more to von Rundstedt's liking. An artilleryman, but well known to von Rundstedt since he was commanding *Wehrkreis* III in Berlin and thus was Gerd's subordinate when selected for the post, von Fritsch made no secret of his distaste for the Nazis but, like von Rundstedt, was a firm believer that the soldier should not become involved in politics. As he declared in 1937: 'I have made it a guiding principle to confine myself to the military domain and to keep aloof from all political activity. I lack all talent for it.'[10]

Von Fritsch could not, however, hide his head in the sand. No sooner had he taken over his new post than a growing crisis began to come to a head. Ernst Roehm, the leader of the Nazi Party's shock troops, the SA (*Sturmabteilungen*), was becoming increasingly vociferous in his belief that, if the National Socialist revolution was to be completed, the SA must be given prime responsibility for the defence of the Reich, with the Reichswehr being made subservient to it. Initially, von Blomberg was prepared to humour Roehm. He instructed soldiers to exchange salutes with SA men when they met and where there were joint parades the SA were allowed to head them. Von Blomberg also did not object to the SA's demand to carry out pre-military training of potential soldiers. On

1 February 1934, however, at a Reich Defence Council meeting, Roehm confirmed to von Blomberg that he intended to relieve the Army of prime responsibility for defence. Alarmed, von Blomberg ordered the *Wehrkreis* commanders to cease co-operation with the SA, but Roehm now went even further. He sent von Blomberg a letter saying that he regarded the Reichswehr as no more than a training organisation and that henceforth the SA would be responsible for mobilisation and the conduct of war. Deeply disturbed by this, von Blomberg took the letter to Hitler. At the same time, in order to demonstrate Reichswehr's loyalty to the régime, he ordered all members to wear the *Hoheitsabzeichen*, the new national emblem of eagle and swastika, above the right breast procket of their uniforms. Further, he ordered the Reichswehr to implement the first of Hitler's anti-Jewish measures, the banning of officials not of Aryan descent. Even though war veterans were exempted and only fifty all ranks in the Army and Navy were affected by this, it was a rash step to take, since it showed that the Reichswehr was prepared to acquiesce to even the most extreme and distasteful of the Nazi policies. No wonder that von Blomberg became known by the Army, according to von Rundstedt, as 'Hitler Youth Quex' after the 1933 Nazi propaganda feature film of that name about the Hitler Youth who was murdered by communists.[11] Eventually, all members of the Reichswehr, like everyone else employed by the State, had to complete forms tracing back their ancestry to prove that it was untainted by Jewish blood. Von Rundstedt scrawled 'Aryan shit' across the file in which he kept his personal papers pertaining to this.[12]

Von Blomberg's actions drove Hitler to call a meeting of SA and Reichswehr leaders for 28 February. Von Rundstedt was one of those present and heard Hitler reaffirm the primacy of the Reichswehr and tell the SA that it must concentrate on political matters, although it would still be allowed to carry out pre-military training and be involved in the protection of Germany's Eastern frontiers. Hitler then ordered von Blomberg and Roehm to sign an agreement to this effect. After the meeting Roehm invited the Generals to his house for lunch, a sumptuous but frosty affair. The Generals then returned to their commands, highly satisfied that the SA's wings had been clipped, once and for all. What none of them appear to have realised, however, was the price which the Reichswehr would have to pay for this. Furthermore, Roehm immediately told his confrères that he was not prepared to observe the agreement and if necessary would have to go against Hitler. One of the SA leaders, Viktor Lutze, who would succeed Roehm after his murder, was horrified at this and went first to Hitler's deputy, Rudolf Hess, and then to Hitler himself, who realised that something more drastic would have to be done. This was further reinforced by a fierce altercation which he had with Roehm at the beginning of June. The result was what came to be known as the Night of the Long Knives, which took place on the night 30 June/1 July, when the SS were unleashed on the heirarchy of the SA.

There is no doubt that the Army knew that something was in the wind. Von Blomberg had shown his son-in-law, General Wilhelm Keitel, a list of people to be arrested and also advised von Fritsch to put his men on the alert. This von Fritsch did, without knowing the real reason, although he suspected that it was in case Roehm mounted a putsch. In von Rundstedt's case, he apparently merely armed his batman and driver and, like his fellow senior commanders, awaited events.[13] What he certainly did not do, as wartime Allied propagandists asserted, was to offer his men as firing squads or sit on a drumhead court-martial of victims of the purge.[14] As it happened, matters got out of control, with Himmler, Goering and Heydrich using the operation to settle personal scores. Thus it was not just the SA members gathered for a conference called by Roehm at Bad Weissee near Munich, nor those still in Berlin, who were liquidated, but others elsewhere in the country. For von Blomberg and von Reichenau the Night of the Long Knives was good in that it had finally removed the threat of the SA without the Reichswehr having to dirty its hands. Accordingly, on the next morning, von Blomberg issued an order of the day praising Hitler for his courage in dealing with the SA. But the affair had left something of a sour taste in the Army's mouth. Among the victims were Kurt von Schleicher and his former assistant in the Defence Ministry and von Reichenau's predecessor, Kurt von Bredow. Many soldiers found it hard to swallow that two of their kind should have been put on the same level as the SA thugs whatever their political dabblings. Some, notably Erwin von Witzleben, now commanding *Wehrkreis* III in Berlin, Wilhelm Ritter von Leeb, von Rundstedt's fellow Group Commander, and even von Reichenau went to see von Blomberg to demand that von Fritsch institute court-martial proceedings against those responsible.[15] Other sources assert that von Rundstedt also joined in these demands,[16] but in the witness box at Nuremberg he implied that he did no such thing: 'In the first place, Reich President von Hindenburg was still at the Head of the State. In the second place, I was not the senior officer. We had a Commander-in-Chief of the Army [von Fritsch] and a Minister of War [von Blomberg] for a purpose of that sort.'[17]

But now came the penalty which the Army had to pay for the final removal of the SA threat. On 2 August, the venerable von Hindenburg passed away, thus severing the last link with the old régime. On the same day, all members of the Reichswehr were ordered to swear a new oath of allegiance. During the Weimar era the troops had sworn loyalty 'to the Reich constitution, the Reich and its lawful institutions'. In December 1933, Hitler had amended the oath to reflect allegiance to just 'the people and Fatherland'. Now, however, all members of the armed forces were required to swear fealty to Hitler himself as 'the Führer of the German Reich and Commander-in-Chief of the Wehrmacht'. This was drawn up by Hitler with the connivance of von Blomberg and von Reichenau. Yet, no one in the Reichswehr publicly objected to the oath and all meekly took it. Von Rundstedt himself told the International Military Tribunal (IMT) Commission at Nuremberg in 1946 that, as a soldier, he swore his oath 'no matter who was at the head of the state', but 'no other oath in my whole life was such a heavy burden as the one I had to swear to Hitler'.[18] Yet he swore it, probably on the grounds that *Befehl ist Befehl* (orders are orders), and personally administered it to some of the troops under his command.

But von Blomberg had not finished offering concessions to Hitler in exchange for securing the primacy of the Reichswehr. In that same month, August 1934, he proposed that the Armed Forces address Hitler as *Mein Führer*, and the Nazi raised arm salute and the *Heil Hitler!* greeting, although not mandatory at this time, became increasingly common. Furthermore, superiors were no longer to be addressed in the third person. Von Rundstedt said that 'apart from a very few exceptions, we were all very angry about the increasing Nazification',[19] but none took any action. In return, Hitler wrote to von Blomberg on 20 August assuring him that he saw his 'highest duty to defend the existence and inviolability of the Wehrmacht and ensure that the Army would form the bedrock of the nation as the sole bearer of arms'.[20] This proved to be an empty pledge. In September, a formal announcement was made of the formation of the *SS-Verfügungstruppe* (SS Special Purpose Troops or SS-VT) as the military wing of the SS. In order to help organise it a number of retired and serving officers joined, including Paul Hausser, Felix Steiner and Willi Bittrich, who would all attain high SS rank during the war. Even though Hitler stressed, in a secret order dated 2 February 1935, that in time of war the SS-VT would be incorporated in the Army, he did little to prevent growing tension between the two organisations. Significantly, too, when the Saarland was reincorporated into Germany, as a result of the January

1935 plebiscite, Hitler sent his own bodyguard, the SS Leibstandarte Adolf Hitler, now part of the SS-VT, and not the Army to formally welcome the province back into the Reich.

While von Rundstedt regarded the increasing dead hand of Hitler on the Army with gloom, life on the domestic front had some compensation. He and Bila lived in a large twelve room apartment on the fashionable Hardenbergstrasse by the Tiergarten Station in Berlin-Charlottenburg. Hans Gerd, who was still working as an archivist at the University of Berlin, continued to live at home. He had, too, met a girl, Editha von Oppen, sister of an army officer friend and they were married in September 1935. Ditha, as she was always known, was just over a year older than Hans Gerd, had a doctorate in economics and was working at a high-powered job in the Labour Ministry, organising the modernisation of rural housing in order to attract people from the cities to the countryside, a major National Socialist policy. For the first few months after their marriage, Hans Gerd and Ditha lived with his parents while they hunted for a suitable apartment. Ditha quickly became pregnant and, in August 1936, bore a daughter, Barbara. Once she became pregnant, von Rundstedt was very keen that she should give up her job, but since she earned much more than Hans Gerd she was loath to do so. Accordingly, her father-in-law insisted on making up the difference in earnings. Nevertheless, he and Bila continued to live modestly, but did not begrudge expensive tastes in others and were very generous in their presents to their son and daughter-in-law.

Even so, von Rundstedt was unable to avoid Berlin's 'high life'. His two superiors, von Blomberg and von Fritsch, were a widower and bachelor respectively and protocol dictated that without wives they could not give official hospitality. Hence von Rundstedt found himself deputising for them. While he enjoyed the good food and wine, even though he often said that his favourite food was pea soup from a field kitchen, he had little in common with the Nazi Party functionaries and tried to avoid going to official parties whenever he could. The one exception to this was the French Ambassador, André François-Poncet, with whom von Rundstedt became very good friends and especially welcomed his gifts of cognac and cigars. If he knew that François-Poncet would be at a function then he would attend.[21]

Von Rundstedt's main concern at this time was the expansion of the Army. Hitler called for a doubling in strength during 1934 and an increase by half as much again the following year, giving an army of 21 infantry divisions. Initially this was carried out covertly, with the additional manpower being found from one year volunteers drawn largely from the ranks of the SA. In March 1935, however, Hitler announced to the world both the existence of the Luftwaffe and the introduction of conscription. He also declared that he now wanted a 36 division army. This marked the final tearing up of the Treaty of Versailles and was formally accepted by the Western democracies through the Anglo-German Naval Treaty of June of that year. Hitler also reorganised the higher command structure. The Reichswehr now formally became known as the Wehrmacht and Hitler appointed himself Supreme Commander. Directly under him came the Minister of War and Commander-in-Chief of the Wehrmacht with a unified headquarters, the *Wehrmachtamt*, later to be renamed *Oberkommando der Wehrmacht* (OKW). Below this came the three individual armed services, the *Oberkommando der Marine* (OKM), *Oberkommando des Heeres* (OKH), and *Oberkommando der Luftwaffe* (OKL), with the heads of each, Raeder, von Fritsch and Goering, being styled Commanders-in-Chief. Each had a chief of staff, which in the Army's case was Ludwig Beck. The *Gruppenkommando* remained as the next level of command, but by autumn 1935 they had been increased to three and were later retitled *Heeresgruppen* (army groups). Each now commanded a number of army corps. In von Rundstedt's *Gruppenkommando* 1 there were four – I corps (HQ Königsberg – three infantry divisions under von Brauchitsch), II Corps (Stettin – two infantry divisions, two frontier commands – Blaskowitz), III Corps (Berlin – three infantry divisions – von Witzleben), VIII Corps (Breslau – two infantry divisions, two frontier commands – von Kleist). While rank and file manpower was not a problem, that of officers and non-commissioned officers was. To try and overcome this, the training period for officer cadets was reduced from four to two and a half years and, in order to fill the intermediate ranks, 2,500 officers were transferred from the police and 1,800 former officers recalled to the colours. The NCO problem was more difficult and a number of vacancies could not be filled. Another shortage was trained staff officers. In order to overcome this, the *Kriegsakadamie*, whose doors had been closed since 1920, was reopened on 18 October 1935.

Because Hitler demanded that the restructuring of the Wehrmacht must be completed as soon as possible, the Army found itself in no condition to fight any form of war. Yet, as early as the end of March 1935, it was forced to consider the prospects of war with Czechoslovakia. A further scenario was added that autumn, which painted the picture of a French invasion combined with a threatened Czech attack – the classic two front war which Germany had always feared. Neither von Fritsch nor Beck were happy with this and would have preferred to conduct the expansion much more slowly, so that at least part of the Army was always combat-ready. Beck even threatened to resign, but never carried it out. Matters came to a head with Hitler's decision to send troops into the demilitarised Rhineland in March 1936. Von Fritsch, Beck and von Blomberg protested strongly, but to no avail. After the three battalions, all that were available to carry out the task, had crossed the Rhine, the German military attaché in London, Geyr von Schweppenburg, warned von Blomberg that he thought that the British were about to take counter-action. Von Blomberg then suggested to Hitler that the troops be withdrawn, but with no success. From now on von Blomberg was to become increasingly isolated. On the one hand, Hitler viewed him with increasing suspicion, while of the other, the Army saw him as Hitler's fawning servant who would do anything that he was told. By autumn 1935, even von Reichenau had turned against him leaving von Blomberg to replace him in the *Wehrmachtamt* with his son-in-law Keitel, who, at least, could be counted on to support him. Von Rundstedt himself told the IMT Commission in 1946 that all von Fritsch did, time and again, was to order the senior commanders to devote the maximum attention to unit training at the lowest level. Von Rundstedt, although he said that such training was normally the responsibility of junior commanders, agreed that this had to be done. 'One could not take enough care over the training of our scarcely trained troops. We would not have dreamt of war'.[22]

By this time, von Rundstedt was, in terms of service, the most senior officer in the Army. Only von Blomberg was senior to him in rank, having overtaken him by being promoted Colonel General in August 1933. In consequence, Gerd was being increasingly looked on within the Army as its figurehead, as the officer who stood more than any other for the traditional military values. His experience, too, was wide and his talent as bright as ever. Von Fritsch reporting on him in October 1935 described him as:

> 'An exeptionally outstanding officer. The personality of a leader with good foresight and special understanding for large operational questions. In actual fact he will be an excellent commander, provided he sees it through health-wise.'[23]

In April 1936, Hitler promoted von Blomberg General Field Marshal and the following year von Fritsch proposed that von Rundstedt, who was still ranked as General of Infantry, should also be promoted to the same rank in recognition of his seniority. Hitler turned this down because it might be seen as a slight by the Navy and Luftwaffe.[24] He did, however, recognise von Rundstedt's worth and began to make a special effort to cultivate him. Thus, on von Rundstedt's 60th birthday, Hitler gave him a signed photograph mounted in a silver frame and in January 1936 appointed him to represent the German Army at the funeral of King George V in London. His fellow German mourners were von Blomberg, Admiral Albrecht, General Kampisch of the Luftwaffe and Foreign Minister Freiherr von Heurath. It was, of course, von Rundstedt's first visit to Britain and one that he would remember for the rest of his life. He was made an honorary member of the prestigious Marlborough Club for the duration of his stay and attended a reception at Buckingham Palace on the eve of the funeral. Although he never openly admitted it, von Rundstedt was at heart a monarchist; his upbringing and ancestry could not have made him anything else. He must therefore have especially felt the poignancy of the occasion. It may be, too, that he met there, for the first time, Marshal Philippe Pétain of France, a fellow mourner, but would have little imagined the circumstances in which their paths would cross and become entwined in the future.

During 1937, the position of the German Army improved, but, at the same time, Hitler's attitude was becoming more bellicose. In June, von Blomberg issued a Wehrmacht directive laying down that the Armed Forces must be prepared 'in case of outside attacks, to exploit, by military means, favourable political opportunities'. In addition to the French and Czech scenarios, the Wehrmacht was also to plan for an attack on Austria in the event of the Habsburg monarchy being restored, action against Republican Spain, and to take into account the possibility of Britain, Poland and Lithuania intervening in the French and Czech scenarios.[25] Von Blomberg and von Fritsch were, however, deeply concerned over the possibility of war against Britain and France and warned Hitler against this at a meeting held in November over the allocation of raw materials to the Wehrmacht. Von Rundstedt, too, held strong views, especially where Britain was concerned. Addressing a gathering of staff officers in 1937, he warned them that:

'A Continental power wishing to defeat England must have either Russia or the United States as an ally in order to have any chance of victory. If this constellation cannot be obtained, then England must be the ally of any power aiming at predominance on the Continent. She must not be neutral, for even as a neutral she can turn the scales of victory as may suit her convenience. The lesson to be learned from this is that land power is useless if not coupled with command of the sea. But sea-power alone can strangle a Continental power in the long run.'[26]

He fully recognised Germany's difficult geo-strategic position and firmly believed that in any future war she must remain on the defensive. He also considered that the 36 division army had not only been created too quickly, but was not strong enough to carry out an offensive either in the East or the West. Von Rundstedt therefore hoped and believed, at least until 1938, that Hitler saw the Army as merely guaranteeing Germany's security.[27]

In the major manoeuvres of autumn 1937, von Rundstedt commanded the Blue forces. In line with previous major exercises, they were defensive in nature, with von Rundstedt commanding an army defending Pomerania against an attack from across the Polish border. Included in his forces, though, was Germany's new Panzer arm. This had grown from nothing to three Panzer divisions in the space of three years. As with the rest of the Army, its expansion had been carried out by splitting existing units and then splitting again, which created constant instability and affected training. The latter was also not helped by the problems of matching supply of equipment with demand. The 1937 manoeuvres, although they concluded with a spectacular mass attack by all three Panzer divisions, which impressed Hitler and Mussolini, who were present, brought out the problems only too clearly, especially on the logistic side. Von Rundstedt himself later commented that it was only through wartime experience that the Panzer arm learnt its job effectively. He also bewailed the fact that the cavalry was drastically reduced in order to create light and motorised divisions, particularly because he was convinced that cavalry was vital for war in the East.[28] Much of the trouble lay in a lack of clear direction on how the Panzer divisions would be employed in war. The traditionalists, like von Fritsch and von Rundstedt, believed that the tank's prime role was infantry support, in order to help them overcome the 'machine gun paralysis' which had so bedevilled the infantry during 1914–18. Guderian and his fellow armoured commanders thought otherwise. He himself published his thoughts in *Achtung! Panzer!* in 1937. He seized on Hitler's growing love affair with motorisation, quoting from his speech at the 1937 Motor Show: 'This is certain: the replacement of animal power by the motor leads to the most tremendous technical and consequently economical change the world has ever experienced.'[29] He also grasped Hitler's concept of *Blitzkrieg*, which he had first voiced in 1935 at the Nuremberg Party Rally to foreign delegates of the League of German Girls: 'I shouldn't negotiate for months beforehand and make lengthy preparations, but – as I have always done throughout my life – I should suddenly, like a flash of lightning in the night, hurl myself upon the enemy.'[30]

Hitler's belief that the Panzer arm and the Luftwaffe had given him an offensive capability had manifested itself at the 5 November 1937 meeting on raw materials which has been mentioned earlier. Hitler reiterated the aim of completing the Wehrmacht's rearmament programme by 1943, but pointed out that by then much of the equipment being currently produced would be obsolete. It was therefore essential that Germany maintain the initiative. The Wehrmacht's role in this would be to exploit any window of opportunity that occurred in Europe. Such a window might be seen in internal problems in France or even in war between France and Italy. It was also necessary to secure Germany's south-east flank – Austria and Czechoslovakia – and to neutralise Russia, which could be done through Japan, using the November 1936 Anti-Comintern Pact. Time was of the essence and it was important to achieve Germany's territorial aims before the other European powers were able to react. It was this announcement that Hitler was prepared to use the Wehrmacht offensively which brought about protests from von Blomberg, von Fritsch and even von Neurath. But all these protestations did was finally to convince Hitler that the Army High Command lacked drive and determination.

After the 5 November conference, von Fritsch departed on two months' leave to Egypt. He had offered to postpone it in view of the seeming emergency which Hitler had painted, but Hitler told him that the situation was not that urgent. Von Fritsch asked von Rundstedt to deputise for him, but, according to von Rundstedt, did not tell him what had transpired during the 5 November meeting.[31] Furthermore, the day-to-day affairs of OKH remained in Beck's hands and he only briefed von Rundstedt every eight days.[32] It is difficult to believe that von Rundstedt could not have been consulted more frequently if he had wished it. Indeed, had he been, it is possible that he might have been able to do something to forestall the crisis that was about to erupt.

Towards the end of January 1938, von Rundstedt went to East Prussia to attend map exercises being carried out at Königsberg. On the 30th, Beck telephoned him and asked him to return to Berlin immediately as a very serious situation had arisen.[33] Beck wanted von Rundstedt to take a plane back, but he declined, possibly on the grounds that he did not like flying, and took the overnight express train instead. He arrived in Berlin early the following morning and was met by Beck at the railway station.

What Beck had to tell him came, von Rundstedt claimed, as a complete surprise. Indeed, he stated that if he had had any prior knowledge of it he would never have gone to East Prussia.[34] It concerned both von Blomberg and von Fritsch. As far as the former was concerned, on 12 January he had remarried, but unsuitably it transpired, a woman who had a police record of conviction for immorality. Worse, both Hitler and Goering had been witnesses at the wedding. The Berlin police chief, Heinrich Graf von Helldorf, drew Keitel's attention to it and, probably because he disapproved of the match strongly enough to override his natural loyalty as von Blomberg's son-in-law, Keitel referred von Helldorf to Goering. Goering, who coveted von Blomberg's job, and Himmler, who saw him as an obstacle to the strengthening of the SS-VT, presented the evidence to Hitler. He, delighted to have grounds for finally getting rid of von Blomberg, confronted him, dismissed him from his post and sent him and his wife on a year's exile to Capri. At this meeting, von Blomberg recommended Goering as his successor, but Hitler turned this down, probably because it was placing too much power into his hands. Then, on 27 January, Hitler consulted Keitel. He suggested four names, Friedrich Graf von Schulenburg, a Nazi Party member and 1918 Chief of Staff to the Crown Prince's army but now retired for some years, von Rundstedt, Otto von Stülpnagel, then serving with the Luftwaffe, and von Reichenau, but Hitler dismissed them all. On the previous day, however, Hitler had also spoken with his Army adjutant, Colonel Friedrich Hossbach, who had recommended von Schulenburg, von Rundstedt and Beck. Hitler had preferred von Schulenburg, probably because he was a Nazi! but he had immediately turned the post down on the grounds of ill health.

Much more serious in the eyes of both Beck and von Rundstedt was the crisis surrounding von Fritsch. At the same time that Goering and Himmler informed Hitler about von Blomberg's new wife, they also laid another dossier in front of him. This asserted that von Fritsch was a practising homosexual. Hitler immediately authorised Himmler to initiate a Gestapo investigation. They summoned von Fritsch for interrogation, although this was illegal, since he could only be investigated by the military authorities. This news deeply shocked von Rundstedt. But Beck told him that Hitler wanted to see him at the Chancellery at 11am that morning. He was to come to a back entrance in civilian clothes. Beck also asked him whether he was prepared to succeed von Fritsch as Commander-in-Chief of the Army, but von Rundstedt declined.[35]

Von Rundstedt returned to Hardenbergstrasse to change and telephoned von Fritsch to assure him of his support. Ditha, now heavily
pregnant with her second child Gerd, who would be born on 24
February, happened to be visiting her mother-in-law at the time and
was very surprised to see von Rundstedt not in uniform. 'He asked me
to get him a taxi. To my objection that I ought rather to summon his
driver he said: "No, I prefer it like this!"'[36] He did not, however, tell her
where he was going or why. Von Rundstedt saw Hitler alone.

> 'He was in an awful state of excitement, such as I had never seen him in
> before. Something had broken in him and he had lost all confidence in
> people. It was certainly no "theatre". First, I had to calm him down and
> then he started to tell me first about the Blomberg case. He had deceived
> him and put him in an awkward position. Then he railed at him and the
> leading generals because of their timidity during rearmament and the
> occupation of the Rhineland in 1936. It was he who did everything.
> Generals wanted slower rearmament, the strength of 36 divisions was too
> large for them. . . . Thus, the abuse continued for a while.
>
> I then said to him that Blomberg had violated the officer's code of
> honour through his behaviour and had to be put in front of a Court of
> Honour. He brusquely refused – as a private he just did not have any idea
> of the term officer's code of honour. Finally, he conceded that Blomberg
> would have to be erased from the officer *Rangliste* in the future, whatever
> happened.
>
> Now he turned to the Fritsch case. He would have made him War
> Minister if it were not for the accusations of the known kind which
> Himmler had already reported to him years ago. I asked angrily how he
> could keep such vulgar defamations from a senior officer without giving
> him the chance to justify himself. Fritsch was, according to my opinion
> denigrated by "a certain corner", by which I meant Himmler. It was the
> same as I being supposedly working towards the "re-establishment of the
> monarchy", which was surely known to him. To this he only smiled. But
> in Fritsch's case, reasons of foreign policy had been decisive in his silence.
> But now he had to tackle the matter because of Blomberg's succession.
> During a conversation with Fritsch he had given an ice-cold and reserved
> impression instead of exploding. This made him (Hitler) believe in his
> guilt. I said that Fritsch had heard about the impending conversation
> from Hitler's adjutant Hossbach and as a nobleman he was only able to
> display icy disdain.
>
> In the name of Fritsch and in the name of the whole Army I demanded
> an immediate legal investigation and, in the event of proven innocence, of
> which my conviction was as firm as a rock, adequate reparation for
> Fritsch. After some hesitation, he said that he was prepared to do so.'

Hitler then went on to say that now there was no War Minister he
wanted to assume supreme command of the Wehrmacht himself. He

realised that Goering was not acceptable to the Army, but would make him a Field Marshal. He wanted to appoint Keitel as Chief of Staff of the OKW and von Rundstedt agreed with this, but warned that Keitel must not be given command authority since he knew nothing about the Navy and would not dare tangle with Goering's Luftwaffe. Hitler concurred, but then said that he would like to appoint a Generalissimo in the future. Von Rundstedt proposed von Fritsch for this post after his certain acquittal, but Hitler did not react to this.

They then went on to discuss the question of von Fritsch's successor as Commander-in-Chief. Von Rundstedt proposed Beck, which Hitler rejected and came back with von Reichenau. In turn, von Rundstedt turned him down 'in the name of the entire Army'. Finally, Hitler came up with von Brauchitsch, now commanded *Heeresgruppe* 4 at Leipzig. To this von Rundstedt responded that he was an excellent choice, 'a good leader and thoroughly welcome by the Army'. Finally, von Rundstedt broached his own position. He had now held his current command for well over five years and wanted to retire and make way for a younger man. Hitler said that he wanted him to stay on for the sake of the Army and for 'political reasons'. Von Rundstedt said that he would be prepared to do so until autumn 1938. 'In the meantime, he told me, he trusted me. I don't know why.' This ended the meeting and von Rundstedt immediately went and reported the conversation to both Beck and von Fritsch.[37]

Von Brauchitsch himself was an artilleryman, who had, among other posts, served two tours in the *Truppenamt* during the Weimar era, as well as having been a *Wehrkreis* and corps commander. Thus, in terms of experience, he was well suited to the job. He was, however, intending to retire for domestic reasons. He wanted to divorce his wife of over 30 years and marry another woman. His wife, with four children on her hands, would only agree to this in return for a financial settlement well beyond von Brauchitsch's means. Von Brauchitsch therefore tried to bargain with Hitler. He would accept the post of Commander-in-Chief in return for a payment, which turned out to be over 80,000 Reichsmarks. Hitler agreed to this and, in doing so, was able to put von Brauchitsch into an impossible position. First, von Brauchitsch was now personally indebted to him and his second wife, a fervent Nazi, never hesitated to remind him of this. Worse, she herself had a dubious background and he did not need to be reminded of what had happened to von Blomberg. No wonder, then, that Franz Halder described the von Brauchitsch – Hitler relationship as 'like a little cadet standing before his commandant'.[38] Thus, Hitler had got what he

MAP 5. Wehrkreis Boundaries 1939.

wanted, two officers in key positions, Keitel and von Brauchitsch, whom he knew would not stand in his way, but he was not finished yet.

On the following day, von Rundstedt, at his own request, had another interview with Hitler. He wanted to reiterate the urgent need for von Fritsch to have a proper legal investigation and to warn him once more about allowing Keitel executive power. Hitler then asked his views on certain senior officers, 'which, of course, I only expressed in a favourable way'.[39] Von Rundstedt did not, however, seem to have detected what Hitler's purpose was in this. Von Brauchitsch was then summoned to see Hitler and the same questions were asked of him.[40] Von Rundstedt's name was mentioned and von Brauchitsch defended him on the grounds that he and Hitler got on well,[41] which, considering Hitler's parting remark to von Rundstedt at their 31 January meeting, must have merely reinforced Hitler's view of him.

The next step was taken on 3 February, when von Fritsch was formally removed from his post pending the investigation. The following day, von Brauchitsch's appointment as Commander-in-Chief was made public. Simultaneously, a list of senior officers was announced as being retired or posted. No less than sixteen of the most senior were retired. They included one group commander (von Leeb), and five corps commanders (von Kluge, Kress von Kressenstein, von Küchler, von Weichs, von Witzleben). All, apart from Kress von Kressenstein, would be recalled to the colours within the next few months. A further 44 officers were reassigned, including Erich von Manstein, Deputy Chief of Staff of OKH, who was appointed to command 18th Infantry Division. Curiously, when the list of those being retired was published in the *Berliner Tageblatt* on the following day (5 February), von Rundstedt's name was also on the list.[42] Whether this was an assumption on the newspaper's part or whether von Rundstedt's name had been on the list and someone had forgotten to delete it, cannot be ascertained, although it is more likely to have been the latter. As it was, confirmation of von Rundstedt's position came on 1 March when he was promoted Colonel General.

Von Brauchitsch's first task was the disagreeable one of having to organise von Fritsch's court-martial, which was convened on 11 March and presided over by Goering. But, on the following day, German troops marched into Austria and embodied it into the Greater Reich. Von Brauchitsch, although he was not available when Beck and von Manstein, who had not yet been replaced, were summoned to the Chancellery 48 hours before, to be told by Hitler what he wanted, must have known what was in the wind. Indeed, he told von Rundstedt to deputise for him at the celebrations of 125th anniversary of the institution of the Iron Cross, which were to take place in Breslau at that very time. Either he wanted to get von Rundstedt out of the way in case he objected or, more likely, he himself could not get away from Berlin. In any event, von Rundstedt said later that the first he heard of the *Anschluss* was in Breslau after it had happened.

Be that as it may, the von Fritsch court-martial was interrupted and was not re-convened until 17 March. It then transpired that Himmler's Gestapo had, mistakenly or intentionally, confused von Fritsch with a retired cavalry captain of the same name. He was therefore acquitted and von Rundstedt later stated that Goering, according to von Fritsch, had 'behaved in a decent way'.[44] Even so, von Fritsch was not restored to the active list, although, as a sop, Hitler appointed him to the Colonelcy of the 12th Artillery Regiment. A now very embittered man, he resolved to challenge Himmler to a duel and passed this in writing to von Rundstedt to issue.

Duelling itself was still officially considered to be an acceptable way of settling affairs of honour. Indeed, on 1 March 1938, von Brauchitsch, perhaps with the von Fritsch case in mind, issued a circular on the subject, which stated that: 'A challenge to a duel is the ultimate means for the defence of honour. It is only to be employed if personal honour has been gravely injured and if a senior officer is powerless to restore the situation.'[45] Certainly, von Fritsch's case appeared to fulfil these criteria, but von Rundstedt took no action over the challenge. He merely carried it around in his pocket for some weeks and then persuaded von Fritsch to withdraw it. His grounds for this were that 'on Hitler's orders, Himmler would have never faced up to a duel and because the whole affair would have only stirred things up at the expense of the Army.'[46] Von Rundstedt clearly believed that the honour and integrity of the Army as a whole was not worth risking for the sake of one individual member. He also thought, perhaps, that Hitler's trust in him was worth cultivating and that to appear as the bearer of von Fritsch's challenge would put him at odds with him. If this happened, he would be in no position to defend the Army's integrity.

Hitler now believed that, as a result of the purge, all possible Wehrmacht opposition to his plans had been removed. His eye was now firmly fixed on the South-East. On 21 April he ordered Keitel to dust off the plans for Case Green, the pre-emptive attack on Czechoslovakia. One officer within the OKH was still prepared to object. Ludwig Beck began to bombard von Brauchitsch with memoranda warning of the dangers of such an operation. On 28 May Hitler told his commanders that Germany's outstanding problems in Europe had to be solved quickly, before Britain could complete rearmament, which would not be until 1941–42. Beck again warned his superior officer that an attack on Czechoslovakia could lead to general war in Europe, which Germany will be ill placed to win. Hitler now declared that Czechoslovakia must be overcome by 1 October at the latest and this served to increase Beck's protests. Finally, at the end of July, he urged von Brauchitsch to tell Hitler that his generals refused to support him in his madcap expansionist schemes. Von Brauchitsch refused to do this, but did agree to summon the senior commanders to a conference.

In the meantime, a revised mobilisation plan was issued on 1 August and training was stepped up.

The conference itself was held on 4 August. Von Brauchitsch informed those present that he had received orders to prepare for an attack on Czechoslovakia. He read out a paper, which they assumed to have been written by Beck, although the Commander-in-Chief did not come clean on this. In essence, the document declared that the Sudetenland was not worth the risk of general war. Von Brauchitsch then invited the assembled company to put this view to Hitler. In turn the corps commanders said that the mood of both soldiers and civilians within their areas was against war and all agreed that, while an attack against Czechoslovakia would be successful, the Army was not strong enough to take on the major powers. According to von Weichs,[47] only two generals were against a mass objection to Hitler. Von Reichenau, who was commanding IV Corps, based at Munich, and appeared at the conference on crutches, said that from his personal knowledge of Hitler, it would be much better if officers represented their views individually to him. Nevertheless, von Reichenau did not disagree with the general view, which von Rundstedt said surprised him.[48] The other objection came from Ernst Busch, the VIII Corps commander, who said that soldiers should not interfere with politicians. This brought the retort from Beck that trained staff officers had to think in politico-military terms. Von Brauchitsch, however, undertook to represent the views of the meeting to Hitler, although von Rundstedt, according to von Weichs, warned him that he should be careful how he put them across. In Robert O'Neill's view,[49] this was because von Rundstedt was fearful that Hitler might sack von Brauchitsch and replace him with von Reichenau, which, considering von Rundstedt's constant opposition to this notion, is very likely to have been so. He would not, of course, have known of the circumstances through which von Brauchitsch, whether he liked it or not, was bound to Hitler. According to Keitel,[50] what had transpired at the conference quickly reached Hitler's ears, either through von Reichenau or Guderian. The latter was now commanding XVI Corps (the Panzer Divisions) and was forming an increasingly close relationship with Hitler in pursuit of furthering the Panzer arm. Thus, von Brauchitsch received short shrift when he saw Hitler, although he continued to try and influence him throughout September. Hitler then upraided his senior commanders while attending military exercises at Jüterbog. He told them that he would deal with Czechoslovakia by force and that there would be no general European war while Neville Chamberlain and Edouard Daladier, with their policy of appeasement, were at the helm in Britain and France. Beck was then invited to tender his resignation, which he did.

While von Rundstedt supported Beck's sentiments, he was not prepared to make any personal protest over his forced resignation. He merely relied on the 'chain of command' and saw this as von Brauchitsch's duty, as he would constantly do. He therefore urged von Brauchitsch to keep up the pressure on Hitler.[51] In the meantime, he had a role to play in the seizing of the Sudetenland for the Third Reich. Four armies were to be involved. These were, according to the mobilisation plan, to be formed from existing *Heeresgruppen*. Von Reichenau, now promoted to command *Heeresgruppe* 4, was to strike at Pilsen from the north-west with the Tenth Army, while the Twelfth Army, under von Leeb, now recalled to active service, and Fourteenth (List-*Heeresgruppe* 5) would invade from Austria. Von Rundstedt would advance from Silesia in the north with what would become Second Army. His prospects of retiring from active service on 1 October receded into the distance. According to his daughter-in-law, however, the deal that von Rundstedt had made with Hitler during the von Fritsch affair was that he would be recalled in 'times of emergency'.[52] The Sudetenland was clearly such an emergency and hence von Rundstedt accepted the situation.

If Hitler believed that he had, with Beck's resignation, finally removed all military opposition to his plans this was not so. Franz Halder had moved across from being Chief of Operations to OKW to Chief of Staff OKH in succession to Beck. A devout Roman Catholic, he was also horrified at Hitler's policies, but was more circumspect in his opposition than Beck had been. He was already in touch with a circle, both military and civilian, who believed that Hitler must be deposed, although he was careful to use an intermediary, Colonal (later General) Hans Oster, Admiral Canaris's chief of staff at the Abwehr. Among the civilians involved were Dr Hans Goerdeler, former Lord Mayor of Leipzig, Hjalmar Schacht, President of the Reichsbank and Ulrich von Hassell, who had been deposed as Ambassador to Rome in February 1938. The soldiers included Beck and Erwin von Witzleben, recalled to the Colours and now one of von Rundstedt's corps commanders and, according to his elder grandson, his closest comrade.[53] Another well known to von Rundstedt was Erich Hoepner, his chief of staff in Berlin from 1935, who had recently taken over command of 1st Light Division.

In August 1938, the plotters sent an emissary, Major Ewald von Kleist-Schmenzin, a cousin of the General Ewald von Kleist, to

London in order to warn the British Government of Hitler's intentions towards Czechoslovakia and to enlist its support for a coup. While Winston Churchill, then still in the political wilderness, received him warmly, Prime Minister Neville Chamberlain merely noted that von Kleist reminded him of 'the Jacobites at the Court of France in King William's time and I think that we must discount a good deal of what he says.'[54] Thus von Kleist-Schmenzin returned virtually empty-handed, but the plotters were undeterred. As soon as Hitler gave the order to invade Czechoslovakia, von Witzleben, whose headquarters was in Berlin, was to arrest Hitler and secure the capital while Hoepner prevented SS units from advancing from Bavaria. Halder had not, however, approached those who would be commanding armies during the attack.

> 'I knew that at that moment when the veil was removed I could rely on Adam, Bock and also on von Rundstedt. This gave me the conviction to act; I well know that many comrades said it would be impossible to set the Army in motion against Hitler. Anyway it was the last moment when it was possible.'[54]

Certainly, von Bock and von Rundstedt were well placed, while Wilhelm Adam was commandant of the Wehrmacht Academy, and Beck, on 1 September, was placed in temporary command of the First Army on Germany's border with France. Von Rundstedt himself later confirmed that he knew nothing of the plot, telling Liddel Hart that he had already retired by this time.[56] Yet, apart from this not being so, it is surprising when officers as close to him as von Witzleben and Hoepner were involved in the plot that no approach was made or hint given to him. But Halder stated that Adam, von Bock and von Rundstedt had all warned him that they could not be entirely confident of their troops being prepared to act against Hitler.[57] This was to be one of von Rundstedt's justifications for not becoming involved in future plots against the régime, as we shall see.

As it was, Neville Chamberlain's intercessions in September, which culminated in the Munich Pact, swept the carpet from under both the Czechs and the plotters. The German armies crossed the border on 1 October and the Sudetenland was bloodlessly incorporated into the Third Reich. Von Rundstedt recalled that Hitler spent the day with him during the occupation and told him how 'free and liberated' he felt. This, von Rundstedt said, made him believe that Hitler had never wanted war with the Czechs and that finally the 'nightmare was lifted off the German people and also off the Führer'.[58] This was reinforced when, on 1 November, von Rundstedt was finally permitted to retire. Some, notably von Hassell, were, however, convinced that von Rundstedt had been sacked for 'cold feet' over the Sudetenland and believed that, with the retirements of Beck and Adam, which were announced at the same time, the Army had 'suffered enormous losses politically'.[59]

As a parting present, Hitler appointed von Rundstedt Honorary Colonel of the 18th Infantry Regiment, which he had commanded in the 1920s. It was an honour that meant much to von Rundstedt and he would wear its uniform throughout much of the war, although, as his biographer Günther Blumentritt commented, 'it often happened that young officers thus mistook him for a colonel and did not know that it was the Field Marshal standing before them, which Rundstedt always accepted with good humour.'[60] His regiment was to fight in France and Russia, although never under his command, and was decimated in the summer of 1944. Reformed as 6th Volksgrenadier Division, it would end the war in Prague. It was, however, equally proud to have von Rundstedt as its Colonel and, on the 50th anniversary of his joining the Army, presented him with a beautifully bound detailed account of its war history, which today is in the possession of his elder grandson.

The von Rundstedts were now able to return to their beloved Kassel, where they rented an apartment on Skagerrak Platz. 'It's good that I'm out of that pig-sty Berlin', he was supposed to have commented.[61] He was, though, still bound by the 'state of emergency' agreement with Hitler and his retirement would accordingly be brief.

PLATE 1. The young Gerd (left) with his father and brothers, Joachim (on father's knee) and Udo.

PLATE 2. The Cadets – Left to Right – Udo, Gerd, Joachim and Eberhard (on Gerd's shoulders) at Oranienstein. Today, the castle is the headquarters of 5th Panzer Division.

PLATE 3. Lieutenant and Regimental Adjutant.

PLATE 4. Gerd and Bila on their wedding day.

PLATE 5. Hans Gerd and Bila, Kassel 1911.

PLATE 6. German artillery passing through Brussels, August 1914.

PLATE 7. The Narew battlefield, July 1915. Gerd's health broke down again during the fighting here.

PLATE 8. General von Beseler, German military governor of Warsaw and Gerd's chief 1915–16, with his Austro-Hungarian counterpart, Graf Slepycki.

PLATE 9. Eastern Front, January 1918 – Russian and German troops fraternising.

PLATE 10. A cavalryman at heart – Gerd (left) while umpiring the 5th and 7th Infantry Divisions' manoeuvres, Bavaria 1926.

PLATE 11. Reviewing 2nd Cavalry Division, Breslau 1929.

PLATE 12. Gerd, Bila and Hans Gerd on the steps of Hardenbergstrasse 32, Berlin, Spring 1932.

PLATE 13. Von Rundstedt, von Hammerstein-Equord and von Hindenburg, 1933.

PLATE 14. Von Rundstedt (extreme left), von Fritsch (centre) and von Kluge (behind and to the right of von Fritsch), 1935.

PLATE 15. Left to right: Raeder, von Blomberg, Hitler, Goering and von Rundstedt on Hitler's 47th birthday.

PLATE 16. Von Rundstedt (left) with Hitler during the *Gruppenkommando 2* autumn manoeuvres, 1936.

PLATE 17. A grim-faced von Rundstedt takes the salute of his troops as they leave Breslau for the occupation of the Sudetenland, 28 September 1938.

PLATE 18. Poland, September 1939 – German infantry on the march.

PLATE 19. Polish prisoners after the reduction of the Kutno pocket.

PLATE 20. They do not yet know it, but their fate will be grim. Polish Jews being
questioned by an SS officer, 5 September 1939.

PLATE 21. France, May 1940. Elements of Rommel's 7th Panzer Division.

PLATE 22. Reduction of the Dunkirk pocket – British and French prisoners, 27 May 1940.

PLATE 23. Preparations for SEALION. A PzKpfw III undergoing deep wading trials.

PLATE 24. A happier moment – von Rundstedt visiting 18th Infantry Regiment during the winter of 1940–41. (It will be noted that he is dressed as Honorary Colonel of the Regiment. This form of dress was his favourite uniform and in many of the plates in this book he may be seen wearing it rather than that of a Field Marshal).

PLATE 25. Russia – a Rumanian artillery unit crosses the River Pruth, September 1941. Lack of motor transport among the Allied contingents aggravated von Rundstedt's supply problems.

PLATE 26. Autumn rains in the Ukraine with a German horse-drawn supply column in the background.

PLATE 27. Russia – the first snows. Vehicles waiting to cross the Dnieper by ferry. The Russians had destroyed all the bridges.

PLATE 28. German troops fight their way into Rostov-on-Don, November 1941. Their withdrawal before the end of the month would result in von Rundstedt's removal from command.

PLATE 29. 'Very impressive'. Dieppe after the disastrous raid of August 1942.

PLATE 30. Von Rundstedt
visiting Seyss-Inquart,
Reichs Commissioner for
the Netherlands, July 1943.
Seyss-Inquart was executed
for war crimes in 1946.

PLATE 31. Inspecting the Atlantic defences in the La Rochelle area, August 1943.

PLATE 32. Von Rundstedt in April 1944. He is holding his treasured *Interimstab*.

PLATE 33. Tea with Guderian at St. Germain, 1 May 1944.

PLATE 34. A visit to
Marshal Petain. Laval is
behind the doorway.

5
Poland

WHILE VON RUNDSTEDT was enjoying his retirement in Kassel, Hitler had both dealt with the rump of Czechoslovakia and sent his troops to occupy Memel, which lay on the Baltic on the East Prussia – Lithuania border. This done, he now turned his attention to Poland. Early in April 1939, OKW issued *Directive for the Uniform Preparation by the Wehrmacht for War in 1939/40*. This directive was in three parts, covering Frontier Protection (Part I), *Fall Weiss* (Case White – Part II), and Danzig (Part III). Part II was the most significant and appeared a week before the other two.[1] It concerned Poland. The preamble of the directive, which was written by Hitler himself, warned that force might be the only way to solve the Polish problem once and for all. If this was so, the mission of the Wehrmacht would be to destroy the Polish Armed Forces by surprise attack. The Wehrmacht must be ready to do this by 1 September. All three Services were to produce plans by 1 May.

Mobilisation plans had called for two army group headquarters to be formed, one to operate in the West and the other the East. Case White now demanded that two army group headquarters be created for the projected attack on Poland, one to operate from Pomerania and East Prussia and the other from Silesia. The army group headquarters themselves were formed from two of the six *Heeresgruppen* which now existed, the other four, together with a number of the *Wehrkreis* HQs, creating Army HQs. The Army Group responsible for defence of the West was based on *Heeresgruppe* 2, which had its headquarters at Frankfurt-am-Main and was commanded by Erwin von Witzleben. Since the concept was to remain strictly on the defensive in the West while Case White was being implemented, OKH appears to have considered that the commander needed to be well versed in defence. Recognised as the expert was Wilhelm Ritter von Leeb, who had written a widely acclaimed book on the subject[2] but had been retired in

1938 during the von Fritsch affair. Perhaps because he had a good relationship with Keitel,[3] he was earmarked to be recalled to the colours. With regard to Poland, Fedor von Bock's *Heeresgruppe* 1 in Berlin was nominated under the mobilisation plans to become the army group headquarters in the East and in Case White this became Army Group North. Creation of the second army group headquarters was more problematical. To earmark another *Heeresgruppe* for it would mean recasting the complete mobilisation plan and time was limited. OKH thus decided to create the headquarters afresh. To command it they appointed, doubtless with Hitler's approval, von Rundstedt. For security reasons, however, the headquarters was not to be officially formed before war with Poland became inevitable, but much planning needed to be done in the meantime. Hence, at the beginning of May *Arbeitstab von Rundstedt* (Working Staff von Rundstedt) came into existence. Apart from von Rundstedt, there were just two members. The first was Erich von Manstein, who was nominated as von Rundstedt's chief of staff. At the time, as we have seen, he was commanding 18th Infantry Division at Liegnitz, having been posted there from OKH in February 1938 because of his close involvement with Beck and von Fritsch. He had, however, served as chief of staff to von Leeb during the Munich crisis. Von Manstein was pleased to serve under von Rundstedt:

> 'Every one of us knew him. As an exponent of grand tactics he was brilliant – a talented soldier who grasped the essentials of any problem in an instant. Indeed, he would concern himself with nothing else, being supremely indifferent to minor detail. He was a gentleman of the old school – a type, I fear, which is now dying out, but which once added a delightful variant to life.'[4]

In other words, he saw von Rundstedt as the ideal chief of staff's commander, who would give broad directives and then allow his staff to organise the detail with minimum interference. The other member was Colonel Günther Blumentritt, who was appointed 1a (Chief of Operations) of the Working Party. He echoed von Manstein's comments, noting that von Rundstedt liked 'an operational map to be 1:1,000,000, but not on the scale of 1:300,000 and still less 1:100,000'.[5] At the time, Blumentritt headed the training branch in OKH and both he and von Manstein had to work on Case White in addition to their normal duties. Von Rundstedt, on the other hand, worked from home at Kassel and was not formally recalled to the active list until the beginning of June. Their staff, when it was formed, was to come from VII Corps at

Munich, which was, according to the mobilisation plan, to have become Twelfth Army.

Army Group South had been given three armies. The Eighth was to be created from Johannes Blaskowitz's *Heeresgruppe* 3 at Dresden, the Tenth from Walther von Reichenau's *Heeresgruppe* 4 at Leipzig, and the Fourteenth from Siegmund List's *Heeresgruppe* 5 at Vienna. The geographic distance that separated them cannot have made von Rundstedt's task any easier. Nevertheless, his working group quickly buckled down to the task. The original OKH plan called for Army Group North to cut the Polish Corridor between Germany proper and East Prussia and to thrust towards Warsaw from East Prussia. Von Rundstedt was also to advance on Warsaw on a broad front, whilst providing a strong flank guard on his southern flank to ward off Polish counterattacks from Galicia and south-east Poland. His initial planning task was to obtain the comments of his prospective army commanders. These were duly received and von Rundstedt then forwarded them to OKH at the end of May.

The original OKH plan envisaged Tenth Army in the centre making the main thrust on Warsaw and for this reason it was the strongest, being allocated two Panzer, three light, two motorised and six infantry divisions. Eighth Army's (four infantry divisions) initial primary task was to secure Tenth Army's northern flank against the Polish forces in the Poznan area. To this end its initial objective was Lodz. Meanwhile Fourteenth Army (two Panzer, one Light, five infantry divisions) was to seize Cracow and guard Tenth Army from a southern counterattack. Von Rundstedt's main concern was that Eighth Army was ill equipped to perform its flank guard function since it lacked cavalry. This was accepted and Hitler's own bodyguard, the SS Leibstandarte Adolf Hitler, a motorised regiment, was allocated to Blaskowitz.

The final OKH operation order was issued on 15 June. The main task now to be tackled was the deployment of the necessary forces to the Polish border without alerting Poland, and, for that matter, Britain and France, to the degree that they would mobilise. This was to be done in three stages. First, under the cloak of manoeuvres, and here Blumentritt was ideally placed, a number of infantry divisions and supporting units would be moved close to the border, while the mechanised elements were concentrated in Central Germany. These manoeuvres also provided an excuse for calling up reservists on the grounds that these would constitute their annual training. A further cloak was an announced German intention to strengthen the Eastern borders. The second phase was to be built round the 25th anniversary celebrations in

East Prussia of the victory at Tannenberg, which had thrown back the Russian invasion of East Prussia in 1914. This provided a convenient cover, especially for the deployment of Third Army. The deployment timetable was issued by OKW on 14 July and all preparations were to be completed by 20 August.

On 12 August *Arbeitsstab von Rundstedt* assembled at a training centre at Neuhammer in Silesia. Two days later von Rundstedt took the salute at a parade of 18th Infantry Division, which was on manoeuvres and was now saying farewell to its commander.[6] On the 18th, the staff of HQ Army Group South gathered in Munich. The bulk, according to Blumentritt, were reserve officers and it took them a little time to get used to working in a higher formation field headquarters, another symptom of the German Army's very rapid expansion.[7] Next day, von Rundstedt received the first preparatory codeword from OKH. This told him that 19 August was to be the day for the first of the final deployment measures, which meant primarily the deployment of formation headquarters. In HQ Army Group South's case this meant moving to Neisse, which it did on the 21st, taking up residence at the Monastery of the Holy Cross. Neisse, happened also to be Ditha's birthplace.

Von Rundstedt and von Manstein left the setting up of the headquarters to Blumentritt, for they had been summoned to Obersalzberg, Hitler's Alpine retreat, together with the other army group and army commanders and their chiefs of staff. They went by car, stopping overnight at von Manstein's brother-in-law's estate at Linz, and arrived at Obersalzberg next morning, the 22nd.[8] Apparently, probably for security reasons, the generals were ordered to attend in civilian clothes,[9] perhaps the last time some of them would wear them for some years. Von Rundstedt always preferred wearing uniform and never felt comfortable when otherwise dressed, calling plain clothes a 'funny disguise'.[10] The conference itself began at midday. Hitler began by reviewing the political situation. While he would have preferred to deal with the West first, this would merely invite the Poles to attack Germany. They must therefore tackle Poland. In any event, conditions were favourable for settling the Eastern question. The Fascist leaders – himself, Mussolini and Franco – had the toughness and nerve to face the decisions that needed to be made, while their democratic counterparts did not. Britain was too wrapped up in tension with Italy, Japan and in the Middle East; France was a shadow of her former self. These were the only two nations which might be obligated to go to Poland's aid and German-Polish relations could not go on as they were.

Furthermore, and this came as a bombshell to his audience, the Soviet Union had expressed its willingness to sign a non-aggression pact with Germany. Poland was thus isolated, with her only allies too far away in the west to give her any direct help. All they could do was to establish a blockade, which would not work, since Germany had control of the Danube, or assault the West Wall, which would be difficult both militarily and psychologically. Hence 'Poland has been manoeuvred into a position where our military victory is assured'. Hitler exhorted his military commanders to be hard and remorseless in achieving their aim of annihilating the Poles. He gave some particulars of how the campaign was to be conducted and stated that the attack on Poland would probably be launched on the following Saturday morning, 26 August.

What did the Generals make of all this? Von Manstein stated that they did not believe that war was inevitable. The non-aggression pact with the Soviet Union and Poland's resultant isolation made it unlikely that she would be prepared to fight. Furthermore, even with the concealment of Germany's mobilisation on her Eastern borders, this gathering of miliary commanders at Berchtesgaden could not have gone unnoticed by the Poles, and the build up of forces itself could not be totally hidden from them. This must be 'the climax of deliberate bluff'.[11] Von Rundstedt himself stated to the International Military Tribunal (IMT) Commission at Nuremberg after the war that the news of the non-aggression pact much pleased 'us soldiers of the von Seeckt school, I even almost want to say it made us happy. There was a tradition in the Reichswehr of good relations with Russia.' He did not believe that Poland would dare resort to arms and 'left Berghof with the feeling that it would be a flower war as in 1938 in the Sudetenland'.[12] Yet, K J Müller in his book *Das Heer und Hitler* cites von Rundstedt saying to von Manstein: 'That crackpot wants war.' He also stated that both Erwin von Witzleben and von Sodenstern, who would succeed von Manstein as von Rundstedt's chief of staff, both believed that war with the Western democracies was now inevitable. Von Reichenau, apparently, went even further, declaring: 'The man [Hitler] is in the greatest error if he thinks the war will be over in six weeks; it will last six years.'[13] If von Rundstedt and von Manstein really came away with the idea that Hitler was bluffing, then they must have realised that he was bluffing his generals as well. Halder's notes on his speech certainly reveal no indication that Hitler was hoping that the Poles would see sense and accede to his demands; rather the opposite. Hitler's tone seems to have been bellicose throughout and it is difficult to accept that anyone in the audience came away believing that he did not want war with Poland. Yet, his posture had been the same during the Sudetenland crisis. Even so, von Rundstedt and von Manstein in their postwar recollections possibly voiced what they hoped would happen as against what they thought Hitler wanted to occur.

At the end of the session, the generals left for their headquarters. Von Rundstedt and von Manstein travelled back separately, von Rundstedt direct to Neisse, while von Manstein stayed overnight with his family at Liegnitz, 'a measure of my inner disbelief in the likelihood of an imminent outbreak of war'.[14] This stay could, of course, be interpreted in an entirely different way, namely that von Manstein thought that there was a good chance that he might not have the opportunity to see them for some time. On the 24th, von Rundstedt received the order *Befehlsübernahme* (assume command), which meant that Army Group South was now formally brought into existence. He was also given confirmation of a matter that had been raised at Hitler's conference, namely that the standing forces on the Slovakian border with Poland were to be strengthened immediately.[15] On 25 August came the cryptic OHK order '*Fall Weiss 1. Y-Tag 26.8. Uhrzeit 4.30*'. This meant that the following day was confirmed for the attack on Poland and that H-hour was to be 0430 hours. This was received at 1525 hours and it seemed that war, whether it was wanted or not, was inevitable. The troops began to move that evening from their assembly areas to their jump-off positions. But, at 2030 hours there was a telephone call to Army Group from OKH ordering all forward movement to be halted and for the attacking divisions to return to their assembly areas.

The reason for this was twofold. Firstly, on the same day Britain had signed a formal alliance with Poland, thus indicating a resolve for which Hitler had not calculated. At the same time, Mussolini, on whom Hitler was relying to give active support, complained that he was not ready. The order created an urgent problem for von Rundstedt's staff. The deployment was, for obvious reasons, being conducted under radio silence, hence all that could be done in many cases was to send out liaison officers. Most units received the halt order around midnight, although, in one case, a motorised infantry regiment was only halted when the officer carrying the message to it landed in a Feiseler Storch light aircraft in the dark in front of the head of its column. In one case, though, the order did not get through. A highly secret unit, 'Construction Battalion 800', had been formed by Admiral Wilhelm Canaris, head of the Abwehr, from ethnic Germans and other anti-Polish elements living outside the borders of the Third Reich. Their task was to cross the Polish border ahead of the Army, seize vital points and carry out other sabotage tasks. One group in Slovakia, and led by a Reserve Lieutenant, had as its mission the capture of the Jablunka Pass in order to prevent the railway tunnels running underneath it being blown up by the Poles. They successfuly achieved this and it was only when the commander spoke on the telephone at the nearby station to a staff officer from 7th Infantry Division, which was to relieve the group in the Pass, and who had been anxiously hanging on to the telephone at the nearest Slovak railway station, that he realised that he had been premature. He managed to get back across the border, after some firefights with the Poles. Some of his men were captured, though, and it was only after interrogation and submitting to a demand that a German general personally go the the border to negotiate their release that they were returned. It would have been expected that the Poles would increase their alert measures as a result, but there had been so many border incidents during recent months and, in any event, mobilisation was already taking place.[16]

Von Rundstedt's and von Manstein's reaction to the halt order was to believe that the Russo-German non-aggression pact and the concentration of German force on the border had persuaded the Poles to negotiate. Von Rundstedt told the IMT Commission that it merely reinforced his assumption that there would be no war. 'Such halts had occurred before the occupation of the Sudetenland. Therefore, we thought: "Aha, there is a new peace effort going on".'[17] The next few days enabled the Germans to complete the mobilisation of second, third and fourth line units and to deploy the newly formed 10th Panzer Division to the Fourth Army. For those already deployed it was a period of limbo and not a few units spent it helping with the local harvest. The Anglo-French efforts to persuade Germany and Poland to negotiate and Mussolini's offer to mediate need not be gone into here. Suffice it to say that, although OKH was abreast of the diplomatic flurry,[18] von Manstein said that he and his commander were kept entirely in the dark. When at 1600 hours on the 31st they received another cryptic OKH signal stating that Case White was to be executed on the following day at 0445 hours they 'were sceptical, particularly as no mention had been made of negotiations having failed.' They waited until midnight for another cancellation and only then accepted that the die was now cast.[19]

As the German armies crossed the Polish borders next morning at dawn, the Luftwaffe attacked airfields and key points, knocking out aircraft on the ground and impeding the movement of Polish reserves.

In Army Group North's area there was thick mist, but von Rundstedt was luckier. The day was clear, which enabled him to obtain valuable information from air reconnaissance. Initial progress was good. By 0600 hours the advance was up to four miles and this had increased to 15 miles by early afternoon. It was only now that Polish resistance stiffened. The attacking troops began to come across an increasing number of demolitions and there were local counter-attacks. Significantly, there were several reports of civilians shooting at German soldiers.[20] It was the reaction of von Rundstedt's troops to these *franc-tireurs*, usually summary execution, which helped to make him a major war criminal in post-war Polish eyes.

By the end of the second day of the war, Tenth Army had reached the River Warthe, but the Poles resisted fiercely around the towns of Czestochowa and, across the inter-army boundary to the south, Katowice and Nikotow. Von Rundstedt and von Manstein concluded that the Poles were intending to stand firm on the Warthe. Next day, however, Czestochowa fell and the left wing of Fourteenth Army managed to get through the resistance around Katowice and Nikotow. Furthermore, several bridgeheads were secured over the Warthe. The bag of Polish prisoners began to rise rapidly and it was clear that the moment for break-out in the north had arrived. It was also noticeable that the Polish forces in Galicia were beginning to withdraw in order to avoid being cut off.

On 4 September, Tenth Army broke out of its bridgeheads over the Warthe with Reinhardt's 4th Panzer Division in the van. Next day von Reichenau's forces crossed the River Pilica. His increasingly rapid advance, however, stretched Blaskowitz's flank guard to his north. This began to cause von Rundstedt and von Manstein increasing concern, especially since the Poznan Army lay virtually unengaged to the north. In the extreme south, the bulk of the Polish forces were withdrawing towards Cracow, but OKH now ordered Fourteenth Army to destroy the Polish forces withdrawing east across the Vistula. To this end, List was to thrust across the River San to Lublin in order to get in behind them. Cracow fell to List on the 6th and he now began to advance along the line of the upper Vistula.

The growing threat of the Poznan Army caused von Rundstedt to transfer two corps from von Reichenau to Blaskowitz on the 7th. He also once more asked OKH for cavalry to screen his northern flank, but there was none available. Matters were not helped by the fact that, for some unaccountable reason, Blastowitz had deployed his one mobile element, the SS Leibstandarte, on his right rather than left flank. One might have expected von Rundstedt to have insisted from the outset that the Leibstandarte be used in the extreme north. That he did not could have been an oversight, but was more likely part of his policy of giving his subordinates as free a rein as possible. For the moment, though, all remained relatively quiet on the northern flank, and von Reichenau began to create a pocket around the Polish forces which had withdrawn on Radom, 50 miles south of Warsaw. Reinhardt, however, continued to dash to the capital and reached the suburbs on the 8th. That evening, in his situation report, von Rundstedt claimed to have taken Warsaw and also to have established crossings over the Vistula to the south of the city. Army Group North's War Diary noted that 'the drama is approaching its finale'[21] but this proved to be premature. Next day, Reinhardt tried to seize Warsaw single-handed, but was bloodily repulsed, losing 57 out of 120 tanks engaged. Apart from starkly illustrating the vulnerability of tanks on their own in built-up areas, it also showed that the Poles were not prepared to surrender their capital at the first sight of the enemy.

On 9 September, before von Rundstedt and von Manstein could decide what to do next about Warsaw, the attack from the north, which had increasingly worried them, suddenly materialised. 30th Infantry Division, advancing north-east and stretched out for almost 20 miles, reported being attacked by a force estimated as two or three divisions and two cavalry brigades. Blaskowitz sent the other two divisions in the corps to assist and, although 30th Division lost ground and suffered casualties, the situation was stabilised by the end of the following day. That the Poznan Army had committed itself to attacking south rather than withdrawing east did, however, present the opportunity of destroying it, something which was quickly spotted by OKH. Accordingly, on 11 September, von Brauchitsch ordered von Rundstedt to use Eighth Army to destroy the Poznan Army by containing it in a pocket centred on Kotno, while elements of Army Group North, which had been advancing on Warsaw from the north, acted as a backstop. In the meantime, von Rundstedt and von Manstein visited Blaskowitz's headquarters and organised a counterstroke to be mounted by von Leeb's XI Corps (two infantry divisions) against the eastern flank of the Polish penetration.

Elsewhere, Army Group South was achieving some notable successes. Tenth Army had now eradicated the Radom pocket, which yielded some 60,000 prisoners, while Fourteenth Army, having captured Cracow, had now crossed the River San north and south of the ancient fortress of Przemsyl. During the next week, though, the main focus of von Rundstedt's attention was on what became called the Battle of the Bzura, the elimination of the Kutno pocket. Twice, on the 12th and 16th, the Poles made determined efforts to break out of the noose but were repulsed. Eventually, on 17 September, the Luftwaffe was unleashed on the Poznan Army. Its commander, General Kutrzeba recalled:

> 'In point of the number of aircraft committed, the severity of the individual strikes, and the acrobatic daring displayed, the [enemy air operation] represented a record. Every movement, every troop concentration, and all march routes were taken under annihilating fire from the air. . . . It was Hell come to earth. The bridges were destroyed, the fords were blocked, the anti-aircraft and part of the other artillery forces were annihilated.'[22]

Next day the surrenders began, but it took three days of mopping up before the pocket was finally cleared. Even then the equivalent of two divisions managed to escape to the east, leaving 40,000 of their brother Polish soldiers as prisoners, and many others dead.

The German treatment of captured Polish troops would also be laid at von Rundstedt's door after the war. Indeed, with regard to atrocities as a whole, Halder had noted in his diary as early as 11 September the 'enemy propaganda campaign' to this effect and the need for an officer to be sent to investigate 'the accusations' so that the propaganda could be effectively countered.[23] The acts on which the atrocity accusations were based took several different forms. There was, for a start, the treatment of the *franc-tireurs*. The German Quartermaster-General, General Eduard Wagner, reinforced the Army Group South War Diary entry of 1 September with an entry in his personal diary three days later. 'Brutal guerrilla war has broken out everywhere and we are ruthlessly stamping it out. We won't be reasoned with. We have already sent out emergency courts, and they are in continual session. The harder we strike, the quicker there will be peace again.'[24] Not surprisingly, in the light of this, German troops over-reacted and, if shots were fired at them from a village, houses were set alight and innocents as well as guilty found themselves facing firing squads. Looting, too, was widespread. Just as serious were the numerous occurrences cited by the Poles after the war in their case against von Rundstedt and von Manstein of surrendered Polish soldiers in uniform being shot.[25] These varied from the shooting of individuals to what appeared to be virtually mass murder.

There is certainly no evidence that von Rundstedt ever condoned, let alone encouraged these acts. It would have been totally out of character for him to have done so. Indeed, at the end of the campaign he and Blaskowitz complained personally to Halder about Hitler's edict pardoning all soldiers who had been found guilty of looting and other offences.[26] Even so, their complaint was not acted upon. What, however, must be understood is that the German soldiers fighting in Poland were almost all experiencing combat for the first time and, in spite of the traditional discipline of their army, they were understandably nervous. Furthermore, there was no love lost between the Germans and the Poles. The Versailles creation of the Polish Corridor, with resultant isolation of East Prussia, and the Polish attempt, with French encouragement, to take over Upper Silesia in 1921 are but two examples of why this should be so. Even so, von Rundstedt was responsible in the eyes of international law for the conduct of his troops and cannot be totally absolved of the atrocities they committed. Nervous tension arising from inexperience and traditional enmities can never constitute any excuse for breaches of the Geneva Convention or normal military discipline. They are, however, good reasons why a commander must be especially vigilant over the conduct of his troops and why he should issue firm warnings against the perpetration of such excesses before the soldiers are committed to battle.

More sinister were the activities of the SS. The military arm, the SS-VT (later Waffen-SS), was represented in the front line by the SS Leibstandarte, SS Deutschland, SS Germania and SS Artillery Regiments, and a reconnaissance battalion, engineer battalion and a reinforced infantry battalion. In the Army's view, they were lacking in discipline and military skills and also had atrocity charges levelled against them. Thus Halder noted in his diary on 10 September that members of the SS Artillery Regiment, which was under von Küchler's Third Army, had herded Jews into a church and massacred them. They had been sentenced by court-martial to one year's penitentiary, but von Küchler had not confirmed this because 'more severe punishment is due'.[27] Behind the SS-VT, however, came the SS *Totenkopfverbände* under the notorious Theodor Eicke. These were deployed on 7 September in three regiments. They were briefed by Reinhard Heydrich, leader of the SD and Himmler's deputy, that the Polish ruling classes were to be eradicated and the lower classes 'kept down in one way or another'. Furthermore, Hitler told von Brauchitsch that the Army was not to interfere.[28] Since Eicke's men were largely to operate in von Rundstedt's area of responsibility, it is likely that Hitler told him the same thing when von Rundstedt reported to him on his train at Iltenau on 9 September.[29] Eicke's men quickly got to work and it immediately became apparent that the Jews were also a prime target. Admiral Canaris was an early witness. On 10 September he went to view the fighting and was told of numerous incidents of murders of civilians. When he tried to remonstrate with Keitel he was advised not to become involved since it was Hitler's policy.[30] Even so, the Army did not remain a totally passive bystander. One of Eicke's *Einsatzgruppen* (Action Groups) under Udo von Worysch was operating in Fourteenth Army's area. The soldiers were disgusted by its operations and the Army's Operations Section complained to von Rundstedt. He immediately banned von Worysch's action group from the war zone and ordered anti-Jewish measures in the Katowice area to cease forthwith.[31] Unfortunately, this did little to deter Himmler's henchmen. On 21 September, they received fresh instructions from Heydrich ordering them to clear the Jews from the land and to concentrate them in ghettos in the cities.

While the battle of the Bzura was being fought, Fourteenth Army had captured Przemysl and had invested Lvov. Tenth Army had been ordered to secure Lublin and Guderian's XIX Motorised Corps had been unleashed from East Prussia in order to link up with von Reichenau and trap the bulk of the remaining Polish forces east of the Vistula. In addition, attention was being devoted to the capture of Warsaw, which the Poles had declared a fortress. By the 16th the capital was surrounded, with elements of Eighth Army covering the west, Tenth Army the south and Third Army the east. The Luftwaffe, which had been making attacks solely on military targets in and around the city since the first day of the war, now dropped leaflets proposing that negotiations should be opened for its surrender and for the evacuation of its civilian population and foreign embassies. On the following morning, under a flag of truce, an officer from Third Army made direct contact with the Poles, but the commander of the Warsaw garrison, General Rommel (not to be confused with Erwin Rommel) refused to speak to him or accept his written demand to surrender. Further leaflets were dropped that afternoon calling on the civilian population to evacuate the city and guaranteeing a 12 hours ceasefire for them to do this. Polish batteries, however, ignored this and the German guns replied. Next day the Poles broadcast a request that they be permitted to send emissaries to discuss the civilian evacuation. The Germans expressed themselves happy to receive them, but none appeared.

It is now clear that the Polish garrison, strong and largely made up of regular troops, was determined on resistance. Von Rundstedt and other commanders, fearing the heavy casualties that protracted street fighting would produce, were content to starve the city into submission, but Hitler would have none of this. Apart from viewing the continued resistance of Warsaw as an affront to German arms, Hitler had another reason for wanting the capital to be secured quickly. On the 17th, the Russians had invaded Poland from the East and he was keen that Warsaw should be in German hands before the Russians advanced too far to the west. Accordingly, on 18 September the Germans began a continuous artillery bombardment while dive-bombers attacked the water works and other public utilities. Probing attacks confirmed the fears that resistance would be fierce and made little progress. This situation continued for the next few days.

By now Hitler, acting through OKH, had taken personal control of the Warsaw operations and laid down that the city should be attacked from the west. This would drive the civilian population eastwards into the hands of the Russians and save the Germans from having to look after them. After much discussion, OKH eventually decided that Eighth Army, having finally reduced the Kutno pocket, should be responsible for the assault. This was finally mounted on the 26th, but Blaskowitz was told that he must not allow any civilian evacuation, on the grounds that the worsening food situation would hasten surrender. By then the only source of water available to the inhabitants was the Vistula and the other utilities were hardly functioning. That evening, two Polish envoys crossed the lines north of Warsaw and requested a 24 hours ceasefire and surrender negotiations. The Germans would not agree to the former and OKH directed that any surrender must be unconditional. The following morning the Poles accepted this and hostilities ended at 1400 hours. No less than 140,000 Polish troops laid down their arms.

Warsaw occupied a good deal of von Rundstedt's attention, but the Russian invasion created complications in Galicia and east of the Vistula. On 21 September, he was ordered to withdraw his forces west of the Vistula-San line since it was agreed that this would be the boundary between Russian and German occupied Poland. Fourteenth Army was still besieging Lvov, but was ordered to hand this task over to the Russians. As the Germans prepared to withdraw, the garrison, not wanting to fall into Russian hands, suddenly surrendered. This was not the case at Chelm, north of Lvov and also close to the River Bug, and which elements of Tenth Army were trying to reduce. Another complication was local clashes between the Red Army and Fourteenth Army. These were largely cases of mistaken identity, especially since Polish forces were still active in the area, but were resolved on the spot, although there were casualties on both sides.

No sooner had von Rundstedt's troops completed their withdrawal than the demarcation line was changed. On 1 October he was told that henceforth the line would be along the Bug to a point east of Tomaszow, where it was to run west to the San and then down that river to the Slovakian border. Thus he had to advance east again, meeting further pockets of Polish resistance. The most significant of these was at Kock, 80 miles south-east of Warsaw. This did not fall to elements of Tenth Army, which had already been warned off for withdrawal to Germany, until 6 October. Only then could Army Group South's part in the Polish campaign be considered to have ended.

Apart of the capture of territory, Army Group South had reaped some impressive results. No less than 523,156 prisoners of war were captured, together with 1,401 guns and 96 tanks. The cost was 6,554 killed, 20,478 wounded and 4,064 missing. Von Rundstedt's personal contribution was recognised in the award of the Knight's Cross to the Iron Cross which was announced on 30 September. Yet, what satisfaction that he might have got from the successful conclusion of the compaign was soured when, on 5 October, Hitler flew to Warsaw to take the salute at a victory parade. At its conclusion von Brauchitsch, von Rundstedt, Blaskowitz and other commanders took him back to the airfield to meet the commanders of the troops who had taken part in the parade. A table, laid with white table cloth and decorated with flowers, had been laid out in a hangar and, knowing Hitler's preference for very simple food, it was planned to serve soup from a field kitchen. Hitler, apparently took one look at the table, turned about, and joined the troops outside. After swallowing a little soup at the field kitchen and exchanging a few remarks with the soldiers around it he boarded his aircraft without another word to his generals. The snub, von Manstein later wrote, 'inevitably set one thinking'.[32]

By now von Rundstedt had been given another appointment. He was made Commander-in-Chief East and Military Governor of Poland. It was not a job he relished, so he set up his headquarters on a small estate south-west of Warsaw, well clear of the city. Appointed as the head of the Civil Administration was Hans Frank. According to von Rundstedt:

> 'The famous "King of Poland", Frank; Stanislaus the Little as we always called him, was supposed to be Chief of the Civil Administration under me. But that obviously didn't suit him. At any rate, he went off somewhere, and did no administrative work at all, but stayed in Lodz.'[33]

Ignored by Frank and powerless to prevent the increasing depredations of the SS *Einsatzgruppen*, von Rundstedt had little to do. Luckily, salvation was quickly at hand.

Hitler's attention had now turned to the West and how to deal with France and Britain. Von Rundstedt's presence and that of his staff were required. On 20 October he thankfully relinquished his position as C-in-C East, handing over his responsibilities to Blaskowitz.

6

Assault in the West

IN BETWEEN leaving Poland and taking up his new appointment, von Rundstedt would have probably been able to call in at Kassel and see Bila. It would, however, have been only a fleeting reunion. On 25 October 1939, only five days after relinquishing his previous command, he assumed the appointment of Commander-in-Chief of the newly formed Army Group A.

The once-fashionable Hotel Riesen-Fürstenhof in Koblenz was to be his headquarters for the next seven months. He did not arrive here in total ignorance of what his next task would be. On the contrary, on 10 October, after he had remonstrated with Halder over Hitler's intention to pardon all those found guilty of looting and other offences in Poland, he had attended a Führer conference. During this, Hitler made plain his intentions towards the West. The Wehrmacht was to prepare for a 'swift and shattering blow' in order to force the British and French into battle and defeat them. All available forces would be concentrated, especially mechanised forces and air power, to this end.[1] At the same time, the first version of *Fall Gelb* (Case Yellow) was issued. In essence, it was very similar to the von Schlieffen Plan of 25 years before, but this time not just Belgian, but Dutch neutrality as well, was to be disregarded. The main strength, including the bulk of the Panzer divisions, was to be given to von Bock's Army Group B in the north. This would take on the same role as von Kluck's First Army had undertaken in 1914, something which must have set alarm bells ringing in von Rundstedt's mind, given his own experiences in that campaign. Army Group A would conform to von Bock's movement while von Leeb's Army Group C masked the Maginot Line. Plan Yellow was to be executed in mid-November.

Von Brauchitsch was apparently aghast. It was not just the timing, which did not take into acount the necessity to assimilate and put into action the lessons of the Polish campaign, as well as the complete transfer of the necessary forces from East to West, but also the prospect of battle with enemies infinitely stronger and better equipped than the Poles had been. He is supposed to have turned to von Rundstedt and asked him to intercede with Hitler.[2] If this was so, von Rundstedt took no action. Nevertheless, he shared von Brauchitsch's concern that the forces currently available were not strong enough and pressed him for additional time so that they could be reinforced.[3]

On 21 October, while en route to the West, von Manstein called in at OKH at Zossen, south of Berlin, to collect a copy of the orders for the attack. He gained the distinct impression that, while von Brauchitsch and his staff totally disagreed with the concept of Case Yellow, they had been rendered powerless to influence Hitler and had resigned themselves 'to acting as a purely technical, executive organ'.[4] But they were not the only ones. All the senior commanders involved were unhappy. On 25 October, Hitler held another conference, which was attended not just by von Brauchitsch and Halder, but also by von Bock and his two army commanders, von Reichenau and von Kluge. By now Hitler had set his mind on 12 November as the date of the attack. It was, however, von Reichenau who led the protest that this was premature, pointing out that the seasonal fogs would hamper air support and that the standard of training of the troops left much to be desired. Hitler dismissed this, as he did another protest from von Brauchitsch two days later.

On 29 October, a revised directive on Case Yellow was issued. While von Bock still retained by far the strongest force of the three army groups, Hitler envisaged an attack on a broad front by Army Groups B and A rather than the von Schlieffen wheel. Nevertheless, von Rundstedt, while advancing west himself, was still expected to protect von Bock's left flank. To do this he had just two armies, List's Twelfth and Busch's Sixteenth, with 22 infantry divisions, but no armour. Not only was this insufficient, but he and von Manstein considered the whole concept to be fatally flawed. List, too, felt very strongly about it and confided his fears to von Rundstedt before writing a personal letter to von Brauchitsch on 31 October. He considered that 'the military annihilation of the English, French, and Belgians a goal which cannot be attained at present'. Hence Hitler should create the conditions for peace by granting Czechoslovakia autonomy and restoring nationhood to German-occupied Poland.[5] Von Rundstedt, too, wrote to von Brauchitsch on this day, not one, but two letters. In the first he stated that the offensive as it stood 'cannot have a decisive effect on the war' and that it would be better to let the Allies attack first. Indeed, to allow the Army to be frittered away 'for an indecisive and partial objective' made no sense. Rather, like the doctrine of a fleet 'in being', '*an army capable of attacking* [sic] will remain the decisive factor on the continent in the event of a long war'. Unlike List, he stressed that his view was entirely a military one since political aspects were 'irrelevant to the sphere of responsibility of a soldier'. His second missive was somewhat different and took the form of a memorandum on what eventually became known as the von Manstein Plan.

Von Manstein viewed the flaw in Plan Yellow as its aim, the defeat of the 'largest possible elements' of the Allied armies and the gaining of as much territory as possible in northern France and the Low Countries 'as a basis for successful air and sea operations against Britain and as a broad protective zone for the Ruhr'. This was too limited in scope and meant that at best only a partial victory could be achieved. If the operation was to be mounted then its object should be the *total* defeat of the Allied land forces on the Continent. As it was, to use Army Group B as the decisive element made no sense. The fortifications and water-ways in Northern Belgium favoured the defence and, worse, von Bock would be committed to meeting the enemy head on. Furthermore, it invited an enemy counter-offensive against von Bock's southern flank. Instead, Army Group A should make the main attack, a surprise one through the Ardennes. This would cut off the Allied armies deployed in Belgium, after which the remainder of France could be overrun. To undertake this von Rundstedt would need another army and strong armoured forces, but this would also provide an effective counter to an expected French attack in Lorraine. In conclusion von Rundstedt commented: 'Both the danger and the chance of great success lie with Army Group A.'[6]

This barrage of letters never got past von Brauchitsch and he apparently made no mention of them to Hitler or Keitel. Halder himself noted that von Rundstedt's proposal lacked 'positive aspects' and he did not share his view of the likelihood of a French attack in Lorraine.[7] Furthermore, as Telford Taylor has pointed out, for von Brauchitsch to present a new and more effective plan to Hitler at the same time as he was trying to dissuade him from launching the attack during the winter would merely have been pulling the rug from under his own feet.[8] Nevertheless, von Brauchitsch and Halder felt that the time had come for them to go and see for themselves and at the beginning of November visited all army group and army headquarters on the Western Front. Von Rundstedt reiterated his views on the need for his army group to have the decisive role, but von Brauchitsch dismissed these out of hand. The only concession that he made was to agree to release one Panzer division and some motorised elements from the OKH reserves. This, however, merely reflected an idea which Hitler had had on 30 October of using a Panzer and a motorised division in a thrust on Sedan. What the visit did confirm, however, was the current lack of operational readiness. Replacements had not yet been properly assimilated in their units, more training in offensive operations was needed and a lack of spare parts meant that there were serious delays in repairing faulty equipment.

Halder also took the opportunity to sound out the commanders on the feasibility of a revolt against Hitler in order to bring the war to an end. Von Rundstedt was sympathetic, but warned Halder: 'If you order the coup, I can make the attempt, but I cannot tell you for certain that if I draw the sword it does not break in my hand.'[10] In other words, he was not wholly confident that his troops would follow him. Significantly, though, a new member of his staff, Lieutenant Colonel Henning von Tresckow, whom von Manstein had recruited in order to assist Blumentritt in the Operations Section, was strongly opposed to Hitler (even though he had originally been sympathetic to National Socialism) and would later become one of the leading lights in subsequent plots against Hitler's life. Whether he tried to persuade von Rundstedt or not is not known. Even so, the field commanders did not dismiss Halder's proposals out of hand. At the request of von Leeb, he, von Bock and von Rundstedt conferred at Koblenz on 10 November. Von Leeb wanted agreement that the three would refuse to carry out Case Yellow or, at least, resign if Hitler refused to see reason. Neither von Bock nor von Rundstedt agreed to this, viewing it as mutiny.[11] No wonder that Ulrich von Hassell noted later in his diary that the Foreign Office Liaison Officer to the General Staff, Hasso von Etzdorf, considered that von Bock was 'vain', von Rundstedt 'soft in the head' and that von Leeb was the 'only one with whom something might be done'.[12] Nevertheless, General Georg Thomas, Chief of War Economy and Armament, and Colonel Hans Oster of the Abwehr were determined to go ahead if Hitler should give the executive order for Case Yellow to be activated. They intended, as the plan had been in 1938, to arrest Hitler and other leading members of the Nazi hierarchy. As it happened, there was an assassination attempt against Hitler on 8 November, while he was in Munich celebrating the anniversary of the 1923 Putsch, but he had already left the beer hall, where the celebrations were taking place, before the bomb went off. This had nothing to do with Thomas and Oster, whose plans foundered because of lack of support from von Brauchitsch and Halder. As for von Rundstedt, all that was left for him was to continue to work on Hitler through von Brauchitsch, first to postpone the offensive until the spring and then to have von Manstein's plan adopted.

Von Brauchitsch, however, was still getting nowhere. On his return from the Western Front he went to see Hitler in another atempt to get the offensive postponed. All that he received for his pains was the accusation that the Army did not want to fight.[13] One bonus for von Rundstedt and von Manstein, however, was that Hitler decided that the Panzer division and motorised regiment allocated by von Brauchitsch to them were not sufficient for the thrust on Sedan. Accordingly, on 11 November, Guderian's XIX Corps, with two Panzer and one motorised division plus two motorised regiments, was allocated to Army Group A and Guderian was ordered to set up his headquarters in Koblenz, close to von Rundstedt. Apart from merely having Sedan as an objective, Hitler saw this as a means of unlocking the door if von Bock's armour became bogged down in Belgium. In other words, if von Bock's initial attack failed, the initiative would be handed over to von Rundstedt. Thus, even though Hitler was still not aware of the von Manstein option, he was gradually shifting his view towards it. Yet, the addition of Guderian still did not give von Rundstedt sufficient weight with which to thrust to the Channel. Nevertheless, increasingly gloomy weather forecasts did persuade Hitler to postpone the launching of Case Yellow – the meteorologists succeeded where the generals had failed – and this brought time for von Rundstedt and von Manstein to continue to press their case.

Not surprisingly, Guderian was instantly won over to the von Manstein plan. Indeed, Keitel summoned him to discuss the Sedan idea and Guderian, who had fought in the Ardennes in 1914 and had spent time at Sedan while on a staff course in 1918, assured him that there was no problem in passing armour through the region. In subsequent discussions with von Manstein he also advocated that at least seven Panzer divisions were needed to fulfil the Army Group A plan.[14] Hitler, though, felt that his generals needed some fire implanting in their bellies and summoned all commanders involved in Case Yellow down to and including divisional commanders to Berlin on 23 November. He addressed those down to corps commander first and then the divisional commanders. By now the offensive was scheduled to begin on 3 December, but a further attempt by von Rundstedt and von Manstein to win over OKH at a conference of army group and army commanders at Koblenz on 21 November had failed. According to Guderian, Hitler made unfavourable comparisons at the 23 November conference between the political reliability of the Army and that of the Navy and Luftwaffe. So incensed was Guderian that, on his return to Koblenz, he tried to get von Manstein to refute the allegation, but he said that he had already spoken to von Rundstedt who was not prepared to take any action. Guderian now saw von Rundstedt himself. He agreed to raise the matter with von Brauchitsch, but stressed that he was not prepared to go outside the chain of command. Guderian tried to lobby other commanders, including von Reichenau, who said that he was in bad odour with the hierarchy (probably as a result of his outburst at the 25 October conference), but suggested that Guderian go and see Hitler himself. This he did, saying to Hitler that if he did not trust von Brauchitsch he should appoint another C-in-C. Hitler then asked him whom he recommended. Guderian produced a list with von Rundstedt's name at the top, but all were rejected.[15]

To the relief of the generals, the bad weather forced further postponements to the date of the attack. In the meantime, von Rundstedt and von Manstein continued their pestering of von Brauchitsch and Halder. On 27 November, von Rundstedt, Busch and Guderian attended yet another Hitler conference and it would appear that the von Manstein plan was raised and that Hitler showed some sympathy with it, although he was not prepared to commit himself. He did, however, agree to two divisions being transferred from von Bock's reserve to that of Army Group A.[16] Encouraged by this, von Rundstedt wrote to von Brauchitsch again on 30 November, pressing for another army to be given to him. He argued that if Guderian was succesful it would tend to draw Army Group A away from B and another army headquarters would be needed to fill the resultant gap. A week later von Manstein followed this up with a memorandum to Halder. No favourable response was forthcoming and so von Rundstedt arranged to confer with von Brauchitsch in Berlin. This meeting took place on 22 December, but again von Brauchitsch would not be moved.

This war of paper was frustrating and exhausting, especially so for von Rundstedt, whose patience, von Manstein noted, was never his strong point. One of the activities which kept him sane was his daily walk, something which became increasingly important to him as the war went on. Von Manstein recalled that every morning during that bitter winter von Rundstedt would walk by the Rhine and his chief of staff would often accompany him. Von Rundstedt 'still wore only a thin raincoat. When I protested that he would catch his death of cold, he merely retorted that he had never possessed a greatcoat in his life and was certainly not going to buy one at his age.'[17] Another relaxation was detective novels, with which Bila kept him regularly supplied. As he later told the IMT Commission at Nuremberg: 'In general, I am not a friend of literature, I prefer to read works of fiction. I love detective stories best.'[18] Von Manstein noted that he would read these at his desk while awaiting verbal reports from the staff, but 'since he was rather shy about this taste of his, he regularly read the novel in an open drawer which could be quickly closed whenever anyone came to see him.'[19]

In January the paper bombardment of OKH was resumed. Von Rundstedt submitted yet another memorandum to von Brauchitsch on the 12th. He reverted to the drawbacks of the aim of Case Yellow, reiterating that merely to defeat the Allied forces in northern France and Belgium and occupy the Channel coastline was too negative and would not bring about a speedy end to the war. Instead, the object should be the 'annihilation' of the Allied land and air forces so as to 'eliminate the continental sword of the English' and then to attack England by land and sea. The decisive blow would be the throttling of her Atlantic lifeline and to accomplish this the whole of the French coast needed to be occupied. Furthermore, a partial victory would not 'justify the bad political repercussions which the breach of the neutrality of three states [Belgium, Holland and Luxembourg] will certainly entail'. He also requested that the memorandum be shown to Hitler since he 'has reserved to himself the right to determine the point of concentration in executing the operation – meaning that OKH is not free to make operational decisions.' Stung by this last comment, von Brauchitsch sent a prompt letter of rejection, saying that Hitler was only concerned with coordination with the Luftwaffe and that he would act on von Brauchitsch's recommendations. Even so, he did concede that Case Yellow as it stood only covered the initial attack and that provision was being made to give Army Group A another army once the operations had begun.[20]

Two days before von Rundstedt's latest broadside, Hitler, encouraged by a more favourable long range weather forecast, declared that the attack would now be launched at first light on 17 January. It was also mooted that the Luftwaffe might carry out attacks against enemy airfields on either the 12th or 13th. On that same day, 10 January, however, a German Me108 communications aircraft force-landed in fog near Mechelen in Belgium. On board was a staff officer from Luftflotte 2, who had with him, among other papers, the Luftflotte Case Yellow operational order. He tried to burn the documents, but was only partially successful and the charred remains fell into the hands of the Belgian authorities. It was not until the 12th that OKH and OKW began to fear that the plan could have been compromised, and on the next day Hitler ordered a postponement until the 20th. Then the weather began to worsen and Hitler laid down that, for security reasons, he would set no more dates in advance, but that the Case Yellow forces were to be prepared to launch the attack within 24 hours of receiving the executive order. Once again, the Case Yellow revisionists had been given more time, but, as Halder noted, at the expense of waning confidence among the troops.[21]

Von Rundstedt and von Manstein saw the situation as one. Indeed von Manstein later paid his commander a significant tribute for the support he gave in getting the von Manstein Plan accepted. 'I would stress that my commander, Colonel-General v. Rundstedt . . . agreed with my view throughout and that v. Rundstedt backed our recommendations to the full with his own signature. Without his sanction we could never have kept up our attempts to change OKH's mind by these repeated memoranda.'[22] Guderian, the other driving force behind changing the plan, proved a more difficult problem. As his biographer has pointed out, he did not share the traditional Prussian view that the Army should stay out of politics and, as we have seen, was quite prepared to bypass the chain of command and speak direct to Hitler, something which von Rundstedt was loath to do since this would bypass the chain of command. Furthermore, von Rundstedt's more conservative views meant that he could not yet accept the concept championed by Guderian that armour, if used with sufficient boldness, was the decisive arm. Rather, and this pertained particularly to the projected Sedan operation, to allow the Panzer divisions to get too far ahead of the main body was foolhardiness and there had to come a point where they must halt to allow the infantry divisions following in their wake to catch up. Von Rundstedt probably recalled only too clearly what had happened when 4th Panzer Division had tried to take Warsaw single-handed. Matters were not helped by the fact that Guderian was even more impatient than von Rundstedt and was not afraid to show it. This is well illustrated by a letter which he wrote to his wife on 21 January:

'The recent evening with Herr v R began quite pleasantly and ended with a debate started by him and Busch about the *Panzertruppe*. It was a debate which I thought impossible in its lack of understanding and, in part, even hatefulness after the Polish campaign. I went home deeply disappointed. These people will never see me again. It is completely fruitless ever to

expect anything from this well-known group of "comrades". To these
people can be traced back the reason for our irreplaceable equipment
standing immobile out of doors for months on end to perish in the extreme
cold. The damage arising from this is inconceivable.'[23]

This last accusation was hardly fair since it was the numerous alerts
and high state of readiness demanded by Hitler which caused the tanks
to be left outside rather than kept in their depots. Even so, the letter
does reflect Guderian's concern that his corps was not going to be used
as he wanted it to be.

Guderian had another opportunity to raise the matter of the Sedan
thrust on 7 February. This was at a map exercise organised by von
Manstein at Koblenz and attended by Halder. Guderian now had a
motorised corps, von Wietersheim's XIV Corps, following in his wake,
although it did not set off until some time after the armour. Guderian
expected to reach the Meuse in three days and wanted to force a
crossing 48 hours later with the assistance of von Wietersheim alone.
Halder conceded his demand for an additional Panzer division and
agreed that von Wietersheim must follow closely behind him, but
considered forcing the Meuse so early to be over-ambitious. He
believed that it would not be possible to mount a 'concerted' crossing of
the river before the ninth or tenth day of the offensive. He noted that
von Rundstedt and von Manstein agreed with this.[24] Both, however,
used this as an argument for the army group to be given an additional
army. Significantly, though, von Rundstedt forgave Guderian for his
outburst of three weeks earlier. Guderian noted: 'Apparently von R
himself has the feeling that I was right to defend myself recently. At the
meeting [map exercise] he was kindness itself . . .'[25]

This exercise was von Manstein's swan song at HQ Army Group A.
He had just been notified that he was to be given command of an
infantry corps. The official reason for this was that it was time that he
held another field command, but it is certain that von Brauchitsch and
Halder had become increasingly fed up with the waves that he was
creating and had decided to shift him to a post where he was unable to
continue to make a nuisance of himself. Von Manstein recalled that at
the end of the map exercise 'v.Rundstedt thanked me in front of
everyone present for all I had done as his Chief-of-Staff. His choice of
words on this occasion reflected all the kindness and chivalry of that
great commander.'[26] Two days later he left Koblenz for some leave
prior to assuming command of XXXVIII Corps. But he still had one
more trump card to play.

Von Manstein's successor as Chief of Staff Army Group A was Georg von Sodenstern, a protégé of Halder's and probably selected by him as being less likely to rock the OKH boat. Guderian rather disparagingly described him as rather 'prosaic'[27], but Blumentritt considered him 'calm' and 'clever'.[28] Certainly, though, he was to serve von Rundstedt well and would remain at his side for almost two years.

It was Hitler himself who took the next step towards modifying Case Yellow. On 13 February, he queried the sense of using so much armour amid the Belgian fortifications and wondered whether it would not be better to concentrate it against Sedan, where the Allies would be unlikely to expect an attack, particularly as they were probably aware of the details of the existing plan, thanks to the Mechelen incident. He ordered the OKH Operations Section to study this. Next day, another map exercise took place, this time at Mayen, List's headquarters. Once again Halder was present. He was not impressed with the deployment of Guderian's corps in line. It indicated that there were insufficient infantry divisions forward and confirmed his belief that a major attack over the Meuse could not take place until the tenth day. He also recorded Guderian's and von Wietersheim's pessimism over the plan as it stood.[29]

On the evening of 17 February von Manstein, four other newly appointed corps commanders and Erwin Rommel, who was leaving Hitler's personal staff to take command of 7th Panzer Division, had dinner with Hitler. After the meal, von Manstein expounded his plan once more and Hitler indicated his complete agreement. Events now moved quickly. On the following day, Hitler announced a change of plan to OKW and OKH and on the 24th the details were given to the army group and army commanders.

The new plan, however, not only switched the *Schwerpunkt* to von Rundstedt but also gave him not just one but two additional armies. Von Bock was to pass across both von Kluge's Fourth Army and von Weichs' Second Army. Furthermore, von Rundstedt now had seven Panzer and three motorised divisions, as opposed to von Bock's three and one. The redeployment was to be completed by 7 March. Yet, having now got even more than he had been demanding for the past few months, von Rundstedt seems to have suffered from an attack of 'cold feet'. At the conference on 24 February, he expressed scepticism about the effectiveness of the armoured wedge, fearing that the follow-up forces would not be able to keep up with it.[30] At the same time, von Sodenstern and Blumentritt expressed doubts in the opposite direction. They thought that the closeness of the terrain in the Ardennes and the defences being constructed in Luxembourg and Southern Belgium might prevent the armour from breaking out and wondered whether it might not be better for the infantry to lead initially. Von Sodenstern sent Halder a letter on the subject in early March but was told to discard his 1914–18 mentality and be prepared to take risks.[31]

This appears to have settled the issue and after von Brauchitsch and Halder had attended a conference at Koblenz on 13 March, and the Army Group A commanders had presented their plans to Hitler on the 15th, Hitler expressed his satisfaction that all was well. The only question left to be answered was what the armour was to do if it managed to break through at Sedan. Hitler posed this question to Guderian on the 15th and was told that he intended to push westwards. All that he required from the High Command was an objective, either Amiens or Paris, although he himself favoured Amiens and the coast. Busch, according to Guderian, then interjected that he did not think that Guderian would be able to get across the Meuse, to which Guderian replied that Busch need not worry as his army would not have to force a crossing.[32] Significantly, Hitler announced on the 17th that he was reserving any decision as to what would happen once the Meuse was crossed.[33] By now, though, he was increasingly turning his attention to Scandinavia and the pressure came off the Western Front for the next few weeks.

A major problem that continued to worry commanders at all levels was how to maintain the offensive spirit in their troops during this long period of *Sitzkrieg*. One method was the use of the Third Reich's extensive propaganda machine. To this end, a number of senior commanders were encouraged to write uplifting articles in the newspapers. Thus von Brauchitsch contributed an article on the soldiers of Frederick the Great in the leading Nazi party newspaper, the *Völkischer Beobachter* in January, and one under von Rundstedt's name appeared in early March in the same publication. Entitled *To Heroes Memorial Day 1940: Sacrifice for Germany*, it exhorted the German soldier to emulate his forbears of 1914–1918, and reminded him that 'the heroic death of a German soldier is not something to be forgotten. Instead it should inspire everyone who remembers it to die in the same way, to be as strong, unswerving, and obedient, to go happily and as a matter of course to his death.' Furthermore, the present war had been forced on Germany and it was a struggle for justice and freedom.[34] It is highly unlikely that von Rundstedt himself wrote this. It has the hallmarks of a professional propagandist and all that von Rundstedt was probably asked to do was to lend his name to it. Hans Gerd, too, was now involved in this field. He had been conscripted into the Army and was working in the OKH Historical Section in Berlin, mainly compiling biographies of the leading commanders, including his father.[35]

On 9 April, German forces invaded Denmark and Norway. This meant that, because sizeable Luftwaffe assets had to be transferred to that theatre, Case Yellow would have to be delayed until a successful outcome was certain. Not until 30 April did Hitler pronounce that the forces in the West had to be ready to execute Case Yellow any time after 5 May. Unsettled weather, as had so often been the case during the winter, now intervened and caused some postponement. Eventually, on the morning of the 9th, Hitler resolved on action the following day. That night, the codeword 'Danzig' was promulgated. The long months of waiting were about to end.

Von Rundstedt later recalled: 'I can still see us in Koblenz, drinking coffee in the hotel at 4 o'clock in the afternoon; the order: "it will start early tomorrow morning" came through at 2 o'clock in the afternoon.'[36] That evening, he left Koblenz and set up his forward headquarters at Bitburg, 80 kilometres west-south-west of Koblenz and just 20 kilometres from the Belgian border. No record exists of what he actually felt now that the moment of truth had arrived, but probably it was relief that the months of inactivity were at an end.

Von Rundstedt's spearhead, his Panzer divisions, had been organised into three corps under a Panzer Group headquarters commanded by Ewald von Kleist, his successor in command of 2nd Cavalry Division. The corps themselves were commanded by Guderian (XIX Corps), Reinhardt (XLI) and Hoth (XV). Sedan remained as Guderian's intitial objective, while Hoth was to reach the Meuse north of Dinant and Reinhardt, in the centre, at Monthermé. This represented an armoured thrust with a frontage of some 40 miles. Behind the Panzer corps came von Wietersheim's motorised corps. Von Kleist himself was initially placed under Twelfth Army which, in conjunction with Fourth Army, was to advance on the line Namur-Sedan. Sixteenth Army's initial task was to swing south to cover von Rundstedt's southern flank and keep contact with Army Group C. Second Army would initially be in reserve.

At 0300 hours on the 10th the Luftwaffe went into action, attacking Allied airfields in order to win the air superiority battle. Just under two hours later, the German armies crossed the borders of Holland, Belgium and Luxembourg. During that day the Panzer divisions swept westwards through the Ardennes, meeting hardly any opposition. However, that night the first sign appeared of nerves on the part of the higher command. Von Kleist was a cavalryman, with little experience of armour and he now became nervous of a French cavalry threat to Guderian's left flank. He wanted a Panzer division diverted to counter it. This Guderian considered totally unnecessary since cavalry could do little to stop tanks and it might delay his main thrust to the Meuse. He made some alteration to the axis of advance of his left-hand division, pulling it in closer to his centre line, but this only served to interfere with the advance of the other divisions, which cannoned into one another, causing stalls.

On the 11th, resistance began to stiffen a little. Demolitions on the narrow winding roads of the Ardennes became more frequent, causing temporary halts while they were overcome. These were aggravated by List's belief that the close country needed infantry to assist the tanks and caused Halder to note that the armour should be accompanied by mechanised infantry.[37] Even so, the tanks did reach the Meuse on schedule. By the evening of the 13th, both Guderian and Hoth had established footholds across it, assisted by the Luftwaffe. During the night, bridges were built and the tanks began to cross next morning, while Allied aircraft, with little success, sacrificed themselves in trying to take out the bridges. At the height of this von Rundstedt went to Sedan to see for himself. Guderian recorded the 'general delight' with which his appearance was greeted, especially since an air attack was in progress. Guderian:

'I reported our position to him in the very middle of the bridge. . . . He asked drily: "Is it always like this here?" I could reply with a clear conscience that it was. He then spoke a few deeply felt words in appreciation of the achievements of our gallant soldiers.'[38]

Von Rundstedt had not lost his coolness under fire.

But now the decision, left unresolved during the revision of Case Yellow, had to be made. What was the armoured wedge to do once across the Meuse? With the best of Allied forces, the French First and Seventh Armies and the British Expeditionary Force (BEF) drawn into Belgium, as prearranged in the Anglo-French Plan D, the answer could only be that it must drive for the English Channel. Halder sent orders to this effect by teleprinter on the afternoon of the 14th. As for the infantry armies following up behind, Fourth Army would sweep west along the Franco-Belgian border towards the coast, with Second Army to be inserted on its left flank. Twelfth Army was to swing south-west towards the Oise and Sixteenth would turn south in order to cover the army group's open left flank. Von Rundstedt and von Sodenstern were not totally happy about this. They wanted Second Army inserted between the Twelfth and the Sixteenth, but this was rejected by OKH. Von Rundstedt then spoke to von Brauchitsch, saying that he could not accept any responsibility for the resultant chaos if Twelfth Army was made to change direction southwards. His objection was sustained.[39]

By the close of 15 May, the Panzer divisions had broken out of their bridgeheads and were racing west, brushing aside all opposition, including half-hearted efforts by French armour to launch counter-strokes against them. On the 16th, however, fears over the army group's increasingly exposed southern flank began to surface again. While von Kleist and his corps commanders were keen to get across the Oise as soon as possible, so as not to allow Allied resistance to congeal, von Rundstedt, as the army group war diary noted, considered it a risk which 'does not seem justified' and a temporary halting of the armour would enable 'a certain stiffening of the threatened flank'.[40] In fact, he later stated that he expected the overall Allied commander, Gamelin, whom he had met at King George V's funeral and by whom he had been much impressed, to make a flank attack from the direction of Verdun.[41] The upshot was that von Kleist ordered Guderian to halt by last light on the 16th. By this stage he had reached the River Serre and Reinhardt, to his north, the Oise. Guderian, determined not to be stopped, issued orders for a resumption of the advance the following morning. Unfortunately, Panzer Group Headquarters was monitoring his radio nets and overheard this. The next thing that Guderian knew was an order from von Kleist ordering him to remain where he was and to meet the Panzer Group commander early the following morning. Von Kleist expressed his displeasure in no uncertain terms. Guderian, displaying his usual impetuosity, then said that he would resign his command, to which von Kleist retorted that he was to hand it over forthwith. Guderian now informed Army Group Headquarters of his resignation, but was ordered to stay where he was until an emissary arrived. This turned out to be no less than the Army Commander, List, who told Guderian that, on von Rundstedt's personal instructions, he was to remain in command, but, while his headquarters was to stay where it was, he could conduct reconnaissance in force forward. This last was on order of OKH, List said.[42] This was indeed so to an extent, since Halder had spoken to von Sodenstern and ordered him not to halt on the Oise but push on in the direction Valenciennes – Cambrai – Saint Quentin and seize canal crossings there. The southern flank was merely to be guarded by echelonned forces.[43] This axis of advance, however, referred more to Hoth and Reinhardt than it did Guderian and the inference was that XIX Corps should merely cover the southern flank.

In this way von Rundstedt was able, through his quick diplomacy, to smooth the ruffled feathers of both von Kleist and his subordinate and prevent Guderian from taking a step which might have had a very detrimental effect on operations at this critical stage. It did not, however, mean that von Rundstedt was now any less concerned over his southern flank. Neither were others. In the afternoon of that same day Hitler came to Headquarters Army Group A, now at Bastogne (a town that would be of particular significance to von Rundstedt four and a half years later), to assure himself that the army group C-in-C was implementing the necessary measures. He approved of what von Rundstedt had done, but emphasised the need to guard the flank with infantry divisions, even if they were on their feet, which, of course, all but von Wietersheim's corps were. He then went on, as von Sodenstern recorded in the war diary, to underline especially

> . . . the significance the southern flank has, not only for the operations of the whole Army, but also politically and psychologically. Under no circumstances must a set-back occur at this moment anywhere, a set-back that would give a fateful rise [in spirit] to our adversaries, not alone to the military, but above all to their political leadership. Thus the decision, for the moment, rests not so much in the rapid forward push to the Channel, but much more . . . in the speediest establishment of absolutely *defensive* [sic] readiness on the Aisne . . . and later on the Somme. . . . Toward this purpose all measures are directed even if time is lost temporarily in the push toward the West [and the Channel].'[44]

While Hitler was conferring with von Rundstedt, Halder told von Sodenstern that he was to receive Hoepner's XVI Panzer Corps (two Panzer and one motorised division) under command, as well as an additional infantry corps, the Waffen-SS Motorised Division, 9th Panzer Division and the SS Leibstandarte. All these formations were to be placed under Fourth Army. That night, though, von Brauchitsch, who, together with Halder, did not see the threat in the south in the same light as Hitler or even von Rundstedt, telephoned the latter to tell him to continue to advance to the Line Le Cateau – St. Quentin. He was presumably worried that von Rundstedt had been unduly swayed by Hitler's afternoon visit. It was, in Halder's words, 'an unpleasant day. The Führer is terribly nervous. Frightened by his own success, he is afraid to take any chance and so would rather pull the reins on us.'[45]

As it happened, the French did begin to mount an operation against the southern flank on the 17th. It was a thrust by the just formed 4th

French Armoured Division under Charles de Gaulle. His spearhead, one battalion of heavy and two of light tanks, struck Guderian's 1st Panzer Division at about 1600 hours, just at the time that he was having his audience with List. The flank screen was brushed aside and de Gaulle's tanks entered Montcornet, through which ran 1st Panzer's main supply route. But, lacking infantry, artillery and fuel, they were forced to withdraw, harried by the Luftwaffe. This was regarded as of such little significance that even von Kleist, who was told about it, did not bother to report it upwards.

Even so, next day, with the Panzer divisions entering St Quentin and Cambrai by mid-morning, Hitler continued to fret, demanding that the armoured spearhead must thrust north-west instead of west, thus reducing to the minumum the exposed right flank. As Halder put it: 'He rages and screams that we are on the best way to ruin the whole campaign and that we are leading up to a defeat.'[46] He sent an emissary to von Rundstedt in the shape of the Chief of Staff of OKW, Wilhelm Keitel, to reinforce his concern for the southern flank. It was to be the first of many visits. Commenting on them, Keitel wrote: 'General von Rundstedt also wisely recognised the difficulties of my position at the time and listened with great understanding to the tactfully moderate "hints" I gave him, hints that had, in fact, originated from Hitler.'[47] By this time, though, von Rundstedt was well aware that Keitel was a mere cipher and message carrier, and that it was not worth being anything but courteous to him. Keitel, on the other hand, a commoner and a Hannoverian, who, in terms of service, was many years von Rundstedt's junior and was below him in rank seniority, was bound to be obsequious to the doyen of the Prussian officer corps.

On this same day, however, it became clear from von Bock's reports that the Allied forces which had entered Belgium on the 10th were now in retreat. As a result, that evening Halder gave Hitler a situation report and requested permission for the armoured wedge to thrust for Arras and the coast so that these forces could be cut off. Hitler agreed, but it left a sour taste in Halder's mouth: 'So the right thing is being done after all, but in the atmosphere of bad feeling and in a form calculated to give the outside world the impression that it is a plan conceived by OKW'.[48]

The thrust for Arras was to be the responsibility of Hermann Hoth's corps, since the town lay on its axis of advance. To Hoth's south, Reinhardt and Guderian were to take a wider sweep aiming for the Channel. Rommel's 7th Panzer Division had seized Cambrai by the evening of the 18th and had then halted in order to get supplies up and give his men their first rest for almost ten days. His next objective was the high ground south-east of Arras and he intended to make an advance by night. On the afternoon of the 19th Hoth visited him and initially objected to his plan, on the grounds that Rommel's troops were not sufficiently recovered. Rommel's retort was that they had had twenty hours in the same place and a thrust by night would save casualties. Hoth relented and at 0140 hours on the 20th Rommel was on his way once more.[49] Guderian, on the other hand, had not halted at all and on the 20th made his longest daily advance of the campaign – 56 miles from the Canal du Nord to Abbeville and the Channel coast. Even so, he had to drive 2nd Panzer Division hard in order to do it since they were very tired and pleaded for a halt on the grounds of shortage of fuel.[50] Rommel's drive through the night went well, except his motorised infantry had not followed the tanks as closely as they should have done, and he himself had to drive back in order to hurry them forward. The armour itself reached Beauvais and its objective by 0600 hours, but Rommel was unable to take any immediate advantage of this because French elements had infiltrated his lines of communication and it was only after an infantry regiment, supported by artillery, had been moved up to protect his flank south of Arras that he was able to proceed. By this time it was the afternoon of 21 May and intelligence had been received that strong British and French forces were in the Arras area. Hoth's plan was for Rommel to sweep round the south of Arras while 5th Panzer Division advanced across its eastern side. Both divisions would then continue north-west. To protect his left flank, Hoth gave Rommel Eicke's SS Totenkopf Division. At 1500 hours Rommel set his Panzer regiment going, although he admitted that it was by now much reduced in strength because of breakdowns and casualties.[51]

It was now that the British launched a counter-stroke, which became known as the Arras counter-attack. This was carried out by the 1st Army Tank Brigade, with two battalions of infantry tanks. An infantry division was also supposed to have taken part, but got left behind by the tanks. These initially hit the SS Totenkopf, now converted to a combat role after its infamous involvement in the Polish campaign. 7th Panzer Division also became heavily involved and, for a short time, there were signs that the British were causing considerable panic and that Hoth's renewed thrust was being knocked totally off balance. Unsupported, however, the British tanks were unable to sustain the attack and by evening had been forced to withdraw, having inflicted just over 100 casualties on the SS Totenkopf and almost 400 on 7th Panzer.

A determined Allied counter-stroke into the flank of the armoured wedge was what, of course, the German high command had increasingly feared as it advanced ever deeper west. That this attack had been carried out with more determination than the French attempts in the south meant that the momentary reverberations it caused up the chain of command were out of all proportion to the numbers which took part. Von Rundstedt immediately halted the advance of the remainder of his forces until the situation was resolved. Later he said that it was the critical moment of the entire campaign.[52] By midday on the 22nd, however, the situation was looking promising once more. That night OKH issued a fresh order to von Rundstedt. His immediate task was to 'complete the encirclement of the enemy in northern Belgium and France' by narrowing the pocket in which they were already trapped. His armoured forces were to drive north-east from the line Bethune – St Omer – Calais to Armentières – Ypres – Ostend, while his infantry seized the high ground Lens – St Omer.[53] In other words, the infantry was to provide a firm shoulder in the south while the Panzer divisions swept up the coast driving the Allied forces towards Army Group B. This was set in train on the 23rd and Halder expressed himself pleased with initial progress. He did, however, note that Fourth Army, on von Rundstedt's right wing, was thin on the ground. Later in the day, however, he commented: 'The developments of the past few days show that AGp.A is indeed experiencing considerable difficulties in managing this unwieldy mass of seventy-one divisions. I have a good idea that its staff has not been energetic or active enough.' The answer, which he immediately implemented, was for OKH to place its own liaison officers with 'the several armies' to ensure that its orders were being executed.[54] Given the speed at which events were taking place, the many different directions that Army Group A was having to look, and that von Rundstedt's span of command encompassed four armies, it is not surprising that command and control were becoming very stretched. Liaison officers would certainly help, but the danger in this was that OKH would be tempted to bypass Army Group HQ and deal with the armies direct.

It was on this day, 23 May, that a series of events began to unfold which would lead to the major controversy of the campaign, the so-called Halt Order. At 1730 hours, the OKH Liaison Officer to von Kleist, von Gyldenfeldt, spoke to Halder and expressed von Kleist's concern over the situation. There was still heavy fighting around Arras and his tank losses as a whole were now 'as high as 50 per cent'. In the light of this, he felt unequal to tackling the assault on the Allied pocket in the north. Halder reassured him by saying that the 'crisis will be over

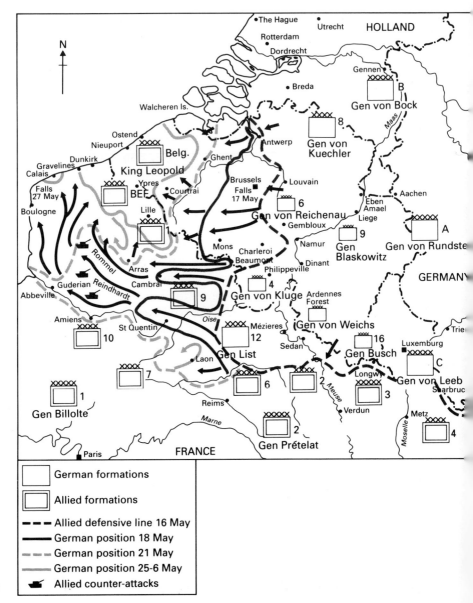

MAP 7. The Drive to the Channel, May 1940.

in 48 hours' and that he must carry on.[55] At much the same time, von
Kluge was voicing similar concerns to von Rundstedt and proposed
that his motorised elements be allowed to halt next day so that the
situation around Arras could be tidied up and the infantry given the

opportunity to catch up. This von Rundstedt agreed to and gave orders for Fourth Army to halt for the following day.[56]

Less than two hours after this, new orders came from OKH at the instigation of von Brauchitsch. He now wanted von Bock to take over control of operations against the Allied pocket. To this end, Fourth Army was now to revert to his operational control. Halder strongly disapproved of this, rightly believing, since there were two army groups involved, that only von Brauchitsch could exercise unified command at this juncture. To express his disapproval, he refused to sign the order.[57] But he was not the only one who was unhappy. When von Sodenstern received the order he objected to von Greiffenberg, Chief of the OKH Operations Section, and said that he could not view 'the prospective change in the command organisation at this time as a happy one'. He also put his estimate of the situation at this time in writing so that it could be used as ammunition when complaining in the morning to von Brauchitsch and Halder, who, since it was now midnight, had presumably gone to bed.[58]

Another seed had also been sown on the 23rd. Major Engel, Hitler's Army Adjutant, noted in his diary: 'Führer has telephone conversation with Goering. Field Marshal believes Luftwaffe would face great task: annihilation of British in Northern France. Army can merely occupy. We are angry. Führer enthusiastic. Jodl says: "That bloke's [Goering] talking pretty big again."'[59]

Next morning Hitler, Jodl and Schmundt, Hitler's Wehrmacht Adjutant, flew to see von Rundstedt, whose headquarters was now at Charleville. Von Rundstedt explained the situation in the light of the OKH order of the previous evening, complaining about the sudden transfer of the bulk of his armour to von Bock. Hitler and Albert Jodl (Chief of Operations at OKW) apparently expressed surprise, having not been informed of the OKH order. Hitler told von Rundstedt that the transfer of von Kluge was to be suspended until he had talked to von Brauchitsch. As for von Rundstedt's intention to halt everything for the day to give the armour a chance to refurbish and for the infantry to catch up, Jodl noted that Hitler was in complete agreement. Hitler went on to remind von Rundstedt that it was necessary to look ahead to the next phase of the campaign, Case Red, the defeat of the Allied forces south of the River Somme, and that it was important to husband the armour for this. Furthermore, if the northern pocket was made too tight, the operations of the Luftwaffe would be severely restricted.[60] Accordingly, von Rundstedt immediately issued an order stating that Hitler had decreed that the general line Lens – Bethune – Arras – Aire –

St Omer – Gravelines was not to be crossed north-west of Arras and that the Panzer divisions were to close up to the Aa Canal and use the day for repairs and maintenance.[61]

As it happened, von Kleist's Panzer divisions had already been on the move on the morning of the 24th. Guderian's 1st Panzer Division had even secured a crossing over the Aa Canal just south of Gravelines, while Reinhardt had one at St Omer. This indicates that, because of the OKH order transferring him to von Bock's command, von Kluge may not have put the temporary halt order agreed with von Rundstedt the previous evening into effect. Guderian says that he was 'speechless' when he heard of it, but did not initially know of the reasons for it.[62] What seems clear, though, was that von Rundstedt viewed it merely as a temporary measure, primarily designed to give the armour a chance to draw a quick breath before its final assault on the pocket. It is probable, too, that he did not take Hitler's remarks about the Luftwaffe particularly seriously, although, of course, it was the Luftwaffe which had been decisive in the destruction of the Kutno pocket in Poland.

The question remains as to whether von Rundstedt was being over-cautious in halting the armour at this stage. Guderian clearly thought so, and von Gyldenfeldt considered that von Kleist's gloomy estimate of his tank casualties was unfounded, since he did not realise 'that large numbers of tanks were returning to their units after a short repair time. This is a fact, but at the time it was perhaps inexperience.'[63] Yet, Reinhardt's XLI Corps war diary for 23 May states that the Panzer divisions had each suffered some 2,000 casualties and 30 per cent of the tanks, and that losses in other weapons systems had been heavy.[64] We have also seen Rommel's acknowledgement that his tank losses were high prior to his drive on Arras, and 1st Panzer Division's plea to Guderian during the thrust to the coast. In addition, von Rundstedt, in a postwar interview, stated that the mobile workshops responsible for repairing tanks had fallen a long way behind and roads congested by infantry moving to guard the southern flank delayed the moving up of replacement tanks.[65] There were thus justifiable grounds for a temporary halt, especially since there was no evidence to suggest that the enemy, especially the British, would not do everything possible to avert their threatened annihilation.

Hitler, on his return from Charleville, summoned von Brauchitsch to see him at OKW. Halder saw von Brauchitsch back at OKH after the interview, which was apparently 'very unpleasant'. The OKH order of the previous evening was to be cancelled and the halt order confirmed. Hitler also told the Commander-in-Chief that the Luftwaffe would now complete the destruction of the Allied forces in north-eastern France.[66] Indeed, he had already confirmed this with his Directive No 13 issued the previous day. Halder, however, was not prepared to let matters rest and seems to have persuaded von Brauchitsch to tackle Hitler again on the subject, which he did on the morning of the 25th. It proved to be a 'painful wrangle'. Halder's thinking was that, since the enemy's attention had been drawn by Army Group A, giving von Bock the bulk of the armour would enable him to cut into the enemy's rear and 'deliver the decisive blow', while von Rundstedt kept him occupied with 'heavy frontal attacks. It now seemed that political considerations dictated that the final battle be fought in northern France, rather than Flanders. Although Halder did not specify what these were, it appears that Hitler viewed the Flemish as being close to the Germans in their racial characteristics and hoped that they would be willing to become part of the Greater Reich after the end of the hostilities. Having already violated their neutrality, he had no wish to antagonise them further by inflicting added damage on their country. In Halder's view, Hitler had camouflaged this political argument by asserting that Flanders, because of its many water obstacles, was unsuitable for armour. As it now was, von Bock was to be the 'hammer' and von Rundstedt the 'anvil'. But, with Army Group A being held strictly on the defensive, the enemy could turn his attention once more to dealing with von Bock, whose 'progress will be slow and casualties high'. Furthermore, the Luftwaffe, 'on which all hopes are pinned' was dependent on the weather.[67] Von Brauchitsch, according to Jodl, asked Hitler for permission for the armour 'to push forward from the high terrain Vimy – St Omer – Gravelines toward the West [sic – East] into the level terrain. Fuehrer is against it, but leaves decision to Army Group A.'[68] It now seems that Halder took this as a 'green light'. He told Army Group A that the advance could be resumed once more. Von Rundstedt acknowledged this, but, as Blumentritt noted in the War Diary, instructed that this must not be passed to von Kluge because he wanted to get the motorised infantry divisions up with the armour.[69] This may well seem to reflect von Rundstedt's caution once more, but bearing in mind the terrain and the likely enemy resistance, it made sound tactical sense for the Panzer divisions to have additional infantry available to assist them. Indeed, this is supported by von Sodenstern, who said that his commander, remembering his time in Flanders in 1914, which presumably meant his tour with the military government of Antwerp, was worried about committing tanks on their own across the Canal.[70] On the other hand, the last entry in the Army Group War Diary on that date states: 'The task of the army group can be considered, in the main, to be completed.'[71] Thus, probably in view of Hitler's comments to him, von Rundstedt was now turning his attention to Case Red and saw no reason to incur seemingly unnecessary casualties, with the Luftwaffe so confident of being able to complete the work in the north. Even so, von Kluge did get to hear of the order and his exclusion from it and, according to General Brennecke, his Chief of Staff, they lodged a protest with Hitler via Engel.[72] This certainly represented a change of heart from the von Kluge of 48 hours before and indicates, probably as a result of pressure from the Panzer commanders, that his armour was ready to drive forward once more.

On 26 May Operation DYNAMO, the evacuation of the British Expeditionary Face (BEF) from Dunkirk began. The Luftwaffe, in the meantime, opened its offensive, but found that it was not as easy as Goering had boasted. Lack of advanced airfields, fatigue on the part of the aircrews, the difficulty of obtaining pinpoint accuracy, and unsettled weather, were all to play their part. Perhaps the most significant reason was revealed in Fourth Army's War Diary on the 25th:

> 'For two days, the enemy enjoys air superiority over Group von Kleist and partially above Group Hoth. This is something completely new to us in this campaign and the reason is that the base of the English Air Force is in England and therefore now quite close, while our units on the whole are still based on German airfields.'[73]

In spite of this, General Hans Jeschonnek, the Luftwaffe Chief of Staff, visited and assured OKW that all was well and that they could still 'annihilate' the British, although they would need some assistance from Army Group B.[74] However, Halder clearly had no faith in the Luftwaffe and commented that halting the armour meant that 'cleaning out the pocket may take weeks'. He also noted that von Rundstedt had now become impatient and had gone to see Hoth and von Kleist in order to discuss the renewed advance.[75]

In the early afternoon, all suddenly changed. Von Brauchitsch was summoned by Hitler and told by him that he was now authorised to advance to Dunkirk in order to halt the evacuation of the BEF. In the south of the pocket, infantry were to seize sufficient ground for artillery fire to be brought to bear on the Bailleul – Cassel – Bergues road and armour would thrust between Bailleul and Armentières to link up with Army Group B, under whose orders it would now come, and then push on to Ostend to prevent it being used as an evacuation port. Further armour would isolate enemy forces south of Lille. Various theories have been advanced for Hitler's change of heart. One advanced by Engel, his Army Adjutant, was that he wanted the Waffen-SS to take a prominent part in the final battle in the north. Engel recalled a conversation at the *Felsennest*, probably on the evening of the 25th: 'Hitler had a long talk about the necessity to have SS units participating in the final annihilation. In particular, the so racially arrogant British had to be confronted with some of equal quality; for this "his SS" would be just the right thing.' Engel thought that Hitler was specifically thinking of his own bodyguard, the SS Leibstandarte, who had just arrived at the Aa Canal and had been placed under Guderian's command. This may have been a contributory factor, but Engel also said that the question of a British evacuation had never been considered at OKW until it actually happened.[76] It is more likely that it was the knowledge that the evacuation had started, together with Jeschonnek's acceptance that assistance by the ground forces would be needed, that caused Hitler's *volte face*.

The new orders reached von Rundstedt while he was still forward with the Panzer formations. What Halder had feared now came to pass. The British resistance, and indeed that of the French formations in the pocket, was stiff and progress was slow.[77] Hence DYNAMO was largely successful, although at a cost in ships, aircraft, and in the equipment which the BEF had to leave behind. Goering, however, remained optimistic for some time. The now famous armada of Little Ships was mobilised to take the Allied troops back across the Channel and Goering saw this as a sign of British desperation. At a meeting with Hitler on the 27th he boasted: 'Only fishing smacks are coming across; I hope the Tommies can swim well.'[78] The answer was that they could and did.

Von Rundstedt's postwar comments on the halt order make it very clear that he put the blame entirely at Hitler's door. He told Major Milton Shulman of the Canadian Army that the order was an 'incredible blunder' caused by Hitler's personal conception of generalship, and that his hands were tied by direct orders from Hitler. 'I wanted to send five Panzer divisions into Dunkirk to destroy your force but I had to stand uselessly by and watch you escape.'[79] He also criticised Hitler for wanting to husband the armour for Case Red. 'One must bring one operation to a halt before thinking of the next one.'[80] Blumentritt, in his biography of von Rundstedt, also makes it clear that he and his staff were in total disagreement with the halt order. As for von Rundstedt's own temporary halt order for the 24th, Blumentritt is vague, and even implies that it may have referred to a much earlier stage of the campaign. He also makes the suggestion, one that became popular with historians in the early postwar period before it was disproved, that Hitler wanted the BEF to be saved so that he would have a better chance of bringing Britain to the peace table.[81] Von Rundstedt himself never mentioned his own halt order and indeed consistently asserted that it was Hitler who was unnecessarily concerned over the tank casualties. This, as we have seen, does not represent the whole truth. The fact was that von Rundstedt, for sound military reasons, implemented a pause in order to allow his armour time to refurbish and that Hitler then left the decision to him as to whether to resume on the 25th. Again, von Rundstedt had good operational reasons for delaying the release of his armour for a further 24 hours. However, when he was ready to go, Hitler had applied the brakes once more. There is also no doubt that, with the Channel coast largely secured, he considered that the objective of Case Yellow had been virtually achieved and that, in spite of his postwar comment of finishing one operation before starting another, he was in fact turning his attention to the next phase of the campaign, as were both OKW and OKH. It was logical that they should have done so. To have paused after the destruction of the northern Allied armies in order to plan the subjugation of the remainder would have made no military sense. The fact remains that the Germans would later bitterly regret the escape of the BEF and von Rundstedt himself probably did not wish to be regarded by history as being even partially responsible for it.

Be that as it may, as the last Allied troops slipped away from the beaches there was little time for recrimination, Moves were already afoot for the offensive across the Somme. The original plan for Case Red had been drawn up by Halder and presented to Hitler on 21 May. Army Group C would attack across the Upper Rhine with fifteen infantry divisions and also assault the as yet untouched Maginot Line near Saarbrücken. The bulk of the armour was to be given to von Bock, who would cross the Seine west of Paris, while von Rundstedt, with three infantry armies, passed down to the east of the capital, the idea being to trap the remaining French armies on the Plateau de Langres. Hitler, however, objected and wanted more armour in the eastern thrust. Thus it was back to the drawing board for Halder, who now recast the plan so as to make the main thrust on that flank, delaying von Leeb's offensive until the main drive had approached the River Moselle near Toul.

Hitler discussed the new plan with von Rundstedt and his staff at Charleville on 27 May. Two days later, von Brauchitsch and Halder conferred with von Bock, von Rundstedt and their army commanders, again at Charleville, in order to iron out the final details. On 31 May, they went to see von Leeb. In its final form Case Red gave von Bock four armies and three mechanised corps (six Panzer and six motorised divisions). He would now attack on both sides of Paris, his boundary with von Rundstedt lying just west of Soissons. Von Rundstedt himself was left with three armies, von Weichs's Second, List's Twelfth and Busch's Sixteenth, and two mechanised corps (four Panzer and two motorised divisions) under the newly created Panzer Group Guderian. His main attack was to be carried out by List, with Guderian under command, across the Aisne between Soissons and Reims. The offensive was to open on 5 June. Initially von Bock only would attack, with von Rundstedt then joining in, and finally von Leeb.

Three days before the opening of the second phase in the West, Hitler visited von Rundstedt once more in order to express his gratitude for the victories so far achieved. It was this meeting that probably gave von Rundstedt his first inkling of Hitler's future strategic plans. According to von Sodenstern:

> 'Before the actual discussion began Hitler walked up and down in front of the building in which the officers had assembled. In this connection, ie in more private conversation, he bragged about Russia. "Now that things – England being probably ready for peace – had finally gotten to this point he could begin his settling of accounts with Bolshevism! . . ." In the evening Rundstedt expressed amazement to me. He was convinced that with a campaign against Russia, one could overtax the German forces.'

Von Rundstedt also told him that Hitler's only concern seemed to be how he could justify such an action to the German people.[82] In the light of his experience on the Eastern Front during the First World War, von Rundstedt must have regarded the prospect of war with the Soviet Union with gloom, but, with Case Red about to open, there was little time to ponder on the implications of what Hitler had said.

On 5 June, von Bock duly attacked, initially experiencing some difficulty in breaking through the French defences on the Somme, the so-called Weygand Line. Von Rundstedt's forces joined in on the 9th. He, too, had problems in establishing bridgeheads across the Aisne, a contrast to the Meuse a month earlier. Indeed, he told Liddell Hart after the war that this was the only tough operation that he had during the whole campaign.[83] It was not until after dark that Guderian was able to get tanks across the river and into the one small bridgehead that had been formed. Yet, Halder commented that the crossing of the Aisne was a 'superb achievement, in which the exemplary work of the General Staff officers of this group had a substantial share'.[84] Before Guderian could achieve a break-out, he had to contend with a number of armoured counter-attacks, which were conducted with much greater determination than the French had shown in May. By the 11th, however, he had succeeded in getting sufficient armour across the river and began to beat a path south with increasing momentum. According to Blumentritt, von Rundstedt had worked out a system with Guderian whereby he would transmit codewords based on football terms by radio to confirm Guderian's axis of advance. The three options were a swing eastwards towards Belfort to cut off a French withdrawal from Alsace, straight ahead to Lyons and Marseilles, or turning south-west towards Bordeaux to cut off the forces withdrawing in front of Army Group B.[85] This is indicative that von Rundstedt had less to fear from the now already half-beaten enemy and was prepared to let Guderian have his head more than he had during the first phase of the campaign, which was dominated by the ever present threat to the flanks of the armoured wedge. Eventually, on the 16th, OKH ordered that Guderian should adopt the first option, eastwards towards Alsace.

Once the break-out from the Aisne had been achieved, everything went smoothly for von Rundstedt, as the disintegration of French forces became more and more apparent. Indeed, there seems to have been only one disagreeable moment as far as he was concerned. On the 19th, with the Italians about to mount their own invasion of France, Hitler ordered some of the forces in Army Group A to advance south into Savoy in order to assist them. Von Brauchitsch and Halder accordingly passed the order to von Rundstedt, but specified that the task force should be assembled under List and was to consist of Hoepner's XVI Panzer Corps and some motorised units. Von Rundstedt bridled at this, considering that the organisation and selection of the force should be left to him as the army group commander. Probably viewing this as just the latest of OKH's interferences with his command authority, he telephoned Halder and told him in no uncertain terms what he felt, moving the latter to write in his diary: 'He uses language which one would not think possible between German generals.'[86] As it happened, the force made little difference since the Italians failed to make much impression on the French defences. This, however, was of little consequence. On 22 June, the French signed an armistice with Germany, and did the same with the Italians two days later. The battle for France was over, but, as von Rundstedt was probably well aware, it was by no means the end of the war.

7
Invasion Talk

THE VICTORY over France was greeted by Germans with some joy, but much more, relief that the campaign had ended so quickly, thereby avoiding a repeat of the long drawn out bloodbath of 25 years before. Hans Gerd, still in Berlin, was clearly very excited by the victory and proud of the part that his father had played. Writing to his mother on 26 June, he termed the armistice 'this happy news'. He noted that von Leeb and his two army commanders, von Witzleben and Dollmann, had been awarded the Knight's Cross and wondered whether 'Father is to be awarded the Oakleaves to the Knight's Cross or the Grand Cross or whether he will become a Field Marshal perhaps'.[1] In fact, von Rundstedt was not to be decorated again at this time and would have to wait four more years before receiving the Oakleaves. As for the Grand Cross or the Iron Cross, which had been instituted on 1 September 1939, the only person ever awarded this was Hermann Goering, on 19 July 1940, for the Luftwaffe's services during the recent campaign. Von Rundstedt's efforts did not, however, go unrecognised. On the same day that Goering was awarded the Grand Cross, Hitler announced in the Reichstag the promotion of nine of his leading army generals to the rank of General Field Marshal. Von Rundstedt was No 3 on the list, after von Brauchitsch and Keitel.[2] What von Rundstedt felt about Keitel being given seniority over him is not known. It would not have been in character for him to have commented on it and, even though his regard of Keitel was not high, he would have accepted that a retired officer recalled to active duty was likely to have less clout when it came to promotion than one who was still serving. Nevertheless, von Rundstedt did maintain his seniority over his fellow army group commanders, von Bock and von Leeb, who were also promoted on the same day.

Now that France had been overrun, she had been split into two zones. The north of the country, including Paris and the Channel and Atlantic coasts, was occupied by German troops and placed under military government. The remaining two thirds were put under the jurisdiction of Marshal Pétain, who set up what was to be little more than a puppet government at Vichy. Britain, although the BEF had left all its heavy weapons and equipment behind in France, and had suffered 70,000 men killed or captured, did not seem inclined to come to terms. Hitler had not really prepared for this contingency when he was drawing up Plan Yellow. The assumption had been that, with the Channel coast in German hands, Britain would quail in the face of the twin threats of the Luftwaffe and the U-boat. Now, with his troops gazing at the White Cliffs of Dover from the French coast, Hitler realised that invasion might be the only option, or, as Halder put it, 'Britain probably still needs one more demonstration of our military might before she gives in and leaves us a free hand in the east.'[3] Accordingly, on 1 July, he issued his first military directive on the subject. In this he laid down that he considered an invasion as 'possible, providing that air superiority can be attained and certain other necesary conditions fulfilled'. No invasion date was laid down but all necessary preparations were to be set in train immediately. Hitler stressed that he had not made any decision as yet and that the invasion was to be regarded only as 'a plan'.[4] The planning itself developed rapidly. On the 3rd, Halder designated the coast between Ostend and Le Havre as the launching pad and began examining potential landing beaches. He also optimistically likened the operation to a 'large-scale river crossing'.[5] On 11 July, von Brauchitsch agreed Halder's draft plan and two days later Hitler added his seal of approval. This was in spite of Admiral Erich Raeder, C-in-C of the Navy, expressing grave reservations to him on the 11th. Finally, on 16 July, Hitler issued Directive No 16 for Operation SEALION.

Directive No 16 laid down that there would be three attack forces, based on Cherbourg, Le Havre and Boulogne-Ostend. These were to land in Lyme Bay, west of Weymouth, Portsmouth-Brighton and Hastings-Dover respectively. Thirteen infantry divisions would constitute the first wave, with a further eighteen Panzer, mechanised and infantry divisions as follow-up forces. 15 August was nominated as D-Day. This was a massive force, landing on a very broad front, with little time to prepare, and it is no wonder that Raeder blanched at the thought of protecting its crossing against the ravages of the Royal Navy. The day after Directive No 16 was issued, OKH disseminated orders which detailed troops to tasks. Von Rundstedt was nominated to command the centre and eastern groups, which would comprise Busch's Sixteenth and Strauss's Ninth Armies. The Cherbourg force, which represented von Reichenau's Sixth Army, was to come under von Bock's army group.

Von Rundstedt himself moved from Auxerre, where he was based at the end of the late campaign, and set up his headquarters in the Pavillon Henri IV, a hotel with a first class reputation before the war, at St Germain-en-Laye outside Paris. With the River Seine on one side and the Forest of St Germain to its north, it was a picturesque and tranquil spot and von Rundstedt would quickly become very attached to it. He himself lived in a nearby villa with von Sodenstern and his orderly officer, von Salviati. A retired cavalryman and well known international horseman, von Salviati had been an SS Standartenführer (Colonel) in Hamburg, but had quickly developed a loathing for Hitler and his henchmen and had managed to rejoin the Army rather than become a member of the Waffen-SS, as might have been expected. He was at bottom a monarchist. This was not surprising since he was the brother-in-law of Prince William of Prussia, later to be killed on the Eastern Front. Von Salviati would constantly try and persuade von Rundstedt to join the anti-Hitler plotters.[6]

Von Rundstedt rarely went to Paris, even though it was so close, but did not discourage his staff from doing so. Blumentritt recalled:

'In the good mood in which everyone found himself the young officers hit upon the following idea: in the orderly officer's workroom hung two large maps of Paris; every visitor to the city had to map out his experiences on both of these. One map contained blue, the other red, dots with numbers. The blue dots showed where one could eat particularly well, and the red onces indicated where something for the heart could be found. When the broad-minded Rundstedt entered this room one day he inspected the two maps, whilst the young officers stood near. Rundstedt merely made the laconic comment: "Here, your red map isn't nearly full!"'[7]

SEALION meant, however, that von Rundstedt's staff had only limited time in which to relax and savour the pleasures of victory. They were soon hard at work transforming the grandiose OKH scheme into a practical and detailed plan.

In postwar interrogations and interviews von Rundstedt stated that he viewed the prospect of SEALION with gloom from the outset. He told Liddell Hart that he often thought of how Napoleon had been baffled by the same prospect.[8] To Milton Shulman he said that there was insufficient shipping to transport the force across the Channel and that he and other army commanders involved regarded the whole concept 'as a game'.[9] This is supported by Blumentritt, who said that his chief regarded the venture as 'an impossibility'.[10] Indeed, he appears to have openly expressed the view 'Sealion, rubbish' and to have left most of the planning to Busch.[11] Contemporary evidence also seems to support this attitude. True, von Rundstedt visited Ninth Army at Dieppe at the end of July, and a few days later toured units of Sixteenth Army at Ostend, Dunkirk and Gravelines, but he never attended any amphibious landing exercises. Even when von Brauchitsch and Halder came to see such demonstrations by Sixteenth Army at Le Touquet on 16 August, neither von Rundstedt nor his chief of staff were present, and the army group was represented by Blumentritt, a mere Colonel at the time. According to Blumentritt, von Rundstedt, at one stage in July, did declare that the headquarters should move from its comfortable billet at St Germain to a more spartan existence in a hutted camp in woods near Amiens in order to be closer to the coast, but he never bothered to put this into practice.[12]

Meanwhile Goering's Luftwaffe had been trying to draw the RAF into battle over the Channel, but without success. At the end of July, Hitler accepted that he had been over-optimistic in fixing 15 August as a potential D-day, especially because of the problems being experienced in gathering together from ports and waterways throughout Western Europe the 2,500 barges and other craft needed for the invasion. On 1 August, he issued Directive No 17, which ordered Goering to begin intensive operations to break the back of the RAF. At the same time Keitel issued an instruction to the relevant army commanders laying down that all preparations were now to be completed by 15 September and that Hitler would decide 8–14 days after Goering's renewed air offensive began whether the invasion would take place in September or be postponed until Spring 1941. The Navy, however, continued to object to the Army's plan for landings on a broad front and, at the end of July, Raeder tried to persuade Hitler to postpone SEALION until the spring. On 12 August, Goering switched his efforts from the Channel to RAF airfields and fighter bases and for the three and a half weeks there were desperate air battles in the skies over southern England, actions which the Germans convinced themselves were destroying more British aircraft than they were losing themselves. Yet, the RAF showed no signs of weakening.

On 14 August, von Rundstedt and the other newly promoted Field Marshals attended Hitler at the Reichs Chancellery in order to be presented with their ceremonial batons. Before he left for Berlin, Ditha wrote to her father-in-law: 'Thank the Lord who has brought you home from all these perils. I hope you will live through a few unique hours in Berlin, as a token for what you and your troops have done for us.'[13]

As was inevitable on an occasion like this, Hitler harangued his commanders. The OKM War Diary recorded the gist of what he said as follows:

> 'The Führer stated that he does not intend to carry out the operation if the risk was too great, as he considers that the aim of defeating England is not *exclusively* [sic] dependent on invasion, but can also be achieved by other means. Whatever final decision may be taken, the Führer wishes that, in any case, the threat of invasion be maintained.'[14]

SEALION was still very dependent on the success that the Luftwaffe had against the RAF. But, according to one source, Hitler actually told von Rundstedt in private that SEALION was merely 'a deception'.[15] Even so, Hitler's speech on its own was enough to confirm von Rundstedt's view that the Führer's heart was not in it and that it would not take place.

While in Berlin, von Rundstedt and his fellow Field Marshals attended the first night of a new propaganda film *Sieg im Westen* (Triumph in the West). An American journalist was present and described von Rundstedt as the 'frog-eyed man with a moustache'. He noted that he and von Bock sat in adjacent boxes at the theatre, but exchanged no words. 'They just sat there poker-faced, and gazed blankly into space.' Apart from a possible coldness between the two, as a result of the arguments over Case Yellow, it is likely that von Rundstedt, with his distaste for publicity, was uncomfortable in this gala atmosphere, as was von Bock. The journalist also described their reactions when Hitler's labour minister, Robert Ley, and his wife appeared. They both 'rose stiffly in succession to kiss the hand of the beautiful blonde-haired woman. . . . But they only nodded at the grinning doctor.'[16]

The festivities over, von Rundstedt returned to France, but almost immediately departed on leave. This was at the time when the SEALION preparations were reaching their height, and was confir-mation that he was now convinced that no invasion would take place. It was also the first time that he had seen Bila since well before the invasion of France. There was also another reason for going on leave at this time. He was about to be a grandfather for the third time.

Whether he had the chance to see Hans Gerd and Ditha when he was in Berlin is not known, but it would be surprising if he did not. Ditha, commenting on the general situation in Europe, had written to her mother-in-law: 'How will everything continue with high politics – the calm before the storm [presumably SEALION] really takes one's breath away.'[17] Her condition was not helped by the fact that on the night 25/26 August, RAF Bomber Command raided Berlin for the first time, with fifty aircraft and with further attacks taking place during the following nights, albeit with smaller numbers of bombers. Ditha commented in another letter to Bila:

> 'Though Tommy visits us every night and then cannot tear himself away, we have, thank God, come through everything unharmed. Please keep your fingers crossed that it won't be too awful in the nursing home, because I do not think it much fun having babies surrounded by falling bombs. But these thoughts do not help; Tommy won't be so gentlemanly as to stay away from Berlin during my crucial days.'[18]

Eberhard himself was born on 7 September. His grandfather had been aghast when he had learnt that Ditha was pregnant for a third time and wondered how Hans Gerd and his wife could afford so many children. Ditha reassured him by saying that children attracted generous tax allowances. This they did as part of the Nazi policy for the propagation of the Aryan race. Accordingly, Hans Gerd used to refer to Eberhard as 'our tax bonus'. [19] Von Rundstedt's attitude may help to explain why he and Bila only had one child, but another reason was possibly the memory of his mother's exhaustion after bearing four children in such rapid succession.

While Ditha had withstood the rigours of the RAF's first attacks on Berlin with seeming *sangfroid*, she and her children left the capital the following spring. Her best friend was married to a Swiss and had a house in Goisern in Austria, where the friend's mother was living. The mother found a holiday house there which Ditha was able to rent. Here she settled, returning just once to Berlin for the birth of her fourth and last child. She and the children would remain at Goisern until well after the end of the war.[20]

While von Rundstedt was away from France there were some significant changes to the overall SEALION plan. Most important was a narrowing of the invasion front, although it was still not enough to satisfy the Navy's demands. The Lyme Bay landing was cancelled and Worthing would now be the western boundary. Von Bock's Head-quarters Army Group B was now relieved of any involvement with SEALION and, indeed, was ordered east to Pozen as the first stage of the preparations for the invasion of Russia. Furthermore, on

3 September, Keitel had issued a directive postponing the invasion until 21 September. This would be confirmed on the 11th, with final orders being issued on the 18th. Von Rundstedt thus found himself in sole charge, as far as the land forces were concerned, of an operation which was receding into the realms of theory, merely confirming, even further, his belief that it would never be mounted. His staff seem to have thought the same way. When von Brauchitsch and Halder visited his headquarters on 10 September, whilst von Rundstedt was still on leave, in order to check on the operational planning, Halder complained that it had been done 'much too mechanically'.[21] On that same day, Hitler postponed the operation until 24 September and, four days later, put it back until the 27th, the last day of the month on which the tides would be suitable. By now it was becoming clear to Hitler that the Luftwaffe, in spite of Goering's assertions, had not yet won the Battle of Britain, although he blamed the weather rather than any failings on the part of his air force. Finally, on 15 September, Goering, deluding himself that he now had the RAF on the run, launched an all out daylight attack on London. He lost 58 aircraft, as against 26 RAF fighters. Accepting that he could not overwhelm the RAF by day, he decided to beat the British people into submission through bomber attacks by night. Two days later, Hitler postponed SEALION indefinitely and turned to other things.

No evidence remains of von Rundstedt's reaction to this news, but one suspects that it was one of 'I told you so'. On 1 October, however, he was formally appointed Commander-in-Chief West, tasked primarily with the military occupation of Northern France. Life at St Germain could resume its previous tenor of comparative lightheartedness, although, according to Blumentritt, von Rundstedt himself showed little interest in the fleshpots of Paris. He did, however, grow discontented with life at the villa, perhaps because he felt that he was isolating himself too much from his staff. Acordingly, he moved into two rooms in a detached annexe of the Henri IV. Von Rundstedt maintained a virtually 'open' headquarters, with very little security – no fences, and 'only in the evening did a couple of elderly soldiers go on patrol'.[22] He himself took much pleasure in walking in the neighbouring woods, often totally unaccompanied, and, no doubt, quite willing to practise his French on any local people that he met. All this helped to maintain a relaxed and happy atmosphere, but it was not long before his headquarters was given further planning tasks.

Apart from beginning to prepare seriously for the invasion of the Soviet Union, Hitler's attention had also turned south. On 27

September, he had signed the Tripartite Pact with Italy and Japan by which each country undertook to support any of the others if they were attacked by a country not already at war. The Pact also included mutual recognition of the right to establish the 'new orders' in the Far East and Europe. Two weeks later, Hitler met Mussolini in the Brenner Pass to agree strategy for the future. At the time, the Italians, although they had overrun British Somaliland and secured two small lodgements in the Sudan, had done little to impress their German ally. Their much heralded invasion of Egypt from Libya had come to a halt after 60 miles and British convoys still seemed to be slipping through the Straits of Gibraltar and across Mussolini's supposed *Mare Nostrum*. Africa was the only theatre in which Axis troops were engaged with the British on land and there was also the lure of Middle East oil. Accordingly, during autumn 1940 Hitler drew up grandiose plans for removing the British presence from the Mediterranean and the Middle and Near East. This envisaged a double envelopment around the shores of the Mediterranean. List was to overrun the Balkans and then drive through Turkey, ignoring the fact that she had declared herself neutral, and then thrust for the Suez Canal. A force commanded by von Bock was to take passage from Italy to Tripolitania in order to bolster the Italian forces in Libya. Simultaneously, under the codename FELIX, an army group under von Rundstedt was to move through Spain, capture Gibraltar, cross to Morocco and then drive east to Tunis. This, of course, disregarded the June 1940 armistice with the French, in that French North Africa was part of the Unoccupied Zone. The plan foundered because Franco refused to allow German troops to traverse Spain, but it kept von Rundstedt's staff occupied for a little while.

The spectre of Hitler's plan to invade Russia was beginning to loom large, however. Any German who had read his *Mein Kampf* with any attention realised only too well that Bolshevism was Hitler's ultimate enemy. In this context, the August 1939 pact with Stalin could be seen merely as the measure of temporary expediency that it was. Indeed, it was nothing more than the traditional German policy of trying to avoid simultaneous war on two fronts. By July 1940, while the German commanders in the West were grappling with the problems of SEA-LION, Hitler was already turning his attention eastwards. On the 19th, General Erich Marcks, Chief of Staff of Eighteenth Army, was detailed to produce a study on the invasion of the Soviet Union. He completed it in two weeks. According to Halder, Hitler's justification to the German High Command for invading Russia was that she was Britain's only remaining hope in Europe and that if she were smashed,

Britain must fall.[23] He also laid down the aim as the destruction of Russian manpower and gave the main territorial objectives as Kiev, Moscow, and the Caucasus oilfields. The invasion was to take place in spring 1941. Marcks' plan was based on reaching a final line sufficiently far to the East to put Germany out of range of Soviet strategic bombers. This line he defined as Archangel-Gorki-Rostov-on-Don. He estimated that 147 divisions would be needed. On this basis, OKW issued a directive on 9 August for Operation OTTO, the build-up of the invasion forces in Poland.

As yet, the planning had been carried entirely by OKH, but Jodl and Walter Warlimont, his chief staff officer, worked out their own plan in September. Marcks had laid down the main axis as north of the Pripet marshes and directed on Moscow, with a subsidiary attack to clear the Baltic states and seize Leningrad. He also envisaged a further subsidiary thrust south to Kiev and across the Dnieper, and thence to the Caucasus oilfields. Jodl was less influenced by economic factors and more by Hitler's stated aim of the destruction of Russia's military power. He therefore proposed that the invasion force should be split into three army groups. Two would advance north of the Pripet marshes and the other to the south. The army group objectives were to be Leningrad, Moscow and Kiev. This plan was further refined by Friedrich Paulus, newly appointed OKH Assistant Chief of Staff (Operations) and later to be forced to surrender at Stalingrad. Paulus, however, did raise questions over time and space and pointed to the vast preponderance of Russian manpower. He even queried the popular assumption that Stalin's purges had resulted in poor quality leadership. At the end of November, Paulus conducted a series of war games designed to examine the questions which he had raised and then, on 5 December, Hitler presided over a confirmatory conference with von Brauchitsch and Halder. He emphasised the need to destroy the Red Army by creating pockets and wanted the army group south of the Pripet marshes to be strong so as to better split the Soviet forces. He also stated that Moscow was of no great importance and, although von Brauchitsch and Halder tried to argue the case for the Russian capital as the main objective, Hitler would have none of it. Instead, he declared that the wings of Army Group Centre must be made strong in order to be prepared to exploit north through the Baltic states and south into the Ukraine. It was on this basis that the final plan was drawn up. Before the directive for BARBAROSSA, as Hitler codenamed the invasion after the 12th century Holy Roman Emperor Frederick Hohenstaufen, the army group and army chiefs of staff were briefed at an all day conference in Berlin held on 13 December. Five days later Hitler signed Directive No. 21.

The same team that had won the victory in the West, von Bock, von Leeb and von Rundstedt, was to command the army groups for BARBAROSSA. This time, however, von Bock was to be in the centre, von Leeb would be in the north and von Rundstedt the south. After the war, von Rundstedt said that his initial impression of BARBAROSSA was that it was a contingency against a Russian attack, which was always possible once they had concluded their war with the Finns in March 1940. This, however, runs contrary to what Hitler had told him at Charleville at the beginning of June 1940 (see page 124). Even so, the prospect of war with the Soviet Union, was to him both 'unpleasant and sinister'. He recognised the innate toughness and bravery of the Russian soldier from his experiences on the Eastern Front during the period 1915–1918 and also recalled the difficulties of much of the terrain.[24] Blumentritt, too, stated that von Rundstedt was against an attack on Russia from the outset and considered that if Stalin had intended to atack, he would have done so in May 1940.[25] There is, however, no evidence that von Rundstedt voiced any objections, even when von Brauchitsch conferred with the three army group commanders in Berlin at the end of January 1941. This gave them the outline of the operational instruction for BARBAROSSA, which was issued by Halder on 3 February. Two days later, he was conferring with von Rundstedt and his staff at St Germain. Here von Sodenstern conducted a map exercise on how Army Group South intended to overrun the Ukraine. Halder was clearly pleased with the way that it went, commenting on how well thought out the exercise was and the good discussion. Von Rundstedt had been allocated 41 German and 14 Rumanian divisions. These were to attack on two axes so as to facilitate the double envelopment of the Russian armies facing them. Ewald von Kleist's Panzer Group, von Reichenau's Sixth, and Karl-Heinrich von Stülpnagel's Seventeenth Armies were to attack from southern Poland. Geographically divorced from this blow by intervening Hungarian territory, von Schobert's Eleventh and two indigenous armies would attack from Rumania. What von Sodenstern's planning exercise demonstrated, according to Halder, was that it would be virtually impossible for the northern thrust to carry out any form of envelopment on its own west of the Dnieper, especially since it had to guard against the likelihood of Russian counterstrokes from the Pripet marshes. Also, the southern group tended to advance in too northly a direction too early in its desire to link up quickly with the northern thrust.[26] Von

Rundstedt mentioned this planning exercise to Bila in a letter he wrote to her that evening, but without, of course, telling her the object. He also commented on the wintry weather; 'the poor French must be freezing'. Just over two weeks later, he wrote to her of the worsening food situation in France and remarked that even 'our food stocks will soon be exhausted as well'.[27] His gloom was probably influenced by the harsh wintry weather which prevented him from taking his daily exercise. 'Sleep and mood are suffering', as he told his wife.[28]

On 14 March, Hitler ordered von Rundstedt to Breslau, where, secretly, he was to set up Headquarters Army Group South. His place as C-in-C West was taken by Erwin von Witzleben, who was commanding Army Group D at the time which covered Occupied France south of the River Seine. En route to Breslau, von Rundstedt had to report to Berlin. On 27 March, von Brauchitsch held a day long conference for all army group, army and Panzer group commanders. A number of operational queries were raised, but, it would seem, no basic objections to BARBAROSSA. Three days later, the generals were subjected to a two and a half hour's harangue by Hitler in his office in the Chancellery. After reviewing the war situation as a whole, Hitler went on to say that Britain put her hope in the United States and the Soviet Union. The former would not be on a full war footing for four years. Invading Russia, on the other hand, would provide 'the final and drastic solution to all land problems'. The aims of BARBAROSSA were to 'crush' the Red armed forces and 'break up' the Soviet state. Hitler mentioned the large Russian tank and air forces, but stated that most of their weapons systems were obsolete. The enormous expanse of the Russian terrain meant that the German forces must concentrate on key points. The Luftwaffe also could not cover the entire front and its operations were to be tied closely to those of the ground forces. Not too much could be expected of the Finns and Rumanians. Hitler then went on to describe the coming campaign as a clash of two ideologies. In Halder's diary notes, from which this account of what Hitler said is taken, Hitler described Bolshevism as a 'social criminality'.

> 'We must forget the concept of comradeship between soldiers. A Communist is no comrade before or after the battle. This is a war of extermination. If we do not grasp this, we shall still beat the enemy, but thirty years later we shall again have to fight the Communist foe. We do not wage war to preserve the enemy.'

Having described how German occupied Russia would be organised, Hitler went on to stress the 'extermination of the Bolshevist commissars and of the Communist intelligentsia'. The formation of a new class of the latter had to be prevented.

> 'This is no job for military courts. The individual troop commanders must know the issues at stake. They must be leaders in this fight. The troops must fight back with the methods with which they are attacked. Commissars and GPU [Secret Police] men are criminals and must be dealt with as such. This does not mean that the troops should get out of hand. Rather, the commander must give orders which express the common feelings of his men.'[29]

This was the first mention of what would become the infamous Commissar Order, something which was to haunt von Rundstedt and many of his fellow high commanders in the immediate postwar years. No evidence exists as to what von Rundstedt's reaction to this was at the time. He himself stated after the war that Hitler had said that Commissars were not soldiers according to International Law and hence were not to be treated as normal prisoners of war.[30] Von Manstein, now a Panzer corps commander in Army Group Centre, was not at the conference, but was a recipient of the order when it was formally issued by von Brauchitsch on 8 June 1941. He considered that:

> '. . . from the point of view of international law, the status of these political commissars was extremely equivocal. They were certainly not soldiers, any more than I would have considered a *Gauleiter* attached to me as a political overseer to be a soldier. Neither could they be granted the same non-combatant status as chaplains, medical personnel or war correspondents. On the contrary, they were – without being soldiers – fanatical fighters, but fighters whose activities could only be regarded as illegal according to the traditional meaning of warfare. Their task was not only the political supervision of Soviet military leaders but, even more, to instil the greatest possible degree of cruelty into the fighting and to give it a character completely at variance with the traditional conceptions of soldierly behaviour.'

Even so, von Manstein felt that it went 'against the grain of any soldier' to shoot commissars if they had been captured in battle.[31] As for von Rundstedt, he said that he and his brother senior commanders went 'spontaneously' to von Brauchitsch immediately after the conference and complained.[32] Von Brauchitsch, who had failed in the past to represent the Army's views in a strong enough way, was still not prepared to take any action. Next day he sent a draft of the Commissar order to OKW.[33]

After his morning diatribe, Hitler invited his generals to lunch and continued in the afternoon. Some would have known already, but possibly not von Rundstedt, that Hitler's eye was immediately on the Balkans. In December 1940, he had ordered plans to be drawn up for the occupation of the Balkans in order to secure his southern flank for BARBAROSSA under the codename MARITA. Albania, Hungary and Rumania had already joined the Axis and pressurised diplomacy persuaded Bulgaria also to join at the beginning of March and Yugoslavia on the 25th. On 27 March, however, there was a bloodless coup in Yugoslavia which overthrew the pro-Axis regent Prince Paul and replaced him with a government of national unity, with the youthful Prince Peter being crowned king. The new government immediately signed a non-aggression pact with Russia and expressed interest in creating an anti-Axis coalition with the British. Furthermore, on 7 March, Greece, which had been successfully resisting Mussolini's invasion launched the previous October from Albania, had finally accepted Churchill's pressing offer to send a British force to support them. On hearing of the Yugoslav coup, a furious Hitler immediately ordered MARITA to be put into effect. D-Day for the implementation of the hastily amended plan was to be 6 April. Troops earmarked for BARBAROSSA would have to be used and, as far as von Rundstedt was concerned, this included the use of Panzer Group von Kleist. The conference ended with the commanders giving reports on their preparations. Halder noted that von Rundstedt made a 'clever plea' for the Hungarians to be brought in to attack from the Carpathians. This would give him a more continuous front and remove the problem of the initially exposed left flank of his southern thrust. It was in fact Hitler's intention that the Hungarian Army should take part in BARBAROSSA, but he distrusted the Hungarians because there was still an element of sympathy for Britain in the country. There was also Rumanian antipathy towards Hungary because of the Vienna Award of September 1940. Through this, Hitler had forced Rumania to cede Transylvania to her neighbour in order to pacify the Hungarians and safeguard Rumanian oil supplies to Germany, which had to pass through Hungary. As a result of this, Hitler had decided not to bring the Hungarians into BARBAROSSA until the very last moment.

Von Rundstedt and von Sodenstern set up a small headquarters in Breslau at the beginning of April. The bulk of his staff was, however, based at Cracow, almost 150 miles away and for three weeks von Rundstedt was not allowed to visit them for security reasons.[34] Preparations for BARBAROSSA were further frustrated by both MARITA and the late arrival of the spring thaw. The latter swelled rivers and created a sea of mud, which slowed deployment. On 30 April, Hitler was therefore forced to postpone the launching of the invasion from mid-May until the second half of June. Since the original plan laid down that all objectives had to be achieved by mid-October, before the onset of the Russian winter, the postponement placed increased pressure on those who had to execute BARBAROSSA. Von Rundstedt had even greater difficulties than his two fellow army group commanders. Breslau was a comparatively long way from Rumania. Furthermore, political considerations left the command relationship between himself and the Rumanians vague. General Ion Antonescu, the Rumanian dictator, for reasons of national pride, would not formally place his troops under German command. Von Rundstedt, for ease of command and control, had wanted to put von Schobert, commander of the Eleventh Army, in charge of the southern thrust, but Antonescu's stance made this difficult and the best that could be achieved was agreement that Rumanian forces be placed under von Rundstedt's strategic direction. The Hungarian forces also had to be kept apart from the Rumanians, for reasons stated earlier. The situation was to be further compounded by the allocation of an Italian corps under General Giovanni Messe and a Slovakian motorised division. Furthermore, none of the Allies were to be told about the operation until the last moment, which aggravated the planning difficulties still further. But, given this polygot collection, it becomes understandable why von Rundstedt, with his natural tact and courtesy, should have been appointed to Army Group South.

Operationally, life was made more difficult by the fact that Hitler now decided that the southern prong of Army Group South should be deployed more cautiously. The Pruth and other rivers were natural tank obstacles and he was also fearful that too much activity might attract a Soviet counter-offensive which could threaten the Ploesti oilfields. Consequently, he removed all Eleventh Army's armour and passed it across to von Kleist. The southern wing of his offensive was thus reduced to no more than a slow advance into Bessarabia designed to pin down Soviet forces. This, of course, ran counter to the map exercise that von Rundstedt had conducted for Halder in February, which had demonstrated only too clearly the difficulties of the northern thrust creating pockets on its own. As far as the northern thrust itself was concerned, von Rundstedt had placed his fellow Field Marshal, von Reichenau, in charge. Halder indicates that von Reichenau made difficulties over his plans for handling his armour and that it took some persuasion to get him to allot some of his infantry corps to von Kleist, who would be spearheading the advance.[35]

Von Rundstedt's own overall postwar view of the plans for BAR-BAROSSA was that the main thrust should have been in the north, with Leningrad as the objective. This would have cut the Russians off from the Baltic states and enabled a link-up with the Finns to take place. Once this had been achieved, the German forces could have then tackled Moscow.[36] He also considered that the delay in launching BARBAROSSA was fatal. He told Milton Shulman that he had made the following comment to his staff during the February map exercise at St. Germain: 'Gentlemen, if you are going to conduct a war in Russia you must remember that campaigning weather ends early there. Once winter comes it becomes very difficult. One must start operations in Russia as soon as the swampy period is over, which is usually in May.[37] As it happened, the late spring meant that, Balkans or not, the ground had not dried out sufficiently until June. Furthermore, Hitler remained imbued with an unreal over-optimism that by the time the German armies had closed on the Dnieper, all opposition would have been destroyed.[38]

While von Rundstedt was in Breslau, Ulrich von Hassell (who, it will be remembered, was an active member of the covert opposition to Hitler) gave a lecture on the economic problems of South East Europe during the annual business fair in the city. He recalled in his diary that the Gauleiter of Silesia, Karl Hanke, was sitting in the audience next to a counsellor from the Soviet Embassy in Berlin. The latter turned to his other neighbour, a German industrialist, and said 'with a very naive expression on his face "I think I saw Field Marshal von Rundstedt on the street. Is the Supreme Command located here?"' Von Hassell himself had seen von Rundstedt at an hotel, but had not spoken to him. He had, however, had a word about him with von Salviati who had said that the Field Marshal 'saw clearly almost everything that was wrong, but that was as far as it went'.[39] This reinforced von Hassell's view that there was little point in trying to recruit von Rundstedt for the resistance to Hitler movement. As for the Russian counsellor's comment, this would have certainly been passed back to Moscow and should have set alarm bells ringing there, but Stalin, of course, refused to take seriously the growing evidence of what the Germans were preparing.

On 14 June, Hitler had a final conference of his army group and army commanders at his headquarters in the East, the Wolf's Lair at Rastenburg in East Prussia. Once again, he reiterated that Russia's collapse would force Britain to give in. It is also possible that he may have repeated the Commissar Order and that it was after this that von

Rundstedt and his fellow commanders protested to von Brauchitsch, but certainly Halder makes no mention of it. One point that the conference did finally confirm, however, was the command relationship between von Schobert and the Rumanians. Up until the attack itself, Antonescu would exercise supreme command in his country, with von Schobert's headquarters attached to him as his 'working staff'. In this way it would hold the reins of control, but would pass out all orders in Antonescu's name. The German Military Mission to Rumania would act as liaison between the two. The Hungarians were still not to be told what was about to happen, but merely advised that their defence measures should take the strength of Soviet forces on their borders into consideration. Slovakia, too, would be kept in the dark and only told to organise its troops to repel a Russian attack once BARBAROSSA had been launched. The date of the invasion had already been fixed and now H-hour was confirmed as 0300 hours. On 21 June, the codeword DORTMUND was transmitted by OKH, confirming the following day as D-day. As to what von Rundstedt was thinking, some clue may be gained from a remark he made to von Leeb at the beginning of May: 'So, see you again in Siberia.'[40]

8

Russia 1941

AT 2100 HOURS on the evening of 21 June 1941 a German deserter from von Reichenau's Sixth Army crossed the lines and told the Russians that the German armies were going to invade early next morning. It was but just the latest of a growing number of indicators that the Soviet commanders on Russia's western borders had been receiving during the past days and weeks. Up until now, Stalin had allowed only minimal precautionary measures because he was fearful of provoking the Germans into doing exactly what they were now about to carry out. Further deserters crossed during the next couple of hours and bore the same message. News of this was passed to Georgi Zhukov of the General Staff, who in turn passed it to Semyon Timoshenko, the Commissar for Defence, and to Stalin himself. Stalin at once summoned both across to see him and asked what should be done about it, stressing that he was still fearful of doing anything which might be interpreted by the Germans as provocative. After some discussion, Timoshenko and Zhukov issued an order, timed at 0030 hours on the 22nd, to the frontier military districts warning of the possibility of a surprise German attack during the next 24 hours. Fire positions on the frontier were to be manned immediately, aircraft dispersed and troops not actually on the frontier to be brought to combat readiness, but to be kept dispersed and under cover. It was too little and too late.

At 0100 hours Army Group South passed the codeword WOTAN to OKW indicating that all was ready. Two hours later the attack began on a frontage of some 500 miles, stretching from the Baltic to the Hungarian border. Facing von Rundstedt were, in the north, running from the Pripet marshes to the Rumanian border, the four armies of the Kiev Special Military District. It was commanded by Lt Gen M P Kirponos, who had distinguished himself as a divisional commander in the Russo-Finnish War. On the outbreak of war, his command, which could call on the equivalent of some sixty divisions, was automatically retitled the South-West Front. Kirponos was ill-equipped to meet the initial shock of BARBAROSSA. His static defences were only partially completed and most of his formations were well back from the frontier and dispersed, with his armour well to the rear of his infantry divisions. Nevertheless, he was better prepared than the other front commanders in that he had reacted to the German Sixth Army's deserter by instigating alert measures without recourse to Moscow. Furthermore, Soviet appreciations had always considered that the prime German target would be the Ukraine, because of its abundance of natural resources. Opposite the Rumanian border was the one army of the Odessa Military District, shortly to become the South Front under I V Tyulenev. This was of little consequence during the opening days of BARBAROSSA, however, since the Germans and Rumanians remained on the defensive during the first week.

Von Rundstedt's plan for the northern thrust was for von Reichenau, who had 25 infantry, five Panzer and three motorised divisions at his disposal, to use part of his own Sixth Army as flank protection, advancing from south-east of Lublin eastwards along the edge of the Pripet Marshes. Von Kleist was to aim for Kiev and then turn southeast along the line of the Dnieper, with the remainder of Sixth Army following in his wake, in order to seize the crossings over it and prevent the Russian forces withdrawing across it. Von Stülpnagel's Seventeenth Army would advance in step with Sixth Army on the axis Lvov-Vinnitsa. Von Rundstedt, apart from his concern about the 100 kilometre gap created by the Pripet marshes between himself and von Bock, also faced three other disadvantages at the outset. First, he only had one Panzer group, which meant that large pincer movements were virtually impossible. This was aggravated by the fact that Kirponos had more tanks than the fronts to the north. Also, Army Group South had to tackle more river lines than the other two army groups.

On 22 June itself, von Reichenau's artillery opened with a short, sharp, but accurate bombardment of Soviet strongpoints. Sixth and Seventeenth Armies got across the River Bug, although von Stülpnagel's men did have some problems. But then it became a question of working their way through the lines of incomplete Russian defences. Von Kleist's tanks managed to identify the boundary between the two northern Soviet armies, Fifth and Sixth, and made this their *Schwerpunkt*. Hopes that they would quickly break out and head for Kiev were, however, to be quickly dashed. Kirponos, apart from quickly deploying his rifle divisions, also began to move his armour forward, which consisted of six mechanised corps. They were, however, short of fuel and ammunition, lacked artillery, and the adverse air situation meant that it was impossible to provide them with the necessary air cover. Nevertheless, he deployed the nearest as early as the second day of BARBAROSSA. It had problems with the boggy ground and poor roads and only part of one division actually made contact with First Panzer Group. During the next few days, however, the remaining mechanised corps were committed and the result was four days' worth of concentrated tank battles in the area of Lvov. It was during these the Germans came up against the new Soviet tanks, the KV-1 and the T-34, for the first time and their 37 mm anti-tank guns proved powerless against them.

On 25 June, Halder commented in his diary: 'The stubborn resistance of individual Russian units is remarkable.'[1] Von Rundstedt, too, in his first line to Bila since the opening of the offensive, wrote: 'The Russians are fighting very stubbornly; things will not be as easy as we hoped and as they used to be.'[2] Slowly, von Kleist struggled forward, forcing the Soviet Fifth Army northwards into the Pripet marshes and the Sixth south-eastwards. This pressure was sufficient to prevent the divisions facing the Hungarian border from interfering with the southern flank of the German thrust since they, too, were forced to withdraw. Radio deception had also helped by posing the threat of an attack across the Hungarian border. By 30 June, von Kleist had secured Lvov, but still Kirponos kept throwing in armour. The net result of all this was that Army Group South was now falling well behind schedule. This was in contrast to the other two army groups. Von Bock's spearheads had created a sizeable pocket around Bialystok, which yielded 290,000 prisoners, together with 2,500 tanks and 1,500 guns, when it was eventually reduced on 3 July, and had raced on to the Beresina. Likewise, Army Group North overran Latvia by 2 July. On the same day, von Rundstedt's troops had made enough progress for him to move his headquarters from Tarnow, 50 miles east of Cracow, to Zamosch, the same distance south-east of Lublin. It was not, however, a move that filled him with much enthusiasm. He called Zamosch 'a dirty Jewish hole', perhaps remembering it from over twenty years before.[3]

Because of the delays, von Schobert's Eleventh Army and the Rumanians did not begin their attack until 1 July. It fell on the junction between the Soviet Ninth and Eighteenth Armies. Bridgeheads were quickly secured over the River Prut. Tyulenev, commanding the South Front, had three mechanised corps and ordered them to destroy these

MAP 8. Russia, 1941.

bridgeheads, but to no avail. By the end of the first week, von Schobert had a bridgehead across the Dniester, but Tyulenev was able to do little about it since he was ordered to pass troops across to Kirponos, who in turn had lost two armies to the Western Front north of the Pripet marshes. Nevertheless, the Stavka, the Soviet High Command in Moscow, was still urging Kirponos to deal a decisive counter-blow. To this end, Zhukov was sent to encourage him and the veteran cavalry-man Semyon Budenny, who had been appointed to take charge of both the South-West and South Fronts. By this time, von Kleist had captured Berdichev and was advancing towards Kiev. On the 9th, however, the weather broke – 'terrific thunderstorms, the like of which I have seldom seen', as von Rundstedt wrote. 'The poor troops suffer from the bottomless roads on this black Ukrainian soil which the frequent storms turn to mud.'[4] On the 10th, von Brauchitsch visited von Rundstedt, who was now established at Brody, another 'hole . . . incredibly neglected and dirty'[5] and 100 miles south-east of Zamosch. The reason for this was Hitler's first intervention over the conduct of Army Group South's operations. He now considered that Kiev was no longer a feasible objective for von Rundstedt's armour, the reason being, it would seem, that the population of the city was 35 per cent Jewish and not worth sacrificing tanks for.[6] Von Rundstedt's intention was for von Kleist's northern group to seize Kiev, while the remainder headed for Belaya Tserkov to the south and then south-east. Hitler, however, wanted the whole of First Panzer Group to make Vinnitsa its objective, a much shallower hook, in order to link up with von Schobert. Halder reckoned that this lacked potential, while the deeper thrust that OKH and von Rundstedt envisaged could trap South-West Front in entirety.[7] Von Rundstedt's view, which he discussed with von Brauchitsch, was that the only way to overtake and trap an enemy in a pursuit operation was to strike far ahead of him and that, in any event, the South-West Front seemed to be retreating on Kiev. Even if this proved not to be so, von Kleist could still swing south-east or south-west of the Dnieper or cross it at Kiev and then advance further eastwards. Von Rundstedt persuaded von Brauchitsch to stick to the original plan and Hitler subsequently agreed to this. He wrote to Bila, 'we settled an important point by telegram with "him" [Hitler]'.[8] In fact, it was Halder who had to make the approach to OKW. 'ObdH [von Brauchitsch] will make no decision that would not have the Fuehrer's approval. It is now up to me to get the Fuehrer to agree.' It was 2330 hours by this time, but Halder was unable to speak to him because, unlike Hitler's normal schedule, he had gone to bed. He managed, however, to speak to Keitel, who obtained Hitler's agreement within the hour.[9.]

On that same day, 10 July, Potapov's Fifth Russian Army, supported by elements of three mechanised corps, issued out of the Pripet marshes once more. It struck the rear of von Kleist's panzer group and cut his main supply route. Von Reichenau had to be called in to clear up the mess. Von Rundstedt described the fighting as hard and noted that 'the Russians are attacking everywhere with tanks as though they are crazy.'[10] Potapov was eventually driven back, but from then on von Reichenau was forced to deploy more strength to guard von Kleist's left flank than to give him direct support. On the 16th, von Kleist's tanks reached Belaya Tserkov, south-west of Kiev. Eleventh Army was making good progress to the south and the prospects of finally creating a sizeable pocket began to look good. The weather, however, continued bad and, as von Rundstedt wrote to Bila, 'our movements slow in the mud. The Russians, who are withdrawing can cope better with it. Slowly one turns into a pig.'[11] Things had reached such a stage that when Halder visited HQ Army Group South, now housed in a Russian military school at Stara Konstantinov, on 20 July, he noted that 11th Panzer Division had been forced to leave all its wheeled transport in the rear, because of the state of the roads, and was advancing with just tracked vehicles and peasant carts. Indeed, by now half von Rundstedt's motor transport was out of action and there was a serious ammunition shortage. The situation was also aggravated by the fact that the allied contingents had very little motor transport of their own and leant heavily on the Germans for it. Von Rundstedt himself recalled just after the war:

> 'Transport difficulties were the most serious, even in the summer, or at any rate where I was, owing to the mud. I remember one thing, how a "Panzerdivision" covered 7 km in 12 hours one day. If it begins raining, then that's the end, you simply can[not] get out.'

Another problem:

> 'The maps we got were wrong. There was not one road marked nice and red and thick on the map. There were railways on the map which simply didn't exist. Then the map showed: "There is nothing here", and you were suddenly confronted with an American type town, with factory buildings and all the rest of it.'[12]

Worse, only 11th and 16th Panzer Divisions were forward, the main body being tied up in repulsing attacks in its flank by the Russian

Twenty-Sixth Army south of Kiev. Von Kleist's objective was Kirovo-grad, near the Dnieper, so that he could place himself between the river and the Russian armies withdrawing in front of Eleventh Army. He was already behind schedule and Halder was doubtful if he would arrive in time to catch the bulk of the Russian forces. He was also gloomy about von Reichenau's progress. Having continued to battle with the Russian Fifth Army he was now driving it back north of Kiev towards the Dnieper with the intention of then swinging south and taking the city from the east. This was no good in the eyes of Halder, who was visiting Headquarters Army Group South at the time. Von Reichenau, he said, was to push the Russians away from the Dnieper, and von Kleist must do the same with Twenty-Sixth Army. His spearhead must also be quickly built up so that he could get to Kirovograd in time. With this he departed.[13] Von Rundstedt was clearly somewhat irritated by his visit. He wrote to Bila that evening: 'Today Halder was here with far-reaching plans, but one does not dare to think beyond the next'. Nevertheless, Halder's advice was hearkened. Two days later, von Reichenau was beginning to steer Potapov away from the Dnieper, but von Kleist was still under pressure. Even so, on 2 August von Kleist took Pervomaysk and some twenty Russian divisions were cut off in a pocket based on Uman, a thunderstorm the day before notwithstanding.

By this time, von Rundstedt had moved his headquarters from Stara-Konstantinov to Berdichev, seventy miles to the east and south of Zhitomir. The journey there was 'long and troublesome' and the Field Marshal's humour was not helped by what he found on his arrival. 'B is a fantastically dirty hole.' In spite of this the Red Army battle school which had been earmarked for his headquarters was 'still bearable'.[14] Berdichev, during this last week in July 1941, however, created its own small part in the history of the Holocaust. A weekly report by an SS *Einsatzgruppe* operating in Army Group South's area and dated 30 July noted that 148 Jews had been killed in Berdichev, as well as others at Vinnitsa, Smolensk and Proskurov.[15] This was corroborated by a diary entry made by the diplomat Walther Hewel, who accompanied Hitler on his visit to von Rundstedt's headquarters at Berdichev on 6 August: 'Ruined monastery church. Opened coffins, *execution* [Author's italics], ghastly town. Many Jews, ancient cottages, fertile soil. Very hot.'[16] Von Rundstedt would later testify before the IMT Commission in 1946 that he had been aware of just one atrocity committed by the *Einsatzgruppen* in his area of operations (see page 248) and was probably referring to this incident.

This raises the question of how much knowledge of and control over the SS *Einsatzgruppen* in his area of responsibility von Rundstedt had. As in Poland, it soon became clear that their priority was the eradication of the Jews, but with the additional specific responsibility of identifying and executing the commissars. That the Army had no direct control over them is clear. They were answerable to Heydrich in his capacity as Head of the Reich Security Head Office (RSHA). Indeed, the Army did not even have disciplinary powers over Waffen-SS units operating under its command. That von Rundstedt and his fellow senior commanders had little or no knowledge of their activities is more difficult to justify. Many soldiers witnessed Jewish massacres and some even became directly involved. This was widespread enough for Army Group South to issue a general order on 10 August drawing attention to the fact that soldiers were participating in executions in such an 'undesirable manner' that 'drastic measures' had to be taken. Abwehr officers attached to the armies were to confiscate all photographs taken during 'Jewish operations'.[17] Von Rundstedt told the IMT Commission that he actually prohibited soldiers from watching these hideous events.[18] Certainly, on 24 September 1941, he issued an order forbidding soldiers from actively participating or taking photographs, but this was not quite the same.[19] He also told the IMT Commission that these atrocities only took place in the rear areas, which had been handed over to Alfred Rosenberg's civil administration.[20] This, however, is difficult to reconcile with the Berdichev killings, since it is most unlikely that the site of von Rundstedt's own headquarters would have been under civil administration. Indeed, it was not until 1 September that the Ukraine west of the River Sluch, which runs through Tarnopol and is well to the west of Berdichev, was handed over to the Reichskommissar Ukraine.[21] There is also much primary evidence in the form of orders and reports that troops apprehending Jews and other suspicious or undesirable elements should hand them over to the *Einsatzgruppen*.[22]

The justification for detaining members of the local population was often on the grounds of suspected partisan activity. During the early months of the war in the East, partisan activity was uncoordinated and relatively ineffectual. Nevertheless, there were attacks, usually on communications targets like railways and bridges. In Army Group South's area these were especially on the fringes of the Pripet marshes and the Carpathian foothills. Many of the partisans were Russian soldiers who had been cut off from their units during the advance. Army Group South set up a number of security units, often made up of Ukrainian nationalists, in early August, but they were too few for the expanse of captured territory. During July, in order to try and bring some sense to the growing confusion over who constituted a partisan and who a genuine Red Army straggler, OKH issued a series of directives. In essence they stated that soldiers in uniform, with or without arms, were to be considered as prisoners-of-war and treated as such, as were those in civilian clothes who appeared the right age to be conscripts, whether bearing arms or not. Civilians, whether in part uniform or wholly civilian clothes and bearing arms, were to be considered guerrillas, as were those who aided them. Furthermore, those who gave themselves up by a certain date would be assured POW status. Thus Army Group South ordered all stragglers to give themselves up by 18 August or be considered as partisans.[23]

OKW, however, took a very different view of the whole problem of rear area security. A supplement to Hitler's Directive No 33 dated 23 July 1941 laid down:

'The troops available for securing the conquered eastern areas will, considering the vast expanse of these stretches, suffice only if the occupying power meets all resistance, not by legally punishing the guilty, but rather by spreading that type of terror which is the only means of taking from the population any desire for opposition.

The respective commanders are to be held responsible, together with the troops at their disposal, for quiet in their areas. The commanders must find the means to keep their districts in order by employing suitably draconian measures, not by requesting more security forces.'

A further OKW order, dated 16 September, also decreed that for every German soldier murdered behind the front line 'the death penalty for 50–100 Communists should generally be regarded in these cases as suitable atonement'.[24] Thus, while OKH tried to observe the Geneva Convention and Hague Rules of Land Warfare, Hitler and OKW would have none of it, arguing that they did not apply since the Soviet Union no longer existed as a state in German eyes. OKW had its way, and this is reflected in an order issued by von Reichenau on 10 October 1941:

'The primary aim of the campaign against the Jewish Bolshevik system is the complete annihilation of the means of power and the eradication of the Asiatic influence on European culture.

This situation brings forth tasks also for the troops which go beyond the traditional one-sided soldierdom. In the Eastern Territories the soldier is not only a fighter in accordance with the rules of warfare. He also is the bearer of a merciless national ideology and the avenger of all bestial acts inflicted on German related peoples.

That is why the soldier must fully understand the necessity for hard but just retaliation against Jewish sub-humanity. It has the additional aim to choke off incipient revolts in the rear of the Armed Forces which on the basis of experience are always instigated by Jews.'

He went on to criticise slackness in security matters and said that is was 'mistaken human kindness' to make gifts of food and cigarettes to the local population. Those members of the indigenous population not actively pro-German must be regarded as pro-Bolshevik. Finally,

'The soldier must accomplish two things far removed from all political considerations:
1.) Complete annihilation of Bolshevik false teachings, of the Soviet State and of its Armed Forces.
2.) The pitiless eradication of alien treachery and cruelty thus securing the life of the German Armed Forces in Russia.'

Von Rundstedt was clearly impressed by this. Two days later he circulated the order to other formations under his command. The covering letter, personally signed by him, commented:

'. . . I thoroughly concur with its contents. I suggest for your consideration the issue of analogous orders unless this has not been done already. Considering the impending winter season and the weak forces in the rear areas, the frequently encountered carelessness and softness after the actual fighting should not be tolerated.'[25]

Thus, he appears to have been quite happy to use the partisan threat as an excuse for persecuting the Jews, providing that the dirty work was largely left to the SS *Einsatzgruppen*.

Hitler, however, did not come to Berdichev at the beginning of August to admire the handiwork of the *Einsatzgruppen*. His reasons were diplomatic and military. In the former case, he wanted to thank Antonescu personally for the active support that his country had already given to BARBAROSSA and to decorate him with the Knight's Cross. That the support was so, was in no small measure due to the personal relationship between Antonescu and von Rundstedt. As the Field Marshal wrote to Bila: 'For political reasons Anton [sic] appears as an independent commander although I am responsible for operations and he very nicely agrees to everything.'[26] It was the same with the other allied formations under von Rundstedt's command, especially the Hungarians, who frequently brought gifts to von Rundstedt's headquarters.[27] Nevertheless, having this polygot collection under command was not easy:

'The Rumanian divisions were not bad then, although they were afterwards. The mountain divisions in particular were good and the cavalry brigades. But the leadership was beyond description. The officers and NCOs . . .!

I had Hungarians too. I had an absolute League of Nations "Armee". I had Rumanians, Italians, Hungarians, Slovaks, Croats, Germans. All that was lacking was the [Spanish] "Blue Division" and the French, otherwise I had everything. I had Finns, too. With the Hungarians it was like this; they were represented by a motorised corps. They were good actually, but only wanted to get home again quickly and had no proper enthusiasm, even before the winter began. The Slovaks were very good, first-rate, very unassuming, always there. They only formed one "Division" [actually two divisions and a motorised brigade]. The Croats were a band of robbers, there was only one "Regiment"; they were brave fellows, but undisciplined in the extreme. As for the Italians – let's keep silence; terrible people!'[28]

By the time that Hitler arrived at Berdichev, the Russian resistance in the Uman pocket was almost at an end. When it finally ceased on 8 August, the pocket yielded 103,000 prisoners, 300 tanks and 800 guns. Apart from congratulating von Rundstedt on his success, Hitler wanted to impress his future strategy on him. During the previous weeks, in spite of the spectacular progress made by Army Group Centre, he remained set against the idea of Moscow as the primary objective, despite continued urgings by Halder and others. His eyes were firmly fixed on Leningrad in the north, the overrunning of the Crimea, which he viewed as an aircraft carrier posting a direct threat to the Ploesti oilfields, and the Caucasus. In other words, his objectives were now firmly economic rather than military. Halder was visiting Army Group Centre that day and sent Paulus to represent him at Berdichev. Von Rundstedt raised the question of Moscow (Halder claimed that it was at his prompting), but Hitler, as Paulus reported to Halder, dismissed it out of hand. Instead, Army Group Centre was to lose its two Panzer groups, Hoth to the Leningrad operation and Guderian to assist von Rundstedt in overrunning the remainder of the Ukraine. Hitler then departed, having spent four hours at Berdichev. 'Everything went very harmoniously' and Hitler told him that he would be bringing Mussolini to visit him in ten days time, von Rundstedt wrote to Bila.[29] His letters during subsequent days do, however, indicate a growing gloom over the situation, especially Hitler's grandiose plans for Army Group South. 'I have a horror of winter in this country. Who knows where we will be sitting then' (10 August). 'Two years ago, my staff assembled in Neuhammer. How much longer? I have no great hopes that it will be over soon. The vastness of Russia devours us. . . .' (12 August). 'The poor troops, for eight weeks almost daily fighting, and what kind of fighting' (16 August). The problem was that he was being given too many divergent tasks. Besides destroying the Russian armies in his area, overrunning the Caucasus and capturing the Crimea, Hitler had also got a bee in his bonnet about Odessa, which the Russians were determined to defend to the last.

On 27 August Hitler, accompanied by Mussolini, duly made his second visit to von Rundstedt, now at Uman. The purpose was to inspect Messe's corps. Mussolini was not pleased. He later complained to Dino Alfieri, his Press minister, that he was left talking to 'that old Rundstedt' while Hitler harangued the troops.[30] Bila later sent her husband press clippings of the visit and he remarked: 'Musso looks terribly stupid.'[31] The two men clearly had little regard for one another. In the meantime, the fighting continued without relaxation in its intensity. The Rumanians had been given the task of taking Odessa and put it under siege on 17 August, while the German Eleventh Army pressed on to the Crimea. Guderian had received his orders to drive south and link up with von Kleist east of the Dnieper and Kiev, but was not enthused by the prospect of being diverted from Moscow and doubted whether he would get back in time to continue the drive to the capital before winter set in. Von Brauchitsch and Halder, who had been lambasted by Hitler for objecting to his fixation over the importance of the flanks, seized on Guderian as their last card to persuade Hitler that Moscow must be taken above all else. Guderian flew to Rastenburg to see Hitler on 23 August, an interview arranged by Halder. He got nowhere, Hitler apparently commenting crushingly: 'My generals know nothing about the economic aspects of war.'[32] Guderian returned to an expectant OKH, but dashed Halder's hopes by now stating that he was willing to drive south. This made Halder very bitter.[33] While this had been going on, von Reichenau and von Kleist were battling for crossings over the Dnieper north and south of Kiev in the face of continued furious counter-attacks by the Russians.

The weather, however, continued to be a dominant factor. By 4 September, von Rundstedt was writing to Bila: 'Today a cold mean autumn day with rain . . . things are not going fast enough, and patience is not one of my virtues.' Worse, the Field Post was suffering and 'even the couriers are not operating regularly'.[34] This was of special significance since the Field Marshal tried to write to Bila daily, usually a postcard affixed with a six pfennig stamp, supplies of which

Bila used to send him from time to time. He would use air couriers
going back to Germany to post them once they arrived, thus beating the
normal Field Post system. Bila, on the other hand, had to rely on the
latter, but knowing that she was frequently receiving his news gave him
much strength. Von Rundstedt, like Montgomery, was not one to
involve himself in the minutiae of staff work, but operated entirely
through his chief of staff. It was the 'big picture' that concerned him.
He also took pains to relax whenever he could. His daily walk, unarmed
and usually accompanied just by von Salviati,[35] was very important to
him, as it had been from the beginning of the war. He continued to read
crime novels and enjoyed crosswords, with which Bila kept him
supplied. He also liked a drink and, as we shall see, became increasingly dependent on alcohol as the war went on.

On 5 September, Hitler had yet another change of heart. Moscow
was to be the primary objective after all. Even though von Leeb had not
yet reached Leningrad, he was to hand the bulk of his armour over to
von Bock by the end of the month. Likewise, von Rundstedt was to
return Guderian's Panzer group. First, though, the great pocket east of
Kiev must be sealed. Guderian, followed by von Weichs' Second Army,
made good progress, brushing off a counter-attack by the Bryansk
Front. Von Kleist was turning north to meet Guderian and by 9
September von Stülpnagel's Seventeenth Army was across the
Dnieper. Budenny, and Nikita Krushchev, his political commissar,
now realised the danger that faced them. On the 11th they asked Stalin
for permission to withdraw from the Kiev bend, but Stalin was
adamant and the result was that two days later Budenny was replaced
by Timoshenko. Not until 17 September did Stalin relent, but by then it
was too late. Twenty-four hours earlier, the two Panzer groups had
linked up at Lokhvitsa. They had created a pocket with a diameter of
some 130 miles. During the next ten days it was reduced by Second and
Sixth Armies and yielded 450,000 prisoners, representing four Soviet
armies and parts of two others. Kirponos himself was trapped in the
pocket, but did not get out alive. Kiev fell on the 19th and an SS
Einsatzgruppe was soon busy. During 27–28 September over 33,000 Jews
were taken to Babi Yar, a ravine just outside the city, and murdered.
On this, as on many other occasions, Ukrainian nationalists assisted
the SS. What von Rundstedt knew of this at the time or afterwards is
not clear. Certainly, in 1946, even when confronted by a number of
affadavits to the contrary, he was to tell the IMT Commission that the
Einsatzgruppen were answerable only to Himmler and was emphatic on
his lack of knowledge of Jewish atrocities, apart from what was

probably the Berdichev incident.[36] As far as the fighting was concerned, von Rundstedt was writing to Bila on the 12th that the operation '*could* become a really big thing'. On 22 September he was estimating a bag of 300,000 prisoners, and was pleased with the amount of fresh food which his headquarters had, although 'unfortunately our wine stocks get scarce'. On the 30th, writing from Alexandria, another 'pigs quarters', the weather had made him gloomy once more: 'Weather cloudy and cold. The central heating can't cope. . . . Furthermore one has many different worries about how it is supposed to continue. . . . We all have a horror of the winter.'[37]

Part of his gloom was probably because of the Rumanians, who were making heavy weather of the capture of Odessa, which would not finally fall until 16 October. He was, too, very likely saddened by death of the commander of the Eleventh Army, von Schobert, killed when his aircraft landed on a minefield. His place, however, was taken by von Manstein, who was now proceeding to seize the Crimea. At bottom, though, was the concern over Hitler's inceasing demands to drive his increasingly fatigued troops further and further east. Replacements were not keeping pace with casualties, which were mounting, although more through sickness brought about by the endless daily marches of 25 miles or more in the driving autumn rains. Worse, von Rundstedt was forced to give up no less than nine divisions, including two Panzer and two motorised, for the drive on Moscow, Operation TYPHOON. The further east the war took him, the more von Rundstedt pined for his wife. He was also worried over her safety because of the raids by British bombers. Indeed, Kassel was attacked for the first time on the night 8/9 September, although it would not suffer another major raid for almost a year. Thus, on 2 October he wrote to her: 'How might you be my most beloved one? How is your sleep when there is no alarm? My longing for you gets greater and greater.' Next day: 'I am worried and almost melting through longing for you.'[38] He did, however, now have one consolation. From time to time he was able to have long distance telephone conversations with her.[39]

In the meantime, having tidied up the Dnieper, von Rundstedt's armies were pushing on. Von Kleist, his command now entitled First Panzer Army, was driving south-east towards Maruipol on the northern shore of the Sea of Azov. Von Reichenau was advancing east on Kharkov, while between them von Stülpnagel was aiming for the River Donets south of Kharkov. Von Manstein was clearing the Crimea and securing Melitopol, also on the Sea of Azov. Odessa, too, was finally about to fall. The fact, too, that all eyes were now concentrated on

TYPHOON, which had been launched on 30 September, and was developing well, with large pockets being formed around Vyazma and Bryansk, also kept OKH and OKW off von Rundstedt's back. Even so, the weather continued to frustrate him. By mid-October his headquarters had moved to Poltava, east of the Dnieper, and he was already considering this as a suitable spot to remain during the winter.[40] Indeed, he was becoming ever more concerned about the onset of winter and that his troops were becoming increasingly exhausted. The situation was aggravated by the autumn rains, which arrived in the northern part of von Rundstedt's area of operations on 11 October. Sixth and Seventeenth Armies were quickly brought to a halt. Three days later von Kleist, who, in conjunction with Eleventh Army, had trapped two Soviet armies with their backs to the Sea of Azov at the beginning of the month and was now approaching Taganrog, suffered the same experience. As von Rundstedt wrote ruefully to Bila, 'the weather frustrates all plans'.[41] The supply system was also beginning to come apart again. The railway bridges across the Dnieper had been blown by the retreating Russians and consequently the railheads could not be advanced east of the river. Less than half the motor transport was functioning and the forward troops were forced increasingly to live off the land. Even more frustrating was the fact that the Russians decided to cut their losses by falling back to a shorter front in order to be able to create a reserve. This left the Donets Basin, with its rich coal, iron and steel industries, for the taking. Such was the effect of the weather and the lack of supplies that von Kleist was unable to secure the area before the Russians had largely dismantled the industrial equipment and evacuated it behind the Urals. He did, however, take Taganrog on the 17th, while Kharkov fell to von Reichenau on the 24th. After that, von Rundstedt's armies could go no further. Hitler, however, remained determined that the advance was to continue once the frosts had arrived to harden up the ground. This was not greeted with much enthusiasm. Halder commented in his diary on 3 November that '. . . the difficulties of supply and movement have so reduced the fighting spirit that even Hq. AGp. South has caught that pessimism. Some energetic "persuading" would be in order to kick them'.[42] Perhaps he was referring to von Rundstedt himself. For, on the same day he had proposed to von Brauchitsch, who was visiting him, that a halt be called and the offensive continued in the spring, citing the increasing supply problems. Von Brauchitsch answered that these were well understood, but it was vital that Voronezh, Stalingrad and Maikop, just north of the Caucasus Mountains, be reached. These objectives represented a distance of up to 300 miles from Army Group South's present positions and von Rundstedt later recalled 'we laughed aloud when we heard that'.[43] The situation was not helped by von Rundstedt suffering a heart attack at the same time while in the street at Poltava. It was presumably not serious, though, since he remained at duty, but nevertheless a warning that he needed to take more care of himself.[44] A few days later von Brauchitsch, too, had a heart attack.

On 13 November, winter arrived in the Ukraine. The temperature dropped to -20 degrees celsius and the ground hardened overnight. This brought home even more forcibly the problems facing the supply system. The fact was that hardly any winter clothing had been issued to the troops. According to von Rundstedt, 'it is not entirely true that preparations for a winter campaign were not made. The famous winter clothing was there, but it didn't arrive, owing to rail difficulties and road transport.' What angered him was the campaign then launched by Goebbels among the German people at home for collecting winter clothing to send to the troops, which von Rundstedt called 'revolting propaganda' on the grounds that it gave the impression that the Army had done nothing about it.[45] Be that as it may, on 17 November, amid driving snow, von Kleist launched a thrust on Rostov-on-Don, gateway to the Caucasus. It was spearheaded by von Mackensen's III Corps, which comprised Sepp Dietrich's SS Leibstandarte Adolf Hitler, now a motorised division, and 13th and 14th Panzer Divisions. Three days later, the Leibstandarte and supporting tanks broke into the city, securing it by the end of the 21st. III Corps captured 10,000 men, guns, tanks and even two armoured trains. The Russians, though, had not only fought fiercely around Rostov, but now launched a major counter-stroke. The South Front collected 31 divisions and five tank brigades and struck First Panzer Army in its now long and exposed flank. Seventeenth Army to the north could do little to relieve the pressure and von Kleist, fearful of being cut off, issued orders for a withdrawal to the River Mius. At that moment the Russians paused and von Kleist countermanded his order, but on the 25th the attacks resumed, not just on the flank, but also against Rostov. The situation grew desperate and on the 28th von Rundstedt ordered von Kleist to fall back behind the Mius. The Leibstandarte, its men suffering from frostbite, including Dietrich himself, withdrew from Rostov.

It was not until 30 November that the seriousness of the situation was fully realised at OKH and OKW. At 1300 hours von Brauchitsch was summoned by Hitler and treated to a tirade of abuse for having not countermanded von Rundstedt's order. He seems to have made no effort to defend himself and then, on Hitler's command, issued an order to von Rundstedt for von Kleist to withdraw to an intermediary line still east of the Mius. Halder's comment was: 'These people have no conception of the condition of our troops, and keep grinding out ideas in a vacuum.'[46] When von Rundstedt received the OKH order he asked that it be cancelled and, in von Sodenstern's words, went further:

> '. . . Rundstedt with his own hand entered in the daily report . . . a sentence to the following effect: "Should confidence in my leadership no longer exist, I beg to request someone be substituted who enjoys the necessary confidence of the Supreme Command.". . . When in my anxiety I suggested that, with the existing tension, it was possible that Hitler might agree to the request, the Field-Marshal still held to his decision that the passage he had inserted must stand.'[47]

When this report was shown to von Brauchitsch he appears not to have bothered to discuss it with von Rundstedt, but merely passed it up to Hitler as it stood. At 0400 hours the following morning OKH received three signals from Hitler. One was to von Rundstedt, relieving him of his command; the second to von Reichenau, appointing him in the Field Marshal's place and ordering him to halt von Kleist's withdrawal, while Seventeenth Army was to mount an attack towards Voroshilovgrad in order to help relieve the pressure on First Panzer Army. The third ordered tank reinforcements to be delivered to von Kleist. At 1100 hours that same morning, 1 December, Halder was having a telephone conversation with von Sodenstern when von Reichenau cut in to confirm that he was implementing Hitler's order in spite of von Kleist's objections that he could not hold the intermediary line. Indeed, in some places this line was no more than six miles from the Mius and von Kleist, now under considerable Russian pressure, could not understand why he was not allowed to withdraw this short additional distance to what was a clearly more defendable line. Von Sodenstern could not budge his new commander and so Halder persuaded Jodl to present the facts to Hitler. Ninety minutes later, at 1530 hours, von Reichenau telephoned Halder to say that enemy forces had broken through the Leibstandarte's positions on the intermediate line and asked for Hitler's agreement to a withdrawal behind the Mius that night. This was forthcoming, but Halder commented: 'Now we are where we could have been last night. it was a senseless waste of time, and to top it, we lost von Rundstedt also.'[48]

Von Rundstedt did not leave Poltava immediately, probably because he had received no orders on his future, and was still there when

Hitler visited von Kleist's headquarters on the 3rd to see for himself why his orders had not been obeyed. There he met Dietrich, who according to Keitel, 'stood up honourably and incorruptibly for his Army superior, and it was he who succeeded in eliminating the Führer's lack of confidence on this occasion'.[49] Bad weather on the return flight forced Hitler to stage at Poltava. Von Sodenstern:

> 'At about 5 or 5.30pm Hitler had the situation explained to him. By Reichenau's orders the report came through me and I seized the opportunity to describe the events of the previous weeks in unequivocal language, in the course of which my various telephone conversations with Keitel, by order of the C-in-C, and an imploratory telegram addressed to me by Jodl, did not remain unmentioned.
>
> The circle of listeners – Reichenau, the Operations Chief of the Army Group, Schmundt, Engel and several other persons from Hitler's entourage – stiffened into shocked silence. Hitler countered with the words: "You will understand, General, that I am angry because no one reported any of these occurrences to me." To which I replied: "I can quite understand, Fuehrer, that you have heard nothing in this connection." Hitler rejoined: "Where is Field-Marshal von Rundstedt?" The latter was waiting, in accordance with instructions, in another room. There, as von Rundstedt described to me immediately afterwards, a scene of reconciliation took place, in which Hitler excused himself on the grounds of a "misunderstanding", begged the Field-Marshal to see that his health was restored by a period of sick leave and then once more place his incomparable services at his [Hitler's] disposal.'[50]

Two days later von Rundstedt left Poltava in a special train, with bands playing, a guard of honour, and all the staff there to bid him farewell. He was not the only one to come unstuck at this time. One of his fellow army group commanders was also dismissed. In von Bock's case it was because of the failure of TYPHOON, which had ground to a halt 19 miles short of Moscow and was now facing a furious Russian counteroffensive. Von Brauchitsch, his decline in health aggravated by being used as a football by Hitler and the field commanders, tendered his resignation. Hitler did not replace him, and appointed himself Commander-in-Chief.

No sooner had the Field Marshal returned to Kassel and his beloved Bila than he met with a surprise. On 12 December, his 66th birthday, Schmundt visited him at home. The purpose was to give him a cheque for RM250,000, a gift from the Führer in recognition of his distinguished services. Von Rundstedt was clearly taken aback and embarrassed by this since he did not cash it and still had not done so two months later. He was, however, not the only one whom Hitler financially rewarded at this time. Guderian, von Brauchitsch and Sepp Dietrich were among others who received cheques, although not for such a large amount. The fact that von Rundstedt did not cash his caused a stir in the Reichs Chancellery. Eventually, in 22 February, after being pressured by Schmundt, von Rundstedt wrote to Dr Hans Lammers, Chief of the Reichs Chancellery and Hitler's closest legal adviser, to ask what he should do:

> 'I intended to use the cheque *after* [sic] the victorious end of the war for the purchase of my new home and to leave the cheque in my bank safe until then as one cannot make any purchasing decisions now during the war. And I still hope to be able to somehow serve the Führer and the Fatherland again next spring once my health is restored. I now assume that the cheque must be cashed for technical reasons of clearing and I would be very much obliged to you, dear honoured Reichsminister, if you could tell me briefly what in your opinion I should do with the cheque.'

Lammers, in his reply, explained to the Field Marshal that the sum did not attract income tax, but was liable to property tax whether the cheque had been cashed or not. Hence von Rundstedt should pay it in as soon as possible in order to be able to settle the tax with the interest that it would attract. Consequently, on 5 March, almost three months after he had received it, von Rundstedt finally cashed the cheque.[51] This, however, was not the end of the story. Von Rundstedt himself refused to have anything to do with the money, referring to it in the family as *Saugeld* (dirt money).[52] He passed control of it over to Ditha, who invested it. In spite of the severe devaluation of the German currency, when the Deutschmark replaced the Reichsmark after the war, and its temporary confiscation by the Allies, a sum remained in being. The family never touched it until after Ditha's death in April 1982 when it was used to pay for her funeral, there still being a little left over even after this.[53]

During his time at home, von Rundstedt was required to perform one official duty. This was to represent Hitler at the state funeral of von Reichenau.[54] The circumstances of his death must, however, have caused von Rundstedt a wry smile, bearing in mind his comments on von Reichenau's fanaticism for physical fitness. On 15 January he went for his normal morning jog, but after lunch began to feel unwell and collapsed with a cerebral haemorrhage. He died two days later of heart failure while being flown from Poltava to a clinic in Leipzig. As for von Rundstedt, his recall to active duty was to come more quickly than he expected.

9
Return to France

On 10 March 1942, Hitler summoned von Rundstedt to Rastenburg and informed him that he was to take over from the ailing Erwin von Witzleben as Commander-in-Chief West and Army Group D, since the latter had to go to hospital, suffering from haemorrhoids. No secret was made of his recall and his visit to Rastenburg was broadcast on German newsreels. The Allies, however, concluded from this that von Rundstedt was being given another command on the Eastern Front and did not realise until mid-April that he was in France.

It is difficult to establish just how genuinely enthusiastic von Rundstedt was to be recalled to active duty. Having already suffered one heart attack, and bearing in mind his age, there must have still been a question mark over his medical condition. True, Paris was a little less demanding than returning to a combat command in Russia, but now that America had entered the war the prospect that the Allies might attempt to re-enter the Continent at some stage was more likely than it had been before December 1941. By the same token, the prospects of an early and victorious end to the war for Germany were greatly diminished. Whatever von Rundstedt thought, there is no doubt that the traditional Prussian concept of Duty would have been uppermost in his mind. If his country needed his services once more, then he would give them. Even so, the wrench of parting again from Bila was hard: '. . . I have, like you, to get used to this awful life of separation. *How* [sic] great my longing for you is you can probably judge from yourself, my most beloved one', as he wrote immediately on arrival in Paris.[1]

Von Witzleben himself had already departed for hospital, but suffered a grievous blow in the death of his wife just as von Rundstedt arrived. It would seem, however, that von Rundstedt was appointed only in an acting capacity. 'Now one wracks one's brains over what will happen to me if he [von Witzleben] turns up again, if only to have a job as a distraction. It is rumoured *him*: army group, *I* Commander-in-Chief West. I cannot imagine that the Führer will remove me again immediately after his recent remarks.'[2] The esteem in which Hitler once more held him was reinforced on 22 March, the fiftieth anniversary of the day he first joined 83rd Infantry Regiment. He presented von Rundstedt with a portrait of von Moltke the Elder by Leutebach. Even so, it was not until 1 May that he was confirmed in his posts of C-in-C West and C-in-C Army Group D.

The main and immediate problem that von Rundstedt faced was the complicated command structure that existed in Occupied Western Europe. There was no unified chain of command, but a host of diverse elements, none wholly answerable to him. His authority, such as it was, was defined in Hitler's Directive No 40 dated 23 March 1942.[3] In essence, von Rundstedt held supreme operational authority in the West only for the defence of the coast against invasion. In this respect alone were the naval and Luftwaffe commands answerable to him. Otherwise, Admiral Krancke, commanding Western Naval Group, and Hugo Sperrle's Luftflotte 3 were directly under Raeder and Goering respectively. There were, too, the Military Governors of France and Belgium, Karl-Heinrich von Stülpnagel, who had relinquished command of Seventeenth Army in October 1941 and taken up this new appointment just before von Rundstedt arrived, and Nikolaus von Falkenhausen. Responsible for internal security and political affairs, they took most of their orders direct from OKW. Theoretically under them were the two Higher SS and Police Leaders, Carl Oberg in Paris and his opposite number in Brussels, but these two usually reported direct to Himmler. The German Foreign Office was also involved, especially through Otto Abetz, ambassador to Vichy France, as was Albert Speer (who had recently succeeded as Minister of Armaments and Munitions on the death of Fritz Todt) through the Todt Organisation, which was responsible for constructing the Atlantic Wall.

In the Netherlands, the situation was even more complicated. Here there was no military governor, but a Reichs Commissioner, Arthur Seyss-Inquart. There was a Wehrmacht commander, General Friedrich Christiansen of the Luftwaffe, but he dealt directly with OKW on most matters, being under von Rundstedt's command solely for coastal defence. It was all part of Hitler's policy of 'divide and rule', while he himself provided an all-pervading influence. Given this situation, it is not surprising that von Rundstedt would later make the angry comment to Geyr von Schweppenburg at St Germain: 'You see the guard posted outside. If I want to post him on the other side of the house I must first ask the permission of Berchtesgaden.'[4] No wonder that he became increasingly exasperated. One small compensation was that in April 1942 he was given a very competent chief of staff, General Kurt Zeitzler, whom he knew well from the previous year when Zeitzler was von Kleist's chief of staff. He had had a rapid rise since the beginning of the war when he was a mere regimental commander. According to von Mellenthin he was abrupt in manner, but a master of detail[5], just what von Rundstedt liked in a chief of staff.

At the time von Rundstedt arrived in France, the strength of the forces under him was gradually being increased from a low of 18 divisions during the winter 1940–41 to 25 by June 1942. They were organised into three armies under Army Group D. Responsibility for the coastal defence of south-west France down to the Spanish border was given to First Army. North-western France, from the River Loire to Caen, was covered by Seventh Army, and from there to Zeebrugge by Fifteenth Army. Christiansen was responsible for the Dutch coast. Shortly after von Rundstedt assumed command, on the night 27/28 March, a British amphibious force made a raid on the port of St Nazaire, its aim being to destroy the dry dock there. The aim was achieved, although at some cost in casualties. It was this event, as much as anything, which caused Hitler to order the construction of the Atlantic Wall. His belief was that static coastal fortifications would be sufficient to repel any invader. It was, of course, a mammoth undertaking, and when work began in spring 1942, priority was given to the defence of the Atlantic and Channel ports. Initially, this was von Rundstedt's main concern, but it was a project over which he would become increasingly disillusioned.

Shortly after the end of the war, von Rundstedt wrote a memorandum for the British on the French Resistance. In it he commented:

> 'During the year 1942 the underground movement in France was still confined to bearable limits. Murders and attacks on members of the Wehrmacht, as well as sabotage, were common and trains were frequently derailed. A real danger for the German troops and a real obstruction to troop movements did not, however, exist.[6]'

Even so, when incidents did occur, the occupation forces reacted harshly. Goebbels noted in his diary in April that after the sabotage of a railway line, the military commander had taken thirty hostages – Jews and 'persons close to the perpetrators' – and these would be shot, as well as eight others, and a further one thousand Jews and Communists transported to the East, if those responsible were not caught within three days.[7] It is not clear whether von Rundstedt was directly involved at this stage in this policy, but bearing in mind the command structure, it was probably authorised by the Military Governor. Certainly von Stülpnagel's predecessor, his cousin Otto, had set the precedent of shooting hostages, especially after the first murder of a Wehrmacht member, a naval officer, in the Paris Métro in August 1941. However, the Resistance would make its presence increasingly felt.

After the Eastern Front, France did have its compensations. On arrival, von Rundstedt had commented to Bila: '. . . it is totally peaceful here, the thousands of people who are taking their afternoon stroll look very elegant and content. What a difference from Kassel and Berlin!'[8] He was also once more able to send food parcels to her, Ditha and the grandchildren, and at one stage 'soap, a toothbrush and a sponge',[9] an indication of the increasing shortages in Germany. On 28 April, Ditha gave birth in Berlin to her fourth child, a daughter also called Editha. That same month, Hans Gerd was posted to The Hague. He seems to have been able to make a number of visits to his father and even persuaded him to accompany him on visits to places of cultural interest. Unfortunately, von Rundstedt's headquarters was no longer at St Germain, but in Paris itself, and he was dissatisfied with this. He records going to have lunch with Blaskowitz, now commanding Fifteenth Army, at his 'charming' headquarters in Fontainebleu. In comparison, Paris was a 'dirty hole' and 'atrocious, especially during the holidays when it gets so crowded'. He may, however, have been more than usually irritated since earlier that morning he had been kept awake from 0330 hours by 'constant air explosions'.[10] This probably referred to a raid by twenty RAF Whitley bombers on the Gnome & Rhône aero-engine factory at Gennevillers on the outskirts of Paris. The first hotel in which they were quartered proved to be 'not good enough for the spoilt staff', and they moved to another, but 'I only wish we could be back at St Germain', the Field Marshal wrote to Bila on 6 May.[11] Eventually, however, he did get his way and the headquarters returned to the Henri IV.

On 9 July 1942, von Rundstedt received a telegram from Hitler. It warned of the likelihood of enemy landings in his area of operations. The evidence for this was the assembly of landing craft on the south coast of England, agents' reports and reduced RAF activity during the past few days. Hitler considered that the most likely areas were the coast between Dieppe and Le Havre, Normandy, Brittany and the southern part of the Dutch coast. In addition, an airborne threat existed against main supply routes, airfields and headquarters. In order to help counter this Hitler had ordered the transfer to the west of two SS divisions, the Leibstandarte and Das Reich.[12] The Germans were correct to deduce that the British were up to something, and, according to von Rundstedt, had had their suspicions since mid-June.[13] They had, however, no idea of the specific target, which was Dieppe. The operation itself, originally codenamed RUTTER, had been under consideration since March, but was not formally presented to the British Chiefs of Staff for approval until mid-May. Mountbatten, then Chief of Combined Operations, wanted to explore the problems of an opposed landing and RUTTER seemed ideal as a vehicle for this. Selected to carry it out was 2nd Canadian Division, then under command of Montgomery's South-Eastern Army, and he conducted two landing exercises during June. It was probably the assembly of landing craft for these which first aroused German suspicions. The attack itself was planned for 4 July, but after a spell of bad weather, it was decided on the 7th to postpone it until August, although Montgomery now wanted to cancel it entirely, since the troops taking part had already been briefed and there was a danger of compromise. Now came a spell of waiting, not just for those taking part, but for the Germans as well.

Von Rundstedt clearly felt the strain of this. On 14 July he wrote to Bila that 'this waiting for the "others" is getting on my nerves' and saw it as the exact opposite to the weeks at Koblenz leading up to 10 May 1940.[14] In view of the number of possible places where the attack could come, he was careful to position his mobile forces so that they could quickly get anywhere in the threatened areas of coast. At the time when the threat first became apparent, there were only two Panzer divisions in France, 10th, which had arrived from Russia in May to refit in the Amiens area, and 27th, which was just being formed and was still very incomplete. Von Rundstedt would therefore have much welcomed the two SS Panzergrenadier divisions which Hitler had promised him. They arrived towards the end of July under Paul Hausser's I SS Panzer Grenadier Corps. The SS Leibstandarte paraded in Paris on the 29th, with von Rundstedt taking the salute, and was then deployed to the Evreux-Dreux area west of Paris, while the SS Das Reich was sent to south-west France. Von Rundstedt himself visited the Leibstandarte on 13 August and apparently stayed talking to Dietrich until midnight. The Leibstandarte's official historian used this as evidence of the high regard in which von Rundstedt held Dietrich.[15] The Field Marshal's post-war view on him was that he was 'decent but stupid'[16] and that SS commanders 'like Sepp Dietrich looked to us for support because they felt very uncertain as regards their commands, and none of the "Divisionskommandeurs" or GOCs [General Officers Commanding] or whatever they were, knew what to do'.[17] Bearing in mind the crucial role which the Leibstandarte had, it is probable that he wanted to make certain that Dietrich understood the plans. On the other hand, he would have known of Dietrich's intervention with Hitler after the Rostov withdrawal and may well have wanted to thank him personally. Dietrich's cognac and his respect for senior officers of the 'old school' would have also been appreciated.[18]

During this period of waiting, von Rundstedt issued an order, which was to become the basis of one of the war crimes with which he was charged after the war. Dated 21 July 1942 and entitled *Principle Order of the Commander-in-Chief West No 13* it read in part:

> '*Enemy Parachute and Airborne Landing Attempts*:
> For the treatment of parachutists the following is ordered: Parachutists who are taken prisoner not in connection with battle actions have to be transferred immediately to the nearest office of the Gestapo with information to the competent counter-intelligence office. In this connection it is unimportant whether the arrested are in uniform or not. The purpose of this measure is to prevent speedily the civilian population from assisting the enemy in its sabotage, terror, espionage and destructive efforts. Parachutists and airborne troops which come into the custody of the troops in connection with battle actions are treated according to the present orders, except for saboteurs and spies who are recognised as such by the troops and who have to be treated accordingly.'[19]

This, of course, was in advance of Hitler's infamous Commando Order of October 1942. Two points should, however, be made. First, given the airborne threat which existed at the time, it made sense to spell out the difference between organised bodies of troops and agents of the Special Operations Executive being dropped to assist the Resistance. Secondly, von Rundstedt's brief did not cover internal security and it was logical that agents, whose purpose was to organise espionage and unrest among the civil population, should be handed over to the competent authority for disposal. Where the order was legally more questionable was over the handing over of uniformed personnel operating behind the lines, in spite of the implication that this was in the context of stirring up the civil population.

Meanwhile, the troops in the West continued to wait. On 15 August von Rundstedt was considering an attack to be even more likely, 'especially after Churchill's visit to Moscow',[20] where he had been to inform Stalin that there would be no Second Front in 1942. Four days later, Operation JUBILEE, as the raid on Dieppe was now called, finally took place. The disaster that befell the Canadians has been recounted many times and it is not necessary to go into it again. Suffice to say that 10th Panzer Division was correctly positioned and able to react quickly and few of the attackers got off the beach. It seems that von Rundstedt had been planning a trip somewhere, but had to cancel it because of the raid and was 'pretty busy from early to late'.[21] Zeitzler visited Dieppe the following day and reported that 'it looked incredible, mountains of dead Englishmen, sunken ships, etc'. Two days later, von Rundstedt himself visited and handed out Iron Crosses, noting that the battlefield was '*very* impressive'. He was, however, surprised to receive a congratulatory telegram from Marshal Pétain, with whom he had had no contact until now, and to which he was allowed to reply. 'Funny, isn't it?', he commented to Bila.[22]

No sooner had the dust settled over Dieppe than von Rundstedt began to worry about Bila's safety. This was with justification, since on the night 27/28 August Kassel was attacked by over 300 bombers, which caused widespread damage. Writing to his wife next day, von Rundstedt considered that things would probably become 'lively' now that 'Churchill the swine is back in London'.[23] Two weeks later, he reported to Bila that the British had 'got cheeky again'.[24] He was probably referring to a raid made by one of the crack British Commando units, the small Scale Raiding Force (SSRF), Operation AQUATINT, on the Normandy coast just east of what in June 1944 would be Omaha Beach. It went disastrously wrong with all the landing party being killed or captured, apart from one officer. The graves of the three who were killed are in a churchyard of the village of St Laurent. That of the commander, Major Gus March-Phillipps, records that he was killed in action on 12 September, but the other two indicate that his companions were shot on the following day. The exact circumstances are difficult to establish, but it is possible that they may have been shot in pursuance of von Rundstedt's Parachutist order. If this was so or not, in October 1942 Hitler issued his secret Commando Order. This had been triggered by another SSRF raid, this time on Sark in the Channel Islands on the night of 3/4 October. During the course of it, the Commandos bound some German soldiers they had captured in order to make it easier to get them back to the waiting boat. Some had to be abandoned and hence the Germans discovered what had happened. German propaganda held this up as just the latest atrocity practised by the Commandos and ordered the fettering of almost 1400 British POWs in retaliation. Hitler resolved to retaliate in kind, and hence the Commando Order dated 18 October 1942. The most significant part of it read:

> 'From now on, all men operating against German troops in so-called Commando raids in Europe or in Africa, are to be annihilated to the last man. This is to be carried out whether they be soldiers in uniform, or saboteurs, with or without arms; and whether fighting or seeking to escape; and it is equally immaterial whether they come into action from ships and aircraft, or whether they land by parachute. Even if these individuals on discovery make obvious their intention of giving themselves up as prisoners, no pardon is on any account to be given.'[25]

The first victims of this order were captured members of No 2 Commando who had taken part in an abortive operation against a power station at Glomfjord in northern Norway in September. In December, however, came Operation FRANKTON, an ambitious and successful raid against German blockade-runners at Bordeaux. It was carried out by ten canoeists, led by Major 'Blondie' Hasler, who paddled their way ninety miles up the Gironde to reach their target. Two members of the team were drowned, and two, including Hasler himself, eventually got back to England, by courtesy of the French Resistance. The other six were captured and shot. After the war the Allies used this as a basis of another of the charges against von Rundstedt, in that it was evidence that he had been responsible for the execution of the Commando Order. It would appear, however, that it was the German Navy who had captured and shot these men. Although Admiral Doenitz testified that von Rundstedt had authority over tactical operations on land by the Navy, no evidence exists that he ordered the executions and, bearing in mind his very restricted authority over Navy Group West, it is likely that the Navy carried out the executions on its own accord.[26] At Nuremberg von Rundstedt himself declared that not a single man had lost his life in the West as a result of the order. When asked why, in that case, he had, in 1944, informed OKW that the Commando Order had been carried out, von Rundstedt replied that the words that he actually used were 'the Order has been followed'. If he had openly refused to obey it he would have been dismissed and hence he had tried to evade the issue by using the word 'followed' rather than 'carried out'.[27]

During this time von Rundstedt had become occupied in a new development, which significantly affected his area of responsibility. On 8 November 1942 the Allies landed in French North Africa and the Vichy regime in Algeria, Morocco and Tunisia, after little more than a gesture of resistance, went over to the Allied side. Apart from rushing reinforcements across the Mediterranean to Tunisia, Hitler ordered von Rundstedt to put into a effect a contingency plan for which the German forces in the West had been prepared since 1940. This was Operation ANTON, the military occupation of Vichy France. On the 11th, German troops moved in. Von Rundstedt himself went by train to Vichy to give Pétain formal notification of the occupation. They met in the Hotel du Parc, von Rundstedt accompanied by the German minister to Vichy, Krug von Nedda, and Hitler's personal liaison officer to the Vichy Government, von Renthe-Fink. Pétain then read out a note of protest:

> 'I have during this night received a letter from the Führer, in which he informs me that the military necessities force him to take measures which have the effect of destroying the content and basis of the [June 1940] armistice agreement. I solemnly protest against decisions which are incompatible with the armistice conventions.'[28]

With that he handed the note to von Rundstedt, who did not reply, but, according to Jean Perré, Director-General of the Republican Guard who was present, 'stated his readiness to receive it, folded it in four, tucked it into the cuff of the sleeve of his uniform. The two diplomats who accompanied Marshal von Rundstedt and who realised the significance of this note tried to indicate that he must refuse it, but were too late.'[29] Von Rundstedt then returned to his train, while Pétain arranged for the text of the note to be broadcast on Vichy radio. Plunged as he was into unfamiliar waters, the incident had starkly revealed von Rundstedt's political naivety. Worse, though, was in store for the Vichy French. Hitler now ordered Pétain to disband what was left of the French Army on the grounds that the German occupation of the rest of France had disaffected it. On 10 December, the Marshal had an interview with von Rundstedt in order to make a protest. Martin Du Gard, a Toulouse journalist based at Vichy, described in his diary what took place. Pétain warned that the dissolution of the Army would create anarchy and was 'an absurd vengeance, unworthy of the German Army'. France had been defeated, but Germany also now risked losing the war. All Pétain had wanted to achieve was for his country to live with Germany without it becoming a tragedy for France. Above all he wanted their two countries to be reconciled. Von Rundstedt appears to have said little if anything and the interview lasted just fifteen minutes and was in French, which von Rundstedt understood 'well', although, according to Du Gard, he did not speak it very fluently. The Field

Marshal then left the room 'with his eyes watering'.[30] Von Rundstedt
held Pétain 'in the highest regard' and believed that if he had not taken
charge in 1940, 'Hitler would have certainly robbed France of all
independence and made a kind of "protectorate" of her'.[31] Thus he had
the utmost sympathy for Pétains's position and was very taken by the
dignity with which he pleaded his case. The two men now began to
develop a very special relationship, the cement that bound it being their
mutual respect for one another as soldiers. Not only would von
Rundstedt do his utmost to ensure that France did retain some form of
army, but he also tried to persuade Hitler to give a guarantee that
France would be accorded a special position in the New Europe which
Hitler planned to create after the victorious end to the war.

Von Rundstedt was not, however, prepared to become involved in
French politics. General Alexander Freiherr von Neubronn had been
appointed as his liaison officer to Vichy after ANTON. Pétain was
desperately keen to get rid of his prime minister, Pierre Laval, whom he
had already sacked in December 1940, but who had been reinstated at
German insistence in April 1942. The grounds for this were Laval's
general unpopularity. Pétain explained this to von Neubronn and
asked him to enlist the Commander-in-Chief's help. Von Rundstedt,
however, refused to have anything to do with it, saying that the matter
would have to go through the German Embassy. He told von Neubronn
that in future he was to concern himself solely with military matters.
Even so, the Embassy got to hear of von Neubronn's 'meddling' and complained to von Rundstedt, who successfully protected his emissary from
trouble. The Field Marshal also, according to von Neubronn, shut his
ears to the growing complaints over executive power in France increasingly being handed over to the SS, Gestapo and Party organisations.[32]

The military occupation of Vichy France also produced another
complication, this time with the Italians. The area east of the River
Rhône was their sphere of influence, but the Germans were naturally
concerned about the defence of the French Riviera against amphibious
assault. Delicate negotiations were carried out between Berlin and
Rome and it was agreed that the Italian Fourth Army, which covered
the coast from the frontier to just east of Marseilles, should be placed
under von Rundstedt's operational command for coastal defence only.
To this end, an Italian liaison team under General Marazzini, who had
commanded the Celere Motorised Division in Russia and was known to
the Field Marshal, was attached to his headquarters. General Vercellino, commanding the Fourth Army, made an early visit to Paris and,
on his return, his chief of staff wrote to von Rundstedt's chief of staff

saying that Vercellino had described the German High Command in Paris as 'a splendid binomial – the highest character, on the one part; the most lucid intelligence, on the other'.[33] The first compliment referred to von Rundstedt, the second to Günther Blumentritt.

The reason for Blumentritt being so praised was that he had now taken over from Zeitzler as Chief of Staff. The cause of this was Halder's growing disillusionment with the way that the war on the Eastern Front was being conducted by Hitler. By September 1942, Hitler had become mesmerised by Stalingrad and an increasing number of troops were being diverted from what had been the main aim for 1942, the overrunning of the Caucasus, in order to support the drive by Sixth Army, now commanded by Paulus, on Stalingrad itself. Halder increasingly objected to this and so Hitler cast around for someone whom he thought would be more pliable. Just before or on 20 September, Schmundt had visited von Rundstedt 'in the name of the *Obersten* [highest – Hitler]' and told him that he was to lose Zeitzler. 'Very sad', wrote von Rundstedt to his wife. 'On the other hand, I am thankful that old Blumentritt was sent to me.'[34] Halder, in fact, resigned on 24 September, four days after von Rundstedt had written to Bila and it would seem that if he had not done so he would have been sacked. Zeitzler replaced him, holding down the post amid ever more mounting frustrations until July 1944. As for Blumentritt, since leaving von Rundstedt's staff in Autumn 1940, he had been Chief of Staff Fourth Army on the Eastern Front and then, from January 1942, headed the Operations branch of OKH. He was now to forge an intimate relationship with von Rundstedt which would last right up to the latter's death.

By the beginning of 1943, the tide was on the turn for the Axis. Rommel had been driven out of Libya and the Axis forces in North Africa were now facing the Allies on two fronts in Tunisia. Bad weather was restricting the U-boats in the Atlantic and the remorseless build-up of American forces in Britain continued. At Casablanca, Churchill and Roosevelt had declared their policy of unconditional surrender. It was on the Eastern Front, however, that the news was grimmest. The German Sixth Army was fighting for its life in the Stalingrad pocket, a life that was to be finally extinguished on 2 February. Bodo Zimmermann, von Rundstedt's chief of operations, recalled how the Field Marshal reacted to the news:

> '. . . the Field Marshal, when I entered his office, was as spruce and youthful as ever. No matter what the circumstances, Rundstedt always

managed to look as neat as a new pin. But this morning his manner was one of deep depression. His first words told me why: "Stalingrad," he said, "has fallen. Now what?"'[35]

What it did do was to rekindle the smouldering embers of resistance to Hitler, and it was natural that those so involved should again try to bring von Rundstedt actively on to their side. While Sixth Army was still fighting, Helmut Groscurth of the Abwehr, who was in the pocket, persuaded a friend of his, Major Count Alfred von Waldersee, to fly to Berlin and to ask Ludwig Beck to visit von Rundstedt. He himself would write to von Manstein to help get Hitler deposed so that Paulus's men could be saved. Apparently, both von Manstein and von Rundstedt refused to act.[36] Then, in February 1943, von Manstein rowed with Hitler over the latter's insistence that he should hold on to the Donets basin, now an exposed salient, as a result of the Russian post-Stalingrad counter-offensive. This moved Engel, still Hitler's Army Adjutant, to visit von Rundstedt, whom he knew well, having been his orderly officer on several occasions.

> 'In a frank way I reported everything which has recently taken place and said that his intervention and demands were expected. I declared that Führer would give in if HE [sic] made himself the spokesman of all the Field Marshals. Result is shattering. Von Rundstedt rejects everything, and resignedly says literally: "Why always silly old me? Just let von Manstein and von Kluge do it." He said he was too old and had had enough. The only thing he still wanted was to die in harness.'[37]

A few days later, Goebbels noted in his diary: 'We must certainly be on our guard about the old Wehrmacht and Reichswehr generals. We have very few good friends among them. They are trying to play us off one against the other.'[38] Perhaps, therefore, von Rundstedt may have been right not to display overt support for the plotters at this stage. Even so, according to an Italian naval officer interrogated by the British in September 1943 and who had visited von Rundstedt's headquarters before it moved back to St Germain, the Engel visit was openly discussed among his staff and von Rundstedt made no secret of his own attitude. Indeed, he allowed his staff to openly criticise the régime, although he himself was careful of his own utterances.[39]

Von Rundstedt had other problems on his mind at this time. The question of how to smooth Pétain's ruffled feathers continued to bother him. On 10 January, he had had a meeting with the Marshal and expressed his sympathy for the latter's desire to keep the 'armistice army' in being. Indeed, he agreed to handing back training centres in southern France to the French, and tried to make more modern arms available in the hope that this new army would help the Germans guard the coasts of France. He also agreed that the Milice, the Vichy police force which had already achieved a notorious reputation for its pursuit of those French people who were determined to resist the occupying forces, as well as its growing persecution of the Jews, should be allowed to form small units for the protection of the Vichy Government. He would not, however, allow them to be equipped with weapons from the disbanded French Army.[40]

Of greater concern was his primary task, that of defending occupied Western Europe against Allied invasion. Von Rundstedt believed from the outset that the only way to counter an amphibious invasion would be to defeat it on the beaches. This required mobile reserves so deployed as to be able to react with sufficient speed, as 10th Panzer Division had at Dieppe. However, Hausser's reserve of seasoned SS mechanised divisions, had returned to the Eastern Front at the beginning of 1943. 10th Panzer Division, too, had been taken from him, sent to Tunisia to hold back the Anglo-American forces there. In return, OKH had agreed, in autumn 1942, to the formation of two motorised divisions in France, but both were low calibre. The only other mobile troops available to the C-in-C West were two SS Panzer Grenadier divisions, 9th and 10th, which also began to form in France in the early spring. It would be some while before these could be considered ready for action. In the meantime, von Rundstedt was left with no viable reserve to cover the lengthy coastlines. A further problem was that, in the aftermath of the Stalingrad débâcle, Hitler, who loathed to have any formation struck off the order of battle, ordered that the divisions lost there be reformed. Von Rundstedt received a total of two Panzer, three Panzer Grenadier and six infantry divisions. This looked impressive on paper, but they arrived as just skeleton cadres and, having been brought back up to strength, were all posted away by the autumn. Another aggravation was that some of his better battalions were also transferred piecemeal and all he received in return were low-grade elements of 'Eastern volunteers', a motley collection consisting largely of former prisoners of war, Russians and others.

Hitler, absorbed as he was by the Eastern Front, believed that the Atlantic Wall was enough to keep the invader at bay. Von Rundstedt, on the other hand, took a more cynical view. He is reported to have called it 'an illusion, staged by propaganda to deceive the German people and the Allies'.[41] Even so, shortage of material and labour meant that progress in constructing it was slow. At one point, in October 1942, von Rundstedt had, perhaps in desperation, proposed that Russian POWs be used 'if no political or other reasons are opposed to this move, which I cannot judge'. The advantages of using the Russians were that they were 'satisfied with very little' and hence easy to 'feed and house', they were simple souls not vulnerable to propaganda, they did not speak French and hence were easier to control and 'if he does not behave, he can simple be shot'.[42] This proposal was to form the basis of another of the war crimes charges later levelled against him.

Von Rundstedt's frustrations drove him to drink increasing amounts and his staff became concerned, especially over his tendency to speak his mind too much in evening telephone conversations, especially with OKW. They feared that some of his franker comments would reach Hitler's ears and bring about his demise. None of them, not even von Salviati or Blumentritt, could get through to him and hence it was arranged that Hans Gerd should take over as his ADC.[43] There is, however, evidence that von Rundstedt was also becoming fed up with being pestered by von Salviati to join the anti-Hitler plotters and that this may have contributed to von Salviati being relieved of his post.[44] As it was, von Salviati was posted as riding instructor, but was arrested after the July 1944 Bomb Plot and summarily executed. Bila, too, had become concerned over her husband's health and arranged with her son for a medical report to be sent to her. He himself wrote to her on his father's medical conditions in early March 1943:

> 'Surely you have already looked at the report about Father's medical condition which you asked for . . . Dr Mock in a thoroughly frank discussion emphasised that Father's physical condition was faultless, heart and lungs are healthy. He considers that the momentary lapse in Father's constitution as primarily psychological, as a consequence of heavy and difficult responsibilities. Of course, he [Mock] has little influence, whereas I have more as the son. He thinks that my main task is to create a cheerful atmosphere around Father and I am supposed to visit very often. . . . In view of his good constitution, Dr Mock does not consider the consequences of a somewhat plentiful nicotine and alcohol consumption, together with not enough food, as worrying. . . . Thus, I believe, dear Mother, that you don't have to worry seriously. . . . Of course it is a pity that you can't be here to take care of Father.'[45]

The implication of this is that von Rundstedt was depressed and goes someway to explain what he had said to Engel when he visited in February.

Shortly after this von Rundstedt's headquarters moved back to St Germain, and Hans Gerd was able to report to Bila that the Field Marshal 'immediately feels much better again than in Paris'.[46] Hans Gerd and Dr Mock, a Major in the Medical branch (*Oberstabsartz*), whom Hans Gerd described as 'a very sympathetic man from Freiburg',[47] had been working hard, however, to get the Field Marshal away for a cure. Presumably on Mock's recommendation, they chose a sanatorium at Bad Tölz. It was successfully engineered and, on 5 May, von Rundstedt received a signal from OKH's Personnel Branch informing him that Hitler had granted him sick leave.[48] On the eve of von Rundstedt's departure, Hans Gerd wrote to Bila, who was going to join her husband at Bad Tölz: 'Perhaps it won't always be easy when father rails about the treatment. But if the cure is really to have an effect he just has to hold out for at least four weeks at Tölz.' The Field Marshal was not to be excited and 'has to eat and sleep regularly and dedicate himself to the cure'. Hans Gerd had also arranged for Ditha to come and join them on 9 June. She, too, needed a break, coping as she was with four children from ages of seven downwards, often without help, since her maids seem to have had a tendency to fall ill.[49] Hans Gerd instructed his mother not to tell his father this yet, since he must not have an excuse to become excited.[50] As it happened, Ditha was not able to get away and would not see her father-in-law again until well after the end of the war.

Von Rundstedt duly departed from his cure and it was probably at this time that his staff arranged to have an underground air raid shelter constructed at the headquarters. Von Rundstedt had shown no interest in this or in his personal security. Perhaps he was reassured by an occurrence which, according to Bodo Zimmermann he recounted in the headquarters mess. Apparently he was taking his daily walk in St Germain when the air raid sirens began to howl. Meeting an elderly Frenchwoman carrying her shopping he asked her why she was not frightened. 'Why should I be afraid, *mon Maréchal?* They won't bomb St Germain. It has no military significance, for nothing ever happens here.' Zimmermann also said that on von Rundstedt's return from his cure there was an air raid warning and, after much difficulty Hans Gerd eventually persuaded his father to go to the shelter. Zimmermann was busy on the telephone and forgot about the Field Marshal. 'An hour later my telephone rang. It was the Field Marshal who simply asked, in his usual courteous fashion: "Zimmermann, can I please come out now?"'[51]

Von Rundstedt's cure seems to have gone well. On completing it, he and Bila moved to Wasnerin, a picturesque spot south-east of Salzburg and near the Grundlesee in the Austrian Salzkammergut. This happened to be only some 40 miles from Berchtesgaden, where Hitler was at the time. According to Blumentritt,[52] Hitler invited von Rundstedt to visit him there before he returned to France. Zimmermann, on hearing of this, urged von Rundstedt to bring up the question of the defence of the West. On 22 June von Rundstedt was driven in his own staff car to Hitler's mountain retreat,[53] arriving there after lunch. If he hoped that Hitler would discuss the West with him, he was to be disappointed. He was merely treated to a two hour monologue, much of it on the forthcoming Operation CITADEL, designed to destroy the Kursk salient. It was then time for tea during which official topics were forbidden. Von Rundstedt thus left empty-handed, but resolved to produce a thorough survey of the situation in the West in order to force Hitler to take action. Before he could complete this, however, another urgent problem demanded his attention.

On 10 July 1943, the British and Americans invaded Sicily, thus bringing the war to the Italian homeland. Two weeks later, the Fascist Grand Council in Rome arrested Mussolini and King Victor Emmanuel asked Marshal Badoglio to form a new government. Hitler ordered German troops into northern Italy and also told von Rundstedt to make a 'goodwill' visit to the Italian Fourth Army in order to try and find out whether the Italians were about to ask for an armistice. Von Rundstedt's good relations with the Fourth Army convinced him, according to Walter Warlimont, who was Deputy Chief of Operations in OKW, that the Italians should be kept in the war, a view which Rommel, who was conducting the deployment to northern Italy, shared.[54] As it was, the Italian armistice negotiations with the Allies were, understandably, kept highly secret. On 3 September, an armistice was signed at Cassibile near Syracuse, the day that Montgomery's Eighth Army crossed the Straits of Messina to land in the toe of Italy. Eisenhower announced it five days later, just as the Allies began to land at Salerno, and the Germans moved in immediately, securing Rome on the 10th. Von Rundstedt's role in this was to disarm the Italian Fourth Army, an operation which went smoothly, largely thanks to the tact with which he carried it out. Nevertheless, some Italian coastal units and, among others, Vercellino, the Fourth Army commander, volunteered to remain on the German side. Von Rundstedt, however, stated after the war, and in contrast to what Warlimont wrote, that this army had been a 'most highly unwelcome addition', poorly equipped and trained and guilty of widespread looting, which merely increased

French hatred for it.[55] He was thus relieved to see its demise. In its place a new German army, Nineteenth, was formed under von Rundstedt's former chief of staff, von Sodenstern. Even so, this was probably small consolation for the divisions that he now had to hand over to the Italian front. In July he had already been ordered to send a Panzergrenadier division to Sicily. Now he had to deliver further good quality formations to Italy, including a Panzer and five infantry divisions.

Hitler, however, seems now to have begun to realise in what a parlous state the West was. Goebbels wrote in his diary on 23 September, after a talk with Hitler: 'As regards the West, we have seventeen divisions there at the moment. This, of course, is not enough to ward off a large-scale enemy invasion. But the Führer will earnestly press for the increase of these divisions.'[56] Hitler's sudden concern may well have been prompted by an operation mounted by the Allies in the English Channel on 8 September. This was part of the elaborate deception plan that was being created to deflect German attention away from Normandy as the landing area for the Allied invasion of Europe. The exercise, under the blanket codename of STARKEY, was an embarkation one on the Kent coast designed to make the Germans believe that a cross-Channel attack was about to take place and to draw the Luftwaffe up into the air. The Germans did not react, because, as von Rundstedt said after the war, they realised that it was a bluff.[57] Even so, it was possibly enough to give Hitler a jolt.

Another growing problem was the French Resistance. Von Rundstedt viewed 1943 as 'a serious turning point in the interior situation of France'. The supply of arms from Britain increased 'every month' as did the threat against German troops and the sabotage of railways and supply lines. By the end of the year, 'it was already impossible to dispatch single members of the Wehrmacht, ambulances, couriers or supply columns without armed protection to the 1st or 19th Armies in the South of France'. Matters became so bad that Headquarters Army Group G at Toulouse was 'at times cut off'.[58] During August 1943 there had been a spate of assassinations in the Paris area, and in one incident von Rundstedt himself is supposed to have had a narrow escape.[59] Earlier, too, in May, there was an attempt to blow up von Rundstedt's train as it passed through St Etienne, but the charge went off half an hour too early.[60] In April, von Neubronn had delivered a protest from von Rundstedt to Laval that he had not done enough to suppress attacks by the Resistance. On 27 August, von Rundstedt had a long meeting with Pétain. They were joined by Laval for lunch. The concept of raising a new French Army had come to nothing, since Hitler was too distrustful. Pétain now proposed once more that the Milice be equipped with modern weapons so that they could better combat the Resistance threat. Laval also wanted one or two people in each village to be armed so as to guard the harvest against sabotage attacks. In turn, Pétain undertook to order French people not to attack German troops in the event of an Allied invasion. Both stressed the need for greater understanding between the French and German peoples, but said that this could only come about if Hitler made a clear statement on France's position in postwar Europe. This was something with which von Rundstedt wholeheartedly agreed and he recommended that such a statement, albeit non-committal, should be made. In his report of the discussion, he stressed his impression that Pétain's and Laval's appeals were made 'in good faith' and should be granted.[61] In the event, nothing was to come of them.

It was on 28 October 1943 that von Rundstedt finally submitted his survey on the defences in the West to OKW. With some 1600 miles of coastline to defend, there was no way in which a solid barrier against the allies could be created. With the limited number of troops that he had available, von Rundstedt could only 'cover', but not defend the Atlantic coast, if he was to produce any form of effective defence on the more vulnerable Channel coast. He accepted that the Atlantic Wall was 'indispensable and valuable for battle as well as for propaganda', but since a 'rigid' defence was impossible for any length of time, 'the outcome of the battle must depend on the use of a mobile and armoured reserve'.[62] This was precisely what he lacked, especially since the last of the re-vamped Stalingrad divisions had now returned once more to the Eastern Front and all he had were three SS Panzergrenadier divisions, one of which had only just begun to form.

The effect of this report on Hitler was immediate. On 3 November, less than a week after von Rundstedt submitted his report, he issued Directive No 51. The preamble reflected his dramatic change of heart, especially his recognition that Germany was now on the defensive:

'The hard and costly struggle against Bolshevism during the last two and a half years, which has involved the bulk of our military strength in the East, has demanded extreme exertions. The greatness of the danger and the general situation demanded it. But the situation has since changed. The danger in the East remains, but a greater danger now appears in the West; an Anglo-Saxon landing! In the East, the vast extent of the territory makes it possible for us to lose ground, even on a large scale, without a fatal blow being dealt to the nervous system of Germany.

It is very different in the West! Should the enemy succeed in breaching our defences on a wide front here, the immediate consequences will be unpredictable. Everything indicates that the enemy will launch an offensive against the Western front of Europe, at the latest in the spring, perhaps even earlier.

I can therefore no longer take responsibility for further weakening in the West, in favour of other theatres of war. I have therefore decided to reinforce its defences, particularly those places from which the long-range bombardment of England will begin. For it is here that the enemy must and will attack, and it is here – unless all indications are misleading – that the decisive battle against the landing forces will be fought.'

The emphasis was to be on increasing mobility and anti-tank weapon and artillery holdings in the theatre.[63] This was reassuring for von Rundstedt, but he became confused when two days later Hitler ordered Rommel to carry out a comprehensive inspection tour of the coastline from Denmark round the Low Countries and France.

Rommel himself was commanding Army Group B, which was at the time nothing more than a headquarters. The original intention had been that Rommel should command the German forces in Northern Italy, but he lost the debate with Kesselring, who wanted to conduct a fighting withdrawal up the length of the country rather than just defend the north, as Rommel advocated. Consequently, Kesselring was appointed commander-in-chief in Italy and Rommel's headquarters was sent to France. Von Rundstedt wondered whether this indicated a change of command in the West:

> 'When Rommel was ordered to the West I hoped [*hoffte*] to be replaced by him as C-in-C West! Then Keitel visited me before the end of November and told me that by order of Hitler Rommel would never become my successor if I could not do it any more on health grounds. Rommel was suitable for "Seydlitz type attacks as at Rossbach", but not for larger strategic operations. Only FM v.Kluge could be considered as a suitable replacement for me.'[64]

At the time, though, von Kluge, who had been commanding Army Group Centre, was recovering from serious injuries incurred when his car overturned on the Minsk-Smolensk road in October 1943.

It was not, however, until 19 December that Rommel reported to von Rundstedt at the conclusion of his tour and was invited to lunch. Zimmermann recalled:

> 'Rundstedt outlined the situation briefly and sceptically, speaking of the poor quality of the troops, the dangerous weakness of the Air Force, the almost total absence of naval craft and stressing particularly the main defect of our defensive organisation, namely the complete lack of a

Plate 35.
Von Rundstedt
and Blumentritt
say farewell to
Rommel after a
visit to his
headquarters at
La Roche Guyon.

Plate 36. Von Rundstedt with General Vercellino, formerly the commander of the
Italian Fourth Army, who elected to remain on the Axis side after the Italian armistice,
Toulon, early 1944.

PLATE 37. Von Rundstedt with his erstwhile chief of staff, von Sodernstern,
when the latter was commanding the Nineteenth Army in Southern France.

PLATE 38. Sepp Dietrich points out his dispositions to C-in-C West.

PLATE 39. The beginning of the end – Allied troops coming ashore, Normandy, 6 June 1944.

PLATE 40. Von Rundstedt on reassuming as C-in-C West in September 1944. On his right is Hans Gerd and in the centre, Blumentritt, who was about to depart.

PLATE 41. Planning conference for the Ardennes counter-offensive. Left to right: Model, Krebs, Westphal and von Rundstedt.

PLATE 42. Speer visits von Rundstedt on the eve of WATCH ON THE RHINE.

PLATE 43. The last flourish in the West fails – a German prisoner being escorted past a 'brewed up' PzKpfw V (Panther).

PLATE 44. February 1945 – von Rundstedt with Schlemm, whose First Parachute Army fiercely resisted Montgomery's advance to the Rhine.

powerful reserve. He ended with the words: "It all looks very black to me."' [These last words were apparently said in English][65]
Afterwards the two Field-Marshals lunched together. A few senior officers, of whom I was one, were present. We expected one or other of the Field-Marshals to open the conversation, but neither showed any inclination to do so. Both were apparently preoccupied with their thoughts, which after their discussion can only have been of the most sombre hue. It was a strange, silent meal which will never be forgotten by any man who was present.'[66]

Rommel wrote to his wife that evening, however, that von Rundstedt 'seems very pleased and I think it's all going well'.[67] It is probable, though, that this initial meeting was stiff. Von Rundstedt did not know Rommel well, although, of course his 7th Panzer Division had been in Army Group A in France in 1940, and the laurels that he had won in Africa, regarded as a mere sideshow by those who had experienced the 'real war' on the Eastern Front, would not have particularly impressed him. Rommel, too, was always in the public limelight, while von Rundstedt abhorred publicity. Furthermore, Rommel would contact Hitler directly on the telephone, something which von Rundstedt never did. Von Rundstedt regarded Rommel as 'a brave man' and good at conducting low level operations, but 'not really a High commander'.[68] The German propaganda machine, on the other hand, heralded the creation of this new partnership in glowing terms. Von Rundstedt and Rommel 'could attach everlasting glory to their flags in all theatres of war'. Von Rundstedt was a 'guarantee for the security of Fortress Europe against all attempts by the Americans and British to infiltrate', while Rommel was the man of action who led from the front.[69] The Allies, though, believed that von Rundstedt was the real danger and an October 1943 article in an American journal dubbed him the Allies' 'real enemy No 1'.[70]

It was not until after Christmas, on 27 December to be exact, that Rommel presented his findings to von Rundstedt. He concluded that the Allies would most likely make their landings in the Pas de Calais, or between Boulogne and the River Somme. Allied air superiority would make it difficult for central reserves held well inland to get to the coast in time to prevent beachheads being secured. At present, the Atlantic Wall would not stand up to the sea and air bombardment to which it would be subjected, and once the enemy had secured beachheads, it would be very difficult to drive him back into the sea. Rommel therefore concluded that the enemy must be defeated on the beaches. The defences, especially between Boulogne and the mouth of the Somme, must be strengthened and he intended to do this through the laying of extensive minefields and littering the foreshore with obstacles. Two reserve divisions must be positioned close to the Boulogne–Somme coast to react quickly to any landing.[71] Von Rundstedt's own view was not too dissimilar. He agreed that the priority was to defeat the enemy on the beaches. If this failed local reserves should be deployed, but that there should also be a strong mobile reserve to be used to destroy what enemy was left after the local counter-attacks. He also concurred with Rommel that the Boulogne–Somme area was a likely enemy target, but that the Pas de Calais, being the shortest route across the Channel, was equally likely. What concerned him at this time was not Rommel's ideas for defence but his role in it. Keitel may have confirmed that Rommel was under to his command, but he still had direct access to Hitler. Consequently von Rundstedt sought clarification from OKW. The reply confirmed that Rommel was under von Rundstedt's command, except in the event of an invasion of Denmark or a need to occupy Hungary. In mid-January this was further clarified in that Hitler gave Rommel control of the coast from Holland to the mouth of the Loire.[72] Even so, there were still complications, which surfaced when von Rundstedt departed on leave towards the end of January. Sperrle was still officially the Deputy C-in-C West and he, Rommel and Zimmermann all issued orders, which created some confusion.[73]

Rommel set to with a frenzy of activity, constantly travelling up and down the coast, and soon began to achieve results. Von Rundstedt, however, had not just the coastline to worry about, but also the situation in the interior of France. Resistance activity was increasing daily. In February 1944 he issued a severe order on the hunting down of 'terrorists'. In it, he stated that if innocent civilians were shot, it was 'deplorable', but the fault lay with the terrorists.[74] Many of those arrested for anti-German activities were deported as forced labour to Germany. Up until now, the military commanders in the West had resisted becoming involved in this labour trafficking. The driving force behind it was Fritz Sauckel, Reich Plenipotentiary for Labour Mobilisation, and he operated through the French and German police forces, which were not under control of the military. Originally, a deal had been struck with the Vichy Government by which a French prisoner-of-war would be released for every Frenchman sent to work in Germany. In practice, the proportion was one prisoner for every three workers and the round-ups merely drove many young Frenchmen into the arms of the Resistance. Von Rundstedt himself would later state at Nuremberg:

'Disorderly, irregular behaviour behind the front of the Army must bring
very great misery to the population of the country affected. No army in the
world can tolerate such conditions for any length at time, but in the
interests of the security and protection of its own troops, it must take
sharp, energetic measures. But this should be done in a correct and
soldierly manner.'[75]

Even so, his alleged involvement in the deportation of labour would
form yet another of the war crimes charges against him.

By March 1944 the strategy for the defence of the West had become
the subject of a bitter debate. The particular subject was the handling
of the mobile reserves. Directive No 51 had been followed and von
Rundstedt now had eight Panzer and two Panzergrenadier divisions.
Hitler had appointed Geyr von Schweppenburg to command the
armour, which was formed into Panzer Group West and directly
subordinated to von Rundstedt. At this time, OKW had begun to
consider that areas other than the Pas de Calais and Boulogne–Somme
coast were likely invasion targets. They viewed Normandy especially to
be at risk, but there might also be feints on other coasts, notably the
Mediterranean and Atlantic. Rommel, however, continued to demand
that the mobile reserves be deployed close to the coast. Geyr von
Schweppenburg totally disagreed with this, proposing that Panzer
Group West remain in the Paris area, with all the armour concentrated
under his control, ready to mount counterstrokes in any direction.
Friction between the two grew rapidly and Rommel admitted to his
wife that he had had to be 'very rough' with the Panzer Group
commander.[76] Von Rundstedt, in an effort to heal the split, compromised by allocating some of the mobile divisions to each, but this
satisfied neither, although Hitler expressed general agreement with
what C-in-C West had done. Eventually, Hitler himself was forced to
step in at the end of April and ruled that Army Groups B and G would
have three divisions each while the remaining four would remain under
Geyr von Schweppenburg, but the Panzer Group West divisions could
not be moved without Hitler's permission. Thus, in theory at least, von
Rundstedt had surrendered direct control of all his mobile forces. This,
however, did not mean that he stood idly by. In the British POW camp
at Wilton Park in Summer 1945, there was a revealing eavesdropped
conversation between Blumentritt and von Thoma, erstwhile commander of the Deutsches Afrika Korps, who had been captured at the
end of Second el Alamein. Blumentritt was describing how von
Rundstedt objected to Rommel's deployment of 2nd Panzer Division,
one of the mobile divisions given to him. Rommel wanted to place it

astride the Somme, while von Rundstedt believed that it would be better kept concentrated in the Amiens area. According to Blumentritt:

> 'When Rommel met von Rundstedt he always came in like an unlicked cub. He [von Rundstedt] always called him "cub", he would say "Feld-marshal Cub is ambitious, you see. In Africa things didn't turn out well for him and he would dearly like to be somebody. Take it easy." Then they had a row which old Rundstedt started by saying: "You know, my dear Rommel, I'm too old for these things. Once upon a time we learnt a bit too. This set-up at Abbeville [2 Pz Div astride the Somme], half a division on the right, and half on the left bank, is no good. It ought to be *there* [sic – Amiens], but as far as I'm concerned, do your own blasted business in your own way." That was that. Rommel just looked at him and went out.'[77]

Rommel, on the other hand, had developed a healthy respect for the Western Allies in North Africa and considered that the Eastern Front generals were grossly underestimating the quality of threat that they were facing in the West. Fritz Bayerlein, who had been with him in Africa and was now commanding the Panzer Lehr Division in France, recalled Rommel commenting to him:

> 'Our friends from the East cannot imagine what they're in for here. It's not a matter of fanatical hordes to be driven forward in masses against our line, with no regard for casualties and little recourse to tactical craft; here we are facing an enemy who applies all his native intelligence to the use of his many tactical resources, who spares no expenditure of material and whose every operation goes its course as though it had been the subject of repeated rehearsal. Dash and doggedness no longer make a soldier, Bayerlein; he must have sufficient intelligence to enable him to get the most out of his fighting machine. And that's something these people can do, we found out in Africa.'[78]

What Rommel feared more than anything else was the overwhelming air superiority that the Allies were likely to enjoy. On 23 April, he made this plain in a letter to Jodl: 'With the heavy enemy air superiority we can expect, any large-scale movement of motorised forces to the coast will be exposed to air attacks of tremendous weight and long duration.'[79] There is no evidence that von Rundstedt or his staff really appreciated this point. But not even Rommel really woke up to how the Allies were using their airpower in spite of his warning to Jodl. Apart from attacking all Luftwaffe airfields within range of Normandy, they had launched a prolonged attack against communications designed to cut Normandy off from the remainder of France. Yet, in spite of their clashes, Rommel and von Rundstedt did become reconciled. It is probable that this was at a lunch given by Rommel for C-in-C West on 20 May. Rommel's naval liaison officer, Ruge, noted that von Rundstedt was 'visibly pleased with the invitation. In addition to many service matters, we talked about Karl May and detective stories . . .'[80]

Von Rundstedt's irrascibility at this time was not merely because of irritation with Rommel. Probably more wounding to him was that his very loyalty to the Fatherland had been called into question. It began with one of the Generals who had been captured at Stalingrad, von Seydlitz-Kurzbach, a corps commander under Paulus. A number of senior officers in the Sixth Army had, partly through Russian pressure and partly through resentment that Hitler had abandoned the defenders of Stalingrad, agreed to take part in an anti-Hitler propaganda campaign. Von Seydlitz himself wrote letters to a number of senior commanders on the Eastern Front, including Model, Lindemann and von Küchler, pleading that they stop the war against Russia and join the Free Germany Movement then being fostered in Moscow. For a time their authenticity was doubted, but Hitler and OKW became convinced that they were genuine. Hitler now became concerned over the loyalty of the most senior German commanders as a whole. Schmundt, in order to reassure him, decided to draw up a written declaration of loyalty and to get six Field Marshals – von Rundstedt, Rommel, von Kleist, Busch, von Manstein and von Weichs – to sign it. Schmundt flew to Paris on 3 March and saw von Rundstedt, who apparently 'having made up his mind that there was no doubt' over the authenticity of the von Seydlitz letters, signed the declaration. That evening he went on to see Rommel, who also signed,[81] before then travelling to the Eastern Front to get the others to do likewise. Von Manstein was the last to sign what he later termed this 'rather curious document', and did so because the others had signed and refusal to do so would imply that he supported von Seydlitz. 'All the same, I told Schmundt that I considered the declaration quite unnecessary from a soldier's point of view.'[82] Worse was to follow. On 19 March the signatories were summoned to Berchtesgaden and ordered to declare their view of von Seydlitz to Hitler. Von Rundstedt then read out the declaration and handed it to him in the presence of a gathering of senior members of the Wehrmacht. According to von Manstein, 'Hitler appeared deeply moved'.[83] Von Rundstedt, and possibly the others, were supposedly invited to stay for tea. Apparently, after some five minutes, having hoped to raise the situation in the West, he stormed down to Berchtesgaden railway station muttering: 'What's the point? The Führer wouldn't let me open my mouth, so I walked out on him.'[84]

Yet some were still taking von Rundstedt's name in vain when it came to loyalty to Hitler. The movement for deposing Hitler had grown since Stalingrad. It remained centred around Beck and Goerdeler, but had drawn in an increasing number of other individuals, both civilian and military. Von Rundstedt's predecessor, von Witzleben, remained deeply implicated, as were von Falkenhausen and the military governor of Paris, von Stülpnagel. Among the younger members of the movement, although it must be emphasised that one of its major weaknesses was lack of organisation, were Helmuth von Moltke, a lawyer working in the war ministry, and Adam von Trott zu Solz, a Foreign Office official and kinsman of von Rundstedt's wife. Von Moltke made repeated attempts to gain American support, while von Trott, who had been a Rhodes Scholar at Oxford, did the same with the British. The latter, in particular, or at least the British Foreign Office, regarded the resistance movement as of little consequence. Nevertheless, von Trott persevered and, at the beginning of May 1944, made contact with Allen Dulles, who ran the US Office of Strategic Services (OSS) base in Switzerland. Goerdeler had also recently talked to Dulles and among the names they mentioned as being implicated in the opposition to Hitler was von Rundstedt.[85] There is no evidence that von Rundstedt ever showed the slightest willingness to support the aims of the plotters, whom, as we shall see, he regarded as traitors. Von Neubronn recalled a conversation he had with him in August 1943:

> 'Our plan had been to declare the Army in the West autonomous, as had happened a few times under the Roman Proconsuls, and to march against Berlin with it. Through the mediation of the English ambassador to Madrid, Sir Samuel Hoare, we hoped to reach an understanding with the Allies. But this possibility had to be left unconsidered because the troops were not secure enough in the hands of the leadership. Thus, as I reported to von Rundstedt, only the means of direct intervention with Hitler remained. Rundstedt listened to me calmly and replied that Falkenhausen had suggested the same to him a few days earlier. These proposals were useless. It was impossible to put Hitler under pressure. "I'll be executed. But with that you won't advance one step." I urged him still more: "Herr Feldmarschall, the German people will one day call you to account if you don't act now." But neither this argument nor the repeated statement I made to him not on my own but on behalf of several generals could shift him from his view that the situation would not be improved by his intervention with Hitler and that the sacrifice of his person would not lead to success.'[86]

One can only presume that von Trott mentioned von Rundstedt's name in the hope that it would impress the Allies and that he might be able to win him round through the family connection.

In contrast, Rommel was prepared to do something. According to his chief of staff, Hans Speidel, von Stülpnagel and he met at a country house near St Germain on 15 May 1944. Von Stülpnagel deplored von Rundstedt's resigned attitude to the situation and said that Rommel was now the only officer of sufficient standing to act as the figurehead for the 'autonomous army' concept. Rommel agreed to this and brought his subordinate commanders into the secret. He had a further meeting with von Falkenhausen on 2 June, but the Normandy landings took place before the plans for opening negotiations with the Western Allies could be completed.[87]

The waiting for the invasion to take place was probably getting on von Rundstedt's nerves, as it had done before Dieppe. With the waiting, the uncertainty as to where the Allies would land also increased. On 8 May, he produced a lengthy appreciation of the situation. He noted that most agents forecast the invasion for the first half of May. He considered that the Allied preparations were complete and that the first wave would comprise 20 divisions. The main force concentrations were between Southampton and Portsmouth and landings could be anywhere between the Scheldt and the tip of Brittany, although the most likely area was Boulogne-Normandy.[88] The Allies were not, of course, as advanced in their preparations as von Rundstedt and his staff believed, and he himself relaxed a little once the danger time had past. There are several indicators of this.

On 19 May the Field Marshal visited Pétain at the Chateau Voisons at Rambouillet, not far from Paris. He brought with him an invitation to the French Marshal to accompany Rommel and himself on a tour of the Atlantic Wall on the following Sunday, the 21st. Martin du Gard:

> 'Military curiosity uppermost, Pétain accepted; he would have also inspected the last English dispositions before the landing! The political aspect of the trip escaped him. When Tracou pointed out to him the meal that Nazi propaganda would make of his visit, the confusion that it had provoked among his followers, he realised his heedlessness. It was necessary to cancel the engagement. The danger must be emphasised, the possible bombardment. And von Rundstedt, who himself had thought only of the pleasure of discussing military art with a "colleague", did not insist'.[89]

Nevertheless, von Rundstedt was probably disappointed as he had become fond of Pétain, but the fact that he had proposed such a trip indicated a belief that the danger period for the Allied landings had passed. Furthermore, on 30 May he informed Hitler that there was no indication that the invasion was 'immediately imminent'.[90] In the light of this, von Rundstedt agreed that Rommel could return to Germany for a few days leave, which he did on 5 June, intending also to go and see Hitler and request the transfer to the West of additional forces.[91] Von Rundstedt himself planned a four day inspection trip around the south-west part of the Cotentin peninsula. It was to begin on 6 June.[92] Eugen Dollmann, commanding Seventh Army, summoned most of his senior commanders to a map exercise at Rennes on 5 June.

OKW was not, however, quite so confident that the time of high threat had passed. On 2 June Keitel sent von Rundstedt an order reminding him that in January and February Hitler had declared certain islands and coastal areas as *Festungen* (fortresses) and that their commanders were answerable only to him – another restriction on C-in-C's authority. On the same day OKW asked von Rundstedt why he had not increased the alert state. The Field Marshal replied that if he did it would only really affect the French railways. All rolling stock would become dedicated to transporting reinforcements and supplies and this would mean that the French themselves would be left with nothing. This would surely damage the economy and lead to increased unrest. He therefore preferred to delay this step as long as possible. In all other respects, he assured OKW, his command was prepared and ready for invasion.[93]

As Rommel left for Germany, Eisenhower, who had been forced to postpone D-day by 24 hours because of bad weather, made his final decision. The Normandy landings would take place in the early hours of the following morning, Tuesday 6 June.

10

Normandy and the Bomb Plot

AT 2115 HOURS on 5 June the French Service of the BBC began to broadcast its nightly set of coded messages for the French Resistance. Included in them was the following announcement:

> To-day the Supreme Commander directs me to say this: In due course instructions of great importance will be given to you through this channel, but it will not be possible always to give these instructions at a previously announced time. Therefore you must get into the habit of listening at all hours.'[1]

This, and the fact that the messages were transmitted for longer than the usual five or ten minutes, immediately alerted Abwehr suspicions. Within 30 minutes they had informed von Rundstedt's headquarters and he issued an order for heightened alertness and warned of the likelihood of increased sabotage activities. At 0130 hours, the first reports of parachute landings, on the east side of the Cotentin Peninsula, were received by Ob West (*Oberbefehlshaber West* – Commander-in-Chief West), and the next stage of alert was ordered. Within two hours it became clear that this was no mere raid. The invasion had begun.

One of von Rundstedt's first reactions was to telephone OKW and demand that the Panzer reserves be placed under his command. This produced no reaction on the grounds that Hitler was asleep. Accordingly, at 0425 hours, von Rundstedt sent a written signal stating that if this was a major landing the change of command must be quickly agreed and the Panzer Lehr and 17th SS Panzer Grenadier Division be given marching orders.[2] There was no immediate reply to this, but, in anticipation, the Flak units of both divisions, which had been detached, were given a warning order to make ready to join their parent formations. By now it was 0530 hours and, under heavy naval bombardment, the Allied landing craft were beginning to approach the beaches. The only immediate mobile reserve which the Germans had was Edgar Feuchtinger's 21st Panzer Division. He himself could not initially be located when the alert orders were given – it seems that he was dallying with a lady friend in Paris[3] – but, even so, the division was ready to move by 0200 hours. Yet, it was not until 0800 hours that the first Panzer battalion began to move north towards Caen to counter the British landings, and it seems that the blame for this must lie partially with Rommel's chief of staff, Hans Speidel, and with Feuchtinger himself, who apparently did not return to his headquarters until after 0600 hours. Even then, it was only thanks to the one-legged General Erich Marcks, commanding LXXXIV Corps, that the first elements of the division actually made contact with the invaders. He led them in his staff car towards the coast until he came under fire.[4] In the meantime, the static divisions on the coast were left to cope as best they could.

At 1000 hours, Keitel, having spoken to Hitler, telephoned von Rundstedt's headquarters. The request to have the Panzer reserves placed under his command was firmly rejected. The only concessions made were that he could move the 12th SS Panzer Grenadier Division (Hitler Youth) nearer the coast, but that OKW would control its commitment to battle, and that the Panzer Lehr could remain on immediate stand-by. By now the Allies were ashore on all five beaches and 21st Panzer Division was being committed piecemeal both to tackle the British airborne forces on the River Orne and to counter the advance by the British 3rd Infantry Division towards Caen. To von Rundstedt and Blumentritt it was clear that every hour the Allies were given to consolidate their beachheads, the more difficult it would be to drive them back into the sea. They thus kept up their demands of OKW – 'What is still possible today – also by using the dull weather – could be too late tomorrow', as the Ob West war diary noted. Eventually, at 1430 hours, OKW gave way to von Rundstedt's demands. He was told that he could have not only 12th and 17th SS Panzer Grenadier Divisions and the Panzer Lehr, but also Sepp Dietrich's I SS Panzer Corps. Dietrich, however, only had two divisions under command, 12th SS, which was already being moved up, and the SS Leibstandarte, which was still refitting in Belgium and would not be ready for action for some time. Nevertheless, at least this made a higher Panzer headquarters available. Accordingly, von Rundstedt put the Panzer Lehr, which was based in the Chartres area, and 21st Panzer under

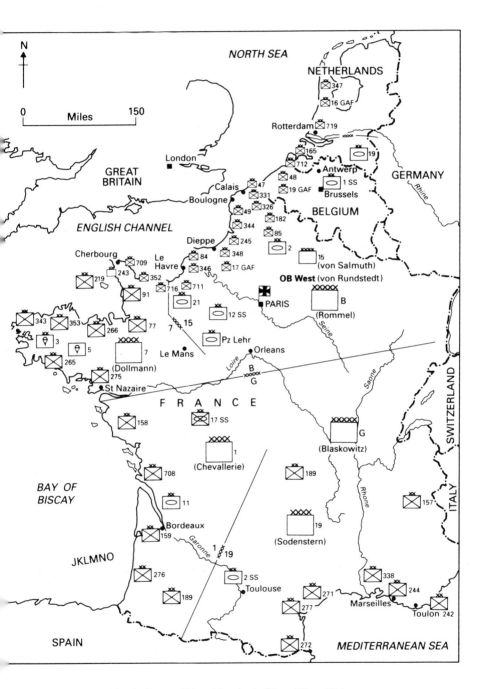

MAP 9. German Dispositions in the West, 6 June 1944.

Dietrich's command, sending 17th SS to assist against the Americans in the west.

That it had taken over twelve hours for OKW to release the Panzer reserves now meant that, as the Ob West war diary put it, the 'greatest acceleration' was needed if there was to be any chance of eradicating the beachheads. This was easier said than done, especially since the day was now far gone. Dietrich's headquarters began its move from the Paris area at 1600 hours, and reached Rouen that night. He hoped to be able to mount a coordinated counter-attack early on the 7th, but this was soon to prove overly optimistic. Air attacks interfered with the move of 12th SS Division, and only one of its regiments had arrived by nightfall. 21st Panzer had found itself committed piecemeal to the support of 716th Infantry Division, which was bearing the brunt of the British and Canadian landings, and the luckless Feuchtinger had little idea of the whereabouts of his units. Part of the reason for this was that he had gone on a visit to Headquarters 716th Division but had failed to take a radio with him. No wonder that an Ob West report criticised him for his failure to use the technical aids available to him for commanding his division.[5] As for the Panzer Lehr, Dietrich had no idea of its progress since efforts to establish contact with it through his parent formation, Seventh Army, failed.[6] Thus, by the end of the day, the six infantry and one Panzer divisions available to Dollmann to defend almost 200 miles of coast, from the west side of the Cotentin Peninsula to the Seine, were simply not enough to prevent the Allies from landing and consolidating their initial gains. All that they had been able to achieve was to deny the Allies their laid-down ultimate D-Day objectives, including Caen.

If Hitler had released the Panzer reserves as soon as von Rundstedt had asked for them, the Allies would have experienced a much harder day on 6 June than they did. The marginal weather and the fact that Allied eyes were initially concentrated on the beaches would have meant that Panzer deployment would have proceeded much more smoothly than it did and they would have probably been able to counter-attack during the afternoon. Yet, there were two Panzer divisions (2nd and 116th) north of the Seine which were under Army Group B's command. They were certainly closer to Normandy than Panzer Group West and hence could have arrived even earlier. Von Rundstedt, however, refused to move them or any other formation from Fifteenth Army. That he took this course was largely thanks to the elaborate Allied deception plans. Neither he nor OKW were convinced that the Normandy landings were the only ones and still thought that they might be a feint, with the main landing being made in the Pas De Calais. It was about the only point on which the two headquarters agreed and they would maintain this view for some days to come.

Not until the morning of the 8th was Dietrich able to put in his counter-stroke and then it was but a shadow of what had originally been envisaged. In the meantime, Rommel, who had returned hotfoot from Germany, had decided that I SS Panzer Corps should be subordinated to Panzer Group West rather than Dollmann. Such was the state of radio communications, though, that it was some time before Dietrich was aware of this. The attack itself consisted in the end of little more than one battle group from the Panzer Lehr. The reasons were two-fold. By this time 716th Division had been decimated and both 12th SS and 21st Panzer were forced to deploy increasing amounts of their strength in defence in order to hold the ring against the Allied advance. Also, thanks to effective Allied air interdiction, the Panzer Lehr had been seriously delayed in its move from Chartres, had suffered casualties and was short of fuel.

By now von Rundstedt was beginning to gain a grasp of the Allied intentions. Captured orders had confirmed that Cherbourg was an initial objective and he and his staff concluded that the enemy would use the port as a base from which to thrust towards Paris. On the 8th, the same day as Dietrich's counter-attack, von Rundstedt sent Blumentritt to HQ I SS Corps in order to get a better feel for the situation. By chance, Rommel was visiting at the same time. Blumentritt concluded that piecemeal commitment of forces was no answer and that the situation could only be stabilised by making counterstrokes in strength. This meant that large reinforcements of both armour and infantry were needed. Furthermore, as Dietrich made clear, Allied air supremacy was proving decisive and the Luftwaffe must also be strongly reinforced. 'We have to clear up the situation in Normandy because otherwise there will be far-reaching consequences', Blumentritt wrote. Another grave shortfall was that threequarters of the radios in Panzer Group West were inoperative. On Blumentritt's return, von Rundstedt demanded further reinforcements of OKW and began to realise that he would have to draw troops from von Salmuth north of the Seine.[7] Zimmermann even telephoned Speidel that night to say that von Rundstedt . . . 'thinks we're going to have to strip other fronts recklessly in order to provide further strength'. Jodl, too, had now come round to the same way of thinking, and told Rommel's headquarters that he no longer believed that the Allies were going to make further landings elsewhere.[8]

Rommel, however, was not so convinced and still refused to transfer forces from Fifteenth Army.

After the war, at Nuremberg in 1946, von Rundstedt was to say that it was at this juncture that he realised that Germany had lost the war.[9] Rommel, too, was now even more convinced that an approach had to now be made to the Western Allies. As he wrote to his wife on 13 June: 'It's time for politics to come into play, we are expecting the next, perhaps even heavier, blow to fall elsewhere in a few days. The long-husbanded strength of two world powers is coming into action. It will all be decided quickly.'[10] Yet, while a British Foreign Office official noted on 8 June that von Rundstedt would not be prepared to listen to any Allied overtures until he had accepted that the invasion had been successful,[11] the Field Marshal was certainly not prepared to have any unilateral dealings with the Allies. As he wrote after the war: 'The soldier is only an instrument of politics.' All he could do was to bring about a favourable military situation such as to allow the politicians 'to reappear on the stage'. On the other hand, 'if the situation has turned out unfavourably, the right moment for politics has passed by in most cases'.[12]

Allied propaganda was, however, trying to drive a wedge between von Rundstedt and Rommel. A Swiss newspaper article of the time believed that this could be fact, pointing to the supposed differences between their concepts for the defence of the French coastline. Von Rundstedt was supposed to have favoured fixed defences inland, while Rommel wanted the defences on the beaches so as to prevent a landing. The fact that he had failed to do so merely aggravated the supposed schism. Furthermore, their characters were entirely different. While von Rundstedt was typical of 'that officer caste which made Prussia and later on Germany great', Rommel was accused of making his career in the Nazi Party. While von Rundstedt was a 'brilliant organiser', Rommel was 'a rough, uninhibited daredevil; a typical Party man, who does not shy away from anybody or anything but who knows how to help himself in difficult situations by an instinct for improvisation'. The conflict was one of tradition versus the 'German Revolution'.[13] Yet, as we have seen, they had made up their differences, at least on the surface, before the invasion began. On the other hand, Speidel noted:

> 'Rundstedt was an eminent strategist, a master of the rules of war, but in the last few years he had lost with advancing age the creative impulse and the clear sense of responsibility to the nation. Symptoms of his lapse were sarcastic comments or indifference. Of course, he despised Hitler and referred to him in all private conversations, as Hindenburg did, with the nickname "the Bohemian Corporal". But he seemed to think that the

height of wisdom was to make studied representations and write grave situation reports. He left action to others. When Rommel sought to move him to send joint demands to Hitler, Rundstedt exclaimed: "You are young. The people know you and love you. You do it!" It was not only as a general that Rundstedt withdrew into himself. His character, personality and mobility were failing, and at a time when supreme efforts were demanded, Rundstedt remained unknown to the soldier at the front, while Rommel ceaselessly exerted his remarkable powers of leadership on the soldiers personally, sparing himself not at all.'[14]

Part of the reason for this was von Rundstedt's refusal to speak direct to Hitler. By now he also tried to avoid talking to Keitel and Jodl, whom he regarded as 'yes' men, preferring to delegate this to Blumentritt.[15] Age, too, had indeed made him less active. In any event, with Rommel actually commanding the forces in Normandy, it was best to let him do his job. Even so, the two did see eye to eye over the conduct of the defence in the west and they would shortly jointly represent their point of view face-to-face with Hitler.

Hitler and OKW were adamant that not an inch of ground in Normandy was to be given to the enemy, but with the air situation and the lack of troops this was impossible to achieve. On 11 June von Rundstedt was forced to warn Keitel that unless the front was stabilised, the situation might 'force fundamental decisions', by which it seems clear that he meant a wholesale withdrawal from Normandy to a more defendable line. Alluding to OKW's tendency to tell Hitler only what they thought he wanted to hear, he wrote: 'I feel obliged to report things as they are and as I judge them to be . . . I want this report to be presented to the Führer without any alteration . . .'[16] Cherbourg was already under threat and Hitler was beginning to demand counter-action so as to deny it to the Allies. Yet, with no reinforcements yet available, because of continued fears of another Allied landing, the only way that this could be done was by withdrawing troops from in front of the British Second Army, but in von Rundstedt's and Rommel's eyes the long-term threat here was very much greater. Indeed, von Rundstedt had already pointed this out to OKW on 11 June, stating that he believed that the Allies would make their main thrust into the interior of France from between the River Orne and Vire. Lack of troops meant that he could only remain on the defensive for the time being, especially since his Panzer divisions were now committed in the line and hence he had no mobile counter-attack force.

The heavy hand of Hitler and OKW became more and more apparent. On 11 June, again, von Rundstedt is recorded asking for elements of the SS Leibstandarte to be placed under his command, feeling forced to specify each regiment and battalion that he wanted by name. The day before, he had received the following from Jodl:

> 'As a consequence of an enemy press report from 7.6. that the Allied soldiers surprised the German defenders in their underpants, the Führer demands a responsible report on the following points:
>
> 1) When did Ob West receive the report about the issuing of the B[coded] message through the English terrorist communication centre?
>
> 2) What was carried out and when?
>
> 3) When did the subordinate commanding officers receive the alert order?
>
> 4) What level of alert was in force when the first enemy paratroopers and gliders landed?
>
> 5) Which part or staffs of 716, 352, 709, 91 Inf Divs, 6th Para Rgt, 21 Pz Div were surprised and attacked by paratroopers without being ready for combat?
>
> 6) How did the commander of 91 Inf Div do? Was he surprised in his battle headquarters?'[17]

This was the type of demand that von Rundstedt, with his attention concentrated on the desperate battle in Normandy, could have well done without, although there is no evidence that he did anything about it. As it was, he had already criticised Feuchtinger, but OKW took no notice of this. They knew that he was a particular favourite of Hitler's, having officiated at many of the prewar Nuremberg Rallies. Hence Feuchtinger remained in command of his division until early 1945.[18] As for the commander of 91st Division, General Wilhelm Falley, he had been ambushed and killed by American paratroopers while on his way back from the Rennes map exercise. This all-pervading and suffocating influence of OKW was another reason for von Rundstedt's seeming lethargy. As he remarked after the war: 'I could have stood on my head but I still would not have been able to budge a division if Hitler disagreed with my judgement.'[19]

By 14 June, the Americans in the Omaha and Utah beachheads had linked up, captured Carentan and were now preparing to turn west to liberate the Cotentin peninsula. In the eastern sector, both the British and Canadians had made efforts to capture Caen, but had been foiled. This was largely thanks to the fanatical defence by the 12th SS Division (Hitler Youth) and the eventual transfer of 2nd Panzer Division from Fifteenth Army. This arrived just in time to fill a critical gap in the overstretched defences. The dilemma that now faced von Rundstedt and Rommel was that the only way that they could mount any form of effective counter-stroke to relieve the increasingly heavy pressure was a concentrated attack by armour. Yet, with all their available Panzer divisions now in the line, they could not do this until they were relieved by fresh infantry formations. They repeatedly pointed this out to OKW and pleaded for Hitler to come to France and see the situation for himself. This he eventually agreed to do and met the two Field Marshals at Margival near Soissons on 17 June.

The site of the meeting was a railway tunnel in and on top of which a collection of concrete bunkers had been constructed as a Führer field headquarters for SEALION. There was just one stool, on which Hitler sat, while von Rundstedt, Rommel and their Chiefs of Staff, Blumentritt and Speidel, stood. Also present were Keitel, Jodl and Schmundt. Hitler had arrived, having flown from Berchtesgaden to Metz and then motored, and, according to Speidel, looked 'worn and sleepless'.[20] His first utterance was that Cherbourg must be held at all costs and he demanded that the garrison be reinforced. As von Rundstedt later commented: 'Instead of trying to pull the troops out of a hopeless trap, Hitler wanted to send more men into it. Of course we paid no attention to the order.'[21] Von Rundstedt then made some introductory remarks and handed the floor to Rommel. He gave a detailed review of the situation and warned Hitler that the fall of Cherbourg was inevitable and the whole *Festung* (Fortress) concept a waste of manpower. Indeed, while the conference was in progress, there was a telephone message from von Rundstedt's headquarters stating that the Americans had begun their attack into the Cotentin Peninsula. Rommel then went on to reiterate his belief that the Allied plan was to break out from the Caen-Bayeux area and the Cotentin Peninsula and thrust to Paris, with a subsidiary operation designed to cut off the Breton Peninsula. He warned Hitler of the rate of Allied reinforcement and that there was no prepared defence line on which the German forces could fall back. He then went on to propose a new plan. The Panzer divisions would be relieved and, with reserve formations, assembled on the flanks. A limited withdrawal would then be made to draw the enemy out of range of his supporting naval gunfire, and the armour would strike him in the flank. Once more he demanded more air, armour and naval assets. Furthermore, and in this von Rundstedt strongly supported him, Rommel said that they must have freedom of action in the West in order to fight the battle as they wanted. Hitler took little notice of what Rommel had said and launched into one of his monologues, this time on the V-1 flying bomb offensive against England which had opened four days before. Both Field Marshals asked if the V-weapons could be directed on the Normandy beachhead and the English south coast ports from which the reinforcements for Normandy were setting sail. This was ignored and Hitler launched into another tirade culminating in the boast that Britain would be devastated by V-weapons and jet aircraft.

At this moment, aptly or otherwise, there was an air raid warning. The meeting moved into Hitler's air raid shelter. According to Speidel, Rommel took the opportunity to tell Hitler that the Western Front could not be held and the same applied to Italy and the Eastern Front. With Germany thus isolated Hitler must bring the war to an end. Hitler's response was: 'Don't you worry about the future course of the war. Look to your own invasion front.' Blumentritt confirmed that the political factor was raised, but that Rommel brought it up again when he was walking with Hitler to his car at the end of the conference. Hitler apparently told him that putting out peace feelers was no option since the Allies were bent on unconditional surrender – 'fanatical resistance' was the only answer. Von Rundstedt recorded after the war: 'After we had explained the situation, we told the Führer that something had to happen militarily, in other words away from the coast, and politically. Consequently he left the room and Generaloberst Jodl said: "No other Field Marshal could have told him this."'[22]

The conference did little to raise von Rundstedt's spirits. This was in contrast to Rommel, who wrote next day to his wife: 'A quick enemy breakthrough to Paris is now hardly a possibility. We've got a lot of stuff coming up. The Fuehrer was very cordial and in a good humour. He realises the gravity of the situation.'[23] There were a number of reasons for this. First, Rommel seems to have been uplifted by Hitler's almost hypnotic delivery. Jodl had also assured him that reinforcements were on their way, including Hausser's II SS Corps which was being transferred from the Eastern Front. Furthermore, Hitler had agreed to visit him at his headquarters at La Roche Guyon on the following day. As it happened, a defective V-1 crashed close to Margival that evening. So upset was Hitler that he and his entourage immediately left for Berchtesgaden. He did not bother to inform von Rundstedt or Rommel of this and this was the trigger that probably caused Rommel to finally lose any faith in Hitler that he might have had left.

The American attack into the Cotentin Peninsula went as predicted by Rommel. By 22 June, Cherbourg had been invested and the garrison surrendered five days later. Previously, on the 20th, Hitler had sent a directive to von Rundstedt ordering an armoured counter-attack to be mounted under Geyr von Schweppenburg's control. Hitler laid down that I and II SS Panzer Corps and XLVII Panzer Corps (von Funck) were to take part. Rather than adopting Rommel's idea of a withdrawal followed by a counter-attack into the flanks of the following up Allies – the voluntary surrender of ground had become an anathema with Hitler – this operation was to attack the Anglo–US boundary at Caumont in order to drive a wedge between the Allies. Once again Hitler was directing operations himself and making von Rundstedt and Rommel mere post offices, although Rommel was to be responsible for the detailed planning. His post-Margival optimism now changed to one of utter pessimism, he wrote on 23 June to Frau Rommel: 'Militarily things aren't at all good. The enemy air force is dealing extremely heavily with our supplies and at the moment is completely strangling them. If a decisive battle develops, we'll be without ammunition. You can imagine how worried I am.'[24] Certainly, the SS Leibstandarte had a frustrating move from Belgium, being forced to detrain in Paris because of the air threat. 2nd SS Panzer Division (Das Reich), which OKW had agreed could be released from southern France, suffered difficulties of another kind in the form of the French Resistance. Such was their frustration that one unit ran amok in the village of Oradour, murdering men, women and children. Von Rundstedt's conclusion was that, in view of the difficulties, the counterstroke could not be mounted before 5 July. But on that same day, 24 June, Hitler ordered him to examine an attack against the rear of the American forces besieging Cherbourg with a view to relieving the garrison. Von Rundstedt immediately replied that this was not possible and that Caen must remain the priority.[25] Hitler, however, would not leave this particular bone alone. On 26 June, having detected the arrival of the Panzer reinforcements through Ultra, Montgomery launched Operation EPSOM; the object was to break through the German lines and pre-empt the planned German counter-stroke. That afternoon von Rundstedt and Blumentritt visited Rommel's headquarters and sent a further reiteration to OKW of the impossibility of the Cherbourg option and stated that priority must lie with resisting the British attack. The OKW reply of the following day showed Hitler to be unconvinced by this argument. 'The Führer holds firmly to the idea of attacking not the strength, but the weakness of the enemy west of Vire where weaker American forces are located on a broad front.' Von Rundstedt, having spoken to Rommel, replied by return. Ignoring

Hitler's view he demanded that commanders be given latitude to withdraw to more favourable positions to avoid encirclement. Further: 'In conjunction with Field Marshal Rommel, I therefore ask for a free hand to order even extensive adjustments of the front . . . and for a corresponding directive.'[26] Both von Rundstedt and Rommel had had enough of Hitler's interference. He, likewise, was becoming fed up with their complaints.

That same evening both received a message from OKW summoning them immediately to Berchtesgaden. They were not allowed to fly or go by train and were forced to make a 600 mile car journey. The conference that they were to attend began at 1800 hours on the 29th, which cannot have given them much, if any time to recover from their journey. Blumentritt, however, wrote that von Rundstedt arrived to be informed that the time of conference had been put back, and then further postponed, which did little for his temper.[27] Present, initially, were Hitler, the two Field Marshals, Keitel and Jodl, but later Goering, Doenitz, who had relieved Raeder as C-in-C of the Navy in January 1943, and Sperrle joined in.

As was now always the case with Führer Conferences, most of it consisted of a long monologue delivered by Hitler which did little to address the practicalities of the true situation in the West. Once again, it was dominated by the new 'miracle weapons' which Hitler was convinced would turn the tide. As for Normandy itself, the Allies must be halted and then the beachhead cleaned up. The Luftwaffe strength must be increased and jet and rocket fighters (Me262 and Me163 respectively) deployed to the theatre. To counter the Allied naval gunfire, which the Germans treated with a respect only just short of that for the overwhelming air supremacy, special bombs were to be used against battleships. The Navy was to play its part in mining operations and the use of all available craft, both surface and sub-surface, to harry the Allied shipping. He glossed over the question of further ground reinforcement. The truth was that on 22 June the long expected Soviet summer offensive had been launched and was already threatening to break the back of Army Group Centre. Hence, such reinforcements as were available were being rushed eastwards. Von Rundstedt and Rommel probably realised this, for they do not seem to have pushed their demands for a further strengthening in the West.

The two Field Marshals did, however, make one concerted protest. On arrival at Berchtesgaden they had been informed that General Eugen Dollmann, commander of the Seventh Army, had died that day of a heart attack. This was, in part, caused by the strain of the previous weeks, but also on account of Hitler's demand for a witch hunt over the fall of Cherbourg and the sending to Normandy of a commission to investigate the circumstances. Hitler had wanted court-martial proceedings to be instituted against Dollmann, which von Rundstedt refused to do, but clearly the imputed slurs against his name were the last straw for the Seventh Army commander. The two Field Marshals now demanded that Hitler halt the investigation. Rommel, certainly, and, according to his postwar testimony to the IMT Commission, von Rundstedt as well, also raised the issue of peace terms, which was once more dismissed out of hand by Hitler.[28]

Von Rundstedt and Rommel arrived back at their respective headquarters late on 30 June. Awaiting them was a fresh directive from Hitler. It demanded an immediate counter-attack against the EPSOM offensive. Whatever happened, Seventh Army must not allow itself to be driven out of the bocage and into the more open country to the south. Rommel, however, had reports from Geyr von Schweppenburg and Hausser, who had just taken over Seventh Army, demanding permission to withdraw their forces from Caen so that they could take up a new line out of range of Allied naval gunfire. Breaking with his normal practice, von Rundstedt promptly telephoned OKW to tell them this and ordered Rommel to make preparations for a withdrawal. The Commander-in-chief followed this up with a letter stressing the need for I SS Panzer Corps and 21st Panzer Division to be 'released in good time from an ever narrowing encirclement' and 'thus be free for further operations. These troops, which are our best, must be preserved east of the Orne at fighting strength; this decision is urgently necessary, lest valuable forces once again be destroyed by the enemy.' He received the OKW answer at 1740 hours on 1 July. There were to be no withdrawals.[29]

For von Rundstedt this was the last straw. He immediately telephoned Keitel. As to what he actually said has been the subject of debate. The most popular version, which was recounted by Blumentritt, who was present in the room, to Shulman, was that Keitel said: 'What shall we do? What shall we do?' Von Rundstedt is supposed to have replied: 'What shall we do? Make peace, you idiots! What else can you do?' He then hung up.[30] Blumentritt in his biography of his chief stated that von Rundstedt's reply was not quite so insulting and that he merely told Keitel that he should end the war.[31] This is supported by a report on an interrogation of Blumentritt in January 1946.[32] Von Rundstedt himself told the IMT Commission that what he said to Keitel was: 'Please rescind this order. If you don't do it, I have to assume that you have no trust in my person anymore and I have to say get someone else.'[33] Schmundt, however, recorded in his diary on 1 July: 'Field Marshal v. Rundstedt tells Field Marshal Keitel that he does not feel able to cope in the long run with the increased demands. Consequently, the Führer has decided on a change in the high command . . .'[34] It is probable that von Rundstedt was irrascible to Keitel over the telephone and also intimated that he had had enough and mentioned his health. It seems likely, however, that von Rundstedt had already spoken about his health while at Berchtesgaden on 29 June and that the decision to replace him had been made then. His successor was, as Keitel had told him the previous December, von Kluge, who had been summoned to Berchtesgaden on 30 June, while von Rundstedt was on his way back to St Germain. Thus, whatever he said or did not say to Keitel on the telephone on the evening of 1 July, made no difference; the decision had already been made.

The next morning, 2 July, von Rundstedt and Rommel attended Dollmann's funeral in Paris. Von Rundstedt was told by OKW that one of Hitler's adjutants, Lieutenant Colonel Borgmann, was on his way to see him with a letter from Hitler. According to Warlimont, Keitel also told von Rundstedt that he 'gave the impression of being much in need of rest and had therefore better take a long leave'.[35] Borgmann duly arrived, bringing with him the Oakleaves to the Knight's Cross which he bestowed on the Field Marshal on Hitler's behalf. As for Hitler's letter, von Rundstedt said that it was 'very cordial' and explained that it was merely the 'impaired state of my health' that was causing him to be replaced.[36] On the same day, he was officially transferred to the Reserve, although the accompanying news release said that Hitler would employ him on 'special assignments' in the future.[37] He was not the only commander in the West to be removed at this time. The axe fell on Geyr von Schweppenburg and on von Sodenstern, who was still commanding Nineteenth Army in southern France. On 3 July, von Kluge, who had been sufficiently 'brainwashed' at Berchtesgaden to be convinced that von Rundstedt and Rommel were unnecessarily pessimistic over the situation, arrived at St Germain to take over the Western theatre. That same day von Rundstedt issued a special order of the day:

'As a consequence of my notification, which I made dutifully and with a heavy heart, that at the moment, because of reasons of old age and the present state of my health, I am certainly not up to the physical strains, as one can expect them, resulting from the developments on the Atlantic front, the Führer has ordered my transfer to the Führer Reserve OKH from 2 July 1944. From the same day he appointed General Field Marshal v.Kluge as Commander-in-Chief West and at the same time Commander-in-Chief Army Group D.

When I say goodbye during the hour of crucial test for the three branches of the Wehrmacht on the Western Front which are subordinated to me, I feel urged to express my thanks and recognition for the work during the years of preparation for defence against the invasion.

The first weeks of the unbelievably hard battles on the Atlantic front have shown that this work has not been in vain. We are still at the beginning of the struggle. We don't know how long it will last and what shape it will take. We only know that the Anglo-Saxons won't spare any means to achieve a decisive success. But we also know that, whatever the extent of the enemy's efforts, the heroic resistance of our troops and our unshakeable belief in the final victory will defeat all the enemy's efforts to achieve operational and war-deciding success.'[38]

Next day, accompanied by Hans Gerd, he left St Germain for the last time. He called in at Rommel's headquarters to say farewell and, according to Speidel, told Rommel that he would never accept another command.[39] He then motored to Bad Tölz to take a further cure. Bila probably joined him and Hans Gerd almost certainly took the opportunity to go and see his family in Austria. Once more, von Rundstedt was not to be left in peace for long.

Von Kluge, after an immediate clash with Rommel, soon realised that he and von Rundstedt were right about the situation in Normandy and matters quickly began to go from bad to worse. Then, on 17 July, while returning from a visit to Dietrich's headquarters, Rommel was badly injured when his car was shot up by a marauding Allied fighter. Three days later, far off in East Prussia, a bomb exploded in the middle of a Führer Conference at Hitler's headquarters at Rastenburg.

Many words have been written on the July Bomb Plot and its subsequent failure and it is not proposed to describe it in detail here. What should be stressed, however, is that while the plotters included members of all the key headquarters, as well as a number of distinguished retired officers, the plot had a critical weakness in that no active field commander was directly involved. Consequently, they had few if any troops upon whom they could call directly in order to consolidate their hold on the country once von Stauffenberg's bomb had exploded. Thus it was that Goebbels was able to turn the tables on Fromm and Olbricht, commander and chief of staff of the Replacement Army, in Berlin by bringing a single Army (and not SS) battalion commander, Major Otto Remer of the Berlin Guard Battalion, on to his side. It was soldiers, and not SS men, who made up the firing squad, on Fromm's orders (in a desperate attempt to save his own skin), that executed von Stauffenberg, Olbricht and others, and despatched Ludwig Beck after he had bungled his suicide attempt. True, von Stülpnagel in Paris was able to arrest all the SS elements in the capital, but failed to gain von Kluge's support, since the C-in-C West had heard that Hitler had survived the attempt. In consequence, von Stülpnagel was forced to release them all. Zimmermann later stated that the events of 20 July had had no effect on the troops fighting in Normandy.[40] They had matters of more immediate concern to occupy their minds.

Hitler's reaction to the attempt on his life was to become even more suspicious of the Army. On 23 July, he decreed that from henceforth the Nazi salute would finally be mandatory for all ranks of the Wehrmacht. This was something that von Rundstedt himself was able to evade by merely giving a wave with his Field Marshal's service baton (*Interimstab*). Hitler's heavy hand on the conduct of operations would also become even more weighty. In the meantime, the Gestapo, under Ernst Kaltenbrunner, Heydrich's successor as head of the RSHA, set about rounding up all those who had been even remotely involved in the plot.

On 2 August 1944, General Wilhelm Burgdorf (who had succeeded Schmundt, one of the fatalities of the 20 July bomb, as Hitler's Wehrmacht Adjutant in OKW) noted in his diary that Hitler had ordered the setting up of a Court of Honour to investigate all army officers suspected of being involved in the plot. It was to assemble on the 4th.[41] Among its members were to be Keitel and Guderian, who had taken over from Zeitzler as Chief of Staff, albeit in an acting capacity on the grounds of the latter's ill health, on the evening of 20 July. Guderian himself had been quick to condemn the plotters. In a national radio broadcast on 23 July he accused them of having 'lost courage and by an act of cowardice and weakness preferred the road to disgrace to that of duty and honour'. Six days later, he issued an order which stated: 'Each General Staff officer must be a National Socialist. That means he must show and prove himself by way of exemplary conduct in political questions, through active instruction and advice to younger comrades on the thoughts of the Führer in the political field as well as a member of the "selected few" . . .'[42] According to his biographer, Guderian made these utterances in order to 'attempt to maintain the status of the Army and that of the General Staff, along with resistance to further encroachment by OKW and the SS in the province of OKH'.[43] Although no firm evidence exists, it is more than possible that Guderian suggested the Court of Honour to Hitler in the first place, though he himself managed to avoid taking part in its proceedings for some time, pleading pressure of work, and sent General Heinrich Kirchheim to represent him. Among the first defendants were Field Marshal von Witzleben and Generals Hoepner and Stieff. Being at the centre of the plot they were found guilty, stripped of their ranks, and arraigned on 7 August in Berlin in a court presided over by the notorious Nazi judge Roland Freisler. Pronounced guilty, they were strung up on meat hooks in the Plötenzee prison.

The premise on which the Court of Honour was based was that upon which it always had been, that an army officer could not be tried by a civilian court. Hence, for this to happen he had first to be dismissed from the Service. Hitler, however, clearly believed that the Court needed added status. So, on 9 August, he laid down that von Rundstedt was to preside over it and no further sittings would be held until the 14th.[44] Von Rundstedt, still at Bad Tölz, was informed of this on the 11th. He gave his own views on the plot when appearing for a witness for the defence in the trial of the German High Command and General Staff at Nuremberg in 1946:

'I would never have thought of such a thing, that would have been base, bare-faced treachery, and could not have changed the situation. The Army and also the people still believed in Hitler at that time, and such an overthrow would have been quite unsuccessful. Even if I, perhaps with the aid of the Allies, had brought about an overthrow, the fate of the German people, according to the famous statement of the Big Three, would have been exactly what it is now, and I would have emerged and been considered for all time as the greatest traitor to my Fatherland.'[45]

Further, during one of his postwar interrogations he declared:

'If anything at all like that is done with a likelihood of success, it can only come from the troops. That is, if the armies in the East and in the West don't act together to a certain extent – what can the stupid crowd at home do? They can't do it. Thank God I was never approached as commander in the field or otherwise.'[46]

As for the Court of Honour itself, he told the IMT Commission:

'The Court of Honour to which I belonged, despite not being an active soldier, had to prejudge the assassinations.
The following had to be considered:
Somebody who was brought in front of the court in Berlin, guilty or not guilty, could not be a soldier any more. If the person in question expected a certain sentence by the court, having been found guilty on the grounds of his own evidence, and it could only be prison or death, we had to sentence him to expulsion from the army.

If, on the contrary, there was the possibility that the person in question
was not guilty, we only sentenced him to discharge. This is a game with
words but there is a difference and later on, if the judgement was 'not
guilty', he was reinstated.

Thank God, in many cases we could apply the latter form, just discharge.
The whole Court of Honour was a very heavy burden for me. But, in the
interest of the Army, I could not evade it.'[47]

Earlier, to Liddell Hart, he made it plain that it was not a court martial,
but admitted that the only evidence which the Court had was that
which was laid before it by the Gestapo. The Army had wanted him to
take on the task because they trusted him to 'make the best of a bad
job'.[48] Even so, according to SS Obersturmbannführer (Lieutenant
Colonel) Dr Georg Keisel, who was working in the RSHA Head Office
at the time, the evidence presented was a mere fraction of that available
and the proceedings were unusual in that not a single accused officer
appeared in person to defend himself. Each case lasted 'only a few
minutes'.[49] No wonder that von Rundstedt later said 'it was a terrible
job to take on the task of presiding over that Court of Honour',
especially as it meant sitting in judgement over officers with whom he
had been closely connected. On another occasion he said that it was
'the worst thing I've ever experienced in my military career'.[50]

While von Rundstedt saw clearly where his duty lay, however
unpalatable this might be, others were surprised that he agreed to take
part. Speidel, in spite of Keitel telling the court that Hitler believed him
to be deeply implicated in the plot, which, of course, he was, was one of
those whom von Rundstedt and his fellow members refused to expel
from the Army. Consequently, he was saved appearing before Freisler,
although he spent the remainder of the war in various prisons. Yet, he
found it 'difficult to understand' why von Rundstedt acted as he did.[51]
Another whose life was saved was Halder, although he spent the
remainder of the war in a concentration camp, which goes some way to
explain the coolness of his relationship with von Rundstedt after 1945.
It was thus probably just as well that at the beginning of September
1944, the Field Marshal was summoned once more by Hitler to tackle
yet another task, and one that would give him little time to dwell on the
rights and wrongs of the Court of Honour.

I I
Recalled Once More

By the beginning of September 1944 the situation in the West was grim for the Germans. Apart from the Channel ports, which remained as *Festungen* with orders to resist to the last man, the whole of Northern France had been liberated and Army Group B, or what was left of it, was reeling back eastwards, having been decimated in the disastrous Mortain counter-attack and suffered unparalleled carnage in the Falaise Gap. US Sixth Army Group, which had landed on the French Riviera in mid-August, was now pursuing the Nineteenth Army, now commanded by Friedrich Wiese, up through Central France. Since von Kluge's sacking and suicide on 16 August, Walter Model had been both C-in-C West and Army Group B and was finding it increasingly difficult to cope with both as he grappled with the problem of trying to salvage at least something from the wreckage of Army Group B, a task in which he and his subordinate commanders achieved a near miracle of recovery – so that the Allies soon found that they still had a very tough fight on their hands. Thus Model spent his time at Army Group Headquarters while that of C-in-C West had to be run by Blumentritt. This was not easy, since the two headquarters were not co-located and, by the middle of August, were some sixty miles apart, C-in-C West near Reims and Army Group B near Soissons. According to Blumentritt,[1] he and Zimmermann decided that this situation could not continue and that the only answer was for von Rundstedt to reassume the duties of C-in-C West once more. Blumentritt wrote to Jodl, who asked for confirmation that Model agreed to this proposal. Model, apparently, was delighted. The idea was therefore put to Hitler, who gave it his blessing. On 1 September von Rundstedt was summoned to the *Führerquartier*, where Hitler apparently said to him: 'Field Marshal, I would like to place the Western Front in your hands again.' To which von Rundstedt replied: 'My Führer, whatever you order, I shall do to my last breath.'[2]

Accordingly, on 5 September, von Rundstedt, accompanied by Hans Gerd, arrived at his headquarters, now at Arenberg, near Koblenz. The familiar faces of Blumentritt and Zimmermann, and others, too, were there to greet him. Sadly for both, the reunion with Blumentritt was brief. After von Rundstedt had previously relinquished as C-in-C West, Blumentritt had asked to be given a field command. This had now just come through and Blumentritt was posted to command the newly created XII SS Panzer Corps, which was to be deployed to the northern part of the Western Front. In his place came Siegfried Westphal, who had been Rommel's Chief of Staff in North Africa and held the same post under Kesselring in Italy. Both had praised him highly, as did the defender of Cassino, the highly intelligent von Senger und Etterlin, who called him 'one of the best horses in the stable'.[3] Thus, once again, von Rundstedt was being given an excellent chief of staff and one who had a cavalry background. Even so, just over two weeks after reassuming command, von Rundstedt did make a request for Blumentritt to be returned to him as 'General on Special Duty', but Hitler turned this down,[4] probably quite rightly since it would not have been fair to Blumentritt's new command.

The Allied view of von Rundstedt's reappointment was summarised in a crowing British 21st Army Group intelligence review:

> 'Just as von Rundstedt has never been strong enough utterly to disregard the Party, so has his ability (or his reputation) been too convenient for the politicos to ignore. If his own health has improved, the state of his armies has deteriorated in his absence. To bring back the Old Guard implies that the situation is desperate, and since little can be done about it, it may mean that the Old Guard is to take the blame. The return of von Rundstedt is reminiscent of the description of the role of cavalry in modern war: 'to add distinction to what otherwise might be a vulgar brawl.' The reappointment is interesting as exhibiting muddle and desperation; but (unlike the cavalry) it doesn't really make much difference. The task of Commander-in-Chief in any German theatre has degenerated into that of local Chief-of-Staff to Hitler and liable to dismissal as much for carrying out quaint orders as for protesting against them.'[5]

Von Rundstedt would have certainly agreed with the last sentence, but, in his eyes, what choice did he have? He had been summoned again and his code would not allow him to refuse, especially in this dark time. To turn his back on the soldiers struggling back to the West Wall would have been desertion.

His own appreciation of the situation was that his main task was 'to stop the entire withdrawal movement and stabilise the front'.[6] This was reinforced by Hitler, who ordered a fierce delaying action in order to buy time for Army Group G to complete its withdrawal from southern France and to enable the defences on the West Wall to be enhanced. However, according to Bodo Zimmermann, von Rundstedt differed from Hitler in the significance of the West Wall as a bastion against the Allied onrush. To him the only feasible defence line was the Rhine and one of his first steps was, discreetly, to secure all crossing places. He would make repeated efforts during the winter to persuade Hitler to think again and not pin his hopes on the West Wall, but in vain.[7] As it happened, Army Group G did manage to get back reasonably intact and took up position on the left of the German line.

The German forces were now organised as follows. The northern part of the front was the responsibility of Model's Army Group B. Under him was Gustav von Zangen's Fifteenth Army, which was being pushed back through Belgium and into Holland by Montgomery's 21st Army Group, Karl Student's newly formed First Parachute Army, now deploying in Holland, and Erich Brandenberger's Seventh Army, falling back through the Ardennes to the German border. Then came Army Group G. This was still commanded by Blaskowitz, but on 21 September he was to be succeeded by Hermann Balck. Otto von Knobelsdorff's First Army covered Lorraine, Hasso von Manteuffel's Fifth Panzer Army, which, after its predecessor had been lost in Tunisia, had been reformed in early August from the remnants of Panzer Group West, was in Alsace, while in the extreme south stood Friedrich Wiese's Nineteenth Army, now recovering its breath after the long withdrawal up through the centre of France.

Hitler told von Rundstedt that his immediate tasks were to prevent the Allies from opening up the port of Antwerp, to create a strong base in Holland and to protect the Ruhr and Saar regions. The city of Antwerp itself had been entered by the British 11th Armoured Division on 4 September, with Brussels being liberated the previous day, but von Zangen still held both banks of the Scheldt and hence the port could not be used. Since the Allies were still relying on Cherbourg for their supplies, it meant that their lines of communication were now overstretched. This had its effect on the momentum of their advance, which now began to slow dramatically, thus giving von Rundstedt a vital breathing space to restore some cohesion. The British Second and United States First Armies managed to get across the Albert Canal and, on 11 September, patrols from the latter crossed the German border for the first time. During the next four days, the Americans tried to punch through the West Wall at Aachen, but with only partial success. Further south, Patton's Third United States Army, suffering from increasing fuel shortages, closed up to the Moselle and managed to cross it opposite Nancy, but in the face of ever stiffening opposition. Montgomery, however, had managed to persuade Eisenhower to allow him to mount a daring airborne operation designed to turn von Rundstedt's northern flank.

Von Rundstedt's own appreciation of the situation on reassuming command was that the main Allied thrust line would be Aachen – Ruhr – Berlin and that the enemy would concentrate his forces in the north in order to achieve this.[8] At the time, his main concern was the mouth of the River Moselle at Trier, close to the Luxembourg border – the closest to the German border that the Allies had reached. Tanks from Courtney Hodges' First United States Army entered the city of Luxembourg on 10 September and the following evening reconnaissance patrols had actually penetrated into Germany. Westphal recalled accompanying von Rundstedt on a visit to the Trier area at this time and that they narrowly escaped capture by American tanks.[9] On 14 September, a more serious threat developed north of Trier. Elements of the US 5th Armored Division began to break through the West Wall at Wallendorf. This happened to be on the boundary between Army Groups B and G and there were few German defenders in the area. A major breakthrough appeared imminent. Next day, von Rundstedt issued a special order of the day: 'The fight for German soil must increase fanaticism. Every pill-box, every village must be defended until the Allies bleed to death. It is no longer a question of operations on a grand scale. The only task is to hold our positions until we are annihilated.'[10] A week's desperate fighting followed, after which the Americans withdrew across the River Sauer. The apparent success was partially achieved by stripping the front to the south in order to deploy reserves to the threatened sector and by constantly keeping the Americans off balance with counter-attacks. The main reason, however, was that Hodges could no longer sustain his offensive because Eisenhower had switched the priority for logistics to Montgomery for his attempt to outflank the Germans in the north.

On 17 September Montgomery launched Operation MARKET-GARDEN with the aim of getting over the Lower Rhine in one quick step. The story of what happened is well known and needs to no re-telling here. It is significant, however, that von Rundstedt, in his report on the operation, admitted that Montgomery did achieve initial surprise, but in turn was surprised by the presence of II SS Panzer Corps in the Arnhem area. He also considered that the main Allied mistake was to spread the airborne landings over three days.[11] The failure to secure the bridge at Arnhem really marked the last chance of the Allies ending the war in 1944 and was to be the prelude to an autumn's grim fighting.

During MARKET-GARDEN, von Rundstedt was also concerned about the situation on the Moselle itself. Hitler had demanded that Patton's bridgeheads should be eliminated and it was this task that Balck faced on assuming as C-in-C Army Group G. Balck himself had had a meteoric rise. He had first distinguished himself as a regimental commander in Rommel's 7th Panzer Division in France 1940, but had thereafter fought on the Eastern Front as a divisional, corps and then army commander. According to Balck's chief of staff, Friedrich von Mellenthin, von Rundstedt had initial reservations over Balck's appointment on the grounds that he had no experience of fighting against the Western Allies, which has echoes of Rommel's view on the commanders in the West prior to the invasion. Von Mellenthin, however, had known von Rundstedt from before the war and regarded him as 'a man one could honour and respect'. He also knew Westphal well and this perhaps helped to quickly develop 'extremely cordial' relations between the two headquarters.[12] Attempts to eradicate the Nancy bridgehead had begun on 19 September with the committal of a Panzer brigade. Next day, another Panzer brigade joined the fray, but Allied air supremacy quickly proved decisive and both brigades were virtually destroyed. After further demands from Hitler, the counter-attacks were resumed on the 22nd, but the result was the same. Von Rundstedt realised that to continue was merely to waste troops, but Hitler refused to listen to him. A further effort was made on the 25th, which initially had some success, thanks to poor weather which kept Allied aircraft grounded. When they did reappear on the 29th, the result was the same as in the previous attacks. Balck said that he would need three fresh divisions if he was to continue, but there were no reserves and hence von Rundstedt ordered him to halt and remain on the defensive. As it happened, in view of the critical resupply situation, Eisenhower had ordered that Patton should halt all offensive operations until the Scheldt was cleared. Hence, there was now a pause, which was invaluable to the hard pressed German forces.

In the meantime, von Rundstedt turned his attention to Aachen, where the Americans were making renewed efforts to break through the

West Wall. The fighting between Courtney Hodges' First United States Army and Student's First Parachute Army and Fifth Panzer Army, which von Rundstedt switched to this area on 14 October, especially in the Hürtgen Forest, was to be particularly bloody over the next two months.

In the midst of these operational crises von Rundstedt was called upon by Hitler to perform another task. On 14 October, Generals Burgdorf and Maisel visited Erwin Rommel at his home at Herrlingen, where he had been convalescing from the wounds he received in Normandy. They brought him a message from Hitler. Either he committed suicide or faced trial for his involvement with the July 1944 plotters, in which case his wife and son would have to face the consequences. Rommel chose the former. It meant that he would be given a state funeral, thus ensuring that his reputation officially remained intact and that his family would be protected. It was, of course, what Hitler wanted him to do since to bring him to trial would not rest easily with the propaganda image of him that Goebbels had so assiduously built up over the past few years. The funeral itself took place in Ulm on 18 October. According to von Mellenthin, von Rundstedt called into Balck's headquarters to say the Keitel had telephone him to tell him that Hitler had asked him to represent him at the funeral and to read the eulogy.[13] This he did and Ruge, who was present, noted that 'although curiously impersonal and somewhat restrained, it was a good speech to those who did not know what was being played out. Just how much von Rundstedt knew I never found out.'[14] Speidel, who was unable to attend since he was now in the hands of the Gestapo, was more forthright: 'Here destiny gave him the unique chance of playing Mark Anthony. The moment found him still impassive.' But, he also commented: 'the old soldier appeared to onlookers to be broken and distracted.' Further, Speidel wrote that von Rundstedt did not any take part in the cremation and did not accompany the other mourners to the Rommel house.[15] In his defence, von Rundstedt was emphatic after the war that he knew nothing of the true circumstances of Rommel's death. As he wrote to Liddell Hart: ' I can swear on oath that I knew *nothing* of *the true case of* Rommel's death. *If I had I would have never taken part* in the memorial ceremony!!'[sic][16] He was supported in this by von Mellenthin, who also said that, like von Rundstedt, he only learnt of the facts after the war was over.[17] According to Ditha, when her father-in-law received Hitler's request he asked 'Why me? Keitel would have been much more suitable.' The reply was: 'Hitler sets great store by you especially, Herr Feldmarschall, performing at the state ceremony.' Von Rundstedt was 'deeply affected' by Rommel's death and acquiesced. As for the funeral oration, the script had been placed on the lectern and von Rundstedt had no opportunity to read it through before delivering it, which would explain Ruge's and Speidel's comments.[18] The Field Marshal had been 'used' once more by Hitler to cloak his actions with respectability.

Meanwhile, the Allied pressure on the Western Front was maintained. Aachen fell to the United States First Army on 21 October, but since it lay on the most direct route to the Ruhr it was essential that the Americans were held. First Canadian Army was clearing both sides of the Scheldt and on 1 November, Montgomery launched a successful amphibious assault on the island of Walcheren, which lies at its mouth. Dempsey's Second British Army was clearing eastwards towards the Rhine from the salient created by MARKET-GARDEN. In Army Group G's area, Patton, now receiving the lowest priority for supplies within the United States 12th Army Group, was battling to reduce the ancient fortress of Metz. This lay in an exposed salient, which von Rundstedt wanted to abandon, but Balck considered that it was better to allow the Americans to wear down their strength against the fortress, provided that the garrison was able to withdraw in good time.[19] Von Rundstedt allowed Balck to have his own way. In any event, Hitler would not have countenanced a withdrawal and, indeed, in early November declared Metz a *Festung*. Von Rundstedt's view of the situation at this time was that 'the soldier can do nothing but buy time for the political leadership to negotiate. He can do nothing but preserve the military power as much as possible.'[20] Conservation of force had to be his watchword, but he must have realised that there was no hope of Hitler being prepared to negotiate with the Allies. Towards the end of October, however, he was to be faced with a bombshell.

On 20 October, Hitler summoned von Rundstedt and Model to Rastenburg, but then amended the order. Instead, Westphal and Model's chief of staff, Hans Krebs, were to attend. They did so and, on the 26th, returned to their headquarters to brief their respective commanders on what had transpired.

The concept for what became known as the Ardennes counter-offensive or, more popularly, the Battle of the Bulge, had been born in mid-September when Hitler, at one of his conferences, announced his intention to strike from the Ardennes for Antwerp, splitting the British 21st Army Group from the United States 12th Army Group. On 25 September, he ordered Jodl to prepare an outline plan, stressing the paramount importance of surprise and the need to take maximum advantage of the winter fogs so that the employment of Allied air power would be restricted. On 9 October, Jodl presented his draft plan. He had blanched at the idea of a thrust on Antwerp, and instead proposed five less ambitious options, consisting of double envelopments from Düsseldorf in the north to the Belfort Gap in the south. Hitler, not surprisingly, was unimpressed and told Jodl to think again. Two days later he presented an acceptable solution. It accurately reflected Hitler's original concept and was to be carried out by three armies under Model's command with von Rundstedt exercising overall supervision. The offensive would be spearheaded by two Panzer armies. In the north Sepp Dietrich's newly formed Sixth Panzer Army, which was built round four SS Panzer divisions, now re-formed after the long mauling they had received in France, and Hasso von Manteuffel's Fifth Panzer Army in the south. Brandenberger's Seventh Army would secure the southern shoulder and Dietrich could call on assistance from von Zangen's Fifteenth Army to his north. Von Rundstedt himself never quite trusted Model since 'he was too temperamental'. 'We had an expression: "to Model", which meant getting everything very muddled. Then there was the word "to de-Model", meaning sorting things out again. The troops invented that one. However he was a very capable man, above all very courageous, but impulsive.'[21] Even so, on this occasion, Model was as aghast as von Rundstedt. Apart from the blatant over-ambition of the plan, they saw its result as merely the creation of a long narrow salient which would invite Allied counter-attacks and would require an inordinate number of men to hold it. As Model remarked: 'This damned thing hasn't a leg to stand on.'[21]

On 27 October, von Rundstedt and Model and their staffs met at Headquarters Army Group B, now at Fichtenhain near Krefeld, to consider the plan. They believed that a much more feasible operation would be one designed to destroy the Allied forces then contained in the salient bounded by Aachen, Maastricht and Liege. These were sizeable, consisting of parts of the American First and British Second Armies and the whole of the United States Ninth Army. This could be achieved by double envelopment, using the Ardennes attack as the southern prong and another attack from the Geilenkirchen area as the northern. Von Rundstedt put what came to be known by the various staffs as the Small Solution, as opposed to OKW's Large Solution, to OKW at the beginning of November. Jodl came and visited von Rundstedt at Model's headquarters on 3 November and made it clear that Hitler considered the Small Solution unacceptable. He went on to describe the plan in more detail and state that Hitler wanted the attack to begin on the 25th.

Westphal now suggested to von Rundstedt that he should go to Hitler himself and personally dissuade him. Von Rundstedt turned this down 'for he considered that Hitler's stubbornness and his habit of conducting hour-long monologues and preventing anyone else from speaking made such personal representations hopeless. He had already had enough of such painful experiences.'[23] However, something had to be done, especially about the date of the attack which allowed totally insufficient time for preparation.

For a start, there was the problem of disengaging many of the formations earmarked for the offensive from the battles being fought around Aachen and the Maas and in Lorraine. Not until the end of October was it possible to withdraw the headquarters of I and II SS Panzer Corps from the front line, which placed a heavy burden on HQ Sixth Panzer Army in re-equipping and bringing the four SS Panzer divisions up to strength. Many of the Panzer divisions themselves had been heavily committed, as had a number of other formations needed for the attack. There was, too, the need to disengage Fifth Panzer Army from the Aachen area. This was done by replacing it by Fifteenth Army from Holland and creating a new army there, Twenty-Fifth, under Friedrich Christiansen. This did bring about one concession to von Rundstedt and Model. It was clear that Model could not both prepare for a major offensive and cover a front that stretched from the North Sea round through Holland and virtually down to the Franco-Luxembourg border. Consequently a new army group was created, H, under Kurt Student, and this took First Parachute, now commanded by Alfred Schlemm, and Twenty-Fifth Armies under command.

Given the heavy losses recently suffered by the German armies in both the East and West, manpower was a critical problem. On 25 July, Hitler had issued a 'total war' directive. Among the measures ordered was the induction of one million recruits for the Wehrmacht. These were comb-outs from industry, and 17 year-olds. Most of them were formed into Volksgrenadier divisions, stiffened by the skeletons of divisions already destroyed. These were slimmer in numbers that the conventional infantry division, just 10,000 men compared to 17,000. Von Rundstedt afterwards declared that this was a mistake, especially the decision to raise some Volksgrenadier divisions from what was called *Volksdeutsch List III*, men of German extraction, and others, domiciled outside Germany:

> 'The quality wasn't the same as it used to be. We had sick men, old men and those not quite fit for active service, besides which we had those

dreadful fellows, taken from "*Volksliste 3*", who were nothing better than deserters in uniform. It was unfortunate: we expected a so-called "*Volksdeutscher*" soldier to give his life and blood whilst his relatives were in a concentration camp in Poland. It wasn't a clever move.'[24]

Even with this new influx at the beginning of December, von Rundstedt reported his command as being 3,500 officers and 115,000 men below establishment. The problem was that reinforcements and replacements were not matching casualties. Morale was a constant concern. The lower grade of the new replacements meant that incidents of self-inflicted wounds so rose that von Rundstedt had to issue a special order warning of the severe penalties that would be meted out to those who took this route to avoid further fighting.[25] At the same time, in a special order of the day, he appealed to the veterans to 'pass on your will for victory and your combat experience' to the new arrivals at the Front.[26]

While the quality of weapons systems remained high, quantity was a problem. True, in spite of the Allied bombing, German war production peaked in 1944, largely thanks to Albert Speer's plan for moving industry away from the cities to carefully camouflaged satellite factories in the country. But losses had risen, too. Also the bombing had severely disrupted communications and the delivery of replacement weapons was taking very much longer than hitherto. In the Panzer divisions, for instance, the establishment of a tank company had fallen from 22 tanks to 17 by early 1944 and to 14 by November. Often, too, assault guns, with their very limited gun traverse, were substituted for tanks. Furthermore, the replacement tank crewmen had received only the most rudimentary training and it was not uncommon for drivers to be posted into divisions at this time who had not as yet driven a tank. The artillery was sufficient in numbers, but the guns were of such varying calibre that ammunition supply, aggravated by the vastly reduced railway system and limited motor transport, together with the fact that, for security reasons its movement had to be tightly controlled, was a nightmare. At the root of the problem was fuel. Germany's stocks were now declining rapidly, both through bombing and the Russian advances in the East. Von Rundstedt calculated that five 'allocations' of fuel were needed, but when the offensive opened only 1.2 – 1.5 allocations were available. The assumption was that the remainder could be brought up from dumps east of the Rhine once the offensive started,[27] contrary to the popular postwar belief that the attacking troops would rely on captured US stocks.[23] One thing that von Rundstedt did insist on, however, was that the troops' rations should not suffer and they continued to get their hot stew. His own staff, on the other hand, were restricted to 1.5 ounces of meat per day. The Field Marshal himself, though, 'a very light eater, would often cut off a tiny piece of his ration for himself and pass the rest to one of his officers'.[28]

Added to these problems was the continuing pressure being exerted by the Allies. This made it very difficult to keep the divisions earmarked for the counter-offensive intact, let alone hold the enemy at arm's length. In the north, von Rundstedt had demanded of OKW from September onwards that he be allowed to withdraw behind the River Waal. He argued that this would shorten his front sufficiently to save five divisions. Hitler turned this down in spite of the Allied crossing of it at Nijmegen during MARKET-GARDEN. The British Second Army's advance eastwards towards the Rhine from the MARKET-GARDEN salient in October created another grave threat and was only stopped by a counter-attack in the Venlo area at the end of the month. On the 29th, von Rundstedt once again urged that Fifteenth Army be allowed to fall back behind the Waal, but Hitler would only concede a withdrawal to the north bank of the Maas. A further concern in the occupied Netherlands was the able-bodied Dutch males of military age, whose numbers were estimated as 600,000. Von Rundstedt was concerned that if the Allied advances into the Netherlands continued, they might well take up arms against his troops and create yet another burden. At the same time, Sauckel was crying out for more manpower to make good the losses in the Third Reich's labour force created by the raising of the Volksgrenadier divisions. It therefore seemed logical to von Rundstedt to use the Dutch manpower to satisfy Sauckel's demands and he issued an order to this effect to army Group B and Christiansen in the Netherlands on 2 November. This order was to form the basis of yet another of the war crimes charges made against him.[29]

Besides the continuing desperate fighting around Aachen, which had forced the transfer from the south of Fifth Panzer Army and saw the British and Americans close up to the River Roer by early December, November brought further crises in the southern part of C-in-C West's front. On the 8th, Patton launched an attack in the Saarland. Six days later, First French Army thrust at the Belfort Gap. US Seventh Army also joined in and the upshot was that, by the end of the month, Balck's army group had been driven back to the Rhine south of Baden Baden, apart from around Colmar, where Nineteenth Army was left in an exposed salient with its back to the river. Patton finally captured Metz and drove First Army back to the River Saar. The condition of many of

Army Group G's divisions was, in von Mellenthin's words, 'deplorable',[30] but the situation might have been much graver had it not been for the bad weather which persisted during the month. The snow and rain slowed the Allied armour and, more significantly, restricted their air power. Even so the net result of all this was that, as early as 21 November, von Rundstedt warned OKW that nine mobile and four infantry divisions would no longer be available for Hitler's Ardennes counter-offensive.[31]

   This von Rundstedt used as a fresh argument for the Small Solution, but Hitler's 'dead hand' began to lie even more heavily on the project. On 19 November, von Rundstedt was sent a 12-page instruction on the assault tactics to be used in the offensive. All subordinate commanders were to be briefed on these and Hitler demanded copies of the briefs,[32] a deeply demeaning intrusion on the authority of C-in-C West. Next day, Model sent a written plea to von Rundstedt to have the Small Solution reconsidered. He argued that the Allies had concentrated a significant amount of force in the Aachen area and that a 'two-pronged pincer movement' against it would be a 'devastating blow' and would create the right circumstances for fulfilling Hitler's overall aim of splitting the Allied armies. He also stated that he considered 30 November as the earliest date on which the attack could be mounted.[33] Hitler rejected this out of hand. Model tried again to get the Small Solution accepted at a conference at von Rundstedt's headquarters on the 23rd, but also said that the Panzer divisions earmarked for the attack would now not be ready before 15 December because he had been forced to commit some of them to the fighting. Again he got nowhere. According to Westphal, von Rundstedt now asked Jodl to come and see him, which he did on the 26th. He was entirely sympathetic to the Small Solution, but said 'with tired resignation' that his hopes of convincing Hitler were slim.[34] The final attempt to make Hitler change his mind came on 2 December. At Model's request, Hitler agreed to see him and his army commanders in Berlin, where he had stopped off for some three weeks en route from Rastenburg to his headquarters in the West. Westphal was also present. Von Rundstedt, however, did not attend. Instead he spent the day watching a map exercise being conducted at Sepp Dietrich's Sixth Panzer Army headquarters.

   Von Manteuffel recalled that Model presented a 'masterly summary' of the issues and that even Hitler was 'visibly impressed'.[35] He was not, however, to be swayed. After the seven hour conference had finished, Hitler had a private discussion with von Manteuffel and said that he accepted that the forces available to reach such a distant objective as Antwerp were probably insufficient. Nevertheless, he was determined on the gamble, so that the situation in the West could be sufficiently stabilised for him to transfer forces to the East, where the Russians were preparing for a major offensive across the Vistula.[36] Significantly, von Manteuffel said that Westphal took no part in the discussions and appeared to display a complete lack of knowledge of Model's dispositions.[37] This would indicate that von Rundstedt had now resigned himself to the inevitable and saw no point in pursuing the Small Solution any further. He may have been influenced in this by his assertion after the war that Hitler annotated the final orders for the attack 'Not to be altered'.[38]

On 26 November, Hitler had declared that the attack would be launched on 10 December. Yet it was only on the 10th that he left Berlin for his western headquarters, the *Adlerhorst* (Eagle's Eyrie), an admission that this date was over-optimistic. On the following day, he formally agreed a postponement to the 15th. This was not just to give Model more time to deploy his divisions, but also because the fuel dumps were still woefully ill stocked.

The *Adlerhorst* itself was situated just one kilometre south of von Rundstedt's headquarters, which were now at Schloss Ziegenberg in the Taunus Hills north of Frankfurt-am-Main. This virtual co-location was a stark indicator that Hitler intended to conduct the offensive himself and that von Rundstedt was to all intents and purposes superfluous. The responsibility for setting up the facilities in the *Adlerhorst* appears to have rested with the army, but Martin Bormann, who was part of Hitler's entourage, complained, on arrival at 0300 hours on the 11th, about the poor preparation, especially the badly installed teleprinters and the lack of facilities for his two secretaries, remarking that 'The proverb "on whom the Lord bestows an office, he also bestows intelligence" certainly does not apply to officers.'[39] On the 11th and 12th, Hitler summoned all commanders, down to and including corps commanders, taking part in WATCH ON THE RHINE (*Wacht am Rhein*), as the offensive was codenamed, for a final 'pep talk', half on each evening. They had to report to von Rundstedt's headquarters first and were taken from there in buses, which, for security reasons, made a half hour long detour for a journey which took only three minutes by the direct route. Von Rundstedt himself had to attend on both occasions, which must have been a trial for him, given his distaste for Hitler's diatribes. Von Manteuffel recalled, too, that: 'the seating accommodation was inadequate and the SS generals politely left the chairs to their senior army colleagues, while they stood.

This created the impression on some of the army generals that an SS officer was posted behind each army officer's chair.'[40] As usual, the monologue itself was lengthy. After a long historical introduction, Hitler announced that new U-boats, the submerged high speed Types XXI and XXIII, were about to become operational and would radically change the face of the war at sea.[41] Furthermore, wars were only decided when one side realised that it could never win. By demonstrating that Germany would never surrender, the Allies would be forced to end the war. Besides, the starkly contrasting political systems of the Soviet Union and Western Allies meant that their coalition was bound to collapse. Finally, he did not believe that the enemy in the West was markedly superior in numbers and claimed that the Americans alone had suffered 240,000 casualties during the past three weeks. In equipment terms, too, the German tanks were markedly superior.[42] Dietrich, who was present on the second evening, also said that Hitler gave the fact that the German people could no longer endure the Allied bombing as another reason for mounting the offensive. He noted, too, that no one else spoke and that when Hitler asked each commander whether he was ready all replied in the negative.[43] It was probably because of this that Hitler relented once more on the 12th and postponed the offensive by a further day to 16 December.

It is most unlikely that many of the commanders, least of all von Rundstedt, were taken in by Hitler's largely fallacious arguments. The die, however, was cast and, in their eyes, there was nothing they could do about it. 12 December was, of course, von Rundstedt's birthday and, following Hitler's conference, the commanders repaired to his headquarters for a celebration. It was, according to Dietrich, a muted affair and by midnight all the Field Marshal's guests had departed.[44] Yet, if the generals were pessimistic, the same does not seem to have been so for their troops. In spite of von Rundstedt's comments on the quality of those that made up the bulk of his forces, there seems to have been a genuine optimism amongst them during the weeks leading up to the offensive, although, of course, it was not until just before it opened that the troops were told what was about to take place. Up until then they had been led to believe that they were preparing for counter-attacks should the Allies break through in the Aachen area. Von Rundstedt had been ordered by OKW on 5 November to ensure that *Volksliste III* personnel whose loyalty was suspect should not be placed in forward positions and that, from 15 November, he was to report all soldiers missing from front line units. Besides being a valuable source of intelligence, desertions to the enemy are a very good indicator of morale. It is therefore significant that during the first twelve days of December only four deserters, all from Volksgrenadier divisions, were notified to OKW.[45]

On the even of the offensive, Hitler issued his final instructions to Model. Primarily, they stressed that his Panzer divisions were on no account to turn northwards while east of the Meuse, thus reminding Model that no attempt to implement the Small Solution would be permitted. Furthermore, Model was to carry out 'all orders from the supreme command unconditionally, and to see that they are followed down to the lowest unit'. Provided Model followed Hitler's concept of operations 'a great victory is assured'.[46] These instructions were sent direct to Model, thereby bypassing von Rundstedt. It was now more than ever clear that the battle was not his to conduct

12

The Last Battles

AT 0530 HOURS on 16 December, the German artillery opened up on the American defences in the Eifel. Half an hour later, the Volksgrenadier divisions responsible for the break-in began their attacks. The Ardennes counter-offensive had begun.

In spite of gaining almost total surprise, the attack began to fall behind schedule on the first day. This was especially so in Sepp Dietrich's Sixth Panzer Army sector, which Hitler had laid down would be the main thrust. Dietrich had planned on the break-in being achieved by the end of the first day. Then five SS armoured battle groups would pass through and race for the Meuse bridges. The infantry experienced unexpected difficulties, both with the terrain and with American units which stood and fought. In consequence, armoured elements had to be committed prematurely to assist the infantry in getting forward. Most of the routes quickly became impassable. By nightfall, only one battle group, led by Joachim Peiper, a regimental commander in the SS Leibstandarte, had actually penetrated the depth of American defences. Von Manteuffel, in spite of having more natural obstacles in the form of river lines to contend with, enjoyed slightly better success, but traffic jams prevented his armour from breaking out as quickly as he wanted. That night, an airborne drop west of Monschau, designed to prevent the Americans bringing in reinforcements from the north, proved abortive. The paratroops, most of whom were novices, were scattered over a wide area. The operations of elements of Otto Skorzeny's 150 Panzer Brigade, dressed in American uniforms and driving captured jeeps, did, however, cause confusion behind the American lines, even to the extent of making Eisenhower a virtual prisoner in his headquarters at Versailles for fear of assassination. Von Rundstedt said that he had never been told of Skorzeny's operations and that they were controlled entirely by

OKW.[1] Certainly, though, Dietrich knew all about them, placing Skorzeny under command of I SS Panzer Corps.[2] Von Rundstedt must have also been aware of the plan for Skorzeny's force since requests for volunteers and captured Allied equipment were passed by OKW to his headquarters and they also sent at least one complaint on the lack of response direct to Zimmermann at Ob West.[3] Yet, von Rundstedt, after the war, also complained to his Allied interrogators that during the offensive Dietrich, whom he referred to as a 'cigarette roller' to Milton Shulman, (whether because Dietrich had once worked in a tobacco factory or, like himself, was an inveterate smoker is not clear) sent his reports directly to OKW, bypassing both Model and himself. They were then relayed to Model.[4] Von Manteuffel, too, complained that he received little information from Sixth Panzer Army, although this was denied by Dietrich.[5] It is possible that Dietrich reported directly on Skorzeny's activities to OKW, but it is very difficult to accept that otherwise he did not keep at least HQ Army Group B informed.

17 December saw Peiper reach Stavelot, 21 miles from his start line, by teatime, but little progress by the rest of Sixth Panzer Army. It was during Peiper's drive on this day that the infamous Malmédy massacre of American troops occurred. Both von Rundstedt and Dietrich asserted after the war that the first that they heard of it was when it was broadcast by the Allied black propaganda radio station *Soldatensender Calais* on 21 December. Von Rundstedt stated that he ordered an immediate investigation. This ties up with what Dietrich told an American interviewer after the war, saying that Model asked him whether he knew anything about it and that he set up an investigation as a result.[6] Given the fact that the suspected culprits were deep behind the enemy lines at the time, and that there were other things to worry about when the survivors did get back to their own lines, it is not surprising that the investigation, if indeed it did take place, got nowhere.[7]

During the next few days, while Peiper experienced increasing frustration, both from the stiffening American defence and, more especially, because an American engineer battalion blew a number of vital bridges in his face, von Manteuffel made increasingly better progress. Even so, pockets of resistance held him up, especially in the towns of St Vith and Bastogne. The latter had been reinforced by one of the only two divisions in Eisenhower's theatre reserve, 101st Airborne. The story of its epic defence of this key communications centre is well known. Out of it came one of the great military quotations of all time,

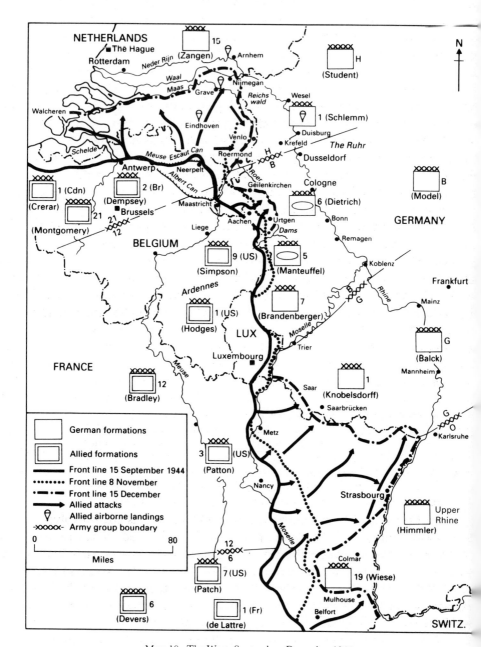

MAP 10. The West, September–December 1944

when Brigadier General Anthony C McAuliffe, the acting divisional commander, dismissed a German surrender demand with the word 'Nuts!'. Army Group B apparently transmitted this to von Rundstedt as *Quatsch* (Bosh), the nearest German equivalent. This must have caused von Rundstedt a wry smile since it was one of his favourite expressions. Blumentritt wrote that 'he used to spit it out when reading some particularly unreasonable order from above'.[8]

By this time, Patton, whom von Rundstedt considered, together with Montgomery, as one of the two best Allied generals of the war,[9] had begun his drive north to relieve Bastogne and it was clear that Dietrich's effort further north was fizzling out. On Christmas Eve, with the fogs clearing and Allied air power making its presence increasingly felt, von Rundstedt realised that the offensive had litte prospect of further success and urged OKW to go on to the defensive.[10] Hitler, though, was determined that it should continue and, in von Rundstedt's words, it degenerated into 'Stalingrad No 2'.[11]

On Christmas Day, there appeared an article in *Life* magazine in the United States. Written by David Cort, it was headlined THE LAST PRUSSIAN. While it made no mention of the Ardennes, the article portrayed von Rundstedt as 'the last and by far the greatest of the Prussian masters who almost won the world for Hitler' and asserted that he had taken over the defence of the West from him. He was 'Germany's last hope'.

> 'Von Rundstedt is as cold, functional and masked as a pillbox. There is no personal dash in him; he does not swagger; he is no Rommel. But beyond the fact that he is a far deadlier foe than Rommel or any Nazi general could have been, von Rundstedt knots in his own person all the crucial clues to the German Army, the Nazi state and the present undercover fight for power in Germany, as well as an omen for the next war.

Cort commented, with some perception, on von Rundstedt's involvement with the bomb plot Court of Honour. He portrayed its victims as having 'broken the sacred law of the Prussian officer corps; they had failed, they had been caught and they had compromised the honor of the Army.' The affair had 'blasted into the open the enormous schism between Hitler and the Prussian officers who own the German Army.' Von Rundstedt and his fellows intended to pin Germany's defeat firmly on Hitler so that they could preserve their honour for the next war. He stressed that von Rundstedt was a defence expert and had conducted the autumn 1944 campaign with 'his usual good sense'. Where the article was lacking in accuracy was in its detailed account of von

Rundstedt's life. Cort had clearly drawn his information from W E Hart's book *Hitler's Generals*, which, as has already been shown, was little more than wartime propaganda, being full of inaccuracies and baseless accusations.

The significance of Cort's article, appearing when it did, is that it reflected the respect, indeed almost awe, in which the Western Allies held von Rundstedt. They were convinced at the time that he had masterminded the Ardennes counter-offensive, and this helped to fuel the crisis that the attack provoked within the Allied ranks. Eisenhower, after the war, wrote that he and his staff always considered von Rundstedt 'the ablest of the German generals'.[12] Montgomery, too, in his notorious press briefing of 7 January 1945, when he claimed that he had pulled the American chestnuts out of the fire in the Ardennes, said: 'I used to think that Rommel was good, but my opinion is that Rundstedt would have hit him for six. Rundstedt is the best German general I have come up against.'[13] All this, though, would have been of little comfort to the Field Marshal, given the increasingly depressing situation and his powerlessness to do anything about it.

On 28 December, Hitler held another of his interminable conferences. Von Rundstedt tried once more to persuade him to halt the offensive and withdraw his forces east of Bastogne in order to save them from Allied counter-attacks on their now very vulnerable flanks. Hitler would have none of it. He accepted that if the counter-offensive had 'not resulted in the decisive success which might have been expected', it had nevertheless brought about a 'tremendous easing of the situation'. The Americans had been forced to weaken the remainder of the Western Front and their defences in Alsace especially had become 'extraordinarily thin'. He therefore intended to take advantage of this by launching a preplanned attack *Nordwind* on New Year's Day. In the meantime, von Manteuffel, who had now taken over most of Dietrich's armour, was to prepare for another thrust at the Meuse and keep Patton tied down in the Bastogne sector.[14] The prospect seems to have filled Hitler's entourage and OKW with renewed optimism. Next evening, Himmler held a reception and among the guests were von Rundstedt and some of his staff. Martin Bormann noted that Jodl danced at it, but it is difficult to believe that von Rundstedt really entered into the party mood. None the less, on the following evening, he reciprocated by entertaining Himmler and Bormann at his headquarters.[15] Perhaps he hoped that he might be able to persuade them to make Hitler see sense.

By now there was another and very much darker cloud looming over the horizon, which reinforced the need to go over to the defensive in the West. All the signs were that the long awaited Russian offensive over the Vistula was about to begin. Guderian had been left grappling with this problem and, deeply concerned by the way in which troops were being frittered in the West, had asked Hitler, on 26 December, to halt the Ardennes attack. Like von Rundstedt, he got nowhere. Thereupon he travelled to the West to plead his case in person. First, however, he visited von Rundstedt and Westphal and asked for their help in getting divisions transferred to the Eastern Front. 'They showed,' he later wrote, 'as so often in the past, complete understanding of the needs of the other front', and offered up three divisions. Guderian immediately had a warning order sent to these divisions, and, when Hitler and OKW tried to resist, was able to get his own way by telling them that C-in-C West had said that they were available.[16] As it happened, Hitler now became concerned about the situation in Hungary and eventually they, and Dietrich's army, were sent there.

Operation *Nordwind* was duly launched on 1 January. It was conducted by Army Group G, now commanded again by Blaskowitz, who had succeeded Balck on Christmas Eve. Its object was the recapture of the Saverne Gap and the destruction of Patch's United States Seventh Army and the left wing of Lattre de Tassigny's First French Army. The initial attack was carried out by von Obstfelder's First Army, with elements of Army Group Upper Rhine, commanded by no less than Himmler, joining in later. Although it gained some ground initially, it never looked like achieving a decisive success and the Americans and French easily rode the blow. On the same day, the Luftwaffe mounted a virtually suicidal attack, *Bodenplatte* (Baseplate) on Allied airfields in Belgium and Holland in an effort to remove Allied air supremacy from over the battlefield. Although the Allies lost over 300 aircraft destroyed on the ground, it cost the Luftwaffe the same number. While it took just two weeks for the Allies to make good these losses, the Germans never could make up the difference, especially in the aircrew lost. These two failures, and that of not making any impression in the Bastogne area, together with the ever more desperate warnings from the Eastern Front, finally convinced Hitler that he had shot his bolt in the West. On 8 January, he permitted von Manteuffel to withdraw from the nose of the salient which he had created and, a few days later, authorised further withdrawals. Then, on the evening of 15 January, he and his staff left the *Adlerhorst*, boarded his special train and departed for Berlin, leaving von Rundstedt to pick up the pieces.

This did not mean that C-in-C West was to be allowed increased freedom of action now that he no longer had Hitler physically breathing down his neck. On 21 January he issued the following top secret order:

'The following order by the Führer is issued in its original text:

1. The Commanders of armies, corps and divisions will be personally responsible for all the following types of decisions or intentions reaching me early enough to enable me to exercise my influence on such decisions and for a possible counter-order to reach the front-line troops in time:

(i) any decision involving an operational movement,
(ii) any projected attack of divisional size or larger which is not covered by general orders issued by Supreme Headquarters,
(iii) any offensive action on an inactive front exceeding normal patrol activity apt to draw the enemy's attention to that sector
(iv) any projected movement of withdrawal or retreat,
(v) any contemplated abandonment of a position, a fortified town or fortress,

2. The Commanders of armies, corps and divisions, the Chiefs-of-Staff and every single General Staff Officer or staff officers will be personally responsible to me to see to it that any report addressed to me directly or through channels will contain nothing but the blunt truth. In future I will punish drastically any attempt at veiling facts, whether done on purpose or through negligence . . .'[17]

Hitler's noose had been drawn even tighter around the necks of his generals. As one army commander put it: 'The high command has lost all sense of time, space and relative strengths, and has so shackled the field commanders that they go into battle with their hands tied behind their backs and a halter around their necks, for they have to carry out the orders under pain of death; and when the execution of these orders ends in failure they are thrown out in disgrace and condemned as traitors.'[18]

But if Hitler was determined to bind the officer corps even more tightly to himself, he was also concerned about morale. By now the manpower barrel was being scraped dry. The final line of defence was the *Volkssturm*, which had been formed in October 1944 and drew on boys as young as 15 years-old and old men for home defence. Elements of these were now being forced into the Volksgrenadier divisions. Their main weapon was the *Panzerfaust* shoulder-fired anti-tank rocket launcher. Von Rundstedt later remarked that it was 'a real crime to set young hardly-grown-up young men against the enemy' with these weapons.[19] There was a comb-out of convalescents and the medically downgraded. Units were formed from those with similar medical complaints; a 'Stomach battalion' fought against the British and Canadians in the Reichswald in February. With such low calibre troops as this, and in the light of both the failure of *WACHT AM RHEIN*, and the success of the Russian offensive over the Vistula (which was launched on 12 January and was across the German border before the end of the month) it is not surprising that morale had plummeted from the level it had been in early December. As von Rundstedt commented in early February, 'the troops are pretty well fed up to the back teeth'.[20] In order to encourage them, decorations were lavishly distributed and Hitler even suggested that von Rundstedt should present photographs of himself to deserving soldiers. He did go as far as exploring the views of his subordinate commanders to this, but their reactions were predictable and he did not pursue the matter further.[21] There was also personal sadness for him at this time. His only nephew, and Joachim's only child, was posted as missing on the Eastern Front.

Having pushed the German forces back to their start line in the Ardennes by the end of January, the Western Allies could now turn their attention once more to their next major objective, closing up to the Rhine and crossing it. Eisenhower continued with his broad front policy. In the north, the Canadians were to clear the area south-east of Nijmegen and move up to the Lower Rhine (VERITABLE and BLOCKBUSTER). Simpson's United States Ninth Army, which was under Montgomery, would then advance towards Düsseldorf and link up with the Canadians (GRENADE). As a preliminary to these operations, the British Second Army would clear the Roermond triangle (BLACKCOCK) and this began on 16 January. In the American sector, Omar Bradley's 12th Army Group was to clear the Eifel and close to the Rhine between Cologne and Mannheim, while Jacob Devers's 6th Army Group was responsible from south of Mannheim to the Swiss border.

Von Rundstedt still believed that it would be better to conserve his forces and withdraw across the Rhine in order to hold the Allies on it. He also continued to believe that the Ruhr was the primary enemy objective. Hitler, however, would not countenance this, arguing that, given the destruction of the German communications system by the Allied bombing, the Rhine was vital for the movement of what raw materials Germany was still producing to the factories in the centre of the country. To this end, the West Wall had to be held at all costs. Von Rundstedt therefore continued to balance his strategy between his and

Hitler's wishes. Luckily, he still had some tough subordinates. In late January, Blaskowitz had been shifted sideways to take over Army Group H from Student, who now became his deputy. First Parachute Army, commanded by Alfred Schlemm, was to make the Canadians and British fight for every inch of the way to the Lower Rhine, especially in the Reichswald. In the centre, Model remained in command of Army Group B, with von Manteuffel and his fifth Panzer Army as the bulwark and sandwiched between the predominantly infantry armies of von Sangen (Fifteenth) and Brandenberger (Seventh). To Model's south remained Army Group G, now commanded by veteran SS General Paul Hausser, with First Army (Förtsch) and Nineteenth Army (Wiese).

VERITABLE opened on 8 February and, two days later, von Rundstedt was stressing to Blaskowitz the importance of holding well forward, especially around Cleve, in order to prevent a breakthrough to the Lower Rhine.[21] Eugen Meindl's II Parachute Corps carried this out to the letter and Montgomery's drive to the Rhine became a bloodstained slog. Further south, the American Seventh and French First Armies had removed that thorn in the Allied side, the Colmar pocket, and Nineteenth Army had withdrawn across the Rhine, Hitler's permission having been given. In the centre, Hodges' First and Patton's Third United States Armies remorslessly pushed Model's forces back to the river, but as in the north, resistance was stiff.

On 13 February, von Rundstedt issued another of his special orders. Addressed to the 'Soldiers of the Western Front' it told them that the Allies' main objective was the Ruhr. With the Russians now having overrun Germany's other industrial region, Upper Silesia, the loss of the Ruhr would mean that 'the Wehrmacht would be without weapons, and the country without coal'. His soldiers were to 'protect now your German homeland which has worked faithfully for you, for our wives and children in the face of the threat of foreign tyranny'. They were to keep the 'menace' off the backs of the armies on the Eastern Front so that they could 'break the bolshevist onslaught and liberate again the German territory in the East'. He warned that the 'coming battles' would be 'very hard'. 'Through your perseverance the general attack of the enemy must be shattered. With unshakeable confidence we gather round the Führer to guard our people and our state from a destiny of horror.'[23] Five days later, von Rundstedt received a signal from Hitler stating that he had awarded him the Swords to his Knight's Cross.[24] No doubt this was a gesture to demonstrate Hitler's continued faith in C-in-C West and to further encourage him.

None the less, von Rundstedt realised the impossibility of holding up the Allies for more than a very short period and was now concerned merely to buy time so that he could get his forces back across the Rhine with the minimum of casualties. He also had to prevent any lightning Allied thrust from seizing an intact bridge over the Rhine. This meant drawing up a carefully worked out programme of demolitions and keeping the minimum number of bridges open for his own troops to withdraw across. With the opening of GRENADE on 23 February and BLOCKBUSTER, the final Canadian drive to the Lower Rhine, three days later, the pressure increased significantly. But von Rundstedt was equally concerned about the threat further south, where Patton was clearing the area between the Rivers Moselle and Saar and Patch's United States Seventh Army was driving north into the Saarland.

The West Wall was now penetrated in several places and von Rundstedt began to thin out his forward troops. Hitler accepted this; on 28 February, Goebbels noted in his diary that the Allied press was commenting on von Rundstedt's change of tactics and that he now seemed to be drawing the enemy forces on to defence lines further in the rear, which would be 'highly disadvantageous to the attacking troops'.[25] On 2 March, elements of Simpson's Ninth United States Army reached the Rhine opposite Düsseldorf, but the bridge there had been blown. It was the same further south when Hodges' First US Army reached the river at Cologne two days later. In the north, meanwhile, Schlemm was still conducting a stiff rearguard action and it would not be until 10 March that Montgomery's forces were completely closed up to the river. Thus, there is no doubt that von Rundstedt's plan was working, and working well. Indeed, Goebbels noted on 6 March: 'Rundstedt is again getting high marks in the enemy press. The fact that our troops escaped more or less intact across the Rhine is attributed to him.'[26] Next day, however, disaster struck.

At noon on the the 7th, the leading elements of a task force from First United States Army arrived on the high ground overlooking Remagen, a small town on the Rhine and south of Bonn. To their amazement they saw that the Ludendorff railway bridge spanning the river here was intact. Fighting their way through the town, they reached the bridge some three hours later. The Germans now attempted to demolish it, but without success. Under cover of shell fire the Americans overcame the defenders on the west bank, but further charges were then detonated. These only partially damaged the bridge and the attackers were able to cross it, cutting all demolition cables as they did so. Thus, the

Allies had achieved what von Rundstedt had been so desperately trying to prevent, the capture of a bridge over the Rhine.

The reverberations of this disaster quickly made themselves felt on the German side. Von Rundstedt immediately sent an order to Model: 'Situation must be cleared up tonight and bridge destroyed. 11 Pz [Div] to be used. Bridge to be bombed from the air and naval special detachment [divers] to come from Army Group G. Investigate neglect of duty.'[27] Hitler, when he heard the news, was furious and decided that a new C-in-C West was needed. He turned to Kesselring, who had recently returned to Italy after recovering from the effects of a car accident which took place the previous October. He received an order on 8 March to report to the Reich Chancellery on the following day. In the meantime the efforts to destroy the Ludendorff bridge failed and the Americans were able to reinforce their small bridgehead on the east bank.

On 9 March Goebbels recorded in his diary Hitler's intention 'possibly' to replace von Rundstedt with Kesselring, but that he needed to speak with him first. As for von Rundstedt, 'he has become too old and works too much on First World War ideas to master a situation such as is developing in the West' – a marked contrast to Goebbels' crowing of a few days earlier. Kesselring duly had his interview and Hitler explained to him that a 'younger more active commander' was needed in the West. Von Rundstedt' s name was not mentioned and Hitler made no disparaging allusions to him.[28] Hitler then telephoned von Rundstedt and told him that he was to be relieved forthwith. Von Rundstedt later recalled:

> 'Hitler had simply had enough of me and was tired of me. As a camouflage, he said on the telephone that he wanted to save me the annoyance of flying courts martial, which could issue summary death penalties for cowardice, desertion etc, being active in my area. He said that he knew that I did not want to participate in such a bloodbath.'[29]

As it happened, Hitler had, that same day, ordered the setting up of Special Flying Tribunal West under SS Gruppenführer Rudolf Hübner to root out the Remagen culprits and deal with them. Next day, Kesselring arrived at HQ C-in-C West, still at Schloss Ziegenberg, apparently greeting the staff with the announcement: 'Well, Gentlemen, I am the new V.3.'[30] Von Rundstedt, who had been transferred to the Führer Reserve with effect from the previous day, now took his leave, driving away with Hans Gerd, his driver Irtel, and Amos, his batman.

The Field Marshal was unable to go directly to Bila, much as he wanted to, for he had been summoned to Berlin for a final audience with Hitler. Goebbels wrote on the 11th that Hitler was to see von Rundstedt that evening. 'Rundstedt is of course a highly respected officer who has done us great service, particularly in the liquidation of 20 July. The Führer therefore wants – I impressed this on him forcibly – Rundstedt's relief to be carried out in a decorous manner.' But he also complained that the Field Marshal came 'from a school that is unsuited to modern warfare' and that Model had been 'unable to operate properly' under him. Indeed, if Model had been C-in-C West 'his army group would not be in the state it actually is.' Ten days later he was writing that von Rundstedt's leadership was 'definitely bad' and that if Kesselring had not had his car accident he would have replaced von Rundstedt months earlier. On the other hand, he wrote that Hitler did not see Model as a candidate for the command, sharing von Rundstedt's view that he was 'too impetuous and impulsive'. Goebbels concurred with this view,[31] thereby displaying a complete *volte face* from his previous diary entry. This was perhaps indicative of the growing confusion in Berlin as the world in the *Führerbunker* under the Chancellery, in which Hitler was spending increasing amounts of time, took on an increasingly unreal hue.

Von Rundstedt duly had his interview with Hitler, whom he told Liddell Hart after the war looked very ill, with bent back and shaking hands.[32] Hitler presented him with the Swords and thanked him for his loyalty.[33] That concluded the last meeting between the two.

Irtel now drove von Rundstedt, his son, and batman to Kassel to see Bila. Von Rundstedt decided, however, not to remain there for what were clearly the last weeks of the war. The reason for this was probably the Allied bombing. There had been a major raid on the city on the night 8/9 March, the first since October 1943, and the Field Marshal perhaps feared that the Allies intended to destroy it. The party, with Bila among them, therefore went to Solz, a village lying some 25 miles south-east of Kassel. Here Bila's relations, the von Trotts, offered them accommodation on their estate. They remained here for some two weeks, while Hans Gerd went off to Austria to see Ditha and his children. When Hans Gerd met his parents again, on 3 April, they had moved on. Perhaps von Rundstedt did not wish to be beholden to the von Trotts, or he found it difficult to live with the fact that Adam von Trott, the July 1944 bomb plotter, had been executed. There is no clear reason.

The von Rundstedt's next stopping place was Weimar, where they hired a suite of rooms in the Hotel Elefant. This, of course, was further east and it may have been the fact that the British and Americans were now breaking out of their bridgeheads across the Rhine which prompted this move. Even so, they stayed in Weimar for little more than a week before motoring north-west to the Harz Mountains. The impending Russian offensive across the Oder and on to Berlin, which was to open on 16 April, probably drove them to this. They stayed in the little village of Tinne and Hans Gerd wrote to Ditha from here: 'This refugee status is new to us. It has the advantage that we see parts of Germany which I would otherwise never see.' Their sojourn here was again for little more than a week. Now the threat was from the West once more. On 4 April, American troops had entered Kassel and were now driving east towards the Elbe. To the north, Montgomery's advance was also making rapid progress and only the extreme south-east of Germany was not under immediate threat. So it was here that the party headed, like a ball in a pinball machine, and probably only just avoided the American thrust through Gotha, Erfurt and Jena, which reached the River Mulde south of Leipzig on the 13th. Bayreuth was their next port of call. Kesselring's headquarters happened to be here and von Rundstedt paid a call on his successor,[34] probably to obtain his estimate of the Allied intentions in southern Germany. The Field Marshal's stop was only brief in view of Patton's advance from the north and he and his party left Bayreuth before it fell on the 15th. Before they did so, Hans Gerd wrote to Ditha: 'I hope that we can travel to Upper Bavaria very soon and that I can find something for Mother and Father where they can settle.'[35]

It seems that the last weeks on the road had affected von Rundstedt's health and an arthritic leg was now playing him up badly. Hence the sanatorium at Bad Tölz was to be the party's final destination. Here they waited for the inevitable. It was to come on the evening of 1 May in the shape of the 36th Texas Division, part of Patch's United States Seventh Army. Defending Bad Tölz were a battle group and students of the SS Officer Cadet School based in the town. Both were under command of 17th SS Panzer Grenadier Division. By late evening on 1 May, the Americans had driven off the defenders and entered the town. Among the leading troops were 1st Battalion 141st Infantry Regiment. A patrol from Company A, led by 2nd Lieutenant Joseph E Burke from St Petersburg, Florida, ascertained from a prisoner that von Rundstedt was in the sanatorium and he set out to apprehend him. He entered the sanatorium and there were von Rundstedt, his wife and son seated in front of a fire. They got up from their seats and, after the Field Marshal had expressed surprise, having not expected the Americans to arrive until the following morning, he said to Burke: 'It is a most disgraceful situation for a soldier to give himself up without resistance.' Then, he limped away into captivity, the Texas Division's 30,000th prisoner during the campaign in North-West Europe.[36]

13
Prisoner of War

THE UNITED States Armed Forces' newspaper *The Stars and Stripes* heralded von Rundstedt's capture as 'the Allies' biggest catch of the war'.[1] This was echoed by the London *Evening Standard*.[2] As such, he was an immediate object of intense curiosity and his captors allowed American journalists to interview him. They noted that he appeared frail, but aggressive in manner. Above all, he continued to feel the disgrace of surrendering without offering any resistance. The *New York Times* noted that he had said that if he had not been in hospital recovering from a 'heart attack' [sic] he would not have surrendered without a fight and to do so was 'shameful and despicable'. He also asserted that he would have defeated the Allied invasion of Normandy on the beaches if it had not been for the overwhelming Allied air supremacy and his own shortage of fuel.[3]

In the meantime, there was the question of von Rundstedt's disposal to be tackled. On 2 May SHAEF had signalled the British Foreign Office and informed them that G-2 (Intelligence) Branch were organising a special detention camp at Dunkirk for prominent prisoners recently captured, including Admiral Horthy, the former dictator of Hungary, and Field Marshals von Leeb, List and von Rundstedt.[4] The fact that the German garrison of Dunkirk had still not surrendered probably brought about an immediate change of mind over the location of this camp. On that same day, 2 May, SHAEF ordered Seventh Army to send Horthy and von Rundstedt as soon as possible to Spa. Seventh Army reported on the 11th that Horthy was on his way,[5] but there is no indication that they ever sent von Rundstedt. In any event, by the time they despatched Horthy the location of the camp had changed yet again, this time to the Palace Hotel, Mondors Les Bains, which lies 20 kilometres south-east of Luxembourg. To this camp, euphemistically codenamed ASHCAN, were taken in due course top surviving leaders of the Third Reich who had fallen into the hands of the Western Allies. (Another centre, DUSTBIN, held captured technical experts). The inmates of ASHCAN would be held there until the decision was made as to which individuals were to be tried by the International Military Tribunal (IMT), which was to be set up at Nuremberg. Von Rundstedt himself, Hans Gerd, Dr Hertz, who had been treating him at Bad Tölz, and Irtel seem to have been taken as far as Headquarters United States Seventh Army at Augsburg and then returned to Bad Tölz, where Bila and von Rundstedt's batman, Amos, had remained. The Field Marshal and his son then left Bad Tölz for the American detention centre at Wiesbaden on the 27 May. He would not see Bila again for over two and a half years.[6]

Before the end of 1944, the Poles had formally registered von Rundstedt as wanted for war crimes, 'mass murder, execution of persons without trial, and other crimes' while C-in-C Army Group South during the period 1 September – 30 October 1939, with the Central Registry of War Crimes and Security Suspects (CROW-CASS).[7] This, however, had no bearing on the selection of those who were to appear at Nuremberg, and von Rundstedt, as a field commander throughout the war, was not considered to be close enough to the centre of the Nazi web to merit selection. Keitel and Jodl, in view of their positions in OKW, were the only senior army officers to be tried by the IMT. Even so, when the list of those who were to be so tried was published, there was surprise expressed in some quarters that von Rundstedt was not among them. Thus the London *Sunday Times* felt that he should have been included on the grounds that he was responsible for sending Skorzeny's 'murder parties' behind the lines during the Ardennes counter-offensive.[8] Instead, he and his son remained at Wiesbaden for some six weeks. While there, von Rundstedt was questioned at the Seventh Army Interrogation Center about D-Day.' He was also interviewed by the United States Strategic Bombing Survey team at HQ 12th Army Group's T (Technical) Branch detention centre. The aims of this interview were to establish the German Army's preparedness prior to the war, its supply situation during the war, and to discuss strategic planning and the mobilisation of economic resources. The significant points of this interview have already been brought out, but there was one curious exchange relating to the Field Marshal's retirement in July 1944:

'Question: "Why did you resign at this point of the campaign?"
Answer: "For reasons of health."

Question: "This was the official explanation. Why did you actually resign?"

Answer: "I do not know."'

Two weeks later von Rundstedt and Hans Gerd were moved again, this time to England.[11] It was, however, only now that Ditha received news in a letter from Hans Gerd that he and her father-in-law were alive.[12] Still in Austria with her children, she was apparently very upset that her mother-in-law had not given her any news[13], but given the chaotic situation in Germany at the end of the war it is not surprising that she had heard nothing. One curious footnote to von Rundstedt's movements during the weeks after his capture was that on 8 May, VE Day, a report appeared on the front page of the British *Daily Express*, which gave a graphic account of how von Rundstedt had taken the news of the German surrender. It claimed that both he and Hans Gerd were already in a British POW camp, Grizedale Hall in the Lake District, and that he had wept when he heard of the surrender on German radio, declaring that 'it is not the Wehrmacht which is to blame. The political leaders of our country were *schlecht* – bad.'[14] Certainly, a large group of senior German officers were taken to Grizedale Hall on 30 April, but von Rundstedt had not even been captured at this time.[15]

The Field Marshal himself, together with other high ranking German officers, was brought to England during the second week of July for what would be a three year sojourn. Hans Gerd accompanied him, supposedly with Montgomery's special consent.[16] Their first home was the Combined Services Detailed Interrogation Centre (CSDIC), otherwise known as No 11 Prisoner of War Camp, at Wilton Park, Buckinghamshire (now the School of Army Education). This had been originally set up in 1941 to interrogate captured enemy officers, in the early days largely Luftwaffe and U-boat crews. Its activities were highly secret at the time, but the intelligence gleaned from its often very subtle methods of extracting information was invaluable. Later, after the surrender in Tunisia in May 1943, it had played host to Marshal Messe, the last commander of the Axis forces in North Africa, and other senior Italian officers. Now it housed a large number of German generals, including von Rundstedt, Field Marshal Ernst Busch, who had signed the instrument of surrender to Montgomery on Lüneberg Heath, and Ritter von Thoma, erstwhile commander of the Deutsches Afrika Korps, who had been captured during the closing stages of the Second Battle of el Alamein in November 1942.

Wilton Park consisted of a large white Georgian house set in its own grounds. This was the officers' mess and the prisoners were housed in a concrete one story block which had been built in what had formerly been the nursery garden. There were four long intersecting corridors with cells large enough to hold four beds. All were centrally heated. There were no bars on the windows, many of which looked out on the eight foot brick wall that had surrounded the original garden, but being multi-paned and steel framed they were deemed sufficiently strong to be escape proof. Nevertheless, additional security precautions were introduced just before the arrival of von Rundstedt and his compatriots. The windows were heavily wired, floodlighting installed and an adjoining field turned into an exercise area with high perimeter fence and Bren gun posts. Colonel Grondona, the Commandant, recalled the arrival of his new guests:

> 'When von Rundstedt was shown his room, he took no notice whatever of the heavily wired windows. Even if there had been no bed on which to sleep I don't think he would have batted an eye-lid. The feelings of those Germans as – red-tabbed, gold-braided and erect – they walked inside their barbed-wire-enclosed exercise ground for an hour each morning and afternoon, must have indeed been bitter; but I never sensed that their bitterness was against their captors.'[17]

Von Rundstedt was still not well[18] and neither were von Thoma (who would shortly have to have his leg amputated) nor Busch. Indeed, the last-named died of a heart attack in his bed on 17 July. The War Office informed Grondona that a motor hearse would collect the body next day and take it to Aldershot for interment. Grondona was granted permission to give 'appropriate military honours' to the cortège as it left Wilton Park and accordingly organised a Guard of Honour from the camp guards.

> 'Next morning two lines of troops with heads bowed over their reversed arms were drawn up between the steps of the White House and the hearse on the wide carriage-way; another party stood ready to slow-march ahead of the short column as it moved the 400 yds to the South gate of the inner perimeter. Rundstedt and about 20 generals walked in rear of the hearse, with the British officers behind them. Then, as the gate was approached, there was a brief halt while the advance party formed two lines on either side of the hearse and, as it moved on, they presented arms. Rundstedt raised his Marshal's baton and we all came to the salute till the hearse had passed through the gate – when it accelerated in setting out on its journey.'

The War Office subsequently said that von Rundstedt and eight others could attend the interment. They were taken by army coach, with blinds drawn, to Aldershot, but Grondona could not resist raising the blinds as they passed through Eton, Windsor Castle and Windsor Great Park.

> Von Rundstedt asked me if it was likely that there would be "a firing party from the Brigade of Guards at the funeral". I replied that I had no idea what arrangements were being made by the War Office. I marvelled at the outlook of this man who had seen all our newspapers' gruesomely illustrated accounts of the terrible discoveries made at the concentration camps, and who even yet imagined that a party of the King's Household Brigade would now be detailed as a guard of honour at a German general's funeral. He was soon to be disillusioned on this and other points. The burial was conducted with a minimum of ceremony; and later that day I had a message to say that von Rundstedt would appreciate my visiting him in his room. He rose as I entered and asked me to sit down. Then he said: "Herr Kommandant, you will have received my letter expressing our appreciation of the ceremony which marked the departure of our late colleague's body from this place. Can you tell me why he was today buried with none of the honours due to a soldier and with no respect whatever for his rank?" Speaking with manifest emotion he added: "None of us who were present at Aldershot today will ever forget what was a very bitter experience." I had to explain to him the state of British public opinion at this time.'

Von Rundstedt's reaction to this was to put his head into his hands and to reply: 'We do realise what you say, and have the utmost shame. But I give you my word of honour as a soldier that the revelations have appalled the Wehrmacht even more than the people of Britain.' It was to be the first of a number of conversations that Grondona was to have with him, but at no time did von Rundstedt ever try to excuse or justify himself over the events of the past few years. His good manners also impressed his captors. When the Japanese surrender was announced, von Rundstedt 'made the point of calling on a BAO [British Army Officer] in order to offer him congratulations on a glorious victory. This was done in the courtly manner at which he excels.'[9]

During this time von Rundstedt, von Manteuffel, Blumentritt and Kruse, who had commanded Army Group B's artillery, were interrogated in depth about the Ardennes counter-offensive. The interrogation report on all four noted that von Rundstedt's mind was no longer very alert and his memory was beginning to fail him. It also appeared that he had disinterested himself in the offensive and was therefore not as conversant with it as he might have been, even given his habit of delegating all detail. He himself stressed that all planning had been done by Hitler and the OKW and his own views, presumably the Small

Solution, were ignored.[20] This interrogation was carried out at Wilton Park, although von Rundstedt also spent time at what was known as the London District Cage in Kensington Palace Gardens, which also carried out POW interrogations and had now become the War Crimes Investigation Unit (WCIU) under Lieutenant Colonel A P Scotland. The late 'Bunny' Pantcheff, who was on the staff of the latter, remembered von Rundstedt being there, although he himself did not interrogate him. 'The impression he made was of a traditional, old-style Prussian officer, a good professional soldier, though by then well past his peak, honourable (and honour-conscious) according to those professional lights, stiff and unbending in manner, *sehr korrekt.*'[21]

At Wilton Park itself, some at least of the wartime techniques of extracting intelligence from the prisoners were still used. In particular, eavesdropping of their conversations was employed on a wide scale and much revealing information was gleaned. Thus, at one point Hans Gerd was heard to comment that it was as well that the British had suffered light losses compared to Germany during the war since this meant that there was still plenty of 'Teutonic' blood with which to face the Russians.[22] On the other hand, the Field Marshal, Hans Gerd, Blumentritt and von Manteuffel expressed themselves 'rather pleased' on another occasion, when talking about the Soviet threat, 'at the trouble the British have on hand'.[23] Discussing the July 1944 Bomb Plot, von Manteuffel considered Hans Gerd's view that it would have been 'a stroke of luck' if it had come off as 'unbelievable impudence', damning Hans Gerd as 'this young puppy'. 'He has no idea what would have happened. I'm, sure that I would have used my troops to fire on the rebels.'[24] As for views on von Rundstedt himself, Halder, who was at the camp and on loan from the Americans, considered him more of a Junker than a strategist and blamed him for keeping aloof from the anti-Hitler plots.[25] Even his most loyal supporters, Hans Gerd and Blumentritt, in a discussion with Halder's erstwhile deputy, Müller-Hillebrand, criticised him for 'failing to speak out at times when action and words were needed'. They felt that he had 'a negative attitude to life' and particularly condemned him for his seeming indifference to the current sufferings of the German civil population.[26] Of more immediate significance was a BBC news broadcast in German on 5 October. This reported that the French had branded von Rundstedt a war criminal and were demanding that he be handed over for trial by them if the IMT did not arraign him. It was heard by a number of prisoners, but not von Rundstedt, and caused a 'considerable stir', the attitude being that if the doyen of the officer corps was to be so treated then what hope for the other members? Von Thoma proposed that von Rundstedt should not be told about it for the time being, while Blumentritt thought that the Oradour massacre, perpetrated by the SS Das Reich in June 1944, was at the bottom of it. He and Hans Gerd immediately set about preparing a case for the Field Marshal's defence.[27]

Probably on 19 October 1945,[28] von Rundstedt and a number of others were transferred to another camp, this time in the North of England. Wilton Park itself was converted into a training centre for German re-education and during the next few years was to do much to further Anglo-German understanding. Before he left, von Rundstedt presented Grondona with a walking stick which had been made for him by General Gerd Bassenge, whom Grondona later claimed was the senior engineer officer of the German Army, although he was actually a Luftwaffe air defence specialist who had been captured in Tunisia, and was a fellow inmate at Wilton Park.[29] Von Rundstedt's new home was No 1 PW Camp at Grizedale Hall, the camp in which the *Daily Express* reporter had placed him at the time of the German surrender. The camp itself lay some three miles from Lake Windermere and close by the village of Hawkshead in the Lake District. It, too, was based on an Edwardian country house, (built by a Liverpool shipping magnate but no longer standing today) and its grounds. It was the first officers' camp opened during the war and had initially housed Luftwaffe and U-boat personnel, becoming known to the locals as the U-boat Hotel. It had twice been the scene of escapes by prisoners. In August 1941 the U-boat U-570 had surrendered to a Hudson aircraft of RAF Coastal Command, which had attacked and damaged it in the North Atlantic. Her officers, apart from the Captain, who was detained in London, were taken to Grizedale Hall. So incensed were the inmates that a U-boat should have surrendered that they decided to place the officers before a Court of Honour presided over by top scoring U-boat ace Otto Kretschmer. The First Lieutenant, Bernhard Berndt, was found guilty of a dishonourable act and, in order to clear his name, resolved to escape from the camp and get back to Germany. He managed to get out of the camp, cutting a hole in the wire, but was caught by members of the Home Guard the following day. They decided to take him back to the camp to have him verified. En route he broke away from his escorts, who shot and killed him. Later he was given a full naval funeral and buried in the churchyard of Hawkshead. It was from Grizedale Hall, too, that the Luftwaffe fighter pilot Franz von Werra made the first of his three escapes from Allied POW camps, the third of which, from a camp in Canada, was ultimately successful and he reached Germany by way of the USA and Mexico. By the time von Rundstedt arrived, however, it had become a senior officers' camp and one other Field Marshal, Ewald von Kleist, was already in residence.

The commandant of Grizedale Hall was a Regular officer and Great War veteran, Lieutenant Colonel Ryn Morton MC, the Cheshire Regiment, who apparently used to refer to his charges as 'My Huns' or 'My Boches'.[30] According to Basil Liddell Hart, whom, as we shall see, got to know the camp well, Morton, whom he mistakenly described as an 'ex-ranker', used to boast 'of the way he ticked off the generals in humiliating terms'.[31] Whether this was so or not, John Trevelyan, then Education Officer for the county of Westmorland, in which Grizedale Hall was situated (whose autograph would later become well known to all British cinema-goers when he was official censor to the British Film Board), noted that he treated von Rundstedt very differently. Trevelyan visited von Rundstedt on a couple of occasions in the room which he shared with his son and noted that when Morton took him to von Rundstedt's door 'he stood to attention and said deferentially, "Mr Trevelyan to see you, Sir"'.[32] According to Liddell Hart, conditions were also very cramped with 'six full generals to a room, and as many as eighteen major generals to a hut'. The only furniture in each room was 'a small table and two hard chairs apart from the narrow iron beds with an apology for a mattress'.[33] Certainly there were well over 200 prisoners in this camp by the time von Rundstedt arrived.[34] Ernie Ridgway, who was a guard there from April 1940 until he was demobilised in 1946, recalls that the big house itself had 32 bedrooms and that some 100 prisoners slept in it. The overflow was catered for in five large huts in a compound.[35] It is probable, however, that the vast influx of POWs after the surrender did mean that the camp was forced to accept more than it could cater for in comfort. This is substantiated by the report of an International Red Cross official who visited on 7 December 1945. He commented especially on the overcrowded conditions, but noted that there was a plan to move the prisoners to a camp in the South. The report also stated that all the inmates were losing weight and that the canteen was very sparsely stocked, with basics like toothpaste being unobtainable. Even so, although the prisoners made a number of requests to the official, they lodged no formal complaints.[36]

The von Rundstedts, however, were lucky enough to have a room with a window which had a view. During one of John Trevelyan's visits he asked von Rundstedt whether he felt isolated from the outside world. Taking him to the small window, the Field Marshal replied: 'Yes I often do, but on a clear day I can see from here a little patch of sea, and this makes me feel I am not entirely cut off.'[37] Even so, occasionally von Rundstedt's frustration got the better of him. Once he was seen by a sentry beating the perimeter fence with his stick and he had to point his rifle at him in order to make von Rundstedt stop. Liddell Hart became very concerned for the Field Marshal's safety when he heard about this and asked Morton to ensure that the guards did not shoot at him when he did it, but treated him with sympathy.[38] Nevertheless, the Generals were allowed to walk in the surrounding woods under escort. Ernie Ridgway remembered that von Rundstedt always had a polite smile for his captors and noted the respect with which the other inmates treated him. Another who was there at the time, Joseph Hutchinson, a nurseryman and an old soldier, who had served with the British Army of Occupation in Germany just after the Great War and had picked up a little German, used to converse with von Rundstedt when he was taking exercise, and recalled how approachable he was, probably because it was a way of 'breaking the monotony'.[39]

For von Rundstedt, however, the high point of his time at Grizedale Hall, if it could be said to have had one, was almost certainly his meetings with the eminent military theorist and historian Basil Liddell Hart. The Liddell Harts were at the time living in Ambleside and he soon came to hear of the rich collection of personalities interned in Grizedale Hall. It was too good an opportunity to ignore, especially since here were many of those who had practised in war the ideas which he had preached so vehemently in the 1920s and 1930s. At the time he was somewhat *persona non grata* in official circles, having often attacked British strategy during the war, and there were many who had not forgiven him for his role as *eminence grise* to Leslie Hore-Belisha, the Secretary of State for War, while still a journalist, in the late 1930s. However, his brother-in-law Barry Sullivan was at the time working in the re-education section of the Foreign Office's Prisoner-of-War Division (PWD) and through him Liddell Hart was taken on as a lecturer. This re-education process had been recognised as essential to the future of the German people. They had to be taught what Western democracy was all about and to realise the error of their ways. Prisoners-of-war in Britain would eventually be repatriated, but, for obvious reasons, they had to be politically cleansed before this could happen. One of the first steps taken was to co-opt lecturers who would visit the camps and talk both formally and informally to their inmates.

Liddell Hart had made his first visit to Grizedale Hall on 9 July and by the time von Rundstedt arrived there, he had become a well known figure, driving up in his 1937 Rolls-Royce and being pleasant and courteous to all. He first talked to von Rundstedt on 26 October, spending the whole morning with him and his son and a further one and a half hours in the afternoon. Having denied all knowledge of Halder's plot to overthrow Hitler at the time of Munich in September 1938, because he was retired, von Rundstedt then went through the whole of his war. Elements of this discussion have already been detailed, but from its length there is no doubt that the two quickly established a mutual rapport.[40] Six days later, they had another talk. Liddell Hart's questions on this occasion were more wide-ranging, as much as anything trying to confirm what others in the camp had told him. Von Rundstedt said that none of the Russian generals were any good in 1941, although Zhukov became so later, and spoke of a captured Russian officer referring to Budenny as 'a man with an immense moustache, but a very small brain'. He denied that Hitler had issued an order not to take Russian prisoners and stated that his own army group had captured over one million. As for the best of the German generals, he considered that von Manstein was very good and well above average (Liddell Hart put in his notes 'R. evidently thinks him the best, though he hesitates to say so definitely') and von Brauchitsch, von Kleist, von Leeb and von Weichs were good. Model was also good, but a 'bull', as were von Reichenau and von Bock, although the last-named 'understood operations'. Liddell Hart also asked about the circumstances of his retirement in 1938 and his role in the aftermath of the July 1944 Bomb Plot, both of which have been covered earlier in the book. Liddell Hart's comments on this interview were:

> 'Rundstedt makes an increasingly favourable impression on me on further acquaintance. He has a rather too orthodox mind, not only in the operational sphere, but he has a "good feel" in regard to character, as well as a good mind compared to many others. He is dignified without being arrogant, and essentially aristocratic in outlook – giving that term in its better sense. He has an austere appearance which is offset by a nice smile and a pleasant gleam of humour, which frequently comes out.
> I walked back with him to the compound, and when we reached the door of the Hall I motioned him to go in first, saying "after you". He replied with a smile, "Oh, no, this is MY [sic] house".'[41]

To follow up his interviews, Liddell Hart also passed written questions through the camp interpreter, Captain F S Kingston, who became a firm ally, and the Generals were allowed to reply to Liddell Hart by letter.

Liddell Hart's next meeting with von Rundstedt was on 20 November, when he visited his room after interviewing others on the Norwegian campaign of April 1940.

'He has a small room which he shares with his son. He had been lying down, but seemed very pleased to see me. (The camp staff say that he is becoming more lame, and only goes out for a quarter of an hour a day. It is due to some disease of the circulation that cannot be remedied – at any rate by such treatment as is available here. But he makes no complaints, and puts a remarkably cheerful face on his troubles, and discomforts – a contrast to some of his juniors here.)'[42]

Liddell Hart became concerned by von Rundstedt's health and believed that his thin Army mattress was hardly giving him any comfort. He asked Captain Kingston to try and obtain a better mattress for von Rundstedt from the local hospital. When this failed he offered to lend him a mattress, at least 'until the family comes home for the holidays'. This would at least ease the pain in von Rundstedt's leg and enable him to get some sleep.[43] This offer was taken up, probably because Morton was on leave at the time, but it caused a ruction on his return. Morton was seemingly a believer in regulations, viewing any item in excess of official holdings as illegal, and apparently complained to the War Office. In Liddell Hart's words, 'I was told later that there was a voluminous correspondence about the matter, and that the file was called "The Case of Rundstedt's Mattress"'. The file apparently grew very thick, but von Rundstedt was allowed to keep his mattress.[44]

On 3 December, Liddell Hart gave his fourth and last lecture to the inmates of Grizedale Hall. In his official report, he noted, one suspects with some pride, that there were two Field Marshals in the audience. He commented that most of the questions were on the current political set-up in Europe and the future of Germany, and described his audience as mostly generals of the 'civil service type'.[45] Nine days later and indicative of the regard in which the inmates held him, Liddell Hart was especially invited to attend von Rundstedt's 70th Birthday Party, which was held in his room. There was a cake and General Siegfried Heinrici presented the Field Marshal with a painting of Grizedale Hall on behalf of his fellow prisoners. Later, von Rundstedt's family gave this painting to Liddell Hart 'as a memento of their meetings and as a mark of friendship'.[46]

On 3 January 1946, Liddell Hart had his last talk with von Rundstedt. The main focus of discussion was the portrait of the Field Marshal which 'W E Hart' had painted of the Field Marshal in his wartime publication *Hitler's Generals*. The accusations which the author made on von Rundstedt' activities in the 1920s and 1930s have already been discussed and have been shown to be baseless. According to the

Imperial War Museum, the author's real name was Aron[47] and the flyleaf of his book claimed that he had been an officer in the Reichswehr and had left the country sometime after Hitler came to power. A search of the Reichswehr Army Lists 1920–1930 revealed no officer of that name. The interview concluded with Liddell Hart asking whether the other generals had appealed to him to lead an overthrow of Hitler, which von Rundstedt denied. Liddell Hart added in his notes on the talk: 'While some German generals have complained that they looked to Rundstedt for such a lead, and that he failed them in this respect, those who knew him really well never seem to have expected him to do so. They regarded him as too simply a soldier and too outright [upright?] a man to be suitable for staging a plot.'[48] This was to be the last time that Liddell Hart was to meet von Rundstedt face-to-face, but by no means the end of their relationship. On 6 January, the Generals left Grizedale Hall for a new camp in South Wales, the Hall becoming the home of Austrian officer POWs only. Liddell Hart himself shortly afterwards hurt his leg and was also engaged in moving house. He wanted to continue his discussions in the camp, but the authorities, now the Foreign Office's Political Intelligence Division (PID), which had taken over responsibility for re-education, decided that Liddell Hart was no longer suitable because he spent too much time discussing recent history.[49] He put the material which he had gathered, however, to good use and produced his book *The Other Side of the Hill (The German Generals Talk,* in the United States) in 1948, which was sold widely and has been published in a number of editions over the years. In recent years he has been attacked by a number of historians for twisting the evidence to demonstrate that the *Blitzkrieg* concept was his and that the Germans were much influenced by his pre-war writings on the subject.[50] Undoubtedly there is strong evidence to support these accusations. On the other hand, it is clear that Liddell Hart had a genuine admiration for the leading German commanders, both for their professionalism as soldiers and the dignity with which they accepted defeat. As we shall see, he would shortly become their champion against what he considered to be the disgraceful official treatment of some, notably von Rundstedt, von Brauchitsch and von Manstein, and he would not be a lone voice.

The Generals' new camp was No 11 Special POW Camp at Island Farm, Bridgend in South Wales. Like Grizedale Hall, it had a previous history. It had originally been built as a dormitory camp for workers at the nearby Royal Ordnance Factory Waterton, which manufactured explosives, the idea being that it would save those living in the Welsh

Valleys a long journey to and from work. It was not, however, much used and in 1943 had been handed over to the American Army. After D-Day it became vacant once more and began a new existence as No 198 POW Camp, housing German and Italian other ranks. It was then made an officers' camp and among its inmates were many hardened Nazis. On the night 10/11 March 1945 no less than 66 of them tunnelled out of the camp, the largest escape attempt in Britain during the war, but all were quickly recaptured because the area was a high security one, in view of the existence of the ordnance factory, although one party, including a Luftwaffe pilot, managed to get as far as Birmingham airport.[51] In the immediate aftermath, the prisoners were moved to other camps and Island Farm was once more empty. In November 1945, however, refurbishment work began to make it a senior officers' camp and a fresh commandant, Major Denis Topham, Grenadier Guards, who had had previous experience with senior officer POWs at Trent Park Camp, the original home of CSDIC(UK),[52] appointed. The camp itself consisted of a number of single story buildings, but was roomier than Grizedale Hall and von Rundstedt, as the camp senior, and his son were allocated a suite of two rooms in a hut specially reserved for Field Marshals, of whom there would now be three, since von Manstein had also been sent to Island Farm.

Probably shortly after arriving at Island Farm, von Rundstedt was interviewed yet again, this time by Major Milton Shulman of the Canadian Army. He had been carrying out a series of interviews of senior commanders who had fought in the West and results of his work, would, like those of Liddell Hart, appear in book form, *Defeat in the West*. Shulman's impression of his subject was as follows:

> 'To-day the Field Marshal is tired. This describes his mental and physical condition. The onerous responsibilities of guiding the fate of millions of men, the continuous clash with the dominant wills of Hitler and his coterie, the last few years of heavy drinking in an endeavour to withstand the heavy pressure against him, all have exacted their price. A limp, exhausted body racked by constant pain due to weakened arteries is now the remnant of the relentless figure that once waved a Marshal's baton before a victorious army goose-stepping along the Champs-Elysée. Yet despite the grey, parchment skin, the slightly bent frame and the thinning hair, it comes as a shock to discover that this man, casually flicking cigarette-ash off his purple, prisoner-of-war battle dress, is seventy-one years old. For Rundstedt has a face that is timeless. A straight firm nose, long thin lips and a determined, blunt jaw, give the impression of a sculptured bust, immutable and relentless. The tiny wrinkles and serried lines help to create this impression of chiselled rock. The eyes, however,

bright and restless, reveal the presence of warm blood. An occasional, limited smile coupled with a dry restrained wit confirm the fact that this man is human after all. If stone predominates in the Field Marshal's physical appearance, it probably betrays what has taken place in the spirit as well. This transformation to granite can hardly be wondered at, for only ossification could have withstood the buffeting of howling events that assailed him from all directions.'

Once again von Rundstedt was taken through his career and campaigns. Shulman noted, however, that his subject generally kept strictly to the framework of the questions and tried to avoid political and philosophical matters. One of the few statements he volunteered was that the Canadians had fought well in North-West Europe (he was not the only one of Shulman's interviewees to say this) and that the British were more cautious than the Americans, although he understood that this was because of their more limited manpower. He also agreed with the Montgomery approach that 'an operation should not be undertaken until there was sufficient material on hand to ensure its being successful'. Shulman considered that von Rundstedt was not bitter or resentful of Hitler, but that he reserved his venom for Keitel and Jodl, whom he viewed as 'yes' men. His personal relations with Hitler were 'always polite, impersonal and cool'. Yet, he was the only man in the Wehrmacht who was not forced to stand in Hitler's presence. 'Whenever I visited him, he always brought me a chair, and made old, fat Goering stand. I never knew why.' The Field Marshal momentarily came to life when Shulman asked him about Hitler's appearance at their last meeting.

'He raised himself from his chair and went to the door of the room where he poised himself like an actor about to make an entrance. "When I saw him early in the war," he began, "Hitler used to come into a conference like this." Here he marched triumphantly forward, chest out, head disdainfully turning from side to side, and arms moving vigorously across his body, in a good imitation of the Hitler known to newsreel audiences. "When I last saw him in March 1945," Rundstedt continued, going back to the door again, "he came in looking like this." This time he bent his body forward like a very aged man, his feet shuffled slowly in front of him, and his arms and body trembled violently. The Field Marshal gave this act with a certain ease and familiarity, as if he had done it many times before. He had probably regaled various High Command messes with it on previous occasions, and he was obviously pleased with his performance.'

In conclusion, Milton Shulman commented: 'If there is one impression more than any other that Rundstedt desired his interrogators to carry away with them, it was the overpowering influence of Hitler on all operations, and the helplessness of commanders in the field to make strategic or tactical decisions.'[53]

By the time the Generals arrived at Island Farm, they were becoming increasingly concerned over their future. The decision had been made that not only would the IMT at Nuremberg try the surviving top-ranking Nazis in Allied hands, but also various organisations and bodies. These included the Reichs cabinet, SS, SA, Gestapo and the High Command and General Staff of the Wehrmacht. Should the last-named be found guilty, the future would clearly be bleak for all those senior commmanders at Island Farm and elsewhere. As it was there were already rumours flying around, even one that all the generals and the SS would be banished to Mexico for twenty years.[54] It was a time of great uncertainty, but one thing was clear. The Generals had to defend their collective honour at Nuremberg.

Germany's senior surviving Field Marshal, von Brauchitsch, was already languishing at Nuremberg and had had much time to consider how best the High Command should conduct its case. On 3 January 1946 he addressed a letter to the President of the International Tribunal, the British judge Lord Justice Lawrence. Dr Exner had already been appointed as the defence lawyer for this case, but von Brauchitsch asked that he be replaced by Dr Leverkühn on the grounds that Exner was already defending Jodl and was unable to devote his full attention to the case. He went on to say: 'The defence should be conferred upon an officer belonging to the circle of the higher ranking commanders representing the General Staff. He will be supported by a legal adviser. In the first place the oldest officer of the former German Army, Field Marshal von Rundstedt, comes into question for this purpose.'[55] In fact, it was Dr Hans Laternser who took on the task of counsel for the defence and on 4 February he wrote to von Rundstedt stating that both von Manstein and General Siegfried Westphal had specifically requested that he appear. Not until a month later did von Rundstedt receive the letter, and two days later he wrote to the IMT requesting that he be allowed to appear before it. He had not made such an application before:

'. . . because I had received the impression from various reports by press and radio, that I myself was mentioned as a war criminal [presumably the French demand of the previous autumn to try him as such]. This was indicated by the British side as an "unofficial statement". I shall, however, in my capacity as senior Field Marshal on active service to the end of the war, not withdraw from the request of my brother-officers of the

Army – former Germany *Army* [sic], its generals fighting and leading the frontline and its General-Staff. I have always, during 54 years of active service, sought loyally to serve my *country* [sic] and the *Nation* [sic], without regarding the person at the head of the State to whom every soldier was bound to swear allegiance. Now I consider it the last task entrusted to my life to safeguard the honour of the German Army.'

He also asked that Blumentritt and Hans Gerd be allowed to accompany him in order to assist with the case. The IMT's comment was that should the defence request their presence then they would be called individually.[56] The summons came and on 15 May von Rundstedt, von Kleist, Westphal and Blumentritt, but not Hans Gerd, were flown to Nuremberg. The late Captain Ted Lees, the camp interpreter at Island Farm, remembered von Rundstedt's departure from Island Farm. 'As he came walking slowly towards the main compound gate, he found the entire complement of 185 or so generals and admirals lined up at the salute. One of the senior among them then delivered a short speech asking him "to uphold the honour of the German officer corps at Nuremberg".'[57]

Von Rundstedt arrived in Nuremberg at the time when the individual cases for the defence were being heard. He and his companions were housed in the witnesses' wing of the jail. Before anything could happen Dr Laternser had to make a formal application for von Rundstedt and the others to appear in front of the IMT Commission, which carried out the preliminary review of evidence prior to the case being formally considered in court. In the meantime, G M Gilbert, the official prison psychologist at Nuremberg, visited von Rundstedt in his cell. The Field Marshal asserted that he and Rommel had told Hitler at the beginning of July 1944 that 'it was time to quit'. He objected to the Ardennes counter-offensive being named after him since he had had little to do with the planning. 'If old von Moltke thought that I have planned the offensive he would turn over in his grave'. He also complained:

'All we had was [sic] the run-down old men who couldn't fight and the foreigners who kept deserting. – And Hitler kept hollering, "hold your ground". – Like at Bastogne, just to mention one name – and that was the man who wanted to be considered a great field general! – He didn't know the first thing about strategy! – All he knew was bluff.'[58]

Eventually, on 19 June, von Rundstedt appeared before the Commission.

Much of what von Rundstedt said during this appearance has been referred to earlier, but suffice it to say the questioning was very searching, much more so than anything that he had previously experienced. Much of it was aimed at establishing the culpability of the High Command and General Staff in the decisions and planning to invade Poland, Norway, France and the Low Countries, the Balkans and Russia. Von Rundstedt asserted that he was not privy to these, being a field commander who merely received the orders to carry them out. The Commission then went on to examine the Eastern front and the atrocities there. Von Rundstedt denied that the Wehrmacht had not observed the Laws of War, and that the *Einsatzgruppen* were under army command. Indeed, he only knew of one atrocity committed by them in his army group area and that merely because it had happened near his headquarters – he was presumably referring to the Berdichev massacre at the end of July 1941. There had been no intentional maltreatment of prisoners – what had happened in the rear had not been his responsibility since his was an operational command and not concerned with routine logistic matters. Nevertheless,

> ". . . one has to admit that a lot of these unfortunate prisoners succumbed to exhaustion and hunger, and died. In an encirclement battle [*Kesselschlacht*] the surrounded troops were almost starving because no food could get in and they only had what they carried with them. The number of prisoners of war sometimes amounted to hundreds of thousands and sometimes was larger than the army which captured them. As much as it would have liked to, the German Army could not supply enough food for the poor prisoners from its own stocks, as these were short as well. In addition, the supply system was miserable; railways were hardly trafficable, the roads not at all, because of mud, ice and snow. One tried to feed the poor people with maize, soya beans or whatever from the fields. But in my judgement, the main reason for the death was the lack of provision of shelter for them in bad weather. They had to remain in the open air.'

Von Rundstedt denied that he had given orders for mines to be cleared by prisoners, although he was aware of one occasion when this happened, at Kiev, but believed that it was a regiment which had ordered it. He was also asked whether he knew what went on in the concentration camps, but said that he was only made aware of this through Allied films and publications. Nevertheless, he had known of two camps. Oranienberg had been a show place to which foreign diplomats had been taken to demonstrate how humane the camps were.

> 'Then there was Dachau, which was in the vernacular jokingly called "concert camp", not concentration camp. People were sent there who had

made careless statements or had fallen from favour, like Pastor Niemöller. Two acquaintances of mine who are here in the prison, Halder and Falkenhausen, were inmates of Dachau for a year, and had no idea of the dirty business that was going on.'

The Commission then referred to a statement made by SS Brigade-führer Ernst Rohde that 'an energetic and united protest by all field marshals would have brought about a change in aims and methods' of the war in the East. Von Rundstedt bridled at this, pointing out that if they had made such a protest they would have merely been replaced by commanders more sympathetic to the régime. The only possible option was 'silent sabotage as with the Commissar Order'. In any event, 'I find it outrageous that an SS man dares give judgement on the field marshals in such a way'.

The examination now moved on to France and von Rundstedt's policy towards the Resistance, as well as the infamous Commando Order. The Ardennes followed, with von Rundstedt's knowledge of the Malmédy massacre being examined. The July 1944 Bomb Plot was also brought up and then von Rundstedt was asked why he had taken part in the invasion of Russia if he did not agree with it. He replied that he had sworn on oath as a soldier to do his duty. To the argument that he did not have to keep his oath to a man who had broken his, the Field Marshal replied that 'the soldier is not a villain' but, said his questioner, what if your superior is a villain? Von Rundstedt declined to answer this. He was then asked what he did with the RM 250,000 given to him by Hitler on his 66th Birthday and the other gifts he received from the Führer. When speaking of the von Moltke portrait, he said that he had loaned it to a museum in Kassel. It was, however, in Bila's possession at the end of the war. To discourage the Americans from confiscating it, she removed Hitler's presentation plaque from the frame and passed the picture off as a portrait of a relation. It hangs today in grandson Gerd's house, still with the gap in the frame where the plaque had been. Von Rundstedt also let slip that he had addition-ally received some coffee at the same time, 'which I do not want to mention here'. One suspects that, while he could put the other gifts he received from Hitler out of sight, the coffee was too much of a temptation. He had recently arrived in France as C-in-C West and it is likely that he sent it to Bila to use. The examination ended with a trick question. Von Rundstedt was asked whether he was aware of the old Prussian General Staff watchword 'an officer does not owe obedience to anyone if the order is against his honour'. He denied all knowledge of this, quoting von Moltke the Elder's famous dictum as the only one worth following, 'the general staff officer has to be more than he seems'. The Commission was not convinced by von Rundstedt's denial and put the question to him twice more, but he refused to elaborate. It was then slightly rephrased: 'Do you agree with the words of Field Marshal von Moltke: "The officer bears a completely different responsibility in front of God and his fatherland than merely the order of some superior"?' Dr Laternser objected, and von Rundstedt, clearly angry, retorted: ' I have sworn on oath to say what I know, to the best of my knowledge and conscience. I do not allow anyone to examine me here. I am not a cadet!' Eventually, after more cross-examination in the same vein, von Rundstedt finally replied: 'I hold the same opinion as von Moltke and Elder, that one is responsible for one's actions to God and one's Fatherland', a subtle amendment of the quote as given by the Commission. The examination was now nearly at an end. After a couple of questions on von Rundstedt's attitude to Hitler's coming to power, he was asked his opnion on race theories – 'That was nonsense. You only have to look at the German people' – 'Lebensraum?' – 'We had enough Lebensraum. The only desire we had was to regain our colonies' – 'In the East?' – 'The only thing to achieve was the [Polish] corridor link [with East Prussia]'. There the Commission's examination ended. It had not been a pleasant experience for the Field Marshal.[59]

There was then a further wait and it was another month before Dr Laternser applied for von Rundstedt to appear as a witness for the defence in the case against the High Command and General Staff. Finally, on 12 August, von Rundstedt entered the witness box. Dr Laternser first took him through the ground which had been covered by the Commission in its examination. The most significant answer that von Rundstedt gave was to Laternser's last question, on the senior commanders' attitude to Military and International Law. In his reply he stressed that these were 'always binding for us older leaders' and that 'very severe measures were taken in the case of excesses which in war can probably take place in all armies'. The divisional court-martial records would support him on this point. He then went on to say:

> 'We old officers who lived through the time of cavalry battles and infantry bayonet attacks witnessed the increasing mechanisation of warfare with regret. Today the bravest men and the best troops are helpless against the force of mechanisation. All the more did we leaders believe that where there was fighting on land the old soldierly, decent forms of battle should be maintained, and that they should be impressed on the troops again and again.
> As senior soldier of the German Army, I will say this: We accused leaders

were trained in the old soldierly traditions of decency and chivalry. We lived and acted according to them, and we endeavoured to hand them down to the younger officers.'[60]

It was now the prosecution's turn to cross-examine and the task was given to the British lawyer Peter Calvacoressi. The first part of his questioning was concerned with the relationships among OKH, an army group commander and his army commanders. What he was trying to establish was that the High Command did operate as an organisation in which an overall policy was generated as a result of an interchange of opinions. Von Rundstedt, however, said that this only happened at the operational and tactical level and that political and strategic matters were laid down by Hitler and the OKW and were not open to question. Calvacoressi then tried to get von Rundstedt to admit that the Army was not entirely non-political. It had not supported Kapp because he failed in his putsch, but backed Hitler after he came to power because he was successful. Von Rundstedt admitted that Hitler had tried to make the Army National Socialist minded, but that the senior commanders, although they may have privately held political opinions, never voiced them at an organised meeting or as a body. He also denied that the Army was training for an aggressive war before 1939 and said that the manoeuvres which he had conducted had been strictly defensive, usually taking as a scenario a Lithuanian threat to the then isolated East Prussia, a joint Polish–Czech attack against eastern Germany or a French crossing of the Rhine. Having then tried to make von Rundstedt accept that Chancellor Schuschnigg of Austria had caved in in 1938 because of the might of the Germany military machine, Peter Calvacoressi then changed tack and asked von Rundstedt about the Commando Order. The Field Marshal assured the prosecutor that no one had lost their life in the West as a result of it, but 'if the Commando Order was carried out elsewhere in another theatre of war, then the commander of the unit in question acted in accordance with Hitler's order, which they had to assume as founded on International Law'.[61] After raising the so-called 1941 Severity Order issued by von Reichenau when commanding Sixth Army and that issued by von Schobert's Eleventh Army, which von Rundstedt denied having seen at the time, although copies might have reached his headquarters, Calvacoressi then read out an order sent to Panzerarmee Afrika in June 1942 ordering the immediate shooting of any members of the Free French forces who were German refugees. The fact that it strictly ordered all dissemination of it to commanders to be verbal and not

written proved that whoever wrote it recognised its illegality. Von
Rundstedt was not given the opportunity to comment, for Calvacoressi
then asked him what he knew of Rommel's death. The reply was that he
had had no suspicion that his death had been unnatural. That was the
end of the cross-examination, but Laternser then asked some further
questions on the commander–subordinate relationship to clarify that
there was no form of senior commanders' 'trade union' in operation.
Likewise, von Blomberg's talk of 'the Group of German Staff Officers'
meant nothing to von Rundstedt. There his day in the witness box
ended.

On the impression that von Rundstedt gave at Nuremberg, *The Times*
correspondent commented that he was 'alert in mind in spite of his 71
years' and that he bore 'a strong resemblance in appearance and
mannerisms to Keitel'[62], which would have annoyed von Rundstedt,
given his views on the Chief of Staff of the OKW. Airey Neave viewed
him as 'now a frail old man but dry and aristocratic'.[63] Peter Calvacoressi's recollection of over forty years later was that:

> '. . . he was – and probably exaggerated how much he was – an old man.
> Partly by nature and partly by training, he exhibited the professional
> officer's posture of being half outside the events of his lifetime; his posture
> was dignity achieved through aloofness. He was not going to let on how
> much he and his colleagues had known or done. He did this well – or
> anyway successfully.'[64]

Von Rundstedt himself did not enjoy his stay at Nuremberg. He, von
Kleist and Blumentritt flew back to Britain on 19 August. On arrival
back at Island Farm, von Rundstedt, according to Ted Lees, 'wrung us
all by the hand and assured us that he was glad indeed to be back at his
"Hotel Island Farm". Later he intimated that he would be quite happy
to remain there until his dying day – as long as he was not handed over
to the Americans again.'[65] One of the camp guards also recalled that on
von Rundstedt's return '. . . we saw a big change in him. His face was
gaunt and expressionless and he had aged considerably.'[66] In the end,
the IMT could not find the former German High Command and
General Staff guilty on any count as an organised body, but stressed
that this did not absolve individual members of guilt.

Island Farm itself was not called a 'special' camp just because it
housed senior officers. Many of them were on CROWCASS lists,
including, of course, von Rundstedt himself. Some were handed over to
allies or sent back to the scene of their alleged crimes for trial. Thus, von
Kleist left the camp in October to be tried in Yugoslavia for war crimes.

Two years later he was handed over to the Russians and died in one of their prison camps in 1954. General Kurt Student was handed over to the French and Blumentritt was, as we shall see, taken to Hamburg to be put on trial. Because of this, conditions were much stricter than they were becoming at other camps. Indeed, a PID training adviser visiting the camp in June 1946 had commented in his report that the other ranks in the camp resented these restrictions and objected to serving as orderlies to senior officers whom they regarded as war criminals.[67] These restrictions were tightened considerably in autumn 1946. Classes in English, some of which had been conducted by Hans Gerd, whom a Technical Adviser had described in an April 1946 report as 'fawning',[68] were stopped, as were outside lectures. The grounds given for this were that the inmates were dedicated Nazis and militarists and beyond re-education.[69] One suspects that the British Government did this in the immediate aftermath of the Nuremberg international trials because it feared a renewed clamour from the Soviet Union and the states of Eastern Europe for the handover of many of the senior officers in British hands, especially since the Cabinet was keen to bring war crimes trials to an end.[70] It did not believe that they would have fair trials, but, on the other hand, did not want it to seem that it had 'gone soft' in its treatment of them. The inmates of Island Farm were therefore thrown even more in on themselves, but life would have been much worse if it had not been for a sympathetic commandant and staff. Indeed, von Rundstedt so appreciated Topham's efforts that just before Christmas 1946 he presented him with his treasured *Interimstab*. In his letter of thanks Topham wrote: '. . . I am proud to accept your gift in the spirit in which you gave it, not only as from a very great soldier to a very humble one, but also, I like to think, as from a friend to a friend . . . the baton will always remain a very treasured souvenir, and a reminder of a very gallant officer.'[71] Topham apparently promised that, after his death, the baton would be returned to von Rundstedt's family. Instead he bequeathed it to his regiment. It was placed in the Grenadier Guards Museum, but some years later went missing and has never been traced.[72] When Topham relinquished command of Island Farm, von Rundstedt made a speech of farewell, thanking him 'for the way in which you have fulfilled your difficult task. We thoroughly appreciated your gentlemanlike chivalry which made you always look at us not as criminals and prisoners but only as officers in a really hopeless situation.'[73]

Von Rundstedt himself tended to isolate himself from all but a few, who included the faithful Blumentritt and Admiral Hans Voss, whose

English was impeccable and was accordingly the Liaison Officer between the prisoners and the staff. According to one of his daughters, Voss would talk little of his time in England – indeed, virtually no senior officer who published his memoirs mentioned captivity – but he did have one story of von Rundstedt. The Field Marshal took up painting at Island Farm, rediscovering his boyhood talent, and used to ask Voss for his comments. 'Father's favourite painting, which he described to us with some relish and much affection, was a landscape – a field bathed in the brilliant red light of a sunset. In the middle of the field sat a fox holding a carrot in its mouth!! Father did not offer artistic appreciation.'[74] One suspects that von Rundstedt had inserted a little quiet humour. He also, apparently, became interested in the local flora and fauna and built up a collection of pressed flowers as another means of keeping himself occupied.[75] General Sir Brian Horrocks, Montgomery's favourite corps commander, was in charge of Western Command at the time and Island Farm was in his area of responsibility. He recalled visiting the camp on a number of occasions and talked to von Rundstedt:

> 'To start with, he was suspicious, as he had never heard my name at all, which was hardly surprising because as one of the supreme commanders he dealt in rather higher coinage than British corps commanders . . .
> Von Rundstedt was chronically short of cigarettes but was much too proud to mention the fact. So we used to leave packets on the table by the door when we went out. I felt no particular hatred for the old field-marshal. We were both professional soldiers, and as far as I knew, he had always fought cleanly. He was, however, a typical Prussian general of the old school. I once said to him: "Have you any complaints? Is there anything I can do to improve the living conditions in your camp?" He replied: "Yes. Some of the German generals in this camp are not the sort of people with whom we are used to mixing. I would be grateful if you would have them moved to another camp."
> "Who are those undesirable generals?" I asked.
> "General doctors and general engineers." he said. "It is most unpleasant for us real generals to be forced to live with people like that." Needless to say, no steps were taken to effect his particular improvement, and I left them all to get on together as best they could.'[76]

About the only inmate of Island Farm who did write about his experiences there was Frido von Senger und Etterlin, the defender of Cassino. He agreed with von Rundstedt that prisoners were there who could not really be considered as generals, especially the members of the Labour Service (*Reichsarbeitdienst*). He also noted that the prisoners tended to form three distinct groups. There were those like himself who had been open critics of the régime before the end of the war, those who criticised Hitler only after the fighting had finished and who would not accept that his shortcomings had been noticeable before then, and, finally, the die-hards.[77] Von Rundstedt seems to have kept himself apart from all three groups and according to Hans Guetler, who waited on von Rundstedt at the camp, he especially distanced himself from the SS generals.[78]

In October 1946 there was a new visitor to the camp. He was to become a well known face to the inmates during the next few months and the futures of many became very dependent on him. Repatriation of prisoners-of-war to Germany had begun the previous month, but every man had to be carefully screened. They were placed in three categories akin to the groupings described by von Senger. Otto John was sent to Island Farm to carry out this task. He was uniquely qualified to do so. He had worked as a lawyer for Lufthansa, the national German airline, and had become deeply involved in resistance to Hitler. Heavily implicated in the July 1944 Bomb Plot, he managed to escape by the skin of his teeth, using his Lufthansa connection to take an aircraft to Lisbon, and had finished the war working for Sefton Delmer's radio black propaganda campaign. He took on the job because he 'would have a unique opportunity to clarify the burning question why our senior commanders had served Hitler to the bitter end, although by the time of the great murders of 30 June 1934, at the latest, they must have realised that he was a criminal'.[79] A number of those at Island Farm already knew him since they, too, had been involved in resistance and this broke the ice. While only those who were not members of proscribed organisations, like the SS, or on CROW-CASS lists, were eligible for repatriation, John naturally wanted to interview as many of the prisoners as possible. Not surprisingly, von Rundstedt was very suspicious of him, but apparently, 'opened up completely' when John was able to arrange for Hans Gerd, who had developed a seemingly incurable throat problem, and whom John regarded as having had nothing to do with Nazi ideology, to be repatriated. Hans Gerd left Bridgend on 17 November 1946, and after short stays at two other camps, at Llanmartin, also in Wales, and Hereford, he was released on 30 January 1947 and returned to Germany. In the meantime, Ditha and the children had been having a hard struggle. Because the Allies had separated Austria from Germany, she found herself a foreigner with no rights and could not even obtain identity cards for herself and the children. Without these, they were not entitled to ration cards. Eventually, in August 1946, the Allied authorities ordered them to return to Germany, which they did with three stranded and wounded German officers. Relations in Brunswick had Barbara and Gerd to stay with them, while Ditha and the two youngest children found accommodation in two rooms of a farm near Hildesheim, which is where Hans Gerd was reunited with his family.[80]

Throughout von Rundstedt's first year at Island Farm, he continued to be troubled by the pain from his arthritic hips. He was, however, given treatment for this three times a week at the Bridgend Emergency Service Hospital. The senior physiotherapist there at the time, Elgiva Thomas, recalls that his appointments were always at teatime and that she gave him and Dr Blum, a fellow prisoner-of-war who always accompanied him, a cup of tea after his treatment was finished. Von Rundstedt was very appreciative and in February 1947 presented Elgiva Thomas with a signed portrait of himself inscribed 'for thankful remembrance'.[81]

In February also, the Americans began to indicate that they wanted von Brauchitsch, who was by then in hospital, von Manstein and von Rundstedt extradited for interrogation. They then placed them on CROWCASS List 55 and, in April, made a formal extradition demand. All three had testified for the defence during the IMT trial of the High Command and General Staff. Since then the Americans had unearthed a mass of new evidence against them and, in Telford Taylor's words, wanted 'to "show them up" against their earlier testimony'.[82] To this demand the British Government replied that since the Poles also wanted them, they would have to decide who had the best right to them.[83] It would appear that they were not convinced by the American case and were using this ploy to play for time.

In the meantime, on 17 March, von Rundstedt left Bridgend once more to fly to Germany, this time to Wuppertal to appear as a defence witness for Blumentritt. A member of the War Crimes Investigation Unit (North West Europe) noted that on his arrival 'several German civilians recognised him, but there was no "grand welcome"'.[84] The trial in which Blumentritt was involved was the Poitiers Case. This concerned an operation mounted by the British 1st Special Air Service (SAS) regiment, Operation BULBASKET. A total of 55 troops were dropped into central France with the object of disrupting railways in the Limoges-Orleans-Poitiers-Nevers-Vierzon region. Their base was betrayed and attacked by elements of General Kurt Gallenkamp's LXXX Corps. Thirty-two men were captured and taken to Poitiers prison, where 29 were shot and three, who had been wounded, apparently given fatal injections. This was all in pursuance of the 1942

Commando Order and the two subsequent orders of June 1944. The murders had taken place on or about 7 July 1944, after von Rundstedt had left the theatre but while Blumentritt was still Chief of Staff. In the event, the prosecution offered no evidence against Blumentritt, even though Gallenkamp tried to maintain that he had been absent at the time and that it was Blumentritt or the Operations Section of Ob West which had given the orders. Indeed, Blumentritt was actually called as a witness and denied any knowledge of the matter until a few days before the trial. Although no record of the detailed proceedings appears till to exist, it would seem that von Rundstedt was not, in the end, called upon to testify. Eventually, Gallenkamp and one other were sentenced to death, one was imprisoned for life, another for a lesser term and the remaining four, including Blumentritt, acquitted.[85]

On 9 April, von Rundstedt returned by air to Britain and to Hotel Island Farm. It would seem that during this time the War Crimes Investigation Group in Germany had been investigating von Rundstedt. On 9 May, the Deputy Judge Advocate General's Officer (War Office) informed the POW Division of the Control Office for Germany & Austria (COGA) at the Foreign Office that they did not want him for any war crimes, although they pointed out that both Poland and the United States did.[86] For von Rundstedt, however, the summer was quiet, apart from his ill health, which continued to dog him, so much so that a medical board, towards the end of August, recommended his repatriation.[87] This was not possible since the Field Marshal, together with von Manstein and von Brauchitsch, were now categorised as war criminals to be detained in custody,[88] although they were not informed of this. Von Rundstedt also fell out with his fellow Field Marshal, von Manstein; it is not clear why, although Ted Lees said that it was because von Manstein still had too much of a Nazi stance.[89] It is probable, though, that the mutual antipathy was brought about as much as anything by the environment in which they were living, especially the continued uncertainty over their future. At the beginning of October, however, von Manstein, suffering from a cataract and diabetes, was transferred to No 99 Military Hospital at Stafford, joining von Brauchitsch, who had been a patient there with stomach trouble since April.[90] But while all remained relatively calm at Bridgend, an American bombshell had hit London. It was to cause the British Government almost two years of agonising over the disposal of the German Field Marshals in its hands.

14

War Criminal

On 6 August 1947, Brigadier General Telford Taylor, the American Chief of Counsel for War Crimes, wrote from Nuremberg to Sir Hartley Shawcross (now Lord Shawcross), the British Attorney-General, with a copy to Mr Macaskie, Head of the Legal Division of the Control Commission for Germany (British Element) in Berlin. He had been instructed to do this by the Military Governor of the United States Zone of Germany, General Lucius Clay, earlier in the year. The Americans were in the course of preparing trials of German military commanders in their hands and Clay did not want it to look as if only the United States were charging Generals with war crimes.[1] He reminded Shawcross of the finding of the International Military Tribunal at Nuremberg on the German General Staff, namely that they could not be found guilty as a group, but their leaders were a 'ruthless military caste' who had been 'responsible in large measure for the miseries and suffering that have fallen on millions of men, women, and children . . . Where the facts warrant it, these men should be brought to trial so that those among them who are guilty of these crimes should not escape punishment.'

In the course of preparing for their trials of German military leaders, Taylor's office had come across 'a very substantial amount of evidence' implicating von Rundstedt, von Manstein, von Brauchitsch and Colonel General Rudolf Strauss (who had commanded the Ninth Army in Russia in 1941 and had then been sacked by Hitler) in war crimes. Enclosed with the letter was an 82 page memorandum summarising this evidence. 'This material is forwarded for your information and for whatever action your Government deems appropriate under Control Council Law No. 10 and the Judgement of the International Military Tribunal.' the memorandum itself was wide ranging in its accusations, covering both the Eastern and Western Fronts. They fell into three broad categories – war crimes, crimes against humanity and crimes against peace. The first-named category covered the Commissar Order of 1941, the Commando Order in its various guises, and, referring to Poland and the Eastern Front, murder and ill-treatment of prisoners of war and their employment in dangerous and prohibited labour. Crimes against humanity dealt mainly with the murder and ill-treatment of civilians in the occupied territories of the East, but also referred to von Rundstedt's involvement with conscription and deportation as forced labour of civilians in occupied Western Europe. The final categoy involved von Brauchitsch's and von Rundstedt's connivance in the invasions of Poland, Norway and Denmark, France and the Low countries, Yugoslavia and Greece, and the Soviet Union.[2] In all it was a damning document and one that the British Government could not ignore.

Yet, there was no immediate official reaction. Shawcross himself was on holiday, sailing in his yacht and incommunicado.[3] Not until a month later did he inform the Foreign and War Offices of the Taylor memorandum, but this he sent only to Captain Frederick Bellenger, the Secretary of State for War, warning Ernest Bevin, the Foreign Secretary, that the War Office would doubtless be consulting him.[4] In the meantime, the British Deputy Military Governor in Germany, General Sir Brian Robertson, had read it and commented that he suspected that much of the evidence gleaned was based on the writings of General Franz Halder, who was now in American hands and recording all he knew of the Nazi era for the benefit of history. Halder, Robertson pointed out, was no friend of any of the three Field Marshals. The Foreign Office agreed with this and considered that the Field Marshals could be used in the same way as Halder, a suggestion to which John Wheeler-Bennett, the eminent historian, who was then working in the German Section of the Foreign Office, agreed with alacrity.

'It does not seem entirely just that General Halder, having "sold out" to the Americans, should have the opportunity of establishing a historical monopoly, while these general officers, to whom he was bitterly opposed, are denied a chance of recording their own version of those events with which Halder will undoubtedly deal in his memoirs. In any case, it seems a pity to deprive ourselves of what would clearly be material of outstanding historical interest and value.'[5]

Nevertheless, at this stage the Foreign Office had not yet seen the evidence, which was with the War Office, the government department responsible for prosecuting war crimes. The agreed Foreign Office view was that unless the evidence was 'overpoweringly strong' the matter should not be pursued by the Government but left to the denazification courts on the Field Marshals' return to Germany. Besides, British public opinion, which had been disquieted by the recent trial in Italy of Field Marshal Kesselring, probably would not stand for such a trial taking place at this late stage.[6] On 3 October Bellenger wrote to Bevin giving the War Office view of the Taylor memorandum:

> 'It discloses a strong prima facie case against Field Marshals Brauchitsch, Rundstedt and Manstein and Generaloberst Strauss of responsibility for certain war crimes and crimes against humanity.
> We were all hoping that there would be no more of these trials of German Generals, but we clearly cannot ignore this evidence which has been brought to our notice by the Americans and if these officers were responsible for the war crimes and crimes against humanity alleged against them they ought not to escape trial and punishment merely because the evidence has only now been unearthed.'

There were, however, problems. First, there were clearly vast quantities of documentary evidence held by the Americans, which had to be considered and there would also be the need for a 'good many' interrogations. The War Office did not have the staff to do this and lacked an officer 'possessing the background, experience and linguistic qualifications necessary to interrogate accused of the standing and ability of Brauchitsch or Rundstedt'. Besides, 'the charges which are likely to emerge from this evidence have rather a Nuremberg character and are perhaps more suitable for trial under the United States procedure than by a British military court'. For these reasons, Bellenger recommended that the British not take on the trials. Instead, he suggested that the Poles, Russians, Belgians or Americans pursue the matter.[7] In the meantime, Frederick Elwyn-Jones MP (later Lord Elwyn-Jones), Shawcross's Parliamentary Private Secretary, who had been a prosecuting counsel at the International Military Tribunal, had visited Nuremberg and discussed the matter with Telford Taylor. He was clearly convinced by what Taylor had to say. While the British had tried a number of generals for war crimes,

> 'The fact remains, however, that the leading and perhaps worst offenders in this field have not yet been brought to trial. Now the Americans hope to bring their war crimes programme to an end with a trial of leading German militarists. They want to include in the case those generals who were in the closest planning relationshhip with Hitler, who instigated and planned aggressive wars and wars in violation of treaties and who issued and distributed orders pursuant to which extensive war crimes and crimes

against humanity were committed by the field formations of the German Army.'

Some of these generals – the three Field Marshals and Strauss – were in British hands. The Taylor memorandum 'makes a powerful case' and a prosecution based on it 'would have every probability of being successful'. Few of the documents mentioned had been available at the International Military Tribunal and if they had been 'we could have shown Rundstedt and Brauchitsch . . . to be not only perjurers but also criminals. The new evidence as to their personal involvement seems to me to be overwhelming.' He believed that the options were to either let the Americans try them or to have a joint trial. If the British did nothing it 'might give the impression that we opposed the American effort. The Germans would not be slow to draw false deductions from such a situation.' These views he passed not just to Shawcross, but to the Lord Chancellor, Foreign Secretary, Secretary of State for War and Lord Wright, Chairman of the United Nations War Crimes Commission (UNWCC), as well.[8]

Elwyn-Jones's letter made it clear that the Government had to take a decision quickly. The Foreign Office briefed Bevin that both in terms of resources and the likely public reaction, it was not desirable for the British to try the Field Marshals themselves. Indeed, domestic public opposition would do Britain 'a good deal of harm in Europe, whose memories of the German methods are longer and more vivid than our own, and would needlessly supply the Russians with an effective propaganda weapon'. The other possible course of action was to ask the Americans to try them at Nuremberg, which had 'both the staff and the organisation to cope with the problem'. It should, however, be recognised that the Americans considered that Britain had not played her full part in the trial of the 'more virulent offenders'. An indication of this was that Britain was one of the few countries which had no permanent representative at Nuremberg.[9] The upshot was that Bevin decided that the Americans should be approached, but wanted first to establish the best method of doing this, either through Marshal of the Royal Air Force Sir Sholto Douglas, the British Military Governor in Germany, to the American Military Government or through the British Ambassador to Washington, Sir William Strang, to General Lucius Clay, the US Military Governor, who was on a visit to Washington at the time. Accordingly a telegram was sent to Sholto Douglas on 15 October requesting that he ask the Americans how best to make the formal approach to them.[10]

It was now that problems of coordination among British Government departments began to show themselves. On the same day that the Foreign Office's exploratory telegram was sent to Berlin, a meeting was held by the Lord Chancellor, Viscount Jowitt, with the Solicitor General, Treasury Solicitor and Elwyn-Jones. This had been triggered by a meeting which Jowitt had had with Macaskie, from Berlin, at which Jowitt had indicated no strong feelings on the matter, but felt that the Field Marshals should be handed over to the Americans. He now held this second meeting without reference to the Foreign Office. However, when Elwyn-Jones apparently gave the impression that Bevin had already decided on the matter, Jowitt complained that he had not been consulted.[11]

Lucius Clay clearly got wind very quickly of what was afoot. On 19 October, he signalled Telford Taylor that he had no wish to take von Rundstedt and the others back and would not countenance a joint trial since this would be going back on the Allied decision to proceed unilaterally. The current Nuremberg trials programme was designed to establish a 'precedent for the future' and was not aimed at individuals. 'History will make no distinction between a von Rundstedt and a von Leeb', even though von Rundstedt was better known outside Germany.[12] On 23 October, Sholto Douglas replied to the Foreign Office request of the 15th. Reflecting his increasing distaste for the whole war crimes business, he stated that neither he nor Robertson were prepared to approach Clay until he was satisfied:

> '. . . that the equity of our proposed action has been carefully considered. We apparently do not wish to be concerned in these trials because public opinion in England will be revolted. We know that the Americans will make use of a lot of evidence of very dubious character. Yet we are apparently prepared to send these men, including one who is 73, to trial by the Americans. I frankly do not like this. I feel that if the Americans wish to be critical about our inaction in trying war criminals, I should prefer that they should continue to criticise rather than that we should commit an injustice in order to avoid their criticism.'[13]

Thus, the Americans had still not been formally told what the British decision was and it was hardly surprising that on that same day, 23 October, Telford Taylor should write to Shawcross asking him whether the British Government had officially reacted to his memorandum, which he had sent in early August. He made the point that some of the defendants in the American trial of von Leeb, von Küchler and others had served under von Rundstedt, von Manstein and von Brauchitsch at various times, and that some of the charges against them were based on orders transmitted by these Field Marshals. The defendants, too, might wish to call the Field Marshals as witnesses. It was thus essential to know what the British intended to do before Taylor drew up his indictment. Finally, he enclosed two cuttings from *The Stars and Stripes* on the SS *Einsatzgruppen* trial, then taking place at Nuremberg, which indicated evidence against both von Rundstedt and von Manstein.[14] Shawcross could not give Taylor an immediate reply since the Government had still not finally made up its mind. Thus the Foreign Office, in reply to Douglas's telegram, assured him that no final decision had been reached and that his views would be considered. He must nevertheless find out Clay's views.[15] These Robertson transmitted to the Chancellor for the Duchy of Lancaster, Lord Pakenham (now the Earl of Longford), the minister responsible for the British Zone in Germany at the Foreign Office, on 11 November. Not surprisingly, Clay said that he did not wish to accept the Field Marshals for trial, especially since the indictment for the trial of the generals held by the Americans had been completed. Douglas noted, however, that informally Clay had told him that he was not keen on trying the Field Marshals and hoped that the British would not try them either.[16] On the 15th he followed this up with a letter to Pakenham. He had heard a suggestion from the British Embassy to Moscow that the Russians should be reproached for not having tried Paulus and Seydlitz-Kurzbach, the ill-fated and erstwhile commander of the German Sixth Army and one of his corps commanders, who had been captured at Stalingrad. Better, he suggested, to wait until the Russians criticised the failure to try von Rundstedt and the others. 'This makes a perfect argument to them and with the Americans plainly out of the field should enable us to drop the whole question of a trial as I am sure we are advised to do.'[17] There was, however, a flaw in this argument. Seydlitz-Kurzbach was the very same general whose anti-Hitler public utterances while a prisoner in Russia had sent Schmundt scurrying to von Rundstedt in March 1944 to obtain a written declaration of loyalty from him. Paulus, too, had been used as a Russian propaganda weapon. The Russians could therefore argue that these two had recanted and contributed to the anti-Hitlerite cause. The same argument could not be used in relation to von Rundstedt and his fellow Field Marshals in British hands. Be that as it may, Pakenham replied to Robertson with a reassuring telegram:

'Legal advisers are at present studying the statement of evidence against the German generals held by us which was produced by the Americans.

> Unless there is strong evidence of participation in crimes against huma-
> nity, we are unlikely to proceed with the matter. The possible Russian
> reaction was not a factor affecting our decision but, as you say, their
> failure to try von [sic] Paulus and Seydlitz provides us with a ready
> answer to any objection they might raise.'[18]

Others did not share this view.

Fed up with the now endless pressure from Telford Taylor to find out
what the British Government had decided, Shawcross wrote to Bevin
from New York, where he was visiting the United Kingdom Delegation
to the United Nations, with ill-concealed irritation. The British were
continuing to try 'small fry' in Germany, but 'it would be open to severe
criticism if, while punishing these small fry, we allow the really big fish
in our custody to escape.' He could not understand Sholto Douglas's
assertion of doubtful American evidence since Elwyn-Jones, 'a very
capable lawyer', had concluded that there was 'ample and satisfactory
evidence that these officers were guilty of war crimes'. Further, he had
received a telegram from Telford Taylor stating that Otto Ohlendorf,
commander of the infamous *Einsatzgruppe D* in the Ukraine during
1941–42, had 'heavily implicated' von Manstein in his defence. Finally,
his office had been told by the Foreign Office, following a meeting to
which neither he nor the Lord Chancellor had been invited, to inform
Telford Taylor of Clay's decision not to try the Field Marshals in
British hands. The Foreign Office had taken over the matter, but did
not seem to wish to communicate with Taylor direct. It was, as Bevin
commented in the margin, 'a muddle' and he ordered Sir Orme
Sargent, Permanent Under-Secretary to the Foreign Office, to give the
matter urgent attention, ensuring that all parties were consulted, so
that the Foreign Secretary could make a decision.[19] The wheels now
began to turn more quickly and by 2 December Bevin was writing to
Jowitt, with copies to Emanuel Shinwell, who had recently taken over
from Bellenger as Secretary of State for War, Shawcross and Robertson, that in his view the only option was for a British military court to
try the Field Marshals. Jowitt was 'sorry to hear' that Bevin considered
a trial necessary as he had hoped to 'pack up the whole business' by the
end of the year. Nevertheless, he accepted that 'if the evidence is as
damning as you say' a trial would have to take place.[20] As a next step,
Bevin convened a meeting at the Foreign Office. This took place on 19
December and was attended by Jowitt, Shinwell, Shawcross, the Judge
Advocate General and other members of their departments. Significantly, Jowitt had still not been given a copy of the Taylor memorandum and it was agreed that he should study this before any further

decision was made.[21] Jowitt's view was that there was a *prima facie* case on the summary of evidence, although it was not as strong in the case of Strauss, but he warned that there might be problems in obtaining offending orders actually signed by the Field Marshals and to prove that war crimes had actually been committed on the strength of these orders.[22]

Von Rundstedt and the others were, of course, totally unaware that these deliberations had been taking place. In September 1947 a new commandant, Major Charles Clements MC of the 4th Hussars, took over from Denis Topham at Island Farm. His orders from the War Office made it plain that he was to take full responsibility for the camp and was not to refer any problems to the War Office. His impression was that the War Office 'was bound by red tape and political opinion to treat the Germans with a severity of which they did not approve, and were inhibited from making any official relaxation but that I could do what I thought right in the matter; the important thing was to avoid any publicity'. Having himself been a prisoner-of-war in Germany, he was sympathetic to the Generals' plight. His first act was to remove the live ammunition carried by the camp guards, 'who were soldiers of the lowest calibre'. In terms of his relations with the prisoners he dealt solely with von Rundstedt and Hans Georg von Seidel, formerly the Luftwaffe Quartermaster-General and now Camp Leader. He used to make a weekly courtesy visit to von Rundstedt's room:

> '. . . at the appointed time I knocked at the door of his room and he answered "*Herein*" [come in] and rose to greet me. We sat down and he offered me a cigarette from his slender store. Having discussed the business of the camp, we continued a general conversation for some time and when I rose to leave I left a packet of decent cigarettes on his table; the canteen supply were of very inferior quality.'

Clements was also able to supply the Field Marshal with a little alcohol from time to time. Noting that the new commandant was a cavalryman, von Rundstedt explained how all his family had been the same and that the high point of his military career had been command of 2nd Cavalry Divison.

The Generals, said von Rundstedt, had two major grievances. Unlike in other camps by this time, they were not allowed outside the perimeter except under escort. Clements replied that they could do as they liked provided that they behave as officers and gentlemen and avoided any publicity, warning them that if they abused this they might well find themselves with a new and less sympathetic commandant.

Von Rundstedt replied that, as soldiers, they knew what was required and assured him that there would be no trouble. Consequently, the Generals were seen much more about the neighbourhood and were, in Clements' words, 'extensively entertained by all classes'. None, as far as Clements was aware, abused this privilege, although he did hear a rumour that, on one occasion, one of them had misbehaved and that von Rundstedt had 'effectively dealt with him'. The other complaint was over the regulation that the Generals had to salute junior British officers. Clements explained to von Rundstedt that there was nothing that he could do about this, but he soon found a solution. 'The Generals were shirking around trying to avoid saluting, and so whenever I saw a General I saluted him. Within days they were competing to get their salute in first.'[23]

Von Rundstedt had a more immediate worry on his mind at this time. In June 1947, his son had been admitted to a church hospital in Hannover, suffering from what turned out to be throat cancer. At the beginning of December, the Bishop of Hannover wrote to Pakenham saying that Hans Gerd was likely to die in the near future and asked whether his father could be granted leave on parole in order to go and see him.[24] Pakenham was very sympathetic and passed the matter via Robertson to the Foreign Office. The letter arrived on the desk of Earl Jellicoe, who had recently joined the Foreign Office after a highly distinguished wartime career in the Special Air Service. He noted that von Rundstedt was in a 'frozen' category, pending investigation of war crimes charges. As such he could not be granted compassionate leave since this had been refused to others in this situation. Instead he suggested that von Rundstedt be discharged from the Wehrmacht, arrested as a civilian war criminal and granted parole. At the end of this he could be re-arrested and sent to Vishbek Civil Internment Camp near Bremen, although 'he would be unlikely to survive the conditions there for more than a week'. Understandably, his colleagues did not think that this was a good idea and recommended that the Bishop's request be refused. Jellicoe then had second thoughts. He discovered that none of the other compassionate cases in the frozen category had been of the same urgency. Furthermore, the Judge Advocate General's Branch in the War Office, which was responsible to UNWCC for war crimes cases, had no objection and strongly believed that he should remain a prisoner-of-war and not be discharged into civilian status. Accordingly, it was agreed that von Rundstedt should be flown by air to Germany on a week's compassionate leave and that he should be given a two pounds grant from the Foreign Office funds to buy comforts for his son from the local Navy Army Air Force Institutes (NAAFI) shop. The Generals were, in fact, each paid sixteen pounds per month (roughly equivalent to the pay of a British Army sergeant of the day). This money was held in camp private accounts, but could only be drawn in the form of vouchers, which had no value outside the camp perimeter; hence the need to give von Rundstedt an extraordinary grant.

Having spent the night at the London District Cage, von Rundstedt was flown unescorted to RAF Buckeburg near Hannover on 22 December and accommodated at the British Transit camp at Hannover, but treated as a prisoner-of-war.[25] He was able to visit his son daily and, on Christmas Day, there was a family reunion at which he saw Bila for the first time since he had been handed over to the British. She noted that Hans Gerd seemed a little better while his father was able to visit him.[26] Barbara, who was seeing her grandfather for the first time for six years, recalls: 'I can never forget the sorrow in his eyes when he was accompanied by an English major to see his son for the last time. I felt disappointment that he would never permit himself to cry. I have never seen tears in his eyes; with his iron discipline he kept them back.'[27] Von Rundstedt was thus understandably, as he wrote to Liddell Hart on his return to England on the 29th to thank him for a Christmas card and gift of cigarettes, in 'a great anxiety' and hoped 'that God will do a miracle and heal my poor son'.[28] No such miracle took place and Hans Gerd passed away on 12 January 1948. Three days later von Rundstedt received a telegram informing him of this. It was a blow from which he never really recovered.

There was one small footnote to this sad saga. On von Rundstedt's return from Germany it was discovered that he had spent Fifteen Shillings and Fourpence (77p) in excess of the Two Pound Foreign Office grant. The War Office wrote to the Foreign Office to ask if they would pay this. They in turn tried without success to get the International Red Cross to foot the bill and not until March 1948 did they finally agree to settle it.[29]

In the meantime, the war crimes business rumbled on. It now seemed that the War Office had been saddled with the responsibility of bringing the Field Marshals to trial, but they were not happy about this. In early January 1948, Shinwell arranged to have them examined by an Army Medical board. No sooner had von Rundstedt returned to Island Farm from Hannover than he was taken up to Stafford, where von Brauchitsch and von Manstein were still in hospital, for the medical examination. The Board noted in von Rundstedt's case that he

complained of 'general weakness, giddiness, palpitations and headaches made worse by change in posture; also progressive insomnia,
recurrent pains in the right shoulder, right hip-joint and both hands'.
Examination revealed 'a markedly general senile physique', poor
appetite, and loss of memory for recent events, as well as chronic
arterio-sclerosis and osteo-arthritis. Not surprisingly, the Board concluded that for von Rundstedt to be tried as a war criminal would
'adversely affect his health', as it would the other three as well. Shinwell
sent these findings to Bevin. 'In these circumstances I have formed the
view that these prisoners-of-war, owing to their state of health, should
not be brought before British Military Courts or at all. That would
leave them to be repatriated in the ordinary way and in due course of
time.'[30] This put another fly in the ointment for the Foreign Office,
especially since they were sensitive to the fact that two generals in
Allied captivity, Blaskowitz and Otto von Stülpnagel, chose the beginning of February to commit suicide while awaiting trial at Nuremberg
and Paris respectively. Shinwell's recommendation thus seemed
attractive, even though, as one official minuted: 'The War Office has
never been particularly enthusiastic about trying these Generals, and
we have been at some pains to keep them up to the mark, because of
international repercussions.' It was not unnaturally the latter, in the
Foreign Office view, which might prove to be the stumbling block.
They noted that the Americans did not seem keen on the Field
Marshals being tried at all, although the only evidence for this
appeared to be Clay's off the record comments to Robertson of the
previous autumn, and that the Russians had not requested their
extradition. The Belgians and the French, on the other hand, might be
upset if the charges were not proceeded with. It was therefore decided
that they should be unofficially approached through the British ambas-
sadors to establish what their reactions might be.[31] They were asked to
reply with some urgency since Fitzroy Maclean, who had led the
British mission to Tito to Yugoslavia during the war, had a parliamentary question on von Rundstedt's future down for answer by the
Secretary of State for War in the House of Commons on 17 February.
The reaction from Brussels was that the Belgian Minister of Justice said
that although von Rundstedt was on their list of war criminals they had
concluded since the IMT at Nuremberg that he was not as guilty as
they first thought and he did not think that the Belgian people, apart
from some in the Ardennes, would be unduly disturbed if he was
released. The Political Director at the Foreign Ministry was rather less
sanguine. He believed that public opinion would be upset and that if

von Rundstedt was released it should not be given undue publicity.[32] Indeed, the latter view was supported by an article which appeared in a Belgian newspaper at this time. This gave a paraphrase of a hard-hitting piece written by Elwyn-Jones, which had appeared in the British *News Chronicle*. This had been written in response to a piece which had appeared in A J Cummings' 'Spotlight' column in the same newspaper a few days earlier. Cummings had noted that a former Member of Parliament had written to the Prime Minister asking for von Rundstedt's release. Von Rundstedt's reaction to this news had apparently been: 'What is the good of going back to Germany only to be bumped off by the Americans?' Cummings also noted von Rundstedt's popularity among the local Welsh people and how they had nicknamed him 'Papa Rundstedt'. Elwyn-Jones considered this singularly inappropriate and made several war crimes accusations against the Field Marshal. In view of these, it was hardly surprising that he had no wish to return to Nuremberg. Given Elwyn-Jones's official position and the fact that the Government had still not made up its mind whether the Field Marshal's should be put on trial, it is somewhat surprising that he should have rushed into print in this way. The Belgian article, however, agreed with everything Elwyn-Jones said and, in view of the memory of the 'Ardennes martyrs', also considered von Rundstedt's nickname misplaced.[33] The British ambassador to Paris was more forthright. The French, even though they had not pursued their demands of autumn 1945, still held von Rundstedt to be at least partly responsible for the shooting of hostages while he was C-in-C West and also remembered what went on in the Ardennes. The ambassador noted that there had been unfavourable comment in the left wing newspaper *Franc Tireur* on von Rundstedt's visit to his dying son and that the French had constantly criticised the 'alleged tenderness' to the Germans on the part of the British. He therefore believed that, in spite of his state of health, von Rundstedt's release 'could not fail to arouse indignation' in France.[30] Thus, the Foreign Office had to go back to the drawing board. This was reinforced when, on 11 March, Marshal Sokolovsky, the Soviet Military Governor in Germany, demanded of Robertson the extradition of von Rundstedt, von Manstein and von Mackensen and cited Allied Control Order No 10. Robertson, however, was able to evade this by pointing out that extradition under Control Order No 10 only applied to those suspected of war crimes who were resident in Germany and that von Mackensen, was already serving a sentence for war crimes in the British military gaol at Werl.[35]

The Foreign Office's next step was to convene another medical board, this time, after Cabinet agreement, to be run by the Home Office.[36] This had been prompted by Shawcross writing to 'Mannie' Shinwell about the War Office medical board findings. While he accepted that all save von Manstein were not fit to stand trial, he feared a possible public outcry if they were released and therefore recommended an 'independent medical board'.[37] The Board carried out its examinations on 25 March. The report on von Rundstedt was very different to that of the Army medical board of two months before. He presented himself without sticks and said that his previous dizziness, headaches and pains in the chest no longer troubled him. Indeed he only complained of occasional pain in his right hip joint and leg and some pain in his lower back. He showed signs of physical senility, but nothing abnormal for a man of his age. His mental state was not so good. He told the Board that he was 'sick of life and wanted to be finished with it all, as it no longer held any interest for him'. He never read, listened to the radio or attended any camp entertainments. He was, without doubt, reacting to Hans Gerd's death and was probably desperately frustrated by his powerlessness to give any help to Bila, his widowed daugher-in-law and grandchildren. Not that he did not try. Shortly after von Rundstedt's return from Hannover, Captain Lees's wife, perhaps feeling sorry for him, made up a food parcel and gave it to him. In his letter of thanks von Rundstedt wrote that he hoped to be allowed to send two tins of food from it to his grandchildren.[38] Notwithstanding this, the medical board concluded that he was fit to stand trial, but that he should be regarded as a 'potentially suicidal person', a comment which was later to have unfortunate repercussions for all four. Both von Manstein and Strauss were also found fit and only von Brauchitsch was considered too ill.[39]

Before the Government had had the time to consider the full implications of the Home Office medical board findings, another complication arose. On 10 April, Telford Taylor signalled the Judge Advocate General's (JAG) department, via the American Embassy in London, with a request for von Brauchitsch, von Manstein and von Rundstedt to appear at Nuremberg as witnesses for the defence in the forthcoming American High Command trial. He asked for confirmation that the three were medically fit to travel and suggested that they should not be told the contents of the telegram.[40] Not the least problem was that the timing of this request was unfortunate. On 12 April the Overseas Reconstruction Committee (ORC), the Government's policy making body for overcoming the ravages of war in Europe and elsewhere, decided that war crimes trials would not pursued after 1 September 1948. This was in recognition of the fact that the Western Allied zones of occupation in Germany would have to be given a significant degree of self-government as a means of self-help to get them back on their feet. It would, however, be difficult to achieve this if an atmosphere of rancour persisted. The JAG's department passed the matter over to the Foreign Office on the following day. Two weeks later, Basil Marsden-Smedley of the German Section wrote to the Deputy Judge Advocate General, Brigadier Shapcott. The main drift of his letter was that no answer could be given to the Americans until the Cabinet had decided the future of the Field Marshals and Strauss. The Cabinet could not do this until the JAG's department had produced a paper giving all the factors, something which they had been tasked to do after the Home Office medical board. The JAG's recommendation of repatriation no longer held since, as a result of the recent Russian extradition demand, Robertson had asked that they should not be returned to Germany. Furthermore, if they did testify at Nuremberg it could not be held that they were medically unfit to stand trial themselves and the Russians might well demand their extradition from the Americans. The only way that the Americans could refuse this was to say that they were merely on loan from the British, and 'this will imply that the British wish to try them themselves'. He therefore urged Shapcott to complete his paper as soon as possible.[41]

On 4 May 1948, von Rundstedt and Strauss left Island Farm, their home for nearly two and half years, on transfer to No 231 Prisoner of War Hospital at Redgrave Hall, near Diss in Norfolk. Before he left Bridgend, Charles Clements and the officers of the camp staff gave a dinner in von Rundstedt's honour. This was in contrast to a lunch given by the Liddell Harts, who were passing through Bridgend, a few weeks earlier. They entertained six Island Farm inmates, but von Rundstedt was not permitted to join them because of his frozen category. Knowing von Rundstedt's regard for him, the previous commandant, Denis Topham, was also invited to the farewell dinner. Von Rundstedt did not forget the kindness shown to the prisoners by the local Welsh community. He presented a silver crucifix to St Mary's Church in the local village of Norton, where many of the Generals had worshipped. He also wrote to the Bishop of Llandaff: 'We shall never forget the solemn and edifying hours we were allowed to spend in attending divine services at St Mary's, never the manifold proves [sic] of love and understanding we experienced in your diocese, especially amongst the congregation of St Mary and their dear rector, Dean Gravell.' In addition, he gave his walking sticks to local inhabitants as keepsakes.[42]

The reason for the transfer to Redgrave Hall was not just on medical grounds. The whole population of No 11 PW Camp was leaving, but, apart from von Rundstedt and Strauss, for Germany and freedom. Yet, as von Senger and Etterlin later recorded, it was not without trepidation. They had to make a major adjustment and 'it was hardly to be expected that the German people would receive their generals back with open arms. They would more likely (and rightly) reproach us for not realising the situation and for doing nothing to put an end to the war.'[43]

At Redgrave Hall, von Rundstedt and Strauss were reunited with von Brauchitsch and von Manstein. Their situation did not seem good. 'Our future is very gloomy and uncertain and I feel very bad with my damned leg', as von Rundstedt wrote to Liddell Hart shortly after his arrival at Redgrave Hall.[44] In reply, Liddell Hart tried to reassure him by writing that the prolongation of his stay might well 'turn out to be in your best interests. I cannot say any more for the moment but what I have heard seemed to be reassuring, though for obvious reasons nothing definite can be said'.[45] Bearing in mind all that Liddell Hart had already done for von Rundstedt, it is probable that this letter did give him and the others some comfort. Also, the régime at Redgrave Hall was sympathetic. The owner of the Hall, who had been invalided from the Army after fighting in Burma, managed to persuade the Commandant to bring von Rundstedt to dinner. The owner's son recalls that his father was impressed by von Rundstedt's good command of English and his interesting conversation. His father noted that von Rundstedt 'still had the air and bearing of a General about him, despite being in civilian clothes, but he also had the air of a bitter and disillusioned man'.[46]

On 2 June, the Americans, having accepted that von Brauchitsch was not fit to appear at Nuremberg, reiterated their request for von Rundstedt and von Manstein to attend, as defence witnesses for Generals von Roques and Wöhler.[47] On the 10th, the London *Times* got hold of the story, and also said that the United States legal authorities had been making efforts to secure the arraignment of the three Field Marshals. The British Government, which appeared to have been playing for time, was being gradually forced to reach a final decision on their disposal. On 5 July the Cabinet considered this and the American request. Shinwell said that von Brauchitsch was clearly medically unfit and he did not consider it worthwhile to bring the others to trial. It would need a 'special executive' to collect the evidence and it was doubtful whether the Poles and Russians would assist. There was the

PLATE 45. Von Rundstedt's ultimate downfall – German prisoners on the newly seized bridge over the Rhine at Remagen, March 1945.

PLATE 46. Hans Gerd and Gerd with Major General Frank W Milburn, commander XXI US Corps shortly after their capture

PLATE 47. Von Rundstedt and his son at Wiesbaden, June 1945.

PLATE 48. Arrival at Island Farm Camp, Bridgend, South Wales, January 1946.

PLATE 49. At Bridgend railway station on return from Nuremburg, August 1946. Left to right: Captain Lees, Blumentritt, von Rundstedt, Sergeant Strauss (interpreter), von Kleist and Heinrici (obscured).

PLATE 50. The von Rundstedts at Nordstadt Hospital, Hannover after the Field Marshal's release from

PLATE 51. Von Rundstedt's grandsons, Gerd and Eberhard, with his ceremonial baton on the day of his death.

PLATE 52. The Last Salute, Hannover-Stöcken, 28 February 1953.

cost and, furthermore, it was obviously impossible to complete them by 1 September, the agreed date for ending war crimes trials. He therefore proposed that von Rundstedt and von Manstein be allowed to testify at Nuremberg on the understanding that they were returned to Britain immediately afterwards. All four would then be released on 1 September and returned to Germany, where they would be subject to denazification. He was supported by Jowitt, who stressed the formidable task of collecting the evidence, the possibility that at the end of it all they might be found innocent and that public opinion 'would regard the trial of these elderly and infirm officers as an act of vengeance rather than of justice'. Both Shawcross and Bevin saw matters differently. There was a *prima facie* case, the Polish and Soviet governments had been given the impression that the British would deal with them, and, bearing in mind that some of their subordinates had been tried and executed, the Government 'could be accused of bad faith if the generals were not put on trial'. Besides, although the ORC had set a 1 September deadline, 'these few and exceptional cases', said Bevin, 'could if necessary be completed after that date'. The Cabinet eventually agreed that the trials would take place, and in Germany, and that von Rundstedt and von Manstein would be allowed to appear at Nuremberg.[48] On 9 July, the War Office signalled Eastern Command, under whose military jurisdiction Redgrave Hall came, giving warning of what was in store for the four. They were not, however, to be told, and 'all necessary precautions will be taken against suicide and privilege of unescorted walks will be withdrawn'. The War Office also informed Headquarters British Army of the Rhine (BAOR), stressing that 'special precautions' were required to prevent suicide, especially in von Rundstedt's case. Four days later, Shapcott wrote to the United States authorities in Nuremberg, giving a similar warning. 'It is considered probable that Field Marshal von Rundstedt will commit suicide.'[49] The sudden harding of their treatment boded ill for the four, but it was still some weeks before they were formally notified of the decision to try them as war criminals.

On 16 July, von Brauchitsch and Strauss left Redgrave Hall and were taken by hospital ship to Germany. On arrival they were taken to the camp at Munsterlager, some 75 km south of Hamburg. Since this was the camp from which German prisoners-of-war were released into the outside world, it was understandable that they thought that this was about to happen to them. Six days later, von Rundstedt and von Manstein also left Redgrave Hall. Dressed in dark brown tunics, with two Ukrainians to carry their bags, they were taken by ambulance to the railway station at Diss, where they waited in the stationmaster's office until their train to London arrived. After thanking their escort officer for the kindly treatment they had received at Redgrave Hall, they boarded a first class carriage and began their journey to Nuremberg.[50] After spending the night at the London Cage they were handed over to an American military escort and flown to Nuremberg. On arrival there, they were, as von Manstein wrote to Liddell Hart:

> '. . . lodged in the Military Hospital. The housing, food and medical treatment were good. But we were strictly isolated from everyone, always a guard (a negro) in the room of each of us. Although I have never been an adherent of the silly theory of "*Herrenrasse*" [race], this method of putting a negro as guard at one's bedside seems to me a perverseness of taste.'[51]

Shapcott, however, had sent a letter care of the escort officer to the Secretary-General of United States Military Tribunal No 5 at Nuremberg warning of the suicide danger, especially in von Rundstedt's case.[52] It is thus hardly surprising that the two were subjected to such tight custody.

According to Telford Taylor, the British Government had asked the Americans not to tell von Rundstedt and von Manstein that their indictment was even under consideration. The Americans, however, were firmly opposed to them taking the witness stand in ignorance of this fact.[53] It is not clear from the records exactly what von Rundstedt and von Manstein were told. Von Manstein in his letter to Liddell Hart said that they were told nothing and that he was especially disappointed since he wanted to check the chief prosecution witness, who was a Gestapo man. Lorna Newton of the Foreign Office considered that it 'completely mispresents the position on this point'. She stated that 'the court made an order to the effect that as persons of peril they were not required to give evidence, and they in fact elected not to'.[54] This was so, but it was not the British Government which warned the Americans of the firm intention to try them for war crimes. On 26 July the Presiding Judge, John C Young, issued a court order which stated: 'The Court has been informed by the *Public Press* [author's italics] that von Rundstedt and von Manstein, who were summoned as defence witnesses for certain defendants, are likely to soon be tried by the British.' The defendants were to be warned of this and be given 24 hours to decide whether they were prepared to testify or not. The court would hear their decision on the 28th.[55] The two Field Marshals declared that they would not testify and on that same day, 28 July, were taken to join von Brauchitsch and Strauss at No 6 PW Hospital,

Munsterlager.[56] It would seem that von Rundstedt and von Manstein travelled separately, possibly because of the enmity between them. En route, von Rundstedt, but apparently not von Manstein, was put up for the night at the Officers Mess of the Field Investigation Section of the War Crimes Investigation Group (North West Europe) at Bad Oeyn-hausen, which was also the location of Headquarters BAOR. The Officer-in-Charge of the Section, R A Nightingale, ignorant of the intention to charge von Rundstedt as a war criminal, and his officers entertained him to dinner. Nightingale recalled that they had a discussion on the Ardennes campaign and that von Rundstedt was very affable. 'It was a full-dress affair. A person of his calibre deserved the honour and he was very touched.'[57]

Munsterlager provided another shock for von Manstein and in view of his warm reception at Bad Oeynhausen, especially so, for von Rundstedt. First, they were surprised to find that both von Brauchitsch and Strauss had not been released, but were still there. Secondly, they found themselves under very different conditions of confinement to those which they had previously experienced, except at Nuremberg. Liddell Hart acquired a letter sent by an anonymous National Service-man who had to guard von Rundstedt during his first days at Munster-lager:

'I had to stand in his room, armed with a wooden truncheon, and wearing PT shoes and watch him carefully all the time to see that he did not try to commit suicide. I was ordered not to take my eyes off him for a moment, and I even had to escort him to the toilet, etc. Rundstedt is an old man almost seventy [sic]. Although he walks with the aid of sticks he is still surprisingly upright for his age. He wore a haggard and worn expression on his face and spoke very little to any of us (he speaks excellent English) so you will gather he was not one of the cheerfullest of characters to look after. It was a very monotonous job and I was very pleased when it was all over.'[58]

This was substantiated in von Manstein's letter to Liddell Hart, which has been referred to earlier. While 'the officers are polite', the windows were wired in, all potential suicide weapons, including string, were confiscated and they were only permitted outside exercise for one hour daily. They were allowed to see their wives for one hour per day but only in the presence of an officer. Bila, still in the American zone and now living in two rooms at Solz, was unable to visit. Matters were made worse when, on 10 August, the Commandant received instructions that the four were no longer allowed to see one another, thus placing them under solitary confinement. It was this step which clearly prompted von Manstein to write to Liddell Hart and it would seem that the Commandant was sympathetic to their plight in allowing the letter to be sent. Worst of all was the fact that the four had as yet been told nothing of what was in store for them. As von Manstein wrote:

> 'You will understand that we are deeply depressed by such treatment. Three years after the war we are still POWs, although none of us in command when the war finished. . . . If there be any true case against us, there would surely have been time enough during those three years to tell us something about it and to have made the necessary investigations.
>
> The prolonged uncertainty of our future as to the time of our further confinment is a torture not only for ourselves but even heavier for our wives. No criminal is detained in such a way without giving him the reasons for his detention and notice about the time he will be detained. . . . A criminal who is arrested has a right to hear the next day the reasons for his arrest.'

Von Brauchitsch went on hunger strike for 36 hours, while Ditha received a letter from her father-in-law forbidding her to visit him. 'I don't think that even my trust in God can help me anymore'. Sensing that something was very wrong, she managed to get permission to come to Munsterlager and was shocked by the humiliated state in which she found von Rundstedt; he was to call this period the worst in his life.[59]

The Field Marshals and Strauss were not, however, the only ones who had been kept in the dark. On 7 August, Sir Brian Robertson sent an angry telegram to the Foreign Office, copied to the War Office. He had been told by the Commander-in-Chief BAOR that he had received instructions to confine the four at Munsterlager and to prevent possible attempts at suicide. He was surprised not to have been informed of the Cabinet decision to try them, especially since he had been assured that his views would be taken into consideration before reaching a decision. He went on to say:

> 'Before any further steps are taken, I wish to record my conviction that to bring these old men to trial three years after the end of hostilities will have an exactly contrary effect in Germany from that for which war crimes trials were instituted. All sympathies will be on their side and instead of holding them up to opprobrium as criminals, the trials will turn them into martyrs. I have long been conscious that the public is sick of and wishes to see an end of such trials. Each death warrant that comes before me brings with it a bundle of petitions from religious leaders and I have no doubt that these prosecutions will excite widespread indignation and resentment against us . . .
>
> These men are a spent force in Germany. The only asset which they retain is their dignity which will only be enhanced if we bring them to trial. I

consider that if, at this later stage and at this juncture in the affairs of Western Germany, we bring them to trial we shall undo much of the good work that has done by the ORC decision [to cease such trials after 1 September]. I therefore appeal to you most earnestly to have the matter reconsidered before it is too late. The conditions in which these men are being held pending trial are also causing me grave anxiety. It would appear that *instructions have been given not to inform them that they are being held for trial as war criminals* [author's italics]. In my opinion it is contrary to justice that they should be held and treated as war criminals and yet not told either that they are to be tried or on what charges. They naturally strongly resent the continuous and humiliating surveillance to which they have been subjected. Brauchitsch has already indicated that he will go on hunger strike if this continues. It has been suggested by the War Office that he should be forcibly fed. The case of Rundstedt is particularly invidious. Having once let him out on parole to visit his sick son we must now appear to be playing cat and mouse with him. Pending consideration of my appeal against the trials, I ask most earnestly, that I be authorised to rescind these draconian orders.'[60]

There was no immediate reaction from the Foreign Office and in the meantime the matter became public.

On 16 August The London *Times* published a letter from Liddell Hart, as did the *Manchester Guardian*. The former mentioned the cat and mouse treatment to which the Field Marshals were being subjected and summarised the contents of von Manstein's letter, which the *Manchester Guardian* letter quoted at length. That evening, the London *Star* carried a leader on the subject. Three days later, the *Times* carried a further letter, this time from the well-known academic, Professor Gilbert Murray. It read in part

'. . . what alarms me most is the fear that in the awful conflict now raging in Europe between two standards of human conduct, we, who must by necessity as well as by our traditions, be champions of the higher standard, are being infected by the things we hate. The first defence offered for the incidents mentioned by Captain Liddell Hart is: "Well, what have they done to us?" It is a defence which amounts to a confession.'

On that same day, the 19th, Winston Churchill telephoned Sir Orme Sargent and complained of the decision to go ahead with the trial. Bevin's marginal comment on Sargent's report of this conversation was: 'I do not mind what he does. Most of the others under them have been tried. After all he started this business.'[61] Nevertheless, Bevin was clearly shaken by Robertson's outburst and the fact that the whole business was now being aired in public made it worse. In a letter to Shinwell on the 21st, he expressed his sympathy with Robertson over the conditions of confinement and asked, within the constraints of not allowing the four to collude over evidence and to prevent suicide attempts, that these be made 'no more arduous than is necessary'. He was not, however, prepared to reconsider the trial decision and made this clear in a telegram to Robertson dated 24 August. Again he used the argument that their subordinates had already been tried, but also that the Poles and Russians assumed that the British refusal to extradite was because they intended to try them themselves. In the meantime the War Office was preparing a draft statement for issue to the Press and Bevin had asked Shinwell if the Field Marshals could be informed of the decision to charge them simultaneously with the release of this.[62]

Yet, the wheels of governmental bureaucracy were turning in no way fast enough to stem public outcry. Further letters to the Press followed. Baron Parmoor viewed the situation as having a 'Nazi rather than British flavour';[63] a host of literary figures, including Osbert Sitwell and T.S. Eliot, asserted that the treatment of the Field Marshals was 'alien to all our traditions and likely to damage our national reputation'.[64] Finally, on 27 August, the lunchtime edition of the *Evening Standard* broke the story that the four were to be tried for war crimes. The Government could delay no longer.

That evening the War Office issued a statement:

> 'HM Government has declared that preparations should be made to bring Field-Marshal von Brauchitsch, Field-Marshal von Rundstedt, Field-Marhsal von Manstein,and Colonel-General Strauss to trial as war criminals by a military court in the British Zone of Germany. This court, which will in all probability be convened in Hamburg, will be the same type of court as that before which war criminals have been tried by the British military authorities in Germany.
> These four officers are held in Munsterlager Hospital in the British Zone of Germany as prisoners-of-war. They will now be demilitarised by the appropriate military authorities and will no longer be prisoners-of-war. They will then be officially informed that it is proposed to bring them to trial.
> These four German generals will be defended by German counsel of their own choice, or, in default of choice, by German counsel allocated to them by the British authorities, and will be given sufficient time within which to prepare their defence to the charges.'

The War Office spokesman who handed out this statement also assured the Press that the four were being well looked after. They each had a radio and the families of von Brauchitsch and Strauss were living on the ground floor of the building in which they were housed. Frau von Manstein lived close by and visited daily, while Ditha had recently visited von Rundstedt. Furthermore, a BAOR staff officer had visited the four on the 26th and none had any complaints.[65] Not released to the Press were details of some of the crimes for which a *prima facie* case was considered to exist, although Sir Oliver Franks (later Lord Franks), who had recently taken over as British ambassador to Washington, was informed. These crimes included the involvement of all four with the Commissar Order, the Commando Order (von Rundstedt only), ill-treatment of Allied POWs, 'chiefly Russian' (all four), contravention of the Geneva Convention in employing POWs on prohibited and dangerous work (all except Strauss), and crimes against civilians (all four). Franks, however, was warned that 'the crimes listed are no more than a *prima facie* case since it would be improper to prejudge the decision of the Military Tribunal as to whether the four Generals were in fact guilty of the offences attributed to them'.[66]

If the Government hoped that public opinion would be assuaged by this it was to be mistaken. The *Times* leader which accompanied the War Office statement, while it accepted that if the four had committed war crimes they should be punished, considered that they had 'been held far too long in captivity without trial. Even if no explanation could conveniently be given, it is still difficult to understand why the authorities have delayed the arraignment of these men for so long.' Leading Socialists, including Michael Foot MP, the Jewish publisher Victor Gollancz and Richard Stokes MP, who had during the war several times discomfited the Government over its strategic bombing policy, wished 'to record our shame that so grave an affront to the national traditions should be committed by a Labour Government'.[67] Indeed, the outcry transcended political divisions. Thus Lord De L'Isle and Dudley VC, who had won his Victoria Cross in Italy, fighting the Germans, asked:

> 'If the charges so tardily formulated are for breaches of the recognised laws of war, it puzzles a layman how soldiers can be "demilitarized" before trial and conviction. Or ought we to infer that the prisoners are to be arraigned upon charges of breaking laws that were never formulated until after the Allied victory?'

Furthermore, the charges had not yet been announced and this filled De L'Isle with dismay. 'I fear for the reputation of our country, and I fear for a precedent which is likely to prove not a deterrent but an incitement to further barbarity in war.'[68] On 11 September the Liberal

Party, representing the centre ground of British political opinion, passed a resolution in London viewing with the greatest misgiving the decision to bring the four to trial after such a long delay, as well as deploring their conditions of captivity and the demilitarisation decision. They also demanded an 'adequate explanation' from the Government.[69] Liddell Hart, too, was anything but mollified by the War Office statement. He pointed out that demilitarisation put the four outside the protection of the Geneva Convention and International Red Cross and that he had heard from one of them that there had been no change to their conditions and that they *had* complained to the BAOR staff officer.[70]

In spite of the public outcry and persistent criticism in Parliament, the Government pressed ahead. Contrary to Bevin's wish, it was not until over 24 hours after the release of the War Office statement that the Field Marshals and Strauss were formally discharged from the Wehrmacht and charged as war criminals.[71] The charges, however, were outlined in only very general terms in the formal written notices issued to each of the four. In von Rundstedt's case:

> '. . . the maltreatment and killing of civilians and prisoners of war, including political commissars, killing of hostages, illegal employment of prisoners of war, deportation of forced labour to Germany, economic exploitation of territories occupied by troops under your command, looting of objects of cultural and artistic value from territory occupied by such troops, mass execution of Jews, general devastation and annihilation of territories which was not justified by military necessity and other war crimes, still to be specified.'[72]

Besides removing their prisoner of war status, there were other implications to being designated war criminals. For a start, although this had been standard practice for all war crimes trials, it implied guilt before this had been proved in a court of law. On a more practical basis, Control Council Law No 10 laid down that the occupying authority within its zone of occupation not only had the right to arrest any person suspected of war crimes but that the authority 'shall take under control the property, real and personal, owned or controlled' by the suspect 'pending decisions as to its eventual disposition'.[73] In other words it was confiscated and this meant the freezing of bank accounts and savings, with no allowance made for support of the suspect's family. The payment of 80 Deutschmarks made to each discharged member of the Wehrmacht, which the four did receive, was of little consolation.[74] This served to add further to the burdens being placed on the Field Marshals.

The task of preparing for the trial was mammoth. Apart from the many potential charges outlined in the Taylor memorandum, much of the evidence was still in American, Russian and Polish hands. Also, in line with the ORC decision, the whole war crimes investigation organisation was being wound down. In order to help gather the evidence, the Foreign Office asked Robertson to request of Clay the retention of four American war crimes experts who had been lent to the British and the services of two experienced war crimes attorneys, Paul Niedermann, who had collated the evidence produced in the Taylor memorandum, and Walter Rapp. Clay's response was not very helpful. The United States war crimes apparatus was being wound up on 30 November and the British could not retain any of them after this date.[75] Instead, Otto John was invited to assist as adviser on German law and interpreter. He had spent the first half of 1948 at Nuremberg, at Telford Taylor's invitation, studying German militarism and his involvement in the July 1944 Bomb Plot was another bonus. His own reaction was:

> 'I had neither patriotic or moral scruples in taking on this task. I felt no obligation towards the German generals, but I did feel myself bound by a Christian ethic transcending nationality and it was entirely in accord with this that men who wished to conquer the world by genocide, and had brought about frightful calamity, should be brought to trial and sentenced.'[76]

The Foreign Office also moved to halt the handback to the Germans of the Curio-Haus in Hamburg, the scene of a number of previous war crimes trials, and which had been partially turned into a music school.[77] Luckily for the Government, both Gilbert Murray and Liddell Hart wrote to *The Times* stating that they had heard from the Field Marshals that conditions had greatly improved and that they were now allowed a reasonable amount of privacy and unsupervised family visits.[78] On 24 September, however, all four were transferred to No 94 British Military Hospital at Barmbeck, Hamburg. Again, their wives were allowed to stay in the same building, the hospital pavilion. Von Rundstedt, while he was unable to see Bila, continued to be visited by Ditha and also by his elder grandson, Gerd, who was at a Pestalozzi children's home in Hamburg. Two months later, Munsterlager, its task of processing the release of German prisoners-of-war now done, was closed down.

Criticisms of the delay in bringing the Field Marshals and Strauss to trial still dogged the Cabinet. During much of September the Government continued to 'stonewall' questions put by Members of

Parliament. It was nevertheless determined that the trials should go ahead, in spite of the criticism. At a Cabinet meeting held on 22 September, it was agreed that Bevin should make a statement in the forthcoming foreign affairs debate in the House of Commons. It was recognised, however, that although there was a *prima facie* case it might be impossible to prove since much of the evidence was in Polish and Russian hands. On the other hand, if the case was abandoned there would be no grounds for not handing the four over to the Russians.[79] Bevin made his statement two days later. He related the history of the case, stressing the time needed to establish that there was a *prima facie* case. He did, however, omit to recount the saga of von Rundstedt's and von Manstein's fruitless trip to Nuremberg in July 1948 and, describing conditions at Munsterlager, stated that 'there were no restrictions on them beyond those necessary for their custody'. In response to questions by two Labour MPs, Richard Stokes and Reginald Paget (later Lord Paget), he said that he did not understand their protests. He regretted the delay in bringing the four to trial, but 'it is a very awkward thing to put a Minister in the position of sanctioning the trials of people who carried out their orders and not sanctioning the trials of the people who gave the orders'.[80] Privately, though, the Governmental finger of accusation was pointed firmly at the War Office. Shawcross wrote:

> 'The War Office knew when these generals were captured that they were already on the list of war criminals and I think that, immediately after the judgement of the Nuremberg Tribunal in October 1946, when they were put on enquiry, they should have taken steps to ascertain what evidence was available at Nuremberg.'[81]

Shawcross clearly felt that the War Office was still dragging its feet when, on 6 October, he wrote to Shinwell stressing the need for speed in preparing for the trial.[82] Nine days later Sir Ivone Kirkpatrick was complaining to Bevin that 'no one at the War Office comprehends the domestic political implications of the question or is resolved to get a grip of it'.[83] The truth was that no professional soldier wanted to become involved with the politics of the business and considered it distasteful that high ranking officers, whom they admired professionally, should be degraded with the status of war criminals and that the responsibility for doing this should be placed on the shoulders of the British Army.

If the British Government now hoped that the preparation for the trials could continue without further public outcry it was mistaken. On the evening of 18 October, von Brauchitsch died of a heart attack. He had been unwell now for a long time, and it is surprising that, considering both the War Office and Home Office medical boards had found him unfit to stand trial, the Government had continued to proceed with his case. Von Rundstedt, von Manstein and Strauss wanted to pay their last respects to their old comrade by marching behind his coffin, but this had to be refused. Instead, a military chaplain conducted a military burial service for them in the hospital while the funeral was taking place. This showed sensitivity on the part of the authorities which was lacking in the treatment of von Brauchitsch's family. According to Frau von Brauchitsch, in a letter she wrote to Liddell Hart, she was taken ill at Munsterlager in early September and was moved to Hamburg at the end of the month. To begin with, her husband was not allowed to visit her and it was only after a Protestant Aid Society worker had obtained an interview with the British Regional Commissioner that the authorities relented. The Field Marshal was able to visit his wife twice, the last time on the day of his death. That afternoon, while walking in the hospital garden, von Brauchitsch began to suffer from heart pains. His wife was brought to see him at 5.30 pm, but was refused permission to bring a German doctor with her, which her husband had asked for. She was also not allowed to get their eldest son, who lived one hour's drive away at Neumunster, to come to the hospital and was not permitted to telephone their second son, who was in the United States Zone. The Field Marshal died at 7.15pm. After the funeral, Frau von Brauchitsch asked for a vehicle to transport the urn containing her husband's ashes to Hohenrode, an hour's drive south of Hamburg. She recalled the kindness of the British authorities in getting her across to England the previous autumn to nurse her sick husband. 'Therefore the greater the contrast since my husband's return to Germany on July 16.'[84] Von Brauchitsch's death triggered off another attack in the House of Commons on the Government's handling of the Field Marshals. Richard Stokes considered it 'astonishing' that the three had still had no charges preferred against them and other MPs, both Labour and Conservative, continued to complain of the delays and treatment of the three. All Michael Stewart, the Financial Secretary to the War Office, could do was to repeat the history of the affair and stress the complexities of the case.[85]

Be that as it may, von Brauchitsch's death simplified the task somewhat in that there was one less case to prepare. Even so, since each defendant was to be tried separately and the trial of von Rundstedt, which was to be the first, was estimated to be likely to last for six months to a year, the task, which was codenamed Operation MARCO, was still huge. At the end of October, the Americans completed the last of their trials, Case No 12, of Field Marshal von Leeb and other former high ranking officers, which had opened in February. Of the fourteen defendants, one, Blaskowitz, had committed suicide, two were acquitted, including Hugo Sperrle, and the remainder found guilty on one or more counts. They were sentenced to varying terms of imprisonment, von Leeb getting three years and Warlimont life. On 2 November, the Marquess of Reading moved a motion in the House of Lords that, in view of the long delays, proceedings against von Rundstedt, von Manstein and Strauss should be stopped. Replying for the Government, the Lord Chancellor produced a photostat copy of von Rundstedt's 21 July 1942 Commando Order to demonstrate the fresh evidence that had come to light since August 1947. He also stated that it was hoped to begin the trials in March 1949. Next day, *The Times* carried a leader commenting both on the motion and the Case No 12 findings. The evidence produced 'must, by its gruesome exactness and detail for ever destroy the claim that Hitler's commanders had no responsibility'. In Germany there were signs 'of the belief that the Army can be separated from the guilt of the Nazi system' and the evidence 'will need reiteration if the Germans as a whole are made to understand what it means'. In other words, *The Times* now clearly supported proceeding with MARCO. This brought about another attack from Liddell Hart, Gilbert Murray, Victor Gollancz, and Richard Stokes. In a joint letter to *The Times*, they criticised Jowitt for producing a document in an attempt to prove the case against von Rundstedt while it was still *sub judice*. As for the document itself, no attempt was made to prove its authenticity and, in any event, even given the 'iniquitous record of the Gestapo', they were 'the official security police of the German State'. Thus, if enemy saboteurs had been dropped by parachute on Britain, would it have been a crime if 'the British Commander-in-Chief had given an order that such parachutists had been handed over to [Police] Special Branch, MI5, or any other special body that might have been created for the security of the realm'? The authors were not attempting to prejudge the guilt of the MARCO defendants, but it was 'indecent for conquerors to try the conquered, whatever they may have done, many years after the termination of hostilities, and after years of imprisonment without trial'.[86]

Meanwhile the collation of evidence continued. Requests were made of both the Soviet Union and Poland for documentary evidence, but whereas the latter was prepared to assist, nothing was heard from the Russians. Shortly after the end of the American trials at Nuremberg, literally plane loads of photostat documents were flown to Britain, and vast quantities of relevant captured German files were located in the Pentagon, Washington DC. The only place that they could be stored was in the coal cellars of the War Office, and the job of examining and analysing them was awesome, especially given the lack of German documents experts still in service. There was, too, the question of witnesses. In order to gain evidence against von Rundstedt during his time as C-in-C West in occupied France, the former German Ambassador to Vichy France, Otto Abetz, was flown across to London from Paris, where he was awaiting trial for war crimes. He refused to testify against von Rundstedt unless the British interceded on his behalf with the French. The British refused to do this and instead, bribed with a packet of cigarettes, he was persuaded to write an account of the July 1944 Bomb Plot as experienced in Paris. This was later to provide the basis of a chapter in John Wheeler-Bennett's best selling *Nemesis of Power*.[87] Abetz himself was then returned to Paris, where in July 1949 he was sentenced to twenty years' hard labour.

More crucial to the prosecution's case against all three MARCO defendants was seen to be the testimony of Otto Ohlendorff and six other former *Einsatzgruppe* members. They had been tried and sentenced to death by the Americans in Case No 9, the *Einsatzgruppen* Case, and were now languishing at the American war criminal camp at Landsberg in Bavaria awaiting the results of a review of their case. They had been used as witnesses in the trial against von Leeb *et al* and had been interrogated by the Americans on behalf of the British. Brigadier Shapcott asked the Foreign Office if an application could be made to the American authorities for a stay of execution so that they could appear as prosecution witnesses in the MARCO trials.[88] Lord Henderson, the Under Secretary of State at the Foreign Office, and Shawcross considered this repugnant. Instead, Robertson was asked to approach the Americans to see if they would allow affidavits to be taken in the presence of the three defence counsels.[89] The defence counsels themselves were having a difficult time, as Dr Walter Grimm of Hamburg, who was representing von Rundstedt, indicated to a friend in Britain (probably Liddell Hart, with whom he was having a lengthy correspondence at this time over aspects of English Law):[90] 'With the exception of a small scrap of paper containing some generalising remarks, my client has up until now not been acquainted with any charges'.[91] It is thus not surprising that all three defendants wanted to also be present when Ohlendorff and his confrères gave their evidence and the JAG's department agreed that they could do so. The Americans were asked, in view of the fact that there was no suitable accommodation in Landsberg and that the daily journey from Nuremberg 'would kill von Rundstedt, with the consequent public outcry in this country that his death was caused by British mal-administration', whether it would be possible to bring Ohlendorff and the others to Nuremberg, but Clay rejected this. Consequently, in January the prosecution team, led by Lieutenant Colonel Gerald Draper and Otto John, and the three defence counsels, went to Landsberg without the defendants.[92] While there they had the macabre experience of hearing the sounds of executions taking place in the courtyard overlooked by the room in which they were interviewing the *Einsatzgruppen* men. Invited by the Americans to witness one of these, they declined.

Liddell Hart did his best to try and keep up von Rundstedt's morale, trying to get cigarettes through to him via the International Red Cross and sending him a Christmas card and photograph of himself. In his note of thanks for the latter von Rundstedt wrote: ' I am now 5 months here as a war criminal and always waiting for the trial. It is *very hard* [sic] time. . . .'[93] Yet Liddell Hart's efforts were being appreciated by other German generals. Heinz Guderian wrote to him:

'You, dear Captain Liddell Hart, give proof that you have learned from history by your gentle help you grant to the three [sic] German field marshals, and so does Mr Churchill and the Members of Parliament who spoke in favour of their former enemies. For it seems to be essential to efface former enemies and to establish a long lasting peace . . .'[94]

One German general, Hans von Donat, a transport expert who had served under von Rundstedt in Poland and France 1940, went even further. He wrote to the British Military Government in Hamburg asking to be confined in von Rundstedt's place, or at least share his imprisonment and to suffer any punishment, including death, on his behalf.

'My action is prompted by the fact that from many years of personal contacts with Generalfeldmarschall von Rundstedt I have found him to be a gentleman of the highest integrity and of sterling worth. I believe him to be one of the finest examples of manhood in Germany and I am firmly convinced that he is not guilty of any crime, because his proven qualities as a peace-loving Christian and a chivalrous soldier would make it impossible for him to violate the laws of humanity and decency.'

He did, however, lay down conditions. Firstly, von Rundstedt was to be released as soon as von Donat's offer was accepted and placed 'under the protection of a foreign power', with his family's pension rights restored. Von Donat's own family was not to be penalised in any way or exposed to any form of hardship. Finally, he appointed Victor Gollancz, 'known the world over as a philanthropist and valiant supporter of the cause of peace and humanity', to act as a trustee to ensure that these conditions were carried out. If he received no response, von Donat would approach the Americans for the release of a general (unnamed) as 'righteous and irreproachable' as von Rundstedt.[95] Needless to say, he did not receive any answer.

The wheels were now, however, beginning to turn a little more quickly. On 1 January 1949 von Rundstedt, von Manstein and Strauss were finally formally charged. The indictments were read out to each in turn by Otto John, their defending counsels and Draper being present. Yet, even after all this time, they were merely holding charges and the counsels were little the wiser. John recalled that von Rundstedt's reaction was to lose his temper, bang his cane on the arm of a chair and say: 'This trial and everything else here is only possible because of the occuping authority which lays down the law here. Such a thing would not happen in England.'[96] Not until the end of January were the detailed charges made known to the defendants. Von Rundstedt faced twenty of these. The first three related to three Commando Orders issued while he was C-in-C West. Two others reflected the treatment of Russian prisoners-of-war and captured Resistance members in France. Ten covered Russia and included the Commissar Order and treatment of Russian civilians, partisans and prisoners-of-war. Two of these dwelt specifically with *Einsatzgruppen* activities in Army Group South's area of operations. One charge dealt with the killing of Polish civilians in autumn 1939 and the remaining four covered the maltreatment and killing of Dutch, Belgian and French civilians, and deportations from France and the Low Countries.[97] Significantly, all the charges except three closely reflected the Taylor memorandum. The exceptions were the killing of Polish civilians and the killing and maltreatment of Dutch and Belgian citizens. Since von Rundstedt's case was the first to be tried and it was still hoped to begin this in early April, the defence had little time to prepare. Admittedly, Grimm had succeeded in bringing in the most experienced of the German war crimes defence counsels, Dr Hugo Laternser, who, it will be remembered, had appeared as the defence counsel in the General Staff trial before the International Military Tribunal, to assist him and was also trying to arrange through Liddell

Hart for a British lawyer to join the defence team. Even so, the material covered by the twenty charges was 'vast' and most of the defence witnesses were likely to be German generals, many of whom were not conversant with English.[98]

The prosecution, even though it had a considerable lead time over the defence, was also continuing to struggle. Elwyn-Jones was dealing with the Poles and had established a good rapport with the Polish Vice-Minister of Justice, Lean Chajn, who invited him and Draper to come to Warsaw. He did, however, warn Elwyn-Jones that it would take three months to assemble all the evidence, since it was scattered all round the country. It would thus not be in British hands before the end of March. Elwyn-Jones decided to delay his visit to Warsaw until the evidence had been collected and asked if this could be done by mid-March.[99] With the Russians it was a different matter. The Cold War was now at its height and repeated requests by the British Embassy in Moscow for Russian evidence brought no response. More sinister was an article by A Dymov in the *Literary Gazette* and entitled 'Letters from Berlin–Hitlerites in American Uniforms'. Dymov accused the Americans of refusing to hand over von Rundstedt to the French after the end of the war, but giving him to the British instead. They, in turn, had allowed him to advertise himself through Liddell Hart and had then installed him in their zone of Germany. Here 'the Hitlerite wolf Rundstedt continues to work on Anglo-American tasks'. Furthermore, all three MARCO defendants had been installed in villas with their families.[100] A week later, on 16 February, the Soviet Ministry of Foreign Affairs handed a note to the British Embassy in Moscow demanding the extradition of von Rundstedt, von Manstein and Strauss. In support of the demand, the Russians quoted the Three Power Moscow Declaration of 30 October 1943 and a United Nations General Assembly resolution of 13 February 1946 that war criminals would be sent back to the scene of their crimes for trial. Should the British have evidence relating to war crimes committed by the three on British territory or that of other countries, then this would be taken into consideration during the examination of the case.[101] The initial reaction of the British Government was that it was not reasonable to expect those accused of charges in several different countries to be tried by each in turn, but on reflection it was realised that this was a dangerous argument to use since half the charges against von Rundstedt applied to Soviet territory, as did nine-tenths of those against the other two defendants. Eventually, in April, it was decided that the response should be that the British were grateful for the evidence submitted in the Soviet demand and that the Russians be invited to send witnesses to Hamburg to give oral evidence at the trials.[102]

In the meantime, Shinwell was becoming concerned once more over the health of the defendants, although the Foreign Office was inclined to think that this was merely more War Office foot dragging.[103] Certainly von Rundstedt was unwell again. As early as the previous 30 August, a medical board at Munsterlager had warned that his heart was in danger of giving out. Then, at the end of October, Brigadier F.J.O'Meara, Consultant Physician BAOR, had noted that the Field Marshal's feet and legs were swollen up to the knees and considered him unfit for trial by court-martial. This finding was reiterated by a further board at the end of December 1948. But a medical check-up by HQ BAOR at the beginning of March 1949 indicated that, although still unfit, he was improving. Both von Manstein and Strauss remained fit, although the latter did have a heart condition.[104] Shinwell, however, was clearly still worried. He arranged for another medical board, composed of Army and prison service doctors. This reported that, while von Manstein continued fit, the other two were considered unfit to stand trial. The Board noted that von Rundstedt arose at 11am and remained up until 9 pm, spending his day reading and talking to Bila, who had at last managed to join him.[105] On 31 March the matter was brought before the Cabinet, who agreed that von Manstein should be tried as soon as possible. With regard to von Rundstedt and Strauss there was some debate. The Cabinet itself was unwilling to take a decision since if it did decide not to go ahead with the trials of the two, the Poles and Russians might take this to mean that the British were unwilling to try them. It was therefore agreed that the Secretary of State for War should find out whether it was acceptable for the court itself to take the decision. Should the court rule in favour of medical discharge, the Cabinet agreed that neither would be handed over to another country for trial and that they would be set free. If, in this event, von Rundstedt appeared as a witness in the von Manstein trial, the evidence he gave would be viewed in the light of the grounds on which the decision not to try him was made.[106] The view within the War Office, however, was that only the Cabinet could make the decision as to whether the trials of von Rundstedt and Strauss should go ahead, and there was a feeling that it was ducking the issue.[107]

Public concern was on the increase again. On 30 March the *Evening Standard* carried a piece which commented on the secrecy surrounding the trial preparations. It quoted Liddell Hart that the defendants still had not received details of the charges, which, of course, was now not so. While it had been agreed that British lawyers could assist the defence, no money was offered to them for this. Reginald Paget, himself a barrister who would eventually join von Manstein's defence team, was quoted as asking: 'who can be expected to spend six months or so away from his practice without any pay?' Finally, the newspaper remarked: 'The bungling Government are giving the Germans a poor example of how justice works in democratic countries.' The Peace Pledge Union, although not the force that it had been in the early Thirties, also expressed concern over both the delay in bringing the three to trial and the problems which the defence was experiencing.[108] Further to this, Bishop Bell of Chichester, another constant critic of the morality of some aspects of British wartime strategy, announced his intention of moving a motion in the House of Lords that all war crimes trials be halted and a general amnesty granted.

When the Cabinet considered the matter again on 28 April, it was very conscious of the resurgence of public criticism. It also had before it another medical report from 94 BMH. This warned that, while von Rundstedt was fit to plead, he was very frail and only kept going through constant medical care.[109] Matters were not made easier when Shinwell stated that a court-martial was not empowered under the Army Act to decide questions of physical fitness to stand trial and argued that the decision was one which only the Cabinet should take. The Lord Chancellor, on the other hand, disagreed. King's Regulations did not have to be applied and the decision could rest with the Commander-in-Chief BAOR. The Cabinet, however, did consider it 'undesirable' that ultimate responsibility should be placed on the C-in-C. Bevin was now 'gravely embarrassed' at the failure to bring the three to trial and argued that the medical reports were in some respects conflicting. In the end, it was agreed that the Lord Chancellor would, with the help of the Law Officers and medical 'assessors', obtain evidence from doctors 'who were in a position to express an opinion' on the medical fitness of von Rundstedt and Strauss to stand trial. Significantly, he was asked to report by 5 May, the day that the Bishop of Chichester's motion was to be debated in the House of Lords.[110]

On 4 May, the Foreign Office replied to the Peace Pledge Union letter, making it plain that Bevin was still adamant that the trials should go ahead.[111] That same day, however, the Lord Chancellor recommended that von Rundstedt and Strauss were unfit to stand trial and that the Cabinet should take the decision not to try them. Foreign Office officials prepared a brief for Bevin advising him to accept the Lord Chancellor's recommendations and to also support the immediate release of the two. 'Any further delay will almost certainly lead to criticism in both Houses and Lord Henderson is sure to be asked in the Lords' debate on the 5th May what instructions have been given with regard to their disposal.'[112] The following morning, the Cabinet considered the matter and agreed that the two should be released forthwith. They recognised that nothing could be done to prevent either giving evidence in defence of von Manstein, who would be indicted in the near future. Nothing would be gained by making known to the public the charges against von Rundstedt and Strauss.[113] That afternoon the Bishop of Chichester duly moved his motion in the House of Lords and Lord Henderson then announced the decision to release von Rundstedt and Strauss. He also stated that all further cases of crimes against humanity were to be tried by German courts under the German penal code, with the exception, of course, of von Manstein, and no further crimes-against-peace trials would be carried out by the Allied Control Commission. In exceptional circumstances, where *prima facie* evidence of murder existed, extradition to the country where the crimes were committed would be allowed, but otherwise not.[114]

Thus, after four years in captivity, the last eight months as a war criminal, von Rundstedt was to finally be released. His ordeal, however, was by no means over.

15

The Twilight Years

THE DECISION to release von Rundstedt and Strauss may have been made, but this did not mean that they were immediately freed. As the West German newspaper *Die Welt* noted, they remained at No 94 British Military Hospital, seemingly still under arrest.[1] This was not the intention of the British authorities, but, as much as anything, because the Government's rapid decision had taken them by surprise. There were, however, two other immediate problems. Firstly, both von Rundstedt and Strauss were still unwell and not fit enough to be discharged from hospital and also, especially in von Rundstedt's case, there was the question of where they were going to live. Dr Grimm visited von Rundstedt at 94 BMH on 17 May:

> '. . . for the first time [I] met Fieldmarshal von Rundstedt walking in the garden without the customary watch [guard]. He had had a visit from a British Colonel who officially informed him of his release. I expect in a short time he will leave the hospital as a free man . . .
> I find Fieldmarshal von Rundstedt rather dejected . . . He is much worried, of course, about the fate of Fieldmarshal von Manstein. Furthermore, Generaloberst Strauss had a severe heart attack and is confined to his bed for at least four weeks and not allowed to see any visitors. And Fieldmarshal von Rundstedt has troubles of his own. His old home in Cassel has been seized and is inhabited by others. Besides there are several reaons why we wish to let him remain in the British Zone for the present time.'[2]

Nevertheless, Strauss was released into Barmbeck civilian hospital in Hamburg on 19 May and formally released four days later. He wished to settle in Lübeck and had no intention of leaving the British zone. Von Rundstedt was informed on 20 May that he could remain at 94 BMH until the 26th. His plans were more complicated. He wanted to stay temporarily with his brother Udo at Ratzeburg, 20 kilometres south of

Lübeck,and then return with Bila to Solz. On 26 May, he and Bila were taken by British military transport to Udo's house. There was much German press attention over the next couple of days, with a number of photographs of the three of them taking a walk being published. The Field Marshal's health, however, was still giving cause for concern and on the 30th the German Red Cross took him to the Nordstadt Hospital in Hannover.[3] A small consolation was that Ditha, who had eventually managed to obtain a flat in Hannover, was able to make frequent visits. But the Field Marshal's wish to move eventually to Solz was now to be frustrated and he was also to find himself severely restricted by the conditions of his release.

The cause of these new problems was denazification. In order to eradicate Nazism and militarism in Germany forever, the Allies published Control Council Directive No 39 in October 1946. This split the German people into five categories – major offenders, offenders, lesser offenders, followers, and persons exonerated. Every adult German citizen was to be screened in this way and responsibility for this was initially given over to the four military governors. A year later, this task was largely handed over to the local German state (*Land*) governments, but the categorisation of former members of the German Armed Forces was retained by the military governments.[4] Von Rundstedt's reason for staying first in the British Zone was that he was waiting for the American authorities to give him denazification clearance in their zone. One of his main concerns was that his savings were in the United States Zone and these could only be unfrozen with United States agreement. The Foreign Office, worried that if von Rundstedt was put through the formal denazification process in the United States Zone it might be seen as calling into question the decision not to put him on trial for medical reaons and make him more vulnerable to extradition by the Russians, asked the British Military Government to seek American agreement for him to be excused the denazification process on health grounds.[5] As far as his status in the British Zone was concerned, it was the intention of C-in-C BAOR that von Rundstedt should be given the status of a private citizen.[6] This would enable him to avoid the procedures to which former prisoners-of-war were subjected.

General George Hays, the United States Deputy Military Governor, replied to the British request on 2 June. He saw no reason why von Rundstedt should not avoid being put through the returning prisoner-of-war process if he was released as a private citizen in the British Zone, but denazification was more difficult. If the British were prepared to issue him with a notice of final decision, this would be recognised in the United States Zone. If this was not possible, he would have to go through the denazification process and under the German Law for Liberation from National Socialism and Militarism this was in German hands.

> 'I can inform you that by reason of his general staff experience and his position as head of the military administration of a territory formerly occupied by Germany he is a presumptive major offender under the law and a proceeding would have to be instituted to determine his final status unless such a decision were first made in the British Zone.'

He would also have to apply for a residence permit from the local German authorities. Hays was, however, reassuring in stating that von Rundstedt would not be allowed to be extradited if he settled in the US zone.[7] The Military Government's recommendation to the Foreign Office was that von Rundstedt and Strauss be denazified by the Military Government and placed in Category 5 (exonerated persons). This would enable their property and money to be unfrozen.[8] Ten days later the Military Government began to doubt the wisdom of the recommendation. Bearing in mind that Strauss and von Rundstedt had been released solely on medical grounds:

> 'If we declare them to be exonerated of any charges made against them, it is inevitable, I think, that our decision will be given wide publicity and may invite severe criticism. In the first place we shall probably be accused of bad faith by the Soviet [Union] who have demanded the extradition of von Rundstedt for trial on capital charges in Russia. Secondly it may be thought that we are putting ourselves in an invidious position vis a vis the forthcoming trial of von Manstein on charges similar to those made against von Rundstedt and Strauss and this may make it difficult to proceed with the trial of Manstein.'

The only other option was to tell the two that as long as they remained in the British Zone the British would make certain that no action was taken against them by the German authorities, but if they moved to another zone it was at their own risk. This, however, would not be of much help to von Rundstedt, who was 'penniless'. The Foreign Office was asked for guidance as 'a matter of urgency'.[9]

What was curious about this exchange of telegrams was that Poland was ignored. No official statement of the British Government's decision was transmitted to the Polish authorities and they only learnt of it from the newspapers. They sent what was, under the circumstances, a polite message to the British Embassy in Warsaw on 17 May, stating the effort that had been put into gathering evidence against all three MARCO defendants and asking for verification and an explantion.[10] In order to smooth the Poles' ruffled feathers and enlist their continued help on the von Manstein trial, Elwyn-Jones and a team flew to Warsaw in early June. This did not mollify the Poles, who continued to complain, suggesting that even if the defendants were not medically fit to stand trial, the crimes had been committed and there were such institutions as prison hospitals in which they could be detained rather than released without any form of restraint.[11] The Russian reaction was predictable. A scathing attack in the Soviet publication *New Times* termed the medical grounds for releasing von Rundstedt and Strauss a 'figleaf' and that they were 'only two among hundreds who had been let off and accepted into Anglo-American service'. The decision to release them was 'illegal' and 'their hands were stained with the blood of thousands of sons and daughters of the Soviet People'.[12] This finally stirred the British Government to reply to the Soviet extradition demand of 15 February. Since von Rundstedt and Strauss had been found unfit to stand trial by the British, they could not be tried by another power. The government was committed to trying von Manstein, however, and once more requested Soviet assistance in providing evidence and witnesses.[13]

Meanwhile, deliberation over what status von Rundstedt and Strauss should now be given continued, and it was not until 24 June that Sir Brian Robertson was able to issue instructions. By this time, Strauss had also been forced to return to hospital, in Hamburg, and von Rundstedt remained in the Nordstadt Hospital at Hannover. The Military Government instructed the two relevant British Regional Commissioners, for Hansestadt Hamburg and Lower Saxony, to inform the two that Robertson was not prepared to issue either with notification of final decision with regard to denazification and hence they would remain as war criminals in Category I (major offenders). At the same time, and this appeared to be a contradiction, as long as they remained in the British Zone they would not be subject to denazification or sanctions.[14] J Needham, the Regional Commissioner for Lower Saxony, accordingly sent von Rundstedt a letter to this effect on 27 June. If it was hoped that this would clear the air, it did not. On 7 July von Rundstedt wrote to Needham:

'. . . I have been categorised into Group 1 as a war criminal whilst I was expressly informed by Colonel Adams of the Control Commission in Hamburg that Group 4 [Followers] was appropriate in my case. In order to put an end to this state of affairs, which for me is untenable, and to give me the opportunity to free myself of the accusation that I am an "alleged" war criminal, an expression used in the name of the Commander-in-Chief of Rhine Army in a letter dated 26th May 45, I request that I am transferred to 94 British Hospital at Barmbeck, Hamburg, regardless of my state of health, so that I may appear before the same military court which is sitting to try Field Marshal von Manstein to answer the charge of alleged war crimes.'

He had already asked Dr Grimm to make the necessary preparations.[16] Indeed, von Rundstedt was now in a 'Catch 22' situation, as he explained in a letter written on the same day to Liddell Hart:

'I am still here in the Hospital [Nordstadt] as an old sick man. My situation has turned very gloomy in this last time. The British Government of Hannover has designated me a "War Criminal" in Nazi-Group 1. It is impossible for me to go the American Zone at Solz where my wife lives evacuated in 2 small rooms. I ought and I wish to stay together, in the British Zone. But I cannot find a home for us; I get no pension; I have no money, because my bank account in the American Zone is blocked. It is an awful situation for me and my poor wife. I would like to end this life as soon as possible.'[17]

Liddell Hart passed a copy of this letter to Reginald Paget, who in turn showed it to Lord Henderson, commenting:

'It does strike me as a bit ignoble. We ought not to treat a fallen enemy like this. History will condemn us. Rundstedt was a career soldier. We ought not to deprive him of his pension and private fortune upon a political charge upon which we acknowledge that he is too old and too ill to be put on trial.'[18]

Liddell Hart had replied to von Rundstedt's letter saying that he would give any help that he could and von Rundstedt wrote back to him again on 16 July. He had been told that 'what had been done at Hamburg was not binding for Hannover'. The whole business had got him worked up, which was not doing much for his heart. 'I think the British Authority at Hannover were glad if I die in Hospital at Hamburg like Field-Marshal Brauchitsch!'[19] Von Rundstedt's physical and mental state was confirmed by Dr Grimm in a letter to Liddell Hart. The handling of the affair was 'unfortunate'. Von Rundstedt considered himself 'an honest soldier who has done nothing but serving his country. He is absolutely convinced that if the trial had taken place he would have shown that he is not a criminal. Now he will suffer under the blame of being permanently listed as a criminal and as a leading Nazi.' Ditha had told him that her father-in-law's health had suffered a 'severe shock' and Grimm had the impression that 'this affair has upset him more than anything else before'.[20]

The Foreign Office accepted that the Regional Commissioner's letter to von Rundstedt was 'rather unfortunately worded' in that it implied his guilt, which his medical condition meant that he had no opportunity to disprove.[21] They decided to ask the Military Government to approach the Americans once more to see if they could arrange for von Rundstedt to avoid the denazification process in the United States Zone. General Hays remained adamant, however, that this was purely a matter for the Germans and that it was most unlikely that he would be put in a low enough category, that of lesser offenders as a minimum, to enable his funds to be unfrozen.[22] A possible means of at least giving von Rundstedt some source of income came on 16 July, when the three Western Military Governors agreed that maintenance grants could be paid by the German Lands to former Wehrmacht members, provided they were entitled to pensions prior to 20 August 1946 or had been serving prior to 30 September 1936. Von Rundstedt, of course, met both these conditions, but those deprived of pension rights as a result of legal action or convictions for war crimes or crimes against humanity were ineligible.[23] This exception included those in Category 1. The Foreign Office, looking for a possible loophole, therefore asked the Control Commission in Germany whether von Rundstedt could be eligible on grounds of age and infirmity for this. The grant was DM160 per month, regardless of rank, but since, in June 1948, all savings in Reichsmarks had been devalued by almost 95 per cent, as part of the changeover to the new Deutschmark currency, it represented no insignificant payment. At the same time, they asked whether the local German authorities could find von Rundstedt accommodation in the British Zone.[24] The matter now threatened to become the subject of another public outcry in Britain, when, on 27 July, Richard Stokes asked a question in the House of Commons on von Rundstedt's trial application and the situation on his denazification. All the Foreign Office could do was to say that they were looking into both.

Some light began to appear at the end of the tunnel when Robertson agreed to have the rules on Wehrmacht pensions amended so that von Rundstedt could become entitled to one.[25] But then the German authorities refused to pay it unless the 'no sanctions' clause in von Rundstedt's release terms was confirmed by the British Military Government as making this payment legally permissible.[26] The question of his denazification category was more difficult and one that the

Foreign Office continued to wrestle with. The nub of the problem was that if the British released him from Category 1 it was tantamount to acquitting him of war crimes charges upon which a *prima facie* case existed. In addition, another stumbling block towards getting his funds released from the United States Zone was now discovered. In spite of General Hays' assurances that clearance by the British would be recognised in the United States Zone, the denazification regulations specified that the process could only be applied in the subject's normal zone of residence, which was the American Zone for von Rundstedt, since he had all his assets there. The German authorities in the United States Zone therefore had every right to insist on denazifying him and, as General Hays had warned, were unlikely to grant him a low enough category to enable his funds to be unfrozen. There was also the question of von Rundstedt's accommodation in the British Zone, since it was now increasingly clear to him that he could not return to Solz. Ditha wrote to and then saw the Regional Commissioner of Lower Saxony. She took the line that since the British had suggested that her father-in-law remain in the British Zone, then they should help him find accommodation. She asked whether he and his wife could not make use of some houses at Gehrden, near Hannover, which were partly inhabited by the Army Kinema Corporation. Gehrden did hold attraction for von Rundstedt since Irtel, his former driver, came from this town, was now resettled there and could perhaps give him some help. Indeed, Irtel, who was a butcher by trade, was already giving Ditha and her children material help and Eberhard von Rundstedt remembers to this day the food that he managed to obtain for them.[27] Needham's reply was that housing was a German responsibility, but he undertook to put in a good word with the Ministerpräsident of Lower Saxony. Needham also proposed that von Rundstedt would be happier if he was termed an 'alleged war criminal' rather than 'war criminal' *per se*.[28] General Robertson supported this idea, but considered that von Rundstedt should still remain in Category 1, although his letter to Needham of 7 July indicated that he appeared 'to have objected even to that milder form of status'.[29] It was now the turn of the Foreign Office's Legal Adviser, J L Simpson, to suggest a possible solution. Studying British Military Government Ordinance No 179, the instrument which gave Control Council Directive No 38 legal clout in the British Zone, he noted that Category 1 was divided into five sub-categories. The fifth, entitled 'miscellaneous', applied to von Rundstedt. This covered 'any individual already held in or later taken into custody who is alleged and *later proved* to have committed a war crime, a crime against peace or a crime against humanity'. Hence, Simpson argued, since von Rundstedt had not been tried he had not been proved to have committed such crimes and hence should not be in Category 1.[30] This solution was transmitted by letter to Sir Brian Robertson on 16 August,[31] but the question of the category into which von Rundstedt should now be placed remained unanswered. Within the British Control Commission, the feeling was that the Military Government's retention of the right under Ordinance 110 to review Category 1 and 2 cases should be invoked. Von Rundstedt could then be given Category 5 status, for if he was given 3 or 4 the German authorities would then have the right to review his case, whereas they could not touch him once he was exonerated. The only problem was that this might prejudice the prosecution case against von Manstein. Nevertheless, Needham was now able to reply to von Rundstedt's letter of 7 July. He informed him that he was no longer Category 1, but his new status had not yet been decided. Once again, he confirmed that von Rundstedt would not be subject to denazification in the British Zone, but if he left it it was at his own risk.[32] Von Rundstedt, in spite of the two months' delay in receiving an answer, was pleased with the news. 'I am most grateful to you for all you have done', he replied to Needham, and also confirmed that he intended to settle in the British Zone and asked Needham whether he could find him suitable accommodation. He also mentioned that he was still not in receipt of any pension and that he had offered himself as a defence witness in the von Manstein trial.[33] There the matter rested for the next six weeks. Von Rundstedt remained in his Hannover hospital and Bila in her two rooms in Solz.

On 23 August 1949 the trial of von Manstein opened in the Curio Haus, Hamburg. The President of the Court was General Sir Frank Simpson, GOC Western Command, and the prosecution led by Sir Arthur Comyns Clark, assisted by Gerald Draper. Paget led the defence, supported by Sam Silkin (also, later, a Labour MP and now Lord Silkin) and Dr Laternser. It lasted, with frequent adjournments, until the middle of December. Von Rundstedt was not called as a witness and von Manstein himself was eventually found guilty on nine of the seventeen charges he faced and sentenced to 18 years' imprisonment, later reduced to twelve years on appeal. He was interned in the British military prison at Werl, but was medically parolled in August 1952. It is difficult not to conclude that, bearing in mind the Generals' trial held by the Americans and the inevitability that von Manstein would, in some respects, be regarded as standing trial on behalf of the other MARCO defendants as well, a guilty verdict was virtually pre-ordained. It does give an indication of what would have happened if von Rundstedt had stood trial.

As far as he was concerned, the next development came in mid-October. By this time the Field Marshal was about to be discharged from hospital and there was still neither accommodation nor maintenance allowance for him. This brought about a *cri de coeur* from Needham at Hannover to the British High Commissioner:

> 'Although some co-operation on both these points was offered by the Minister President at the outset the Minister responsible both for housing matters and subsistence grants has now decided to take a strong line. In the first place he refuses to give Rundstedt any priority for accommodation. Secondly he points out that the Niedersachsen Law on the granting of maintenance allowances to ex-members of the Wehrmacht lays down clearly that these grants may not be paid to persons categorised or likely to be categorised 1,2 or 3. He goes on to point out that he can therefore only pay a maintenance allowance if the Control Commission makes an official statement announcing that he is eligible for such a grant and makes it clear that this statement takes the place of the decision of the competent court or denazification court. He hints that such a statement might be inconsistent with the Occupation Statute.'

If the British agreed to house him and his wife temporarily in requisitioned property, the Germans might well react unfavourably. Needham also assumed that no action would be taken on von Rundstedt's categorisation until after the von Manstein trial was completed.[34] The High Commissioner, in turn, passed the matter to the Foreign Office, although not until 5 November. The matter was causing him 'embarrassment'. He therefore proposed to use his authority to place von Rundstedt in Category 4. Once the von Manstein case was completed he would then move him to Category 5.

> 'I do not think that the suggested course of action is likely to bring forth criticism since Ordinance 110 provided that the categorisation of former members of the German armed forces and the imposition of sanctions on them for the purposes of demilitarisation was reserved to Military Government.'[35]

The Foreign Office did not see the matter in these simple terms. Their reply, which was not sent until 25 November, disagreed with the High Commissioner's interpretation of Ordinance 110. Demilitarisation was an entirely separate issue from denazification. Furthermore, the right of the British finally to determine Category 1 and 2 cases had led to German protests and all that they could realistically do was to categorise provisionally and leave the final decision to the Germans.

Furthermore, as Needham had warned, the Occupation Statute had more or less superseded Ordinance 110 and demilitarisation was not a 'reserved subject' in the former. These were 'assumptions', but if correct, denazification should preferably be carried out by the Germans themselves. This, of course, ran entirely contrary to all British undertakings given to von Rundstedt. The High Commissioner was therefore advised to tell the Field Marshal that this was the only way to get his maintenance grant paid and his funds in the United States Zone unfrozen. This was 'entirely a matter for von Rundstedt himself. In view of the importance he has hitherto attached to clearing his name, it is unlikely that he would object to such a course.' This did not provide any guarantee that he would be placed in a category low enough to entitle him to his maintenance grant, but 'I do not, however, think that this need concern us, since his maintenance is a matter for the German authorities . . .' Even if he was placed higher than Category 4, it 'will probably cause no undue hardship in Lower Saxony, as I understand that the denazification procedure in force there now provides for automatic down-grading after a short interval.' The author of this lengthy Foreign Office reply, M L Priss, was presumably referring to the fact that on 30 June 1949 the Lower Saxony Parliament had passed a law that Category 3 former Nazi Party members and officials would automatically have their property unblocked after one year and be placed in a lower category after a further year unless the Public Prosecutor objected. This had produced 100,000 new applications for denazification over three months in Lower Saxony and an outcry from those in Categories 3 and 4 who had had their property blocked for two years or more.[36] Priss's telegram concluded:

> 'If von Rundstedt's denazification leads to renewed criticism of the decision that he should not stand trial for war crimes, this would be easier to counter than the criticisms which might be made if we appeared to be affording him special protection and exceptional treatment. Moreover, with the lapse of time between the decision not to try von Rundstedt and his appearance before a denazification panel the importance of this point would decrease.'

He asked the High Commissioner to comment and to find out whether the German view tallied with that which Priss believed that they would take.[37]

Von Rundstedt had been discharged from hospital on 28 October[38] and was staying once more with his brother in Ratzeburg until he could find accommodation for Bila and himself. The *Ministerpräsident* of

Lower Saxony, Heinrich Kopf, had, however, made it clear to Ditha that no one could force him to lift a finger for a war criminal.[39] All that she could find were two rooms in a Red Cross home for impoverished old people at Oppershausen, near Celle, a small town north of Hannover. The von Rundstedts moved here in November. Virtually destitute and still in the dark about his status, it is not surprising that von Rundstedt should comment on 1 December, when answering an American questionnaire on the command structure in the West in 1944: '. . . I'm old physically and mentally played out cripple. The final straw was the mean treatment I was exposed to after my release [sic] from England last year.'[40] In the midst of his gloom, though, the Field Marshal's attention was drawn to an unlikely quarter.

Early in 1950, Desmond Young's biography of Rommel was published. It quickly proved a best seller. 20th Century Fox bought the film rights and managed to get James Mason to play the part of Rommel. They wanted to portray von Rundstedt in the film and so Desmond Young wrote to Liddell Hart to ask him to obtain von Rundstedt's permission for this. Liddell Hart accordingly wrote to him and received a reply at the beginning of June. The von Rundstedts were still at the old people's home at Oppershausen. Von Rundstedt apologised for writing in German, but he was 'feeling far from well'. Thinking that he himself might be invited to appear in the film, he wrote that he was most unwilling to do so – 'as you know I do not like to appear in public'. He assumed, though, that the film would be made without him since as a 'war criminal *I can and may not* [sic] leave Germany or even the British zone!' Liddell Hart had said in his letter that 20th Century Fox would pay von Rundstedt money for his permission for an actor to portray him, but the Field Marshal would not accept any fee. He finished his letter by apologising again for not writing in English, 'but I am such an old, miserable, mental cripple that I can hardly write German properly'.[41] The film itself was released in 1951 as *The Desert Fox* in the United States and *Rommel – Desert Fox* in Britain. Von Rundstedt was clearly intrigued by it. 'I am very interested to see what the film will bring for the western part of the world', as he wrote to Liddell Hart on 12 January. When it did appear, with Frederic March playing the part of von Rundstedt, that autumn, Liddell Hart was able to assure the Field Marshal that he had been portrayed in a 'very dignified and sympathetic manner'.[42] Indeed, although the film script mistakenly implied that von Rundstedt had been sacked as C-in-C West before the Margival Conference and its chronology for June 1944 was otherwise awry, it did get something across of his cynical humour and showed his relationship with Rommel as courteous. Significantly, too, Rommel's argument for not actively joining the movement against Hitler for so long, was that actually used by von Rundstedt, namely that it was treasonable. Once Rommel had seen the light, Frederic March's von Rundstedt would not join him on the grounds that he was too old. What was especially significant about *Rommel – Desert Fox* was that it was probably the first postwar film to show that some Germans did not agree with Hitler.

There was also British literary interest in von Rundstedt. Early in 1950, the London publishing house of Odhams contacted a Professor Doktor Kurt Hesse and indicated an interest in a biography of von Rundstedt. He, in turn, mentioned it to Blumentritt, who, apart from doing some work for the United States Army Historical Division, for which he had been working prior to his release from captivity, had not been able to find a job. Blumentritt broached the idea to his former commander, but von Rundstedt was not interested. Odhams continued to press the matter and the Field Marshal eventually relented and agreed that the faithful Blumentritt was to receive £500 advances, half of which he gave to von Rundstedt. Unfortunately, the payments were taxed not only by the British, but by the Germans as well and hence only a fraction eventually found its way into Blumentritt's and von Rundstedt's threadbare pockets. By the end of 1950, Blumentritt had completed half the book. He finished it, in German, at the beginning of June 1951. As Blumentritt wrote to Liddell Hart, the book was written 'in a sense of reconciliation' and von Rundstedt had insisted that it should not be used as a vehicle 'to charge any person, country or any government'.[43]

In early August 1951, the von Rundstedts at last managed to escape from Oppershausen. Ditha, after much struggling, had managed to find them a three room third floor flat above a shoe shop in Hannover. The fact that von Rundstedt had at last been granted his pension enabled them to install themselves. Life now became a little more pleasant. Lieutenant Colonel Nawrocky of the United States Historical Division wrote to Blumentritt in early November about a visit he had recently made to von Rundstedt and commented that there was little change in his attitude and bearing. He also reported that another member of the Historical Division had also been to see von Rundstedt, and found him cheerful if a little tired after a party with 'his British friends'. Blumentritt commented to Liddell Hart that they must have had some 'good English whisky'.[44] He himself had visited his old chief at the beginning of October. He told Liddell Hart that von Rundstedt had met him at the railway station and said how content he and Bila were in their new home. They had gone for a walk in a nearby park and Blumentritt noted that 'his spirit is very active and his judgement of all events and situation [sic] in the whole world is very clear and sharp'.[45] Yet the Field Marshal was now beginning to fade. Doktor Freiherr von Siegler of the Munich *Institut für Zeitgeschichte* (Contemporary History Institute) came to the von Rundstedt's flat and interviewed the Field Marshal at the end of November:

> 'He has severe problems with his circulation and can only leave the house with two crutches. It is impossible to trouble him with more than a few specific questions at a time. Neither is it possible to obtain a more lengthy and complete description from him as he emphasises that his memory is considerably weakened.'

Von Siegler asked von Rundstedt about the von Fritsch crisis and his various dismissals, but the Field Marshal revealed little that was new. Von Siegler recommended in his report on the interview that von Rundstedt not be asked to sign it for accuracy.[46]

Von Rundstedt's misfortunes were not, however, at an end. At the beginning of 1952, just before their golden wedding anniversay, Bila had a stroke and was rushed to hospital, with the whole of her right side paralysed. The doctors were not hopeful as von Rundstedt wrote to Liddell Hart, and his small pension was not enough to engage the services of a nurse. In the same letter, von Rundstedt expressed his heartfelt sympathy over the death of King George VI, recalling that he had attended his father's funeral as a member of the German military delegation. He wondered also whether Blumentritt's book would be a success. 'It seems doubtful.'[47] Worse, left on his own and trying to grapple with the housework, he had a fall which badly bruised his ribs and put him in hospital as well. By the beginning of April 1952, however, both were back in their apartment and being cared for by a nurse. Blumentritt did his best to try and obtain financial help for his old and much revered chief. Von Rundstedt himself was particularly concerned to give his grandchildren all the financial help he could and used part of his pension to this effect. Blumentritt was, however, able to obtain a grant of DM1,000 for him for this purpose from the Order of St John of Jerusalem, but even so the von Rundstedts continued to have a hard struggle.[48] The narrow stairs up to the flat, which are still etched in grandson Gerd von Rundstedt's memory from carrying coal up them,[49] allied to the Field Marshal's crippled state of health, was only one of the many burdens they had to bear. In compensation, Ditha and the grandchildren lived close by and there was the pleasure of seeing Blumentritt and others from time to time. One who befriended him was an American journalist, Daniel de Luce, who worked in Germany for the Associated Press Agency. He later claimed that he was the only journalist to secure an interview with the Field Marshal after his release from captivity. During this von Rundstedt related the following tale:

> 'Back in 1940, Hitler was standing on the French coast over the Channel and planning the invasion of England.
> Suddenly he saw a small black cloud soar up from the cliffs of Dover and swirl toward him, growing bigger and blacker as it came.
> As it approached, he was shocked to see the figure of Moses in the cloud, speaking to him with a voice like thunder. And this was what Moses said –
> "Fuehrer, had you treated my people better, I might be showing you the Red Sea trick."'[50]

The old man had not lost his sense of humour, in spite of all his troubles.

In early September 1952, Blumentritt's book was published as *Von Rundstedt: The Soldier and the Man*. Reviews in the British media were mixed. Thus, the Journal of the Royal United Services Institute praised it as 'emphatically not the usual type of whitewashing book, too often written by senior officers after wars. The author has not protected his hero's reputation by blackening that of other prominent Germans, with the possible exception of Hitler who comes in for many hard knocks.' It was a book which 'ought to be read by any serious student of the 1939–45 War'.[51] The *News Chronicle* considered it '. . . likely to be accepted as the most authoritative German complement to Chester Wilmot's *Struggle in Europe*', but George Murray in the *Daily Mail* thought it 'arid' and the *Manchester Guardian* commented: 'Blumentritt confirms what has often been suspected: that Rundstedt was far from being a brilliant commander.' The most vituperative attack came from Arthur Eperon in the left wing *Daily Herald*. He took Blumentritt to task for glossing over war crimes and concluded: 'It is an excellent thing that the book should be published. We in Britain are inclined to forget easily. We might even forget that the German military mind did not die with Hitler.'[52] Nevertheless, the book sold well and was published in a number of countries.[53] Even the publishing house of Markus Verlag in Cologne planned to bring out a German edition, but in the end did not go ahead.

The promising initial sales of the book did little to cheer von Rundstedt. So desperate was he for money that he swallowed his pride and wrote to Liddell Hart asking whether it might be possible after all for 20th Century Fox to pay him a fee.[54] Liddell Hart took the matter up with Nunnally Johnson, the film's producer, who agreed to pay Rundstedt DM3,000 (£250). Sent a legal document and asked by Nunnally Johnson to have his signature on it witnessed, von Rundstedt refused to do so and would not even sign it himself since he feared that this would make him an employee of 20th Century Fox. In the end, Liddell Hart managed to persuade him through Blumentritt to sign a receipt drawn up in his own words and the money was eventually paid to him at the end of August.[55] By this time Bila had little time to live and she passed away on 4 October. She was buried next to her son in Hannover. Her funeral was well attended and among the wreaths was one from the United States Army Historical Division. In order to give him comfort, Blumentritt stayed with von Rundstedt for two days over the funeral.[56] His eldest grandchild, Barbara, also went to stay with him. She recalls that he helped her with her school work, especially her English and French. In the evenings he would offer her a liqueur, while he had a glass of cognac – he was kept supplied with these and cigarettes by admirers abroad. Sometimes they would listen to classical music, but never current affairs, in which von Rundstedt showed no interest, on the radio. The main problem was getting him to eat, but Barbara could usually persuade him to have a bowl of porridge, something which he had grown to like while a prisoner-of-war in England. He never spoke to her of the war.[57]

Yet, in spite of having Barbara to live with him, Bila's death left him with little to live for. Blumentritt reported to Liddell Hart on a visit he and his wife, accompanied by the de Luces, made to the old man two days before his 77th birthday:

> 'My old Fieldmarshal [sic] is not in a very good condition now. I think he suffers too much his loss and sorrow and I feel he is lacking in the strong will to live any longer. He can't find any sleep in the night and we begged him to consult the doctor who will give him a sleeping pill every night.'[58]

By the new year, von Rundstedt was so lame that he could no longer go out because there were too many stairs and was, according to Blumentritt, very lonely.[59] It was clear that the end was not far off. It came, as a result of heart disease, on 24 February 1953 and in his own bed in the apartment. His last public utterance had appeared at the beginning of January in the form of an introduction to an article written by Blumentritt on the Ardennes counter-offensive in the American magazine *Collier's*. Approving it as coinciding with his own view of events, he wrote: 'Nothing can be beautiful or is excused. Unfortunately, all of us make mistakes.'[60]

16

The Reckoning

THE NEWSPAPERS of Germany's former enemies had a field day over von Rundstedt's death. They noted that he died in dingy surroundings with just a nurse in attendance, but their verdicts on him were mixed. The London *Daily Sketch*: 'Prisoner-of-war No 816209 is dead. A Junker of the Junkers, a Prussian aristocrat, a martinet who believes a soldier has only one duty – OBEY [sic].' It also accused him of having lived a 'myth'. The *Manchester Guardian* saw his life as 'an essay in Prussian orthodoxy', while the *Daily Telegraph* commented: 'He had the virtues and failings of the typical Prussian aristocrat.' Even so, in German eyes he 'was a gentleman if there ever was one'. The *Daily Mail* called him the 'Grand Old Man' of the German Army, while the American *San Francisco Examiner*, although mistakenly stating that he was never accused of war crimes, noted that 'after the war ended he became probably the German general most respected by his former enemies'.[1] The Field Marshal's apartment was beseiged by journalists and some press photographers even went so far as to lift the lid off his coffin so that they could get pictures of him in death.[2]

In Germany the reaction was very muted. The Federal Government understandably had no wish to mark the event in a country which was concentrating on looking forward and not back. Even so, although no official attended the funeral, the Minister of the Interior did write a letter of condolence to the family praising von Rundstedt as a great soldier and an upright man.[3] The socialist administration of Lower Saxony, which had refused to help the von Rundstedts find accommodation, also did not acknowledge his death. There was, too, the spectre of the aftermath of July 1944, which caused a bitter outburst from Blumentritt:

'If von Rundstedt had been anything but a loyal soldier and a front-line general they would have been here in their hundreds already. Rundstedt

was in no way responsible for the 1944 affair. But he has had to endure
vindictiveness and jealousy even up to and after the hour of his death.'[4]

In spite of this, on 28 February, some 2,000 people, albeit mainly
former soldiers, attended the funeral at Hannover-Stöcken cemetery.
They, as Ditha commented in a letter to Liddell Hart, recognised her
father-in-law as a 'noble soldier'.[5] True there was no gun carriage,
which von Rundstedt would have probably liked, but a horse-drawn
hearse instead, and no uniforms were in evidence. Those present heard
the officiating clergyman, Dr Ernst Strasser, say:

> 'In deep grief we have assembled around his bier. Not only you the
> relations suffer grief. It is as if the old Germany has wanted to gather
> round him. First of all us, the old soldiers, who wore the field grey under
> him with honour. In addition, comrades from the 18th Infantry Regi-
> ment, whose chief the Field Marshal was and whose uniform he still wears
> in death . . . In memory of his exemplary modesty of character and his
> nobility we feel it an honourable obligation to state at his grave how much
> we loved the Field Marshal. We do not want to remain silent, but to
> express our admiration. Even the enemy lowered his weapons in front of
> him and had to admit that the "Grand Old Man of the German Army",
> the "Last Prussian", as they said over there, was a noble man from his hair
> to his toes in fulfilling his duty as a soldier.
> He tried to hide his inner self and maintain a noble reserve towards others.
> But, like a man, he spoke the truth, which frees him and us when we
> acknowledge: "We all made mistakes, which we should and must forget."
> The Field Marshal knew that all of us on earth are guilty and cannot
> maintain our view because, as he said: "Destiny is stronger than man."

He went on to stress von Rundstedt's acceptance of the hard knocks
which he had received in the last years of his life and stated that he had
always been a religious man and constantly carried a military prayer
book, a trait, Dr Strasser suggested, which came from his mother. He
also commented on von Rundstedt's modesty and said that if he did
speak about himself it was only in an 'ironic way'.[6] And so von
Rundstedt was laid to rest next to his beloved Bila.

Today, while there are numerous German *Kasernen* (barracks) called
after famous German soldiers, Rommel and von Hindenburg to name
but two, there is no *von Rundstedt Kaserne*. The reason is that he remains
officially *persona non grata*, mainly because of his involvement in the post
July 1944 Court of Honour. Apart from his tombstone, the only other
place in which his name appears in public is at a German barracks on a
memorial stone to the 18th Infantry Regiment at the *Rommel Kaserne* at
Augustdorf near Detmold. He is, however, commemorated on the other

side of the Atlantic. On 6 June 1954, the tenth anniversary of the Normandy landings, the United States 29th Infantry Division Association unveiled a memorial stone, brought specially from Normandy, to the Division at Bedford, Connecticut. Beneath it was buried an urn containing one of von Rundstedt's shoulder straps as a tribute to him.[7] This is a reflection of the fact that he is held in higher esteem by the nations he fought against than by his own country.

On the surface, von Rundstedt represented the archetypal Prussian officer in character – stiff, unbending, emotionless. Underneath, as we have seen, lay a very different man. While he was shy and reserved towards those whom he did now know, he displayed warmth and humour when in the company of people who were familiar to him. As Guderian wrote in his obituary: 'He had a sense of humour and tended towards irony, even sarcasm, without being offensive. He was a very good companion and always joined in if there was a convivial session; then his endurance astonished many a younger man.'[8] His modesty, too, was, according to Westphal, 'not the least cause of the respect and affection in which he was held throughout the Army.'[9] This was reflected, too, in his lifestyle. As a husband, father and grandfather he showed deep love and there is no doubt that his family meant more to him than almost anything else. They, in turn, loved and revered him. He liked to have young people around him, whether they were young officers or his grandchildren. Yet outside his family he had no close friends as such, but rather close acquaintances. To all, however, he was courteous and often charming, and he never made a lasting personal enemy. His granddaughter Barbara said that even in the last months of his life, when his arthritis made it difficult for him to stand, he would insist on giving up his seat to a woman when travelling on a tram.[10] Like many of his caste, his philosophy was that of the stoic, who tried to accept events as they happened and to make the best of them. He was not always successful. He was vulnerable to depression, as during the months after his illness in autumn 1914 and his first year as C-in-C West during 1942–43. It was as much this as anything else that influenced his increasing reliance on alcohol and nicotine during his last years in harness. Another character defect, and one that he freely admitted, was impatience. He was also a sceptic and a pragmatist. Thus, under a seemingly cold exterior he was a very human individual. However, he seldom revealed his innermost thoughts, even to his wife.

Von Rundstedt was not a man of great original thought nor an intellect, but never tried to conceal this. On the other hand, he had much commonsense, an ability to see both sides of an argument, and was possessed with clarity of thought, especially when it came to reducing a problem to its fundamental essentials quickly. He also had, at least until his later years, a capacity for hard work. His lengthy experience as a staff officer also made him recognise the ideal relationship between a commander and his staff. The staff presented the options to the commander, who then decided on the correct course of action and was ultimately responsible for it. The commander then delegated to the staff the translation of the decision into detailed orders. This meant allowing the staff to get on with this task without interference, which implied total trust. Crucial to this trust is the relationship between the commander and his chief of staff and von Rundstedt was particularly lucky in this respect during the years 1939–1945. Von Manstein, von Sodenstern, Zeitzler, Blumentritt and Westphal were all gifted staff officers on whom he could place total reliance and leave to get on with their work without interference from him. Blumentritt himself once described his relationship with von Rundstedt as that of a father and his son, stressing that they were both of 'one soul'.[11] This reveals the essence of the ideal commander–chief of staff relationship, namely that it should be so close that the chief of staff can read the mind of his commander and act in his name with total confidence.

Some, however, have accused von Rundstedt of a lack of moral courage. Andreas Hillgruber, apparently echoing Blumentritt, wrote that 'he tended increasingly to avoid clear-cut positions and to vacillate'.[12] General Adolf Heusinger, first Commander-in-Chief of the Bundeswehr and one of the July 1944 plotters, also makes the point that 'Rundstedt would never have the courage to say to Hitler, "Resign. Get out", though this was a liberty that Rundstedt, as senior marshal, might well have taken'.[13] To examine this accusation means to explore von Rundstedt's whole attitude to Hitler and the ethics of the Prussian military caste.

Frederick The Great observed that 'the greatest force of the Prussian Army resides in their wonderful regularity of formation, which long tradition has made a habit; in exact obedience and in the bravery of the troops'. He also noted that 'the Prussians are superior to their enemies in constancy since the officers, who have no other profession nor other fortune to hope for except that of arms, animate themselves with an ambition and a gallantry beyond all test'.[14] Thus he was able to bind the officer corps to himself in a state of virtual feudalism where their rigid observance of honour, duty and loyalty was exchanged for a privileged position in the Prussian State. Frederick also expected the most stringent corporate and individual discipline from all ranks.

Succeeding monarchs had continued to strike this bargain and the result was that the Prussian military ethos became deeply engrained in the officers. Loyalty was to the individual monarch himself rather than the State, and when the monarchy was deposed in November 1918 the officer corps was left rudderless in this respect. In the uncertainty of the Weimar era, the officer corps found it difficult to transfer its loyalties to the State, which, itself, was unstable. Likewise, the figurehead of the State, the President of the Republic, was constantly changing. Hence it turned inwards and pledged itself to one of its own, von Seeckt, who saw the Reichswehr as the State within the State, even though its oath was to the Reich. Only when von Hindenburg became President, did the officer corps consider that it had a state figurehead whom it could equate to the old monarchy. On his passing away and the adoption of a new oath to Hitler's person, the officer corps was trapped into creating what Walter Goerlitz termed a 'false monarchy'.[15] The precept of duty forced the officer corps to obey von Blomberg's order to take the oath. Once taken, it could not be broken, since this would be dishonourable. Thus von Rundstedt, even though he personally despised Hitler, was irrevocably bound to him. The only legitimate way in which he could evade this in his eyes was to retire from active duty. We have Blumentritt's statement that he did indeed attempt to do this in early 1934 but that von Hindenburg and von Schleicher insisted that he should stay on. He tried again during the von Fritsch crisis, but Hitler refused him and when he was eventually allowed to do so, after the occupation of Sudetenland, it was with the proviso that he returned to active duty if a national emergency arose – and that was not long in coming.

Yet within this rigid framework, there was an historical precedent which the officer corps could use to go against its oath of obedience. In December 1811 General Johann von Yorck, who was commanding the Prussian troops supporting Napoleon's invasion of Russia, agreed by the Convention of Tauroggen with the Russians to adopt a neutral stance. This ran totally counter to King Frederick William of Prussia's alliance with Napoleon and, indeed, he initially repudiated the Convention before shortly afterwards declaring war on France. Von Yorck's justification for his action, which he took only after a long mental struggle, was that this was for the greater good of both king and country and one who would have most certainly supported him was Gerd's great grandfather Joachim von Rundstedt, who had been part of the resistance movement against the humiliating terms of the alliance with Napoleon. It was Tauroggen that von Stauffenberg used when he visited von Manstein at the end of January 1943 and tried to persuade him to take over the supreme command on the Eastern Front. According to von Manstein's ADC, Alexander Stahlberg, who overheard much of the conversation, von Manstein initially thought that von Stauffenberg was trying to make him enter negotiations with the Russians, but this was not so. Von Stauffenberg argued that von Yorck had demonstrated 'extreme loyalty'. Unfortunately, Stahlberg, who was having to answer several telephone calls in the outer office, did not hear the reasons for von Manstein's rejection of this argument. He merely heard von Manstein's final comment: 'Criticism is the salt of obedience.'[16] There is no evidence that those who tried to persuade von Rundstedt to take an active part in the resistance movement against Hitler ever used this argument, although it would be surprising if, given his ancestor's involvement in the anti-French movement in Prussia, he would not have been aware of it.

Von Rundstedt constantly disparaged Hitler in private and had done so from very early on – Lieutenant Colonel Eugen Ott, who was working in the Defence Ministry at the time, once heard von Rundstedt and von Schleicher at the beginning of 1934 'revile Hitler in the most dreadful way'[17] and there is General X's 1932 comment on von Rundstedt's relationship with Hitler. The Field Marshal was not, however, prepared to take any direct action against him for a number of reasons. For a start, he was a believer in the principle that the soldier should stay out of politics and it was a field in which he took no overt interest. The few instances in which he did find himself pitchforked into the political arena showed him to be very uncomfortable, as the imposer of martial law in Berlin in 1932 after the removal of the Prussian cabinet, and naive, as evidenced by his first meeting with Pétain. He also claimed to have little in common with those soldiers who did dabble in politics or who wore their political beliefs on their sleeves. To remove Hitler by force would be a political act and on the same level as the Kapp Putsch, which, unlike a significant number of senior officers, von Rundstedt had refused to support from the outset.

There was also the excuse that he frequently made to those who approached him over taking an active part in the anti-Hitler movement that he could not be sure that his troops would follow him. There is some evidence to support this, the most striking piece being the behaviour of Major Remer in Berlin on 20 July 1944. Faced with the choice of obeying the Generals or Goebbels he chose the latter. Remer was a convinced National Socialist, as was a significant proportion of the junior and middle ranking officers and it is quite likely that they would have placed their loyalty to Hitler above that to von Rundstedt if he had openly declared himself. Furthermore, it was really only after Stalingrad that defeat began to stare the German people in the face. Up until then, Hitler's successes had muted the opposition. However, simultaneously with the Paulus's surrender, came the Allied declaration of Unconditional Surrender, something which the Nazi propaganda machine eagerly seized on and used increasingly the more Germany's enemies closed in on her. In addition, the forces in contact with the enemy on both the Eastern and Western Fronts were not directly involved in the July 1944 Bomb Plot, although some officers were aware of what was in the wind. They had more immediate matters on their minds.

Furthermore, von Rundstedt consistently refused to act outside the chain of command. To do so, in his eyes, would be both disloyal and a breach of discipline. Unfortunately, of course, up until the end of 1941 his superior was von Brauchitsch, who was personally beholden to Hitler. Thereafter Hitler himself took over overall command of the Army. Keitel, too, von Rundstedt's other superior, was not nicknamed *Lakaitel* (lackey) for nothing. Nevertheless, von Rundstedt did try and remonstrate with Hitler over the conduct of the war in private audiences with him, but, as he told von Manstein in March 1944, when the Field Marshals were summoned to Berchtesgaden to reaffirm their personal loyalty to the Führer, Hitler would not listen to him.[18] To take action outside the chain of command, even to have Hitler deposed as Commander-in-Chief of the Army, ran totally counter to the Prussian military tradition. As von Manstein said on more than one occasion: 'Prussian Field Marshals do not mutiny!'[19]

The other factor was von Rundstedt's growing old age and ill-health. When he had his heart attack in Russia in November 1941 he was almost 66 years old. It should have been the signal to both himself and the Supreme Command that it was time that he hung up his sword for good. As it was, he may well have had his heart attack at the back of his mind when he offered his resignation over the Rostov affair a couple of weeks later. Hitler, however, did not retire him and placed him on the *Führer-Reserve OKH* instead, and made it quite clear, after personally excusing himself for the so called misunderstanding over von Kleist's withdrawal, that his services would very likely be needed again. The von Rundstedt who arrived in Paris in March 1942 was, however, a different man to the one who had enjoyed such success in Poland, France and even during the early months of the campaign in Russia. He had noticeably slowed up, both physically and mentally, and, in addition to the other grounds for not wishing to be involved with the plotters, he simply could not be bothered. This is reflected in his utterance to Gerhard Engel when he visited him in February 1943. He could, of course, have insisted on being retired, but this ran totally counter to his concept of duty. Besides, as he pointed out, to have done so would have been to desert his troops and would have probably resulted in an officer more sympathetic to the Nazi régime being appointed in his place.

This leaves the question of the 1944 Court of Honour. His involvement in this was something for which some Germans, while they would be and were prepared to forgive him for everything else, could and cannot excuse him. Von Rundstedt was personally ordered by Hitler, as Commander-in-Chief of the Wehrmacht, to preside over the Court. To have refused would have been to disobey an order from his superior, and a dereliction of duty in his eyes. In addition, if he had refused, it would not have prevented the proceedings from continuing and someone more ruthless would have been doubtless found to substitute for him. This is not, however, the justification that he gave after the war for his participation. It is clear from the von Fritsch affair, when von Rundstedt failed to present von Fritsch's challenge to Himmler, that where there was a choice between the collective honour of the Army and that of the individual, he would opt for the former. When he told the IMT Commission at Nuremberg that he could not evade presiding over the Court of Honour 'in the interest of the Army' von Rundstedt was indicating that again it was collective rather than individual honour in which he was primarily concerned. On the other hand, he also asserted that he did his best to protect those whose guilt was in doubt. For those who were clearly guilty he had no sympathy; what they had done was 'base, bare-faced treachery'. Furthermore, he claimed that the majority of the German people and the Wehrmacht were still firm supporters of Hitler. Even if it had succeeded, Germany, because of the Allied demand for unconditional surrender, would have found herself in no better position than she was in May 1945. Therefore, he claimed, as has already been described, if he had been involved in the plot he would have been dubbed the 'greatest traitor'. Although von Rundstedt himself never mentioned it, underlying much of this was the fact that the German people increasingly hoped that the Western Allies would eventually see sense and join Germany in the defence of Western Europe against the real enemy, Stalin's Russia. What probably made von Rundstedt angrier than anything else, though, was that the failure of the July 1944 Bomb Plot merely served to weaken the

Army's position *vis-à-vis* the Nazi régime still further. The freedom of action that he and his fellow high commanders had striven for so long receded even further into the distance and the impending *Götterdämmerung* was merely brought closer.

In summary, von Rundstedt and his brother Prussian officers were trapped by the military ethic which had for so long been their strength and the strength of their country. Hitler was astute enough to realise this and wove an ever smaller mesh in the net that encased them. When Hitler came to power in 1933, the threat to the Army lay not in himself but in his uniformed henchmen the SA, who saw themselves as the National Socialist successors to the Reichswehr. This threat was removed by the Night of the Long Knives, which was nothing more than multiple murder. The fact that two senior army officers, both members of the Prussian aristocracy, were among the victims should have warned the Army. Indeed, as we have seen, some did protest to von Blomberg, but unfortunately he either considered this a small price to pay for the confirmation of the primacy of the Army, especially since he had never been a friend of von Schleicher (the main reason why Hitler had appointed him as Defence Minister in the first place), or he feared that to rock the boat now would put the Army under threat again. The upshot was the oath of allegiance to Hitler in person. Once the officer corps had sworn this it was lost, since to break it would be dishonourable. Unfortunately, von Rundstedt and his fellows, who adhered rigidly to the principle that officers should be apolitical, believed that matters would not get out of hand while von Hindenburg was President. They forget that he was growing ever more senile. When the old man finally passed away, Hitler was too quick for them.

Hitler quickly recognised that the Army viewed von Rundstedt as the doyen of the officer corps. It was he, more than any other, who displayed the qualities of the ideal Prussian officer. If, therefore, he could cultivate von Rundstedt and ensure that he remained on the active list as long as possible, it would go a long way towards confirming the loyalty of the officer corps to himself. He realised, though, that this had to be carried out with some delicacy. He was careful not to be too obvious about it. If he had been, von Rundstedt might have recoiled. The birthday gifts, the attendance at King George V's funeral, and the Italian, Hungarian and Yugoslav orders conferred on von Rundstedt were all designed to ensure his loyalty, but Hitler never tried to make von Rundstedt one of his inner circle or display too much direct attention to him. By the same token, this was possibly one of the reasons why Hitler rejected von Rundstedt's name for

Commander-in-Chief after the demise of von Fritsch, although much stronger grounds were that he was able to place von Brauchitsch in a position where he could blackmail him. Von Rundstedt, on the other hand, would have been another von Fritsch and not the pliable Commander-in-Chief that Hitler considered essential if he was to achieve his territorial and political aims in Europe successfully.

This leads on to the question of why von Rundstedt himself never wanted to be Commander-in-Chief of the Army, which would have been the natural ambition of a dedicated career officer. It would have been logical for him to have succeeded von Hammerstein-Equord in February 1934 instead of von Fritsch, who was, in any event, junior to von Rundstedt. Whether von Rundstedt was asked if he wanted the post is not recorded, but it is more than likely that he was and refused it. Certainly this was what he did at the beginning of 1938 when Beck asked him if he was prepared to succeed von Fritsch. One can surmise in both instances that von Rundstedt rejected the notion for two main reasons. First, he hoped to retire and would be prevented from doing so if he accepted the post, not that this made any difference in the end. Second, he probably feared that it would involve him too much in politics. An additional reason might also have been that he viewed the prospect of working directly under von Blomberg in 1934 and Keitel in 1938 with distaste.

The only senior officer to really voice the view that the officer corps must step outside its rigid code was Ludwig Beck, a Rhinelander of middle class background. In July 1938, when he was urging von Brauchitsch to tell Hitler that his generals would not support him in his expansionist policies, he wrote:

> 'History will indict the highest leaders of the Wehrmacht with blood-guilt if they do not act in accordance with expert and statesmanlike knowledge and conscience. Their duty of soldierly obedience finds its limits when their knowledge, conscience and responsibility forbid the execution of an order.'[20]

It was a prophecy which became largely true seven years later and among those who would pay the penalty was von Rundstedt.

When the Americans captured von Rundstedt in May 1945 there was an initial thought among the Western Allies that he should be screened at ASHCAN as a possible defendant at the IMT at Nuremberg, but this was quickly dismissed. Instead, the Field Marshal became an object of most intense curiosity and his reaction, once he had overcome his initial humiliation at surrendering without offering resistance, was to display courtesy and dignity. This became even more marked when he was handed over to the British, whom he clearly preferred to the Americans. Much of the reason for this was very possibly that he viewed the British officer class as having much more in common with that of the old Prussian Army, In return, his British captors were charmed by him and it served to reinforce their conviction that he was the most outstanding German commander they had fought against.

The relationship that von Rundstedt developed with Liddell Hart was especially close. While the latter quickly formed the opinion that von Rundstedt had too orthodox a mind he quickly grew to like him. Apart from being the Field Marshal's champion during the period of adversity which he was to endure, he remained in close contact with the family until his death. All the von Rundstedt grandchildren individually stayed with the Liddell Harts and Sir Basil took a great interest in their lives.

The British decision to try von Rundstedt and his fellow Field Marshals for war crimes was entirely as a result of external pressures. Their own war crimes investigation on him had found no case to answer and it was only the United States Taylor Memorandum of August 1947 that made Clement Attlee's Labour Government think again. Up until this time, they seem to have ignored the Polish demand to try him for war crimes committed in their country in 1939. There now followed a year's debate as to whether charges should be instigated. Certainly the Taylor Memorandum produced evidence which was new to the British and, on the surface at least, did provide a case to answer. On the other hand, it must be remembered that the Americans had entered the war crimes business late in the war. It was not until the Malmédy Massacre of December 1944 that they began seriously to pursue the matter, while the British had cases on file that stretched back to May 1940. By autumn 1947 the Government was beginning to feel that the time had come to look forward in terms of the reconstruction of Western Europe rather than to continue to dwell on the past. Public opinion in Britain also reflected the same view. The Americans, however, seem to have keenly felt the failure to achieve a guilty verdict in the IMT High Command case and believed that the senior commanders must be indicted if German militarism was to be destroyed for all time.

The year that it took the British Government to make up its mind to put the MARCO defendants on trial provides a sorry saga. It became a long running battle between the Foreign Office, which was very aware of the international political implications of not bringing them to trial, and the War Office, which was responsible for conducting war crimes trials and which viewed the prospect of bringing to trial men whom it considered distinguished fellow soldiers as distasteful. The Government's handling of the affair contravened the traditional British sense of fair play and united all shades of political opinion against it. Further, this opposition laid open to question the ethics of the war crimes machinery as it had been set up. It was in particular the practice of declaring an individual to be a war criminal before he had been tried and the Government's lack of moral courage in keeping the Field Marshals in the dark for so long over their disposal that rankled most. Indeed, it seemed that the Government only took action in this latter respect after pressure by the media.

As for the charges themselves, von Rundstedt had a case to answer, primarily on the principle that a commander is responsible for the actions of his troops. Yet, the Allies were operating double standards when it came to this. In a lecture entitled *The Responsibility of Junior Officers to the Laws of War* given at the Royal United Services Institute, London, in November 1951, the lecturer was asked 'how many generals, admirals, and so on the Allied side, have been tried' by court-martial for war crimes. The lecturer did not give a straight answer,[21] but the truth was that none had been. Yet, if the same ground rules has been applied to Allied senior commanders as to German, more than one distinguished leader would have appeared in the dock. One would have been General George S Patton, whose troops murdered unarmed and surrendered Italian soldiers in Sicily in July 1943. Worse, Patton tried to cover it up by pretending that the victims were snipers or had attempted to escape.[22] Another was Admiral of the Fleet Viscount Cunningham, who had flagrantly violated the 1929 Geneva Convention on Prisoners-of-War, which dictated that as soon as possible after capture they were to be taken to a place of safety. Italian frogmen launched a daring attack on the Mediterranean Fleet in Alexandria harbour in December 1941 and crippled the battleships *Queen Elizabeth* and *Valiant*. The frogmen were captured after they had placed their charges and taken ashore. Cunningham, on his own admission, then ordered them to be put on board the *Queen Elizabeth* and confined them deep in the hull in an effort to force them to reveal where they had placed the charges.[23]

Further strong grounds for indicting von Rundstedt were over the carrying out of illegal orders such as the Commissar and Commando Orders. The Wehrmacht was subject in this respect to Article 47 of the Military Penal Code of 1872, which stated that: 'If through the execution of an order pertaining to the service a penal law is violated, then the superior giving the order is alone responsible. However, the obeying subordinate shall be punished as an accomplice: (1) if he went beyond the order given to him, or (2) if he knew that the order of the superior involved an act which aimed at a civil or military crime or offence.' When the Commissar Order was issued by von Brauchtisch, on Hitler's command, in early 1941, von Rundstedt stated that he immediately complained to the Commander-in-Chief on the grounds that it was an illegal order for a soldier to carry out. On the other hand, he also stated after the war that Hitler had stated that the Commissars were not soldiers and hence had no right to be treated as such. As for his own June 1942 Parachutist Order, which, of course, preceded the more infamous Commando Order issued by Hitler by some four months, it was justifiable except possibly the handing over of those captured behind the lines in uniform to the Gestapo. He must have known what fate was likely to be in store for them. Yet, as Liddell Hart pointed out after the war, it was similar to handing over German parachutists in uniform to the Police Special Branch, which fulfilled much the same role in Britain, albeit without the brutality. However, the only two specific incidents in which British Special Forces members were executed in pursuance of the Parachutist or Commander order during von Rundstedt's time as C-in-C West were those of the SSRF members, who had not landed by parachute, in September 1942 and the FRANK-TON members who fell into German hands. No evidence exists to link von Rundstedt directly with either of these two crimes.

When it came to crimes against humanity, though, von Rundstedt was at the very least economical with the truth at Nuremberg. True, he had no direct jurisdiction over Himmler's *Einsatzgruppen*, but his statement that he was only aware of one massacre of Russian Jews, that at Berdichev, simply does not tie up with the stream of orders emanating from his headquarters forbidding soldiers from participating in these atrocities. Furthermore, his letter of approval of von Reichenau's October 1941 order, which exhorted German troops to revenge themselves on the Jews for atrocities committed against them, was a damning piece of evidence.

As for the practice of taking civilian hostages by occupation forces as military necessity, there was actually nothing in the Geneva and Hague Conventions, as they existed during the Second World War, specifically forbidding this practice, and it was not outlawed until the 1949 Geneva Convention. The same applied to hostages who were shot in reprisal for guerrilla acts, which in themselves had no protection under the Laws of War. Thus, when French Resistance members blew the Antwerp–Paris railway line at Ascq on 1 April 1944, the third time in the same place, it is hardly surprising that von Rundstedt should declare that 'the population of Ascq bears the responsibility for the consequences of its treacherous conduct, which I can only severely condemn' and have 77 of its male inhabitants shot.[24] As one eminent commentator on the Laws of War pointed out, the Resistance might have attacked the railway elsewhere and further away from habitation, ie the forests south of Lille,[25] and it is almost as if they were willing the Germans to take reprisals. As for the forced transport of foreign labour to Germany, it was not a matter which involved von Rundstedt, except in the case of Holland in autumn 1944. There was, however, a sound military reason behind this; the danger of Dutch males of military age rising against the Germans at the same time as the Allies continued their advance into the Netherlands.

If von Rundstedt had stood trial, it is clear from the von Manstein case that he would have been found guilty of some of the charges levelled against him. These are likely to have been the ones that applied to the Eastern rather than Western Front and there is no doubt there would have been some justification for this. As it was, his defence that he merely tried to evade illegal orders and that if he had protested he would merely have been replaced by someone with less scruples was weak.

Yet, he probably suffered more from not having the opportunity to defend himself in court. The humiliations which he underwent during the years 1948–1951 were hard for him to bear and the fact that German officialdom, especially in Lower Saxony, appeared to take the attitude that he was guilty made him feel, according to his granddaughter Barbara, 'deprived of his honour'.[26] It was this that made him try and dissuade his elder grandson from ever joining the Army, saying that he himself had suffered enough for the family's military tradition. Gerd, who had been called 'General's bastard' by his schoolmates in Hamburg, was not deterred and still serves today as a Lt Col in the Bundeswehr.[27]

Von Rundstedt's tragedy, and that of many of his comrades in the German Army, was to have been born fifty years too late. The code of ethics on which they were brought up may have well suited Imperial Germany, but it was too narrow and too rigid in scope to cope with the Weimar Republic and Hitler's Germany. Over the generations it had cocooned them in a cosy little world in which they could concentrate on their profession and unthinkingly obey orders without dirtying their hands in politics. Duty, Honour and Loyalty are excellent precepts, and, indeed, form the motto of the United States Military Academy West Point to this day, but on their own they are too limited and imply unquestioning obedience. If the story of Gerd von Rundstedt has a moral it is that Conscience must be added to the above three tenets if the soldier is to be a truly effective servant of the state. Nevertheless, in spite of this shortcoming, von Rundstedt was endowed with many good and attractive personal qualities and thoroughly merited his title as the doyen of the Prussian Officer Corps, reflecting all that was best in it. He was, however, the last of the line.

APPENDIX ONE

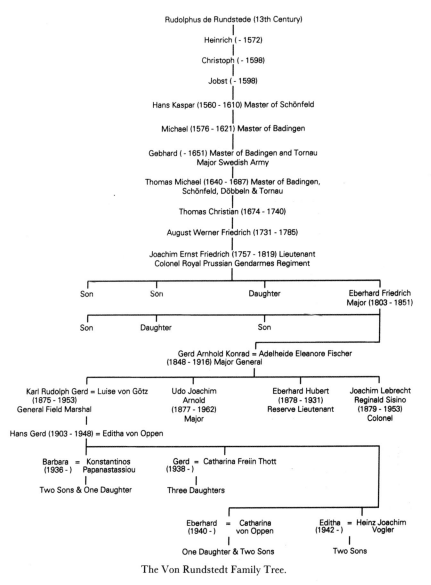

Rudolphus de Rundstede (13th Century)
|
Heinrich (- 1572)
|
Christoph (- 1598)
|
Jobst (- 1598)
|
Hans Kaspar (1560 - 1610) Master of Schönfeld
|
Michael (1576 - 1621) Master of Badingen
|
Gebhard (- 1651) Master of Badingen and Tornau
Major Swedish Army
|
Thomas Michael (1640 - 1687) Master of Badingen,
Schönfeld, Döbbeln & Tornau
|
Thomas Christian (1674 - 1740)
|
August Werner Friedrich (1731 - 1785)
|
Joachim Ernst Friedrich (1757 - 1819) Lieutenant
Colonel Royal Prussian Gendarmes Regiment

| Son | Son | Daughter | Eberhard Friedrich Major (1803 - 1851) |

| Son | Daughter | Son |

Gerd Arnhold Konrad = Adelheide Eleanore Fischer
(1848 - 1916) Major General

| Karl Rudolph Gerd = Luise von Götz (1875 - 1953) General Field Marshal | Udo Joachim Arnold (1877 - 1962) Major | Eberhard Hubert (1878 - 1931) Reserve Lieutenant | Joachim Lebrecht Reginald Sisino (1879 - 1953) Colonel |

Hans Gerd (1903 - 1948) = Editha von Oppen

| Barbara (1936 -) = Konstantinos Papanastassiou | Gerd (1938 -) = Catharina Freiin Thott |
| Two Sons & One Daughter | Three Daughters |

| Eberhard (1940 -) = Catharina von Oppen | Editha (1942 -) = Heinz Joachim Vogler |
| One Daughter & Two Sons | Two Sons |

The Von Rundstedt Family Tree.

APPENDIX TWO

Decorations Awarded to Gerd von Rundstedt

Prior to August 1914

Order of the Crown 4th Class (Prussia)
Knight's Cross 2nd Class Order of the White Falcon (Saxe-Weimar-Eisenach)
Knight's Cross 1st Class Order of Saxe Ernestine (Saxony)
Cross of Honour 3rd Class (Schwarzburg)
Merit Cross 4th Class (Waldeck)

1914–1918
Iron Cross 1st and 2nd Class (Prussia)
Order of the Red Eagle 4th Class (Prussia)
Knight's Cross of the Hohenzollern House Order with Swords (Prussia)
Military Service Cross (Prussia)
Order of Military Merit 4th class with Swords and Crown (Saxony)
War Merit Cross (Lippe)
Military Merit Cross 3rd Class (Austria)
Iron Crescent (Turkey)

1919–1939
Royal Hungarian Order of Merit 1st Class (11/8/37)
Grand Cross of the Order of the Crown of Italy (7/6/38)
Royal Yugoslav Order of Heissen 2nd Class (6/7/39)

1939–1945
Knight's Cross to the Iron Cross (30/9/39)
Oakleaves to the Knight's Cross (2/7/44)
Swords to the Knight's Cross (18/2/45)

And, possibly, Rumanian, Hungarian, Slovak and Italian decorations.

SOURCE NOTES

1. Published works are only cited in full where they are not listed in the Select Bibliography.

2. The following abreviations have been used:

Bundesarchiv Bundesarchiv, Koblenz.

Edmonds Papers The papers of Brig Gen Sir James Edmonds, Liddell Centre for Military Archives, King's College, London.

Freiburg Bundesarchiv Militärarchiv, Freiburg im Breisgau.

IWM Imperial War Museum, London.

IZ Institut für Zeitgeschichte, Munich.

JRUSI Journal of the Royal United Services Institute, London.

LH Papers of Sir Basil Liddell Hart, Liddell Hart Centre for Military Archives, King's College, London.

PRO Public Record Office, London. Classes of papers are CAB (Cabinet Office), FO (Foreign Office), TS (Treasury Solicitor), WO (War Office).

Von Rundstedt Archive Papers held by his grandson, Gerd von Rundstedt

Sayer Archive Private archive of Ian Sayer.

Wheeler-Bennett Papers Papers of Sir John Wheeler-Bennett, St Antony's College, Oxford.

CHAPTER ONE

1. The origins of the von Rundstedt family and Gerd's antecedents are drawn from the *Almanach de Gotha* (1905 edition), Siebmacher J *Grosses und allgemeines Wappenbuch* Vol III.2 (Verlag von Bauer und Raspe, Nuremberg, 1878), *Genealogisches Handbuch*

des Adels: Adele Häuser Vol XI (C A Starke, Limbert and der Lahn, 1971), Blumentritt, *Von Rundstedt: the Soldier and the Man* pp13– 15, Cort, David *The Last Prussian* (Life Magazine, 25 December 1944), and information given to me by Eberhard von Rundstedt.

2. Blumentritt op cit p15.
3. Edmonds unpublished autobiography, Edmonds III/1, Liddell Hart Centre for Military Archives.
4. Most of the material on von Rundstedt's time as a cadet is drawn from Blumentritt pp16–18.
5. Quoted Carver *Twentieth Century Warriors* p92.
6. Introductory Order to the Ordinance on Tribunals of Honour, dated 2 May 1874 and quoted Demeter *The Officer Corps in Society and State 1650–1945* pp313–314.
7. Report dated 1 January 1894, Freiburg Pers 6/16.
8. Report dated 1 January 1896, ibid.
9. Edmonds, Brig Gen Sir James *An Army on the Cheap* JRUSI, February 1951.
10. Blumentritt op cit pp18–19.
11. War Office pamphlet A663 *System of Training Staff Officers in Foreign Armies* (HMSO, London, 1901). A copy of the section covering Germany (pp31–67) is contained in the Edmonds Papers op cit under Edmonds V/5/3, from which my information on entry to the *Kriegsakademie* is drawn.
12. Report dated 1 January 1900, Freiburg Pers 6/16,
13. Report dated 1 December 1901, ibid.
14. Description based on letter to author dated 14 February 1990 from Barbara Papanastassiou, von Rundstedt's eldest grandchild.
15. Report dated 1 December 1903, Freiburg Pers 6/16.
16. Most of my information on the *Kriegsakademie* at the time von Rundstedt was there is drawn War Office pamphlet A663 op cit. Unfortunately, the Kriegsakademie archives were largely destroyed at Potsdam, during World War 2.
17. Edmonds, Brig Gen Sir James *The German General Staff* JRUSI, February 1954.
18. Report dated 1 December 1905 and initiated by Oberst von Schlabrendorff, commanding 83rd Infantry Regt. Freiburg Pers 6/16.
19. Report dated 1 December 1906, ibid.
20. Kitchen *The German Officer Corps, 1890–1914* p6.
21. Because each promotion involved a large number of officers, it was considered important in the Prussian Army to lay down their seniority within each promotion. This was indicated in the *Rangliste* by a special code. The top 25 officers in each promotion were given a single letter A–Z (excluding I), the next 25 a double letter (Aa–Zz), Nos 51–75 a double letter with the figure 1 inserted in between (A1a– Z1z), Nos 76–100 the same with the figure 2 inserted (A2a–Z2z), and so on. The May 1914 *Rangliste* showed von Rundstedt with O9o, which placed him 264th. I am indebted to Klaus Benseler for this explanation.
22. Annual report dated 1 December 1909, Freiburg Pers 6/16.
23. Bodley Head, London, 1904, but originally published in Germany as *Aus Einer Kleinen Garnison* in 1903.
24. Ibid, p276.
25. Report dated 1 December 1913, Freiburg Pers 6/16. One source, W E Hart *Hitler's Generals* p42, states that von Rundstedt 'let it be known that the garrison commander of Colmar consulted him at every opportunity in the preparation of plans of mobilisation' and that he was 'seconded to the staff of the garrison as aide-de-camp' and liked to call himself 'the pocket edition of a chief of staff'. Since his commanders always stressed von Rundstedt's modesty, it is most unlikely that he would have boasted in this way, even if he was consulted unofficially.

CHAPTER TWO

1. *The Advance from Mons* pp121–122.
2. Von Kluck *March on Paris* p76.
3. Ibid p95fn.
4. Isselin *The Battle of the Marne* p148.
5. Ibid p190.
6. Blumentritt op cit p21.
7. Bloem op cit p172.
8. Blumentritt op cit p22.
9. Report on von Rundstedt dated 15 June 1916, Freiburg Pers 6/16.
10. Quoted Kahn, Leo *The Fall of Warsaw*, Purnell's History of the First World War, vol 2 p961.
11. Report on von Rundstedt dated 15 June 1916, op. cit.
12. Report on von Rundstedt dated 1 July 1915, Freiburg Pers 6/16.
13. Reports on von Rundstedt dated 15 June and 1 November 1916, ibid.
14. Blumentritt op cit p22.
15. Report dated 25 December 1916, Freiburg Pers 6/16.
16. Freiburg Pers 6/16.
17. Report dated 20 March 1918, ibid.
18. Report dated 1 August 1918, Freiburg MSg 109/2234.
19. Report dated 22 November 1918, ibid.
20. Report dated 14 December 1918, ibid.

CHAPTER THREE

1. Quoted Benoist-Méchin *Histoire de l'Armée Allemande* Vol 1 p74.
2. Record of service, Freiburg MSg 109/2234. The Deutsche Dienstelle (WASt) in Berlin, which holds records of service of members of the Wehrmacht, has no detail for von Rundstedt during the years 1894–1924 (WASt letter to the Author dated 10 April 1989).
3. Report by Gen Ilse dated 19 April 1919, Freiburg Pers 6/16.
4. Carsten *The Reichswehr and Politics* p86.
5. *The Trial of Major German War Criminals* vol 21 p97. Hereafter known as IMT.
6. Ibid.
7. Quoted Carsten op cit p104.
8. Quoted ibid p114.
9. Report dated 1 November 1921, Freiburg Pers 6/16.
10. Report dated 1 November 1922, ibid.
11. *Hitler's Generals* pp42–3 and reflected, for example, in Brett-Smith *Hitler's Generals* p16.
12. Interview dated 3 January 1946, LH 9/24/132.
13. *Hitler's Generals* p16.
14. Liddell Hart interview with von Rundstedt, 3 January 1946, op cit.
15. Report dated 30 September 1923, Freiburg Pers 6/16.
16. *Die Deutsche Soldatenzeitung* 5 March 1953.
17. *Hitler's Generals* p45.
18. Liddell Hart interview, 3 January 1946 op cit.
19. Report dated 1 November 1925, Freiburg Pers 6/16.
20. Reports dated 1 November 1926, 15 November 1927, ibid.
21. Medical report, January 1948, PRO FO 371/70652, and interview Gerd and Eberhard von Rundstedt, 4 November 1989.

22. Quoted Carr, William *A History of Germany 1815–1945* p305 (St Martin's NY, 1969).
23. Carsten op cit p106.
24. Citano *The Evolution of Blitzkrieg Tactics* pp166–7.
25. *Die Deutsche Soldatenzeitung* 5 March 1953.
26. Vogelsang *Reichswehr, Staat und NSDAP* p159.
27. Letter dated 21 July 1930, Ian Sayer archive.
28. Quoted Citano op cit p183.
29. Interview dated 3 January 1946, LH 9/24/132.
30. *Von Rundstedt* op cit p35.
31. Interview with Gerd von Rundstedt, 4 November 1989.
32. Klotz *The Berlin Diaries* ppxxiii–xxiv.
33. Carsten op cit p326.
34. Klotz op cit pp56–7.
35. Interview dated 3 January 1946, LH 9/24/132. One source, Riess, Curt *Marshal von Rundstedt: German Darlan*, The Saturday Evening Post 2 October 1943, claims that von Rundstedt met Hitler even earlier, in March 1926 when he was commanding 18th Infantry Regiment. A Pastor Ludwig Müller is supposed to have arranged a meeting between the two at von Rundstedt's house at Paderborn. I can find no evidence to substantiate this.
36. Klotz op cit pp87–92.
37. Carsten op cit pp368–9.
38. There is some dispute as to whether soldiers or police were used. Reitlinger *The SS: Alibi of a Nation* p38 states that a police captain and five constables were involved, and this is supported by Carr *A History of Germany* p354. Vogelsang op cit p246 speaks of 'military forces' and von Rundstedt told Liddell Hart that it was a 'small armed party', implying soldiers rather than police (Interview 3 January 1946 op cit). Erfurth *Die Geschichte des deutschen Generalstabes* p236 is the most specific and it is him that I have followed.
39. Klotz op cit p115.
40. Vogelsang op cit p254.
41. Klotz op cit p123.
42. For a detailed exposition of this concept of war see Simpkin, Richard *Deep Battle: The Brainchild of Marshal Tuchachevskii* (Brassey's, London, 1987).
43. Quoted Citano op cit p189.

CHAPTER FOUR

1. John, Otto *Some Facts and Aspect of the Plot Against Hitler* p13, Wheeler-Bennett Papers.
2. Liddell Hart interview, 3 January 1946, LH 9/24/132.
3. IMT p105. Rudolf Steiner (1861–1925) was an Austrian philosopher and founder of the school of anthroposophy which argues that man himself holds the key to understanding the cosmos and that he should therefore find the means to develop his latent spiritual powers.
4. *Revolt Against Hitler* p36. Fabian von Schlabrendorff was later deeply involved in the bomb plot against Hitler of 20 July 1944. Though captured and tortured by the Gestapo, he resisted interrogation and survived. During the war years he served as Aide to Henning von Tresekow, a senior member of the General Staff and an active member of the plotting group, to whom von Schlabrendorff was connected by marriage.
5. Seaton *The German Army 1933–45* p37.
6. Annual Report dated 15 October 1933, Freiburg Pers 6/16.

7. Interview with Freiherr Dr von Siegler, 26 November 1951, IZ 311/52.
8. Goerlitz *The German General Staff* p282 and Craig *The Politics of the Prussian Army* p473.
9. *Von Rundstedt* op cit p35.
10. Quoted Wistrich *Who's Who in Nazi Germany* p84.
11. Liddell Hart interview, 3 January 1946, op cit.
12. Interview Gerd von Rundstedt, 4 November 1989.
13. Andreas Hillgruber in Carver *The War Lords* p190. Hillgruber also asserts that von Rundstedt went with von Witzleben to Hitler to plead for von Schleicher's life. This makes no sense since it is most unlikely that he would have known that he was on the death list.
14. Hart op cit p51 and Riess, Curt *The Self-Betrayed: Glory and Doom of the German Generals* p149 (New York, 1942).
15. Klaus-Jürgen Müller in Barnett *Hitler's Generals* p46.
16. Hoffmann *The History of the German Resistance* p27 and Goerlitz op cit p289.
17. IMT p88.
18. IZ ZS 129.
19. Typescript *Affaire Blomberg-Fritsch 1938*, England, 1946, IZ 311/52.
20. Quoted Seaton op cit p52.
21. My information on von Rundstedts' life in Berlin is drawn from interview with Gerd and Eberhard von Rundstedt, 4 November 1989, and letter from Barbara Papanastassiou dated 3 January 1990.
22. IZ ZS 129.
23. Freiburg Pers 6/16.
24. Taylor *Sword and Swastika* p120.
25. Seaton op cit pp79–80.
26. Hart op cit p55.
27. IMT pp100–101.
28. IMT Commission interrogation, 19 June 1946, IZ ZS 129.
29. Macksey *Guderian: Panzer General* p69.
30. Muller, Albert *Germany's War Machine* p30 (Dent, London, 1936).
31. IMT 88–89.
32. Schall-Riancour *Leben und Wirken von Generaloberst Franz Halder* p39.
33. There is some confusion as to the date of Beck's telephone call to von Rundstedt and those of von Rundstedt's subsequent meetings with Hitler. Von Rundstedt himself in *Affaire Blomberg-Fritsch* op cit states that he was summoned back to Berlin on 3 February and saw Hitler on the 4th. This is supported by his daughter-in-law, letter to Barry Sullivan dated 26 March 1977. Reynolds *Treason was no Crime* p298 n32 states that von Rundstedt's first meeting with Hitler was on 30 January, while Keegan *Rundstedt* p54 says that von Rundstedt saw Hitler on 29 and 31 January. Hillgruber in Carver *The War Lords* p190 even mentions 21 January, but this may be a misprint. I have preferred to follow the chronology given in Deutsch *The Hidden Crisis*, which is by far the most detailed account.
34. *Affaire Blomberg-Fritsch* op cit.
35. Deutsch op cit p115.
36. Letter to Sullivan op cit.
37. The account of the whole conversation is taken from *Affaire Blomberg-Fritsch* op cit.
38. Bond, Brian in Barnett *Hitler's Generals* p77.
39. *Affaire Blomberg-Fritsch* op cit.
40. Seaton op cit p83 states that von Rundstedt was present as well, but von Rundstedt never mentioned this and neither does Deutsch op cit. Indeed, since von Rundstedt's name came up it is most unlikely that he was present.
41. Deutsch op cit pp261–2.

42. This led a number of historians to conclude that he had retired at this time. See, for example, Craig op cit p495, Shirer *Rise and Fall of the Third Reich* pp318–9. Wheeler-Bennett *Nemesis of Power* p373.
43. IMT p89.
44. *Affaire Blomberg-Fritsch* op cit.
45. Demeter op cit p331.
46. *Affair Blomberg Fritsch* op cit and John *Twice Through the Lines* p29.
47. Memoirs, Bundesarchiv H 08-19/5, cited by O'Neill *The German Army and the Nazi Party* pp158–9.
48. IMT commission interrogation, IZ ZS 129.
49. Ibid.
50. *Memoirs* p65.
51. Seaton op cit p109.
52. Letter to Sullivan op cit. Editha also said that another condition was that her father-in-law had found somewhere else to live, but this does not make much sense.
53. Interview with von Rundstedt's grandson, Gerd, 4 November 1989.
54. Lamb, Richard *The Ghosts of Peace 1935–1945* pp70–71. However, he confuses von Kleist with his cousin the General and later Field Marshal.
55. Halder testimony in court, September 1948. Schall-Riancour op cit p244.
56. Liddell Hart interview, 26 October 1945, LH 9/24/132.
57. Schall-Riancour op cit p256.
58. IMT Commission interrogation op cit.
59. Hassell *Diaries* pp19,22.
60. *Von Rundstedt* op cit p38.
61. Hillgruber in Carver *The War Lords* p191.

CHAPTER FIVE

1. Part II was issued on 3 April and the other two parts on 11 April. English translations of all three are in the Wheeler-Bennett Papers.
2. *Abwehr* (Mittler & Sohn, Berlin, 1938) and published in English as *Defense* (Military Service Publishing Co, Harrisburg Penn, 1943).
3. Brett-Smith *Hitler's Generals* p53.
4. Manstein *Lost Victories* p23.
5. Blumentritt op cit p41.
6. Manstein op cit p27. The von Manstein connection with 18th Division was not broken, however. One of his sons was killed while serving with it in October 1942.
7. Ibid p47.
8. Von Manstein stated, Ibid p28, that the conference took place on the 21st, but this is incorrect. See Burdick and Jacobsen *The Halder War Diary 1939–1942* pp28–32, from which my account of what Hitler said is taken.
9. Goerlitz *The German General Staff* p351.
10. Interview Gerd and Eberhard von Rundstedt, 4 November 1989.
11. Manstein op cit pp30–31.
12. Interrogation of 19 June 1946, IZ ZS 129.
13. p411 and cited by Seaton *The German Army 1933–1945* p112n.
14. Manstein op cit p31.
15. War Diary Army Group South, Freiburg RH 19 I/5, and Kennedy *The German Army in Poland* p72, from which my account of the Polish campaign is largely drawn. Kennedy, however, implies that Army Group South was activated on 23 August.
16. A full account of this incident is given by Charles Whiting in *World War II Investigator* April 1988.

17. IZ ZS 129 and Manstein op cit p32.
18. See Burdick & Jacobsen *The Halder War Diary 1939–1942* pp33– 42.
19. Manstein op cit pp32–33.
20. War Diary Army Group South op cit.
21. Kennedy op cit p94.
22. Quoted Cooper, Matthew *The German Air Force 1933–1945: An Anatomy of Failure* p100 (Jane's, London, 1981).
23. Burdick & Jacobsen op cit pp54–55.
24. Quoted Gilbert, Martin *The Second World War* p5 (Weidenfeld & Nicolson, London, 1989)
25. A number of examples are cited by Datner, Szymon *Crimes against POWs: Responsibility of the Wehrmacht* pp22–33 (Warsaw, 1964).
26. Burdick & Jacobsen op cit p69 (diary entry, 10 October 1939) and Lewis, S J *Forgotten Legions: German Army Infantry Policy 1918–1941* p106 (Praeger, Westport Conn, 1985).
27. Burdick & Jacobsen op cit pp52–3.
28. Gilbert op cit p6.
29. Army Group South War Diary op cit.
30. Gilbert op cit p8.
31. Ibid p12 and Mason *To Kill Hitler* pp206–7.
32. Manstein op cit p61.
33. US Military Intelligence Service Report B–826 dated 6 September 1945.

CHAPTER SIX

1. Halder diary entry, Burdick & Jacobsen op cit pp69–71.
2. Guderian *Panzer Leader* pp472–3, Taylor *March of Conquest* p50.
3. Letter dated 21 October 1939 and referred to in the Taylor Memorandum p76, August 1947, PRO FO 371/64474.
4. Manstein op cit p73.
5. Taylor *March of Conquest* p51.
6. Ibid pp 164–5, Manstein op cit pp97–105, Ellis *The War in France and Flanders* p336.
7. Quoted Taylor p165 and Burdick & Jacobsen op cit p76.
8. *March of Conquest* p165.
9. Halder diary entry, 3 November 1939, Burdick & Jacobsen op cit pp75–6.
10. Schall-Riancour *Aufstand und Gehorsam und Generalstab im Umbruch: Leben und Wirken von genraloberst Franz Halder, Generalstabchef 1938–1942* p267. Höhne *Canaris* p392 phrases the quotation a little differently: 'You can order me for all I care, but my instrument of authority would fall to pieces in my hand if I tried to use if for that purpose.'
11. Goerlitz *The German General Staff* p366, Erfurth *Die Geschichte des deutschen Generalstabes* p236.
12. 27 January 1940, Hassell op cit p104.
13. Halder diary entry 5 November 1939, Burdick & Jacobsen op cit p78.
14. Macksey *Guderian: Panzer General* p98.
15. *Panzer Leader* pp85–87.
16. Taylor op cit p169, Ellis op cit p339.
17. Manstein op cit p69.
18. IZ ZS 129.
19. Manstein op cit p70.
20. Ellis op cit pp339–340, Taylor op cit p170, Taylor Memorandum op cit p77.
21. Diary entry 14 January 1940, Burdick & Jacobsen op cit p87.

22. Manstein op cit pp94–5.
23. Macksey op cit p95.
24. Diary entry 7 February 1940, Burdick & Jacobsen op cit pp94– 96.
25. Macksey op cit p95.
26. Manstein op cit p120.
27. *Panzer Leader* p90.
28. Blumentritt op cit p64.
29. Diary entry 14 February 1940, Burdick & Jacobsen op cit pp98– 99.
30. Halder diary entry 24 February 1940, ibid p103.
31. Taylor op cit pp 173–4.
32. Ibid p175.
33. Halder diary entry 17 March 1940, Burdick & Jacobsen op cit p106.
34. 10 March 1940. Von Brauchitsch's article appeared on 24 January.
35. Letter Hans Gerd to Bila, 13 April 1940, Freiburg MSg 1/1893.
36. US Military Intelligence Service Report B-826 op cit.
37. Diary entry 12 May, Burdick & Jacobsen op cit p138. At this stage in the war the Panzer division was built round a Panzer brigade and infantry brigade. The former consisted of two regiments each of two battalions, with a total tank establishment of 562, although the actual figure was some way below this, especially following the conversion of the four light divisions to Panzer divisions after the Polish campaign. The infantry brigade was much smaller, with one motor cycle battalion and a regiment of two motorised battalions mounted in lorries, although a few fortunates did have SdKfz 251 armoured personnel carriers.
38. *Panzer Leader* p105.
39. Halder diary entries 14,15 May 1940, Burdick & Jacobsen op cit pp142–5.
40. Quoted Ellis op cit pp61–2.
41. Interview with Liddell Hart, 26 October 1945, LH 9/24/132.
42. Guderian op cit pp109–110.
43. Halder diary entry 17 May, Burdick & Jacobsen op cit p148.
44. Quoted Ansel *Hitler Confronts England* p70. See also Warlimont *Inside Hitler's Headquarters* p95, and Burdick & Jacobsen op cit p148.
45. Burdick & Jacobsen op cit p149.
46. Ibid.
47. Keitel *Memoirs* p111.
48. Burdick & Jacobsen op cit pp150–1.
49. Liddell Hart *The Rommel Papers* p29.
50. Macksey op cit p115.
51. Liddell Hart op cit p30.
52. Liddell Hart interview, 26 October 1945, LH 9/24/132.
53. Army Group A War Diary, quoted Ellis op cit p397.
54. Diary entries 23 May 1940, Burdick & Jacobsen op cit pp161–2.
55. Ibid p163.
56. Fourth Army War Diary, quoted Ellis op cit p348.
57. Burdick & Jacobsen op cit pp163–4.
58. Army Group A War Diary, quoted Ansel op cit p78fn.
59. Tloke *Heeres Adjutant bei Hitler 1939–1943* p80.
60. Ellis op cit p349, Taylor op cit p259, Ansel op cit pp80–81, citing Blumentritt letter to him dated January 1955, and Meier-Wolcker, Hans *der Enschluss zum Anhalten der deutschen Panzertruppen im Flandern 1940* (Vierteljahreschrift für Zeitgeschichte, July 1954).
61. Meier-Wolcker op cit.
62. Macksey op cit p118.
63. Quoted Meier-Wolcker op cit.

64. Quoted Ellis op cit p151.
65. Interview with Liddell Hart, 26 October 1945, LH 9/24/132.
66. Burdick & Jacobsen op cit p165.
67. Ibid.
68. Diary entry, quoted Taylor op cit p260fn.
69. Ellis op cit p150, Taylor op cit pp260–1.
70. Meier-Wolcker op cit citing letter to him from von Sodenstern dated 1 May 1954.
71. Quoted Taylor op cit p261.
72. Meier-Wolcker op cit quoting letters to him from Brennecke (14 April 1954) and Engel (21 May 1954).
73. Quoted ibid.
74. Engel diary entry, Tloke op cit.
75. Diary entry 26 May 1940, Burdick & Jacobsen op cit p167.
76. Meier-Wolcker op cit quoting Engel statement to him dated 21 May 1954.
77. See, for example the description of the battle for Wormhoudt given in my biography of Sepp Dietrich, *Hitler's Gladiator* pp82–86.
78. Engel diary entry, 27 May 1940, Tloke op cit.
79. PRO WO 205/1020.
80. IWM AL 1325.
81. Blumentritt op cit pp74–78.
82. Letter dated December 1954, Ansel op cit pp108fn,176.
83. Interview, 26 October 1945, LH 9/24/132.
84. Diary entry, 9 June 1940, Burdick & Jacobsen op cit p189.
85. Blumentritt op cit p80.
86. Diary entry, 20 June 1940, quoted Taylor op cit pp306–7.

CHAPTER SEVEN

1. Freiburg MSg 1/1893.
2. The full list, in order of seniority, was von Brauchitsch, Keitel, von Rundstedt, von Bock, von Leeb, List, von Kluge, von Witzleben, von Reichenau. Three Luftwaffe generals, Milch, Sperrle and Kesselring, were likewise promoted. In addition, a further 14 generals, including Hoth, Guderian and von Rundstedt's other army commander, Busch, were promoted Colonel General on the same day.
3. Diary entry 30 June 1940, Burdick and Jacobsen op cit p219.
4. Shirer *The Rise and Fall of the Third Reich* p751.
5. Burdick and Jacobsen op cit p219 and Taylor *The Breaking Wave* p216.
6. Foreign Office Research Department GER/96/49 *20th July (1944) Plot Personalities*, January 1949. Wheeler-Bennett Papers.
7. Blumentritt op cit p89.
8. Interview, 26 October 1945, LH 9/24/132.
9. Shulman *Defeat in the West* p59. Von Rundstedt made the same comment during one of his interrogations shortly after arriving in England in July 1945 (US Dept of the Army G-2 Report B-826 dated 8 September 1945, von Rundstedt Archive).
10. Blumentritt op cit p87.
11. Ansel op cit pp217,256.
12. Blumentritt op cit p88.
13. Quoted SHAEF Psychological Warfare Intelligence Section Background Information Report DE416/D15202 dated 31 May 1945, Freiburg MSg 1/1893.
14. Quoted Taylor *The Breaking Wave* p230.
15. Earl F Ziemke in Barnett ed *Hitler's Generals* p192 quoting Wilhelm von Leeb *Tagebuch aufzeichnungen und Lagebeurteilungen aus zwei Weltkriegan* (Stuttgart, 1976).

16. Smith, Howard K *Last Train from Berlin* pp221–2 (Cresset Press, London, 1942).
17. Letter 2 September 1940, Freiburg HSg 1/1893.
18. Quoted SHAEF PWD report dated 31 May 1945, op cit.
19. Interview Gerd and Eberhard von Rundstedt, 4 November 1989.
20. Letters to the Author from Gerd von Rundstedt, 14 November 1989, and Barbara Papanastassiou, 14 February 1990.
21. Diary entry 11 September 1940, Burdick and Jacobsen op cit p255.
22. Blumentritt op cit p92.
23. Diary entry 31 July 1940, Burdick & Jacobsen op cit p244.
24. Interrogation by the IMT Commission, 19 June 1946, IZ ZS 129.
25. Blumentritt op cit p98.
26. Diary entry 5 February 1941, Burdick & Jacobsen op cit p316.
27. Letters dated 5 and 21 February 1941, Freiburg HSg 1/1893.
28. Postcard dated 8 February 1941, Stephen W Bumball Collection.
29. Diary entry 30 March 1941, Burdick & Jacobsen op cit pp345–46.
30. IMT Commission Interrogation, op cit.
31. *Lost Victories* pp179–80.
32. IMT Commission Interrogation, op cit. Von Rundstedt said that he thought that the conference had taken place in May or June 1941, but 30 March was the only time that Hitler addressed the senior commanders as a group on BARBAROSSA. On the other hand, he may have confused it with a visit which von Brauchitsch made to the army groups in the second week of June, just after the Commissar Order had been issued, or possibly with Hitler's final conference with his commanders on 14 June.
33. Taylor Memorandum of August 1947 p5 PRO FO 371/64474.
34. US Dept of the Army G-2 Report B-826 op cit.
35. Halder diary entry, 19 May 1941. Burdick & Jacobsen op cit p389.
36. Blumentritt op cit pp103–4 and Liddell Hart interview, 9 November 1945, LH 9/24/77.
37. PRO W0205/1020.
38. Shulman op cit, pp75–6.
39. Hassell diary entry 22 May 1941, op cit p180.
40. Quoted by Andreas Hillgruber in Carver *The War Lords* p193.

CHAPTER EIGHT

1. Burdick and Jacobsen op cit p419.
2. Dated 23 June, Freiburg MSg 1/1893. An English translation of extracts of this and several other letters written during the period 1941–2 is to be found in LH 9/24/132. These are clearly based on the extracts found in Freiburg MSg 1/1893.
3. Letter to Bila dated 1 July, Freiburg MSg 1/1893. Von Rundstedt's elder grandson, stresses that this comment did not mean that his grandfather was anti-Jewish. It was merely a traditional German expression. A parallel might be that someone using the English expression 'to work like a black' is not necessarily a racist.
4. Letters dated 9 and 10 July 1941, Ibid.
5. Letter dated 9 July 1941, Ibid.
6. Halder Diary entry 10 July 1941, Burdick & Jacobsen op cit p463.
7. Ibid, 9 July 1941.
8. Letter dated 10 July 1941, Freiburg MSg 1/1893.
9. Diary entry 10 July 1941, Burdick and Jacobsen op cit pp464–5.
10. Letter to Bila dated 13 July 1941, Freiburg MSg 1/1893.

11. Letter dated 18 July 1941, Ibid.
12. US Dept of Army G-2 report B-826, September 1945, op cit.
13. Burdick and Jacobsen op cit pp480–2.
14. Letter to Bila dated 26 July. Freiburg Msg 1/1893.
15. Gilbert, Martin *The Holocaust: the Jewish Tragedy* p173 (Fontana Paperback edition, London, 1987).
16. Quoted Gilbert *Second World War* p221.
17. Höhne *Canaris* p462.
18. IZ ZS 129.
19. Taylor Memorandum, August 1947, p41, PRO FO 371/64474.
20. IZ ZS 129.
21. Ibid pp29–55.
22. Howell, Edgar M *The Soviet Partisan Movement 1941–1944* p53 (US Department of the Army pamphlet 20–244, 1956)
23. Ibid pp57–8.
24. Ibid pp59–60.
25. Taylor Memorandum op cit pp33–35.
26. Letter dated 8 August 1941, Freiburg MSg 1/1893.
27. Letters to Bila dated 30 July and 16 August 1941, op cit.
28. US Dept of Army G-2 report B-826 dated 6 September 1945 op cit. The comments on the Rumanians are echoed by von Manstein in *Lost Victories* pp206–7.
29. Letter dated 8 August 1941, Freiburg MSg 1/1893.
30. Hibbert, Christopher *Benito Mussolini* p174 (Reprint Society edition, London, 1963)
31. Letter to Bila dated 8 September 1941, Freiburg MSg 1/1893.
32. Macksey *Guderian Panzer General* p147.
33. Halder Diary entry 24 August 1941.
34. Letter dated 4 September 1941, Freiburg MSg 1/1893.
35. Blumentritt op cit p115.
36. IZ ZS 129.
37. Freiburg MSg 1/1893.
38. Ibid.
39. SHAEF PWD Int Sect Background Information Report DE416/DIS202 dated 31 May 1945, op cit.
40. Letter to Bila dated 3 October 1941, Freiburg 1/1893.
41. Letter dated 14 October 1941, ibid.
42. Burdick & Jacobsen op cit p552.
43. Seaton *The Russo-German War 1941–45* p197 citing Army Group South War diary, and Military Intelligence Service US War Department Report B-826 dated 6 September 1945, copy in von Rundstedt archive.
44. A January 1948 medical report on von Rundstedt describes the heart attack as 'acute' (PRO FO 371/70652). If it had been so, it is most unlikely that he would have remained at duty.
45. Military Intelligence Service US War Department Report B-826 op cit.
46. Burdick & Jacobsen op cit p571.
47. Quoted Blumentritt op cit pp111–112.
48. Burdick & Jacobsen op cit p574.
49. Keitel op cit p161.
50. Quoted Blumentritt op cit p114.
51. The correspondence surrounding the cheque is found in Bundesarchiv, Koblenz under R 43 II/985a.
52. Letter Editha von Rundstedt to Matthew Barry Sullivan, 26 March 1977.
53. Interview Gerd and Eberhard von Rundstedt, 4 November 1989.

54. Von Hassell in his diary, 24 January 1942, wrote that it was von Brauchitsch whom von Rundstedt represented at the funeral and that he was requested to do so by letter via Schmundt (Hassell op cit p213). Von Rundstedt, however, told the IMT Commission at Nuremberg that it was Hitler whom he represented (IZ ZS 129).

CHAPTER NINE

1. Letter dated 15 March 1942, Freiburg MSg 1/1893.
2. Ibid.
3. Full text if given in Trevor-Roper *Hitler's War Directives 1939–1945* pp111–116.
4. Schweppenburg *The Critical Years* p205.
5. Mellenthin *Panzer Battles* p205.
6. Dated 10 October 1945 and quoted Foot *SOE in France* p224.
7. 21 April 1942, Lockner *The Goebbels Diaries 1942–3* pp128–9.
8. Letter dated 15 March 1942, op cit.
9. Letter to Bila dated 6 August 1942, Freiburg MSg 1/1893.
10. Letter to Bila dated 6 April 1942, ibid.
11. Ibid.
12. Cited Roskill, Capt S W DSC MA RN *The Dieppe Raid and the Question of German Foreknowledge: a Study on Historical Responsibility* JRUSI February 1964.
13. Report on Dieppe dated 3 September 1942, ibid.
14. Freiburg MSg 1/1893.
15. Lehmann, Rudolf *Die Leibstandarte* Vol 2 p317 (Munin Verlag, Osnabrück, 1980).
16. Brett-Smith *Hitlers' Generals* p155.
17. Military Intelligence Service US War Department Report B-826, op cit.
18. For evidence of both see my biography of Dietrich, *Hitler's Gladiator*.
19. Taylor Memorandum p10, August 1947, PRO FO 371/64474.
20. Letter to Bila, Freiburg MSg 1/1893.
21. Letter to Bila, 19 August 1942, ibid. The translations of von Rundstedt's letters for this period found under LH 9/24/132 are prefaced by the comment: 'To judge by his story of the Dieppe raid one would imagine that the Field-Marshal had spent a busy day directing operations. If officers on his staff are to be believed, he was actually suffering from a hangover so severe that it prevented him from reacting in any way.' This was presumably written by Liddell Hart, but I have found no evidence to support this accusation.
22. Letters to Bila dated 21,22,23 August 1942, ibid.
23. Leter to Bila, 28 August 1942, ibid.
24. Letter dated 14 Sepember 1942, ibid.
25. For a full account of the SSRF raids see my *The Commandos 1940–1946* (Kimber, 1985 and Grafton Paperback edition, 1991), which also give the full text of the Commando Order.
26. Taylor Memorandum p12, PRO FO 371/64474.
27. *The Trial of Major German War Criminals* Part 21 pp91, 101–2.
28. Quoted Griffiths *Marshal Pétain* pp311–2.
29. Quoted Whitcomb *France during the German Occupation 1940–1944* p1545.
30. *La Chronique de Vichy 1940–1944* pp309–10.
31. Quoted Blumentritt op cit p121.
32. Neubronn, Alexander Freiherr von *Als 'Deutscher General' bei Pétain* (Vierteljahres-hafte für Zeitgeschichte No 4 1956).
33. Letter dated 10 December 1942.
34. Letter dated 20 September 1942, Freiburg MSg 1/1893.
35. Richardson & Freidin *The Fatal Decisions* p175.

36. Reynolds op cit p219.
37. Diary entry 22 February 1943, Tloke op cit p144.
38. Diary entry 2 March 1943, Lochner op cit pp199–200.
39. Interrogation Report CSDIC/CMF/SIM/AB22 dated September 1943 and cited in Foreign Office Research Department GER/96/49 *20th July (1944) Plot Personalities* Wheeler-Bennett Papers op cit.
40. Blumentritt op cit pp141–2, Whitcomb op cit p795, Godon *Collaborationism in France during the Second World War* p178.
41. Moll op cit p219.
42. Taylor Memorandum op cit p25.
43. Interview Gerd and Eberhard von Rundstedt, 4 November 1989.
44. Foreign Office Research Department GER/96/49 op cit.
45. Dated 8 March 1943, Freiburg MSg 1/1893.
46. Letter dated 10 May 1943, ibid.
47. Ibid.
48. Freiburg Pers 6/16.
49. See letters Ditha to Bila dated 4 November 1942, 19 April 1943, Freiburg MSg 1/1893.
50. Letter dated 10 May 1943, ibid.
51. Richardson & Freidin op cit pp179–180. Blumentritt op cit p92 says that the shelter was built sometime during the winter 1940– 41, but the air threat was only minor at this time and what RAF operations did take place in the Paris area were mainly leaflet raids. I have therefore preferred to follow Zimmermann.
52. Blumentritt op cit p157. Zimmermann mentions von Rundstedt's visit to Hitler, but does not say that he asked him to raise the matter of the defence of the West. Richardson & Freidin op cit p177.
53. Postcard Bila to Ditha, 22 June 1943, von Rundstedt archive. Blumentritt claimed wrongly that von Rundstedt was still at Bad Tölz and that Hitler sent a car for him.
54. Warlimont *Inside Hitler's Headquarters* p374.
55. Undated handwritten comments by von Rundstedt triggered by Zimmermann's *Ob West: a Study in Command* (IWM AL 786), von Rundstedt archive.
56. Lockner op cit p376.
57. Liddell Hart interview, 26 October 1945, LH 9/24/132.
58. Von Rundstedt Memorandum, 10 October 1945, quoted Foot op cit pp233,285.
59. Riess, Curt *Marshal von Rundstedt: German Darlan, The Saturday Evening Post*, 2 October 1943.
60. Aron *The Vichy Régime 1940–44* p434. I have not, however, been able to find out any details of this incident.
61. Du Gard op cit p373, Lottman *Pétain: Hero or Traitor*: p310. Von Rundstedt's report is in the Sayer archive.
62. Cited Wilt, Alan F *An Addendum to the Rommel-Rundstedt Controversy* (Military Affairs, December 1975).
63. Trevor-Roper op cit pp149–153.
64. Written statement dated 1 December 1949, IWM AL 1553/2. Seydlitz was Frederick the Great's cavalry commander. At Rossbach, 5 November 1757, Seydlitz delivered a devastating surprise attack into the flank of the greatly numerically superior Austro-French army.
65. Irving *The Trail of the Fox* p287.
66. Richardson & Freidin op cit p180.
67. Liddell Hart *The Rommel Papers* p461.
68. Liddell Hart interview, 26 October 1945, LH 9/24/132.
69. *Pariser Zeitung* 21 December 1943.
70. Riess *The Saturday Evening Post* 2 October 1943, op cit

71. This is based on Rommel's report to Hitler dated 31 December 1943 and quoted at length in *The Rommel Papers* op cit pp452– 456.
72. OKW Operations War Diary, 31 December 1943, cited Ellis *Victory in the West* Vol 1 p56, and Wilt op cit.
73. Ruge *Rommel in Normandy* p77.
74. Taylor Memorandum, op cit p20.
75. IMT Vol 21 p92.
76. Letter 27 April 1944, *Rommel Papers* op cit p463.
77. CSDIC(UK) Report GRGG 344 dated 21 August 1945, PRO WO 208/4178.
78. *Rommel Papers* op cit pp467–8.
79. Ibid p469.
80. Ruge op cit pp164–5. Karl May was a German writer of adventure stories in the Jack London mould.
81. Schmundt diary entry 3 March 1944, Bradley & Schulze-Kossens *Tätigkeitsbericht des Chefs Heeres-personalamtes ...* pp129–130 and Ruge op cit p90.
82. Manstein op cit p531–2.
83. Schmundt diary entry 19 March 1944, Bradley & Schulze-Kossens op cit p131, and Manstein op cit p532.
84. Irving op cit p306. Irving, however, does not make any mention to the reason why von Rundstedt had been summoned to Berchtesgaden, which would have upset him far more than Hitler not listening to him. Hence this quotation must be viewed with circumspection.
85. Lamb op cit pp275,282.
86. Neubronn op cit.
87. Speidel, Dr Hans *Ideas and Preparations made by FM Rommel for and Independent Termination of the War in the West and Elimination of National Socialist Depositions,* January 1947, MS B-721. Copy in Wheeler-Bennett Papers.
88. Ultra intercept cited in Bennett *Ultra in the West* p50.
89. Du Gard op cit p483.
90. Shirer *The Rise and Fall of the Third Reich* p1036.
91. War Diary Ob West, 1 and 3 June 1944, Freiburg RH 19 IV/40.
92. Ruge op cit p169.
93. War diary Ob West op cit.

CHAPTER TEN

1. Quoted Wilmot *The Struggle for Europe* p247.
2. Ob West reactions are taken from War Diary, Freiburg RH 19 IV/43 and IV/47.
3. Luck, Hans von *Panzer Commander: the Memoirs of Colonel Hans Von Luck* p180 (Praeger, NY, 1989)
4. Report to OKW dated 15 June 1944, Ob West War Diary op cit. Marcks had lost his leg on the Eastern Front. He was killed by an Allied fighter near St Lö on 12 June.
5. Ibid.
6. Further detail of Dietrich's problems is given in my *Hitler's Gladiator* pp123–5 op cit.
7. Ob West War Diary entries, 8 & 9 June 1944, op cit. Dietrich also commented on the British Churchill tank with 6-pdr gun. It could only be effectively attacked at ranges of under 1,000 metres, but its own gun was effective beyond this range. For further details of the communications problems see *Hitler's Gladiator* op cit p126.
8. Irving op cit pp340, 343.

9. IMT p93.
10. Liddell Hart op cit p491.
11. Lamb op cit p280.
12. Undated handwritten notes, von Rundstedt archive.
13. *Die Weltwoche*, Zurich, 16 June 1944.
14. Speidel *We Defended Normandy* p89.
15. Shulman *Defeat in the West* p136.
16. Ob West War Diary op cit.
17. Ibid.
18. Mitcham, Samuel W *Hitler's Legions: German Army Order of Battle World War II* p377 (Leo Cooper, London, 1985). This is confirmed by Luck op cit p181. Feuchtinger was apparently tried by court-martial in March 1945 for dereliction of duty on 6 June 1944 and found guilty, but his sentence was mitigated on orders from above.
19. Shulman op cit p131.
20. The description of the conference is based on Speidel op cit pp105–111, Blumentritt op cit pp233–5, *Rommel Papers* op cit p479, Zimmerman in Richardson & Freidin op cit pp190–1, and Ellis *Victory in the West* Vol 1 op cit p195.
21. Shulman op cit p131.
22. Testimony to IMT Commission, IZ ZS 129.
23. *Rommel Papers* op cit p492.
24. Ibid.
25. Ob West War Diary, cited in Ellis *Victory in the West* Vol 1 pp295–6.
26. Ibid, p296.
27. Blumentritt op cit p238.
28. Conference description is drawn mainly on *Rommel Papers* op cit pp479–80, Blumentritt pp237–8, and IZ ZS 129.
29. Ellis *Victory in the West* vol 1 pp320–1.
30. Shulman op cit p137.
31. Blumentritt op cit p238.
32. ETHINT 73, IWM AL 1556/2.
33. IZ ZS 129.
34. Bradley & Schulze-Kossens op cit p149.
35. Warlimont op cit p438.
36. IMT p94.
37. Ziemke in *Hitler's Generals* op cit p201 citing Domarus, Max *Hitler Reden und Proklamationem 1932–1945* vol 2 p1540 (Munich, 1963).
38. Hans Gerd von Rundstedt's personal copy, von Rundstedt archive.
39. Speidel op cit pp89–90, 119. Ruge op cit p209 says that the visit took place on 6 July, but he was not present.
40. Richardson & Freidin op cit p193.
41. Bradley & Schulze-Kossens op cit p182,188.
42. Macksey op cit pp188–9.
43. Ibid p188.
44. Burgdorf diary entry, Bradley & Schulze-Kossens op cit p195.
45. IMT p93.
46. Military Intelligence Service, US Dept of Army Report B-826, op cit.
47. IZ ZS 129.
48. Interview dated 1 November 1945, LH 9/24/132.
49. *SS Report on July 20*, Nordwestdeutsche Heft 1/2, 1947. English typescript in Wheeler-Bennett Papers.
50. Military Intelligence Service, US Dept of Army Report B–826, op cit.
51. Speidel op cit p90.

CHAPTER ELEVEN

1. Blumentritt op cit pp241–2.
2. Quoted by Ziemke in Barnett *Hitler's Generals* op cit pp201–2.
3. Brett-Smith op cit p180, which also gives comments on him by Rommell and Kesselring.
4. Burgdorf diary entry 21 September 1944, Bradley & Schulze-Kossens op cit p263.
5. Quoted Shulman *Defeat in the West* pp200–1.
6. Quoted Blumentritt op cit p245.
7. Zimmermann *OB West – 9 Questions (June 44 – Mar 45)* 23 October 1947, IWM AL 1556/1–2.
8. Handwritten undated notes by von Rundstedt while a POW in England, von Rundstedt archive.
9. Westphal *The German Army in the West* p174.
10. Quoted Bennett *Ultra in the West* p133.
11. Ibid p150.
12. Mellenthin *Panzer Battles* p373.
13. Ibid p383.
14. Ruge op cit pp247–8.
15. Speidel op cit pp90,159.
16. Letter dated 5 June 1950, LH 9/24/77. Von Rundstedt made a similar declaration at Nuremberg, IMT pp103–4.
17. Mellenthin op cit p383.
18. Letter to Matthew Barry Sullivan, 26 March 1977.
19. Mellenthin op cit p394.
20. Quoted by Blumentritt in *Collier's* 3 January 1953.
21. Military Intelligence Service US War Department Report B-826 op cit.
22. Quoted by Günther Reichhelm, who was on Model's staff, in Pallud *Battle of the Bulge: Then and Now* p20.
23. Westphal op cit p180.
24. Military Intelligence Service US War Department Report B-826 op cit.
25. Cruikshank, Charles *The Fourth Arm: Psychological Warfare 1938–1945* p172 (Oxford University Press paperback, 1981).
26. Dated 1 October 1944, printed copy in the von Rundstedt archive.
27. CSDIC(UK) GRGG 330(G) dated 1 August 1945 *The Ardennes Offensive*, PRO FO 371/46780.
28. Blumentritt *Collier's* 3 January 1953 op cit.
29. Taylor Memorandum op cit p56.
30. Mellenthin op cit p404.
31. Westphal op cit p181.
32. Ellis *Victory in the West* Vol 2 p179.
33. Pallud op cit p31.
34. Westphal op cit p181.
35. Richardson & Freidin op cit p224.
36. Ibid p219.
37. CSDIC (UK) *The Ardennes Offensive* op cit.
38. Ibid.
39. Letter to Frau Bormann, *The Bormann Letters* p148.
40. Richardson & Freidin op cit p232.
41. The first Type XXIII coastal U-boat, U2324, set out on its first operational cruise on 29 January 1945, and was followed by five more before the end of the war. Only one Type XXI ocean going U-boat, ever became operational and then not until the end of April 1945.

42. Pallud op cit pp80–81.
43. *An Interview with Obstgrf 'Sepp' Dietrich: Sixth Pz Army Planning for the Ardennes Offensive* 10 July 1945, US Department of the Army Historical Branch ETHINT 16, US National Archives RG 338.
44. Ibid.
45. Pallud op cit p29.
46. Ibid p81.

CHAPTER TWELVE

1. CSDIC Interrogation report on Ardennes op cit.
2. *Hitler's Gladiator* op cit p150.
3. Pallud op cit pp63–64.
4. Shulman Interrogation, PRO WO 205/1020 op cit, and CSDIC Ardennes Interrogation report op cit.
5. Richardson & Freidin op cit p238 and Dietrich interview, 8–9 August 1945, US Department of the Army History Branch, ETHINT 15, US National Archives RG 338.
6. IMT Commission transcript on von Rundstedt op cit, and ETHINT 15 op cit.
7. The most detailed and accurate account of the postwar investigation of the massacre and the subsequent controversial trial is given in Weingartner, James J *Crossroads of Death: The Story of the Malmédy Massacrea and Trial* (University of California Press, 1979). See also, especially from Dietrich's viewpoint, *Hitler's Gladiator* op cit.
8. *Collier's* 3 January 1953, op cit.
9. Liddell Hart interview, 26 October 1945, LH 9/24/132.
10. Von Mellenthin op cit pp408–9, Westphal op cit p185.
11. Liddell Hart interview, 26 October 1945 op cit.
12. Crusade in Europe (Heinemann, London, 1948) p386.
13. *New York Times* 8 January 1945.
14. Wilmot op cit pp676–7 citing a fragmentary record of this conference.
15. *Bormann Letters* op cit pp155–6.
16. Guderian op cit p385.
17. Quoted Shulman op cit pp9–10.
18. Gen Raus of Third Panzer Army quoted by Seaton *The German Army 1933–1945* op cit p245.
19. Undated handwritten postwar notes, von Rundstedt archive.
20. Quoted Bennett op cit p224n.
21. Shulman op cit pp307–8.
22. Ellis *Victory in the West* vol 2 p263.
23. Quoted Shulman op cit p290.
24. Original signal is in the von Rundstedt archive.
25. Trevor-Roper ed *The Goebbels Diaries: The Last Days* p6.
26. Ibid p57.
27. Quoted Bennett op cit p221.
28. Kesselring *Memoirs* p237.
29. Interview with Dr Freiherr von Siegler, 26 November 1951, IZ 311/52.
30. Von Mellenthin op cit p417.
31. Trevor-Roper op cit pp104–5,194–5.
32. Interview 26 October 1946, LH 9/24/132.
33. Hillgruber in Carver *The War Lords* op cit p199.
34. Ibid.

35. Von Rundstedt's movements during the last weeks of the war are based on letters from Hans Gerd to Editha, von Rundstedt archive. Unfortunately they give no indication of the Field Marshal's thought processes and I have had to surmise the rationale governing his itinerary.
36. This description of von Rundstedt's capture is drawn from *The Fighting 36th Division: A Pictorial History of the Texas Division in Combat* (Battery Press, 1977), *T-Patch* (36 Div's newspaper) 8 May 1945, *The Stars and Stripes* 3 May 1945, and letter from Colonel (Retd) Vincent M Lockhart USAR, author of *T-Patch to Victory*, dated 30 January 1990. Burke was also told that it was for treatment to his leg that von Rundstedt was in Bad Tölz.

CHAPTER THIRTEEN

1. *The Stars and Stripes* 3 May 1945.
2. 2 May 1945.
3. *New York Times* 5 May 1985.
4. PRO FO 371/46777.
5. PRO WO 219/1200A.
6. The evidence for his movements comes from a letter Hans Gerd to Bila dated 23 June 1945 and an entry in von Rundstedt's pocket diary for 1946, both in the von Rundstedt archive.
7. CROWCASS List No 1 (December 1944), PRO TS 26/876.
8. 2 September 1945.
9. SHAEF Interrogation Report dated 3 June 1945, PRO WO 219/1963.
10. US Strategic Bombing Survey Interview No 51 dated 25 June 1945. Copy in the von Rundstedt archive.
11. Searches in both the National Archives, Washington DC and the Public Record Office, London failed to reveal precisely why von Rundstedt was handed over to the British. One can only surmise that it was considered that the British had a stronger claim over him, perhaps because of France 1940 or the 1942 Commando Order.
12. Letter dated 23 June 1945 op cit.
13. Interview Gerd and Eberhard von Rundstedt, 4 November 1989.
14. I am most grateful to Miss Olive Wilson for drawing my attention to this.
15. *Daily Mail* 1 May 1945.
16. I have been unable to verify this. Monty's official biographer, Professor Nigel Hamilton, cannot recall it and points out that it is most unlikely that Monty ever met von Rundstedt in person, especially since the hospitality that he gave von Thoma after el Alamein was considered unseemly in some quarters. Letter to the Author dated 7 September 1989.
17. Grondona, L St Clare *Sidelights on Wilton Park* (JRUSI December 1979) from which much of the material on von Rundstedt's time at Wilton Park is taken. The remainder is drawn from Sullivan *Thresholds of Peace* pp229–231.
18. Towards the end of July he was taken to Shenley Military Hospital for 'observation and diagnosis'. *Daily Express* 26 July 1945.
19. CSDIC (UK) Report GRGG 344 dated 21 August 1945, PRO 208/4178.
20. CSID(UK) *The Ardennes Offensive* dated 1 August 1945, PRO FO 371/46780 and WO 208/4178. A further copy is to be found in the US National Archives under RG 238, Entry 160 – Box 10.
21. Letter to the author, 22 February 1989.
22. CSDIC (UK) Report GRGG 355 dated 15 September 1945, PRO WO 108/4178.
23. GRGG 358 dated 25 September 1945, ibid.
24. Ibid.

25. GRGG 355 op cit.
26. GRGG 358 op cit.
27. GRGG 362 dated 12 October 1945, ibid.
28. The rather uninformative war diary of No 1 PW Camp for September – December 1945 (PRO WO 166/17820) reveals that this was the only date during the period when a sizeable batch of prisoners, 22 in all, arrived from Wilton Park.
29. It is possible that Grondona was confusing Bassenge with General of Engineers (*Pioniere*) Dinter, former Chief Engineer of Army Group Vistula, who was also at Wilton Park at this time.
30. Sullivan op cit p236.
31. Letter to Captain Cyril Falls, 20 May 1946, LH 9/24/155-163.
32. Sullivan op cit p236.
33. Letter to Falls op cit.
34. In September 1945 the total was 223. PRO FO 939/249.
35. Interview by Mrs Jean Feather on the Author's behalf, April 1989.
36. PRO FO 916/1432.
37. Sullivan op cit p236.
38. Ibid and also Author's conversation with Sullivan, who was Liddell Hart's brother-in-law, 14 June 1989.
39. Letters to the Author, 21 and 29 March 1989.
40. *Notes for History: Talk with Field Marshal von Rundstedt. 26th October, 1945*, LH 9/24/ 132.
41. *Notes for History: Second talk with Field Marshal von Rundstedt, 1st November, 1945*, Ibid.
42. *Notes for History: the Norway Move*, Ibid.
43. Letter to Kingston, 29 November 1945, LH 9/24/77.
44. Letter to Editha von Rundstedt, 10 April 1953, LH 9/24/77. Needless to say, this file is not preserved in the Public Record Office.
45. PRO FO 939/283.
46. Sullivan op cit p237.
47. This is the name inscribed on the title page of the IWM's copy.
48. *Notes for History: (4th) Talk with Field Marshal von Rundstedt, 3 Jany. 1946* LH 9/24/132.
49. PRO FO 939/283.
50. The latest of these attacks is Mearsheimer, John J *Liddell Hart and the Weight of History* (Brassey's, London, 1989).
51. The escape is recounted in Williams, Herbert *Come out wherever you are* (Quartet Books, London, 1976).
52. CSDIC was originally based at the Tower of London and moved to Trent Park, at Cockfosters on the northern outskirts of London, at the end of October 1939. In July 1942, it was moved to a purpose built camp at Wilton Park, with the RAF section being housed at Latimer. Air Ministry Report *Intelligence from Interrogation* dated 31 December 1945. Copy in Author's archive.
53. PRO WO 205/1020. The date of this interview report is given as 1 February 1946, but in *Defeat in the West* the only interviews with von Rundstedt to which Shulman refers are October 1945 and October 1946. Unfortunately, the Author has been unable to ascertain from Shulman as to exactly when and where the interview(s) did take place.
54. Sullivan op cit p348.
55. Typescript copy in the Sayer Archive.
56. PRO FO 1019/51.
57. Sullivan op cit p358.
58. Gilbert G M *Nuremberg Diary* pp230–231 (Eyre & Spottiswoode, London, 1948)
59. This account of the Commission's examination is taken from a transcript in German, IZ ZS 129.

60. IMT p94.
61. Ibid, p102.
62. 13 August 1946.
63. Neave, Airey *Nuremberg: a Personal Record of the Trial of the Major Nazi War Criminals in 1945–6* p291 (Hodder & Stoughton, London, 1978).
64. Letter to the Author, 10 February 1989.
65. Quoted Sullivan op cit p358.
66. Quoted Hawthorne *Island Farm* p41. Another account of the history of the camp is Vincent, Jeff *Island Farm Camp* (After The Battle No 67).
67. PRO FO 939/97.
68. Ibid.
69. Sullivan op cit p351.
70. CM 94(46) PRO CAB 128/8.
71. Letter dated 23 December 1946, von Rundstedt Archive.
72. Letter Editha von Rundstedt to Matthew Barry Sullivan dated 26 March 1977, and details of Topham's will in *Sunday Times* 20 October 1961. Gerd von Rundstedt loaned his grandfather's ceremonial baton, presented by Hitler and which he never liked, to the Museum of Military History at Rastatt, Baden, where it is displayed together with his Knight's Cross with Oakleaves and Swords. Letter Gerd von Rundstedt to the Author, 20 August 1989.
73. Original handwritten script is von Rundstedt Archive.
74. Letter Mrs Elizabeth Crookenden to the Author, May 1989.
75. Hawthorne *Island Farm* op cit p42.
76. *A Full Life* pp185–6 (Leo Cooper, London, 1974).
77. *Neither Fear nor Hope* p347 (Macdonald, London, 1963).
78. Conversation with the Author, 14 August 1989.
79. *Twice Through the Lines* p185.
80. Letters to the Author from Gerd von Rundstedt, 14 November 1989, and Barbara Papanastassiou, 14 February 1990.
81. Letter to the Author, 25 July 1989.
82. PRO WO 311/648.
83. Letter to the Author, 7 September 1989.
84. PRO WO 267/601.
85. PRO WO 235/293, which gives a summary of the case.
86. PRO FO 939/194.
87. Dated 24 August 1947, PRO WO 32/15304.
88. Letter War Office to Western Command, 8 September 1947, PRO WO 311/448.
89. British Channel Four Television programme *Jailed by the British* 1982.
90. Letter Lt Col Clements to the Author, 3 June 1989, and medical reports in PRO WO 32/15304.

CHAPTER FOURTEEN

1. Letter Telford Taylor to the author, 27 February 1989.
2. PRO FO 371/64474.
3. Letter Lord Shawcross to the author, 21 March 1989.
4. Letter Shawcross to Bevin, 9 September 1947, PRO FO 371/64474.
5. Minute dated 6 October 1947, PRO FO 371/64474.
6. Various minutes, ibid.
7. Ibid.
8. Letter Elwyn-Jones to Shawcross, 8 October 1947, PRO FO 371/64474.

9. Brief by Marjoribanks, 11 October 1947, ibid.
10. PRO FO 371/64475.
11. Minutes Chaput de Saintoge to Bevin, 15 October 1947, ibid.
12. Smith ed *The Clay Papers* pp440–1.
13. PRO FO 371/64475.
14. PRO FO 371/64474.
15. PRO FO 371/64475.
16. Ibid.
17. Ibid.
18. Telegram, 26 November 1947, PRO FO 1032/2215.
19. Letter dated 17 November 1947, PRO FO 371/64475.
20. Letters Bevin dated 2 December 1947 and Jowitt dated 5 December 1947, ibid.
21. Ibid.
22. Minute Jowitt to Bevin, 22 December 1947, ibid.
23. This account of Clements' arrival at Island Farm is taken from letters written by him to Matthew Barry Sullivan dated 21 March and 15 April 1978, and I am indebted to Lt Col Clements for allowing me to quote from them.
24. Letter dated 3 December 1947, PRO FO 371/64475.
25. Ibid.
26. Letter Luise von Rundstedt to Liddell Hart, 9 February 1948, LH 9/24/77.
27. Letters to the Author, 3 January and 14 February 1990.
28. Letter dated 2 January 1948, LH 9/24/77.
29. PRO FO 371/70652.
30. Letter dated 29 January 1948, ibid.
31. Ibid.
32. Telegram British Embassy Brussels to Foreign Office, 20 February 1948, ibid.
33. *News Chronicle*, 10 & 19 February 1948, *La derniere Heure* 22 February 1948.
34. Telegram to Foreign Office, 14 February 1948, PRO FO 371/70652.
35. PRO FO 1032/2215.
36. PRO FO 371/70797.
37. Letter dated 10 February 1948, PRO WO 32/15304.
38. Letter dated 10 February 1948 and reproduced in Hawthorne op cit p43.
39. PRO FO 371/70798.
40. Ibid.
41. Letter dated 27 April 1948, ibid.
42. Sullivan op cit pp359–360, Clements letters op cit. The crucifix is now held by Dean Gravell's family and the individuals to whom von Rundstedt gave his walking sticks still have them. I am indebted to Dr Tom Jefferson for this information. The letter to the Bishop is quoted in Hawthorne op cit p42. It is dated 5 May 1949 and is addressed from Island Farm which is curious since von Rundstedt had left the previous day. He also wrote in the letter: 'On May 12th we shall leave Bridgend. With the exception of three Generals the Senior Officers will return home.' He does not indicate that he was one of the three.
43. Von Senger und Etterlin op cit p354.
44. Letter 6 May, LH 9/24/77.
45. Letter 21 May, ibid.
46. Letter P J Holt-Wilson to the author, 30 March 1989.
47. PRO WO 311/648.
48. CM 47(48), PRO CAB 128/13.
49. PRO WO 311/648.
50. *Daily Telegraph* 23 July 1948.
51. Letter to Liddell Hart dated 11 August 1948, LH 9/24/156–163.
52. Letter dated 13 July 1948, PRO WO 311/648.

53. Letter to the Author, 27 February 1989.
54. Minute dated 26 August 1948, PRO FO 371/70805.
55. Original transcript copy of the court order in the von Rundstedt Archive.
56. PRO WO 267/28A.
57. Author's conversation with Nightingale, 26 April 1989 and Bower *Blind Eye to Murder* p256. Bower's description of the dinner is slightly misleading in that it could be interpreted that Nightingale was aware of the decision to charge von Rundstedt as a war criminal, but was not prepared to treat him as such. Nightingale was adamant to the author that he had no knowledge of the decision at the time. On the same page, Bower also asserts thay 'the War Crimes Group officers, with a few exceptions, notably Gerald Draper, resigned *en masse* rather than accept the offer of helping the prosecution prepare the case for the forthcoming trial'. Nightingale vehemently denied this to the author, as did others involved in war crimes investigation. Further, the author could find no documentary evidence that this had happened. Given the ORC decision not to proceed with war crimes trials after 1 September 1948, the whole war crimes investigation machinery was being rapidly run down and it was this that probably created the mass exodus, if there was one.
58. Typescript of Letter from X dated 3 August 1948, LH 9/24/132. This description is confirmed in letter Editha von Rundstedt to Sullivan, 26 March 1977.
59. Letter Editha von Rundstedt to Sullivan op cit.
60. PRO FO 371/70804.
61. PRO FO 371/70805.
62. PRO FO 371/70804.
63. *The Times* 24 August 1948.
64. Ibid 25 August 1948.
65. Ibid 28 August 1948.
66. Telegram Foreign Office to Franks, 1 September 1948, PRO CAB 122/1356.
67. *The Times* 3 September 1948.
68. Ibid 6 September 1948.
69. Ibid 13 September 1948.
70. Ibid 9 September 1948.
71. PRO WO 267/28A.
72. Original notice in German handed to von Rundstedt and signed by him, von Rundstedt Archive.
73. Article III Paragraph 1(a).
74. This payment is noted on von Rundstedt's discharge certificate, von Rundstedt archive.
75. Foreign Office to Robertson, 13 September 1948, and Clay's response, PRO FO 1032/2215.
76. Letter Taylor to the author, 10 April 1989 and John op cit p191.
77. Foreign Office to Control Commission, 29 September 1948, PRO FO 1032/2215.
78. *The Times* 17 & 21 September 1948.
79. CM 61(48) PRO CAB 128/13.
80. As reported in *The Times* of 25 September 1948.
81. Minutes to the Foreign Office, 20 September 1948, PRO FO 371/70807.
82. PRO FO 371/70809.
83. Ibid.
84. *Manchester Guardian* 6 December 1948.
85. *The Times* 27 October 1948.
86. Ibid, 16 November 1948.
87. Abetz's handwritten account dated 18 January 1949 is in the Wheeler-Bennett Papers.

88. Shapcott to Marsden-Smedley, 11 November 1948, PRO FO 1032/2215.
89. Marsden-Smedley to Robertson, 19 November 1948, ibid.
90. See LH 9/24/77.
91. *Manchester Guardian* 6 December 1948.
92. Foreign Office to Robertson, 19 November 1948, PRO FO 371/77026, and Foreign Office to Robertson, 11 December 1948, PRO FO 1032/2215.
93. Letter dated 30 December 1948, LH 9/24/77.
94. Typescript copy of letter dated 14 December 1949, Author's archive.
95. Letter dated 3 January 1949, PRO FO 371/77029.
96. John op cit pp191–2 and PRO FO 371/77026.
97. A copy of the charge sheet, presumably sent to Liddell Hart by Dr Grimm, is to be found in LH 9/24/77. Another is held, with those for von Manstein and Strauss, under PRO WO 32/15304.
98. Letter Grimm to Liddell Hart, 9 February 1949, ibid.
99. Chajn to Elwyn-Jones, 22 December 1948, and reply dated 1 January 1949, PRO FO 371/77026.
100. British Embassy, Moscow English language summary of *Literary Gazette* No 12 dated 9 February 1949, ibid.
101. PRO FO 371/77027.
102. Shinwell to Bevin, 4 April 1949, PRO FO 371/77028.
103. PRO FO 371/77026.
104. Medical Boards dated 30 August, 18 October, 30 December 1948, 2 March 1949, PRO WO 32/15304.
105. Medical Board dated 10 March 1949, ibid.
106. CM 24 (49) PRO CAB 128/15.
107. PRO FO 371/77028.
108. Secretary Peace Pledge Union to Attorney-General, 25 April 1949, ibid.
109. Dated 8 April 1949, PRO WO 32/15304.
110. CM 30(49) PRO CAB 128/15.
111. PRO FO 371/77028.
112. Ibid.
113. CM 32(49) PRO CAB 128/15.
114. *The Times* 6 May 1949.

CHAPTER FIFTEEN

1. 10 May 1949.
2. Letter to Liddell Hart, 18 May 1949, LH 9/24/77.
3. Letter Regional Governmental Officer Hansestadt Hamburg to Dr Grimm dated 1 October 1949, von Rundstedt archive.
4. See, for example, British Military Government Ordinance No 110, dated 1 October 1947.
5. Telegram dated 18 May 1949, PRO FO 371/77029.
6. HQ BAOR telegram to Foreign Office, 21 May 1949, ibid.
7. Military Gvt Berlin to HQ BAOR telegram, 3 June 1949, PRO FO 371/77030.
8. Telegram dated 3 June 1949, ibid.
9. Telegram to Foreign Office, 13 June 1949, ibid.
10. PRO FO 371/77029.
11. British Embassy Warsaw telegram to Foreign Office dated 9 July 1949, PRO FO 371/77030.

12. Summary of *New Times* No 21 (18 May 1949) article entitled 'Protectors of the Hitlerite Hangmen' given in telegram British Embassy Moscow to Foreign Office, 23 May 1949, PRO FO 371/77029.
13. British Embassy Moscow note dated 7 June 1949, ibid.
14. Letter dated 24 June 1949, PRO FO 1032/1948.
15. The text of this, which was von Rundstedt's formal release notice and merely said that he would not be brought to trial before a British court, is given in telegram Military Government (Berlin) to Foreign Office, 28 July 1949, PRO FO 371/77031. The original in German is in the von Rundstedt archive.
16. Ibid.
17. LH 9/24/77.
18. PRO FO 371/77030.
19. LH 9/24/77.
20. Letter dated 16 July 1949, ibid.
21. PRO FO 371/77031.
22. Military Government (Berlin) telegram, 29 July 1949, PRO FO 371/77030.
23. PRO FO 1032/1750.
24. Telegram dated 16 July 1949, PRO FO 371/77030.
25. Telegram to Foreign Office, 29 July 1949, PRO FO 371/77031.
26. Regional Commissioner Lower Saxony letter dated 2 August 1949, PRO FO 1032/1948.
27. Interview, 4 November 1989.
28. Regional Commissioner Lower Saxony letter dated 2 August 1949 op cit.
29. Telegram to Foreign Office dated 13 August 1949, PRO FO 371/77031.
30. Minute to Marsden-Smedley, 11 August 1949, ibid.
31. Ibid.
32. Telegram Frankfurt to Lubbecke, 1 September 1949, PRO FO 371/77032 and reply dated 7 September, PRO FO 1032/1948.
33. Letter dated 6 September 1949, PRO FO 371/77032 and von Rundstedt's reply dated 11 September, PRO FO 1032/1948.
34. Telegram dated 19 October 1949, PRO FO 1032/1948.
35. PRO FO 371/77033.
36. Extract from Land Commissioner's Office Hannover Property Control Technical Report
1–31 October 1949, ibid.
37. Ibid.
38. Certificate of Discharge from Wehrmacht dated 18 November 1949, von Rundstedt archive.
39. Information from Barbara Papanastassiou via letter to the Author from Gerd von Rundstedt dated 27 November 1989.
40. IWM AL 1553/2.
41. Letter dated 5 June 1950, LH 9/24/77.
42. Letters von Rundstedt to Liddell Hart dated 12 January 1951 and Liddell Hart to von Rundstedt of 6 October 1951, ibid.
43. Blumentritt–Liddell Hart correspondence, LH 9/24/53.
44. Letter Blumentritt to Liddell Hart, 24 November 1950, ibid.
45. Letter 4 October 1950, ibid.
46. Interview of 26 November 1951 report, IZ 311/52.
47. Letter dated 8 February 1952, LH 9/24/77.
48. Letter Blumentritt to Liddell Hart, 31 July 1952, LH 9/24/53.
49. Interview, 4 November 1989.
50. *San Francisco Examiner* 25 February 1953.
51. JRUSI November 1952.

52. *Daily Mail* and *News Chronicle* of 9 September 1952, *Daily Herald* of 10 September 1952, *Manchester Guardian* of 12 September 1952.
53. Unfortunately I have not been able to establish exactly what the sales figures were. Odhams has had several takeovers and is now part of the Hamlyn Group, which no longer holds any records on the book, which has been long out of print.
54. Letter dated 3 May 1952, LH 9/24/77.
55. Johnson–Liddell Hart correspondence, summer 1952, ibid.
56. Letter Blumentritt to Liddell Hart, 13 October 1952, LH 9/24/53.
57. Letter Barbara Papanastassiou to the Author, 3 January 1990.
58. 15 December 1952, LH 9/24/53.
59. Letter to Liddell Hart, 5 January 1953, ibid.
60. *Collier's*, 3 January 1953.

CHAPTER SIXTEEN

1. All issues dated 25 February 1953.
2. Interview Gerd and Eberhard von Rundstedt, 4 November 1989.
3. Guderian obituary in *Die Deutsche Soldatenzeitung* 5 March 1953.
4. *Daily Express* 28 February 1953. The report also described how 'the victor of Dunkirk . . . lies dead and abandoned in the public building of the Hannover city Cemetery tonight. A cold draught blows through broken windows patched with planks of wood and four-inch nails.'
5. Letter dated 5 March 1953, LH 9/24/77.
6. Typescript of oration, Bibliothek für Zeitgeschichte BZ Z 3890 2.
7. My information for this comes from a German newspaper cutting dated 5 October 1955 in a report of the handing over of von Rundstedt's funeral plot to his daughter-in-law. The money to purchase the plot had been raised by various ex-soldiers' associations. As for the US memorial, 29th Infantry Division Association Past National Commander Charles A Lusby Sr, stated to me in a letter dated 30th March 1990 that he had no knowledge of this and had asked all posts if they knew anything of it. None did, but the Rhode Island post, in whose area the memorial is situated, did not reply.
8. *Die Deutsche Soldatenzeitung* 5 March 1953.
9. Westphal op cit p33.
10. Letter to the Author, 3 January 1990.
11. Letter Blumentritt to Crowe, 21 May 1965, Sayer Archive.
12. Carver *Warlords* op cit p189.
13. Quoted Galante op cit p90.
14. *Instructions for his Generals* pp2–3 (Stackpoole, Harrisburg Penn, 1960 edition).
15. Goerlitz op cit p152.
16. Stahlberg *Bounden Duty* pp 245–6.
17. Ziemke in Barnett *Hitler's Generals* op cit p180.
18. Stahlberg op cit p330.
19. Ibid p290.
20. Quoted Taylor *Sword and Swastika* op cit p173.
21. JRUSI, May 1952.
22. An account of the Pescari massacres is given in Sayer, Ian and Botting, Douglas *Hitler's Last General: the Case against Wilhelm Mohnke* pp355–358. Patton's attempted cover up is taken from Patton's diary, 14 July 1943 and cited in Blumenson, Martin *The Patton Papers 1940–1945* p288 (Houghton Mifflin, Boston, 1974).
23. Cunningham *A Sailor's Odyssey* pp433, 435 (Hutchinson, London, 1951).
24. Quoted Brett-Smith op cit p40.

25. Best, Geoffrey *Humanity in Warfare* pp241–2 (Methuen University paperback edition, London, 1983).
26. Letter to the author, 3 January 1990.
27. Interview, 4 November 1989

SELECT BIBLIOGRAPHY

The Trial of German Major War Criminals: Proceedings of the International Military Tribunal sitting at Nuremberg, Germany – Part 21 (HMSO, London, 1949)

Ansel, Walter *Hitler Confronts England* (Duke Univ, Durham NC, 1960)

Aron, Robert *The Vichy Régime 1940–44* (Putnam, NY, 1958)

Asprey, Robert B *The First Battle of the Marne* (Weidenfeld & Nicolson, London, 1962)

Baird, Jay W *The Mythical World of Nazi War Propaganda 1939–1945* (University of Minnesota Press, 1974)

Barnett, Correlli ed *Hitler's Generals* (Weidenfeld & Nicolson, London, 1989)

Bennett, Ralph *Ultra in the West: the Normandy Campaign 1944–45* (Hutchinson, London, 1979)

Benoist-Méchin, J *Histoire de l'Armée Allemande* Vols 1 & 2 (Editions Albin Michel, Paris, 1964)

Blumentritt, Gen Guenther *Von Rundstedt: the Soldier and the Man* (Odhams, London, 1952)

Bormann, Martin *the Bormann Letters: The Private Correspondence between Martin Bormann and his Wife from January 1943 to April 1945* (Weidenfeld & Nicolson, London, 1954)

Bower, Tom *Blind Eye to Murder: Britain, America and the Purging of Nazi Germany – a Pledge Destroyed* (Deutsch, London, 1981)

Bradley, Dermot & Schulze-Kossens, Richard ed *Tätigkeitsbericht des Chefs des Heerespersonalamtes General der Infanterie Rudolf Schmundt, continued by General d. Infanterie Wilhelm Burgdorf 1.10.42–29.10.44* (Osnabrück, 1984)

Burdick, Charles & Jacobsen, Hans-Adolf ed *The Halder War Diary 1939–1942* (Presidio, Novato Cal & Greenhill Books, London, 1988)

Carsten, F L *The Reichswehr and Politics 1918 to 1933* (Clarendon Press, Oxford, 1966)

Carver, FM Sir Michael ed *The War Lords: Military Commanders of the Twentieth Century* (Weidenfeld and Nicolson, London, 1976)

Carver, Field Marshal Lord *Twentieth Century Warriors: the Development of the Armed Forces of the Major Military Nations* (Weidenfeld & Nicolson, London, 1987)

Citino, Robert M *The Evolution of Blitzkrieg Tactics: Germany defends itself against Poland 1918–1933* (Greenwood Press, NY and London, 1987)

Craig, Gordon A *The Politics of the Prussian Army 1640–1945* (Clarendon Press, Oxford, 1955)

Degener, H A L ed *Wer Ists?* (Berlin, 1935)

Demeter, Karl *The German Officer Corps in Society and State 1650–1945* (Weidenfeld & Nicolson, London, 1965)

Deutsch, Harold C *Hitler and his Generals: the Hidden Crisis, January–June 1938* (University of Minneapolis Press, 1974)

Du Gard, Maurice Martin *La Chronique de Vichy 1940–1944* (Flammarion, Paris, 1948)

Ellis, Maj J F *The War in France and Flanders 1939–1940* (HMSO, London, 1953)

Ellis, Maj J F et al *Victory in the West: Volume 1 – the Battle for Normandy* (HMSO, London, 1962)

Ellis, Maj J F & Warhurst, Lt Col A E *Victory in the West: Volume 2 – The Defeat of Germany* (HMSO, London, 1968)

Erfurth, Waldemar *Die Geschichte des deutschen Generalstabes* (Götingen, 1957)

Erickson, John *The Road to Stalingrad* (Weidenfeld & Nicholson, London, 1975)

Fitzgibbon, Constantine *Denazification* (Michael Joseph, London, 1969)

Foot, M R D *SOE in France* (HMSO, London, 1966)

Galante, Pierre *Hitler Lives – and the Generals Die* (Sidgwick & Jackson, London, 1982)

Gilbert, Martin *Second World War* (Weidenfeld & Nicolson, London, 1989)

Godon, Bertram M *Collaborationism in France during the Second World War* (Cornell Univ Press, 1980)

Goerlitz, Walter *The German General Staff: Its History and Structure 1657–1945* (Hollis & Carter, London, 1953)

Griffiths, Richard *Marshal Pétain* (Constable, London, 1970)

Guderian, Heinz *Panzer Leader* (Michael Joseph, London, 1952)

Hart (Aron), W E *Hitler's Generals* (Cresset Press, London, 1944)

Hassell, Ulrich von *The von Hassell Diaries 1938–1944* (Hamish Hamilton, London, 1948)

Hawthorne, S M and the Pupils Brynteg Comprehensive School *Island Farm: Special Camp 11 for Prisoners of War* (Brynteg Comprehensive School, Bridgend, 1989)

Höhne, Heinz *Canaris* (Secker & Warburg, London, 1976)

Hoffmann, Peter *The History of the German Resistance 1933–1945* (Macdonald and Jane's, London, 1977)

Hoffmann, Peter *Hitler's Personal Security* (Macmillan, London, 1979)

Hibbert, Christopher *Benito Mussolini* (Reprint Society, London, 1963 edition)

Irving, David *The Trail of the Fox: The Life of Erwin Rommel* (Weidenfeld & Nicolson, London, 1977)

Isselin, Henri *The Battle of the Marne* (Elek, London, 1964)

Jacobsen, Hans-Adolf *Dunkirchen* (Neckargemünd, 1958)

John, Otto *Twice through the Lines* (Macmillan, London, 1972)

Keegan, John *Rundstedt* (Ballantine, NY, 1974)

Keegan, John *Opening Moves: August 1914* (Ballantine, NY, 1971)

Keitel, Wilhelm *The Memoirs of Field Marshal Keitel* (Kimber, London, 1965)

Kennedy, Maj Robert M *The German Campaign in Poland (1939)* (Department of the Army Pamphlet 20-255, Washington DC, 1956)

Kesselring, Albert *The Memoirs of Field Marshal Kesselring* (Kimber, London, 1953)

Kitchen, Martin *The German Officer Corps 1890–1914* (Clarendon Press, Oxford, 1968)

Klotz, Dr Helmut ed *The Berlin Diaries* (Jarrolds, London, 1934)

Kluck, Alexander von *The March to Paris and the Battle of the Marne 1914* (Arnold, London, 1920)

Lamb, Richard *The Ghosts of Peace 1935–1945* (Michael Russell, Salisbury, 1987)

Liddell Hart, B H *The Other Side of the Hill* (Pan Paperback, 1978 edition)

Liddell Hart, B H *The Rommel Papers* (Hamlyn Paperback, 1984 edition)

Lochner, Louis P ed & trans *The Goebbels Diaries* [1942–43] (Hamish Hamilton, London, 1948)

Lottman, Herbert R *Pétain: Hero or Traitor? The Untold Story* (Viking, London & NY, 1985)

Macksey, Kenneth *Guderian: Panzer General* (Macdonald & Jane's, London, 1975)

Manstein, F M Erich von *Lost Victories* (Arms & Armour, London, 1982 edition)

Mason, Herbert Macroy *To Kill Hitler* (Michael Joseph, London, 1979)

Mellenthin, Maj Gen F W von *Panzer Battles* (Futura paperback edition, 1977)

Messenger, Charles *Hitler's Gladiator: the Life and Times of Oberstgruppenführer and Panzergeneraloberst der Waffen-SS Sepp Dietrich* (Brassey's, London, 1988)

Moll, Otto E *Die deutschen Generalfeldmarschalle 1939–1945* (Erich Pabel Verlag, 1961)

Morgan, Brig Gen H L *Assize of Arms* (Methuen, London, 1945)

Müller, Klaus-Jürgen *The Army, Politics and Society in Germany 1933–45: Studies in the Army's Relation to Nazism* (Manchester Univ Pres, 1987)

Nash, D B *Imperial German Army Handbook 1914–1918* (Ian Allan, Shepperton, 1980)

O'Neill, Robert J *The German Army and the Nazi Party, 1933–1939* (Cassell, London, 1966)

Oppen, Beate Ruhm von ed *Documents on Germany under Occupation 1945–1954* (Oxford University Press, 1955)

Paget, R T *Manstein: his Campaigns and his Trial* (Collins, London, 1951)

Poliakov, Leon & Wulf, Josef *Das Dritte Reich und seine Diener* (Munich, 1978)

Preradovich, Nikolaus von *Die militärische und soziale Herkunft der Generalität des deutschen Heeres* (Osnabrück, 1978)

Reichsarchiv *Der Weltkrieg 1914 bis 1918 Band 1* (Berlin, 1925)

Reitlinger, Gerald *The SS: Alibi of a Nation, 1922–1945* (Arms & Armour, London, 1981 edition)

Reynolds, Nicholas *Treason was no Crime: Ludwig Beck, Chief of the German General Staff* (Kimber, London, 1976)

Rich, Norman *Hitler's War Aims: the Establishment of the New Order* (Deutsch, London, 1974)

Richardson, William & Freiden, Seymour ed *The Fatal Decisions* (Michael Joseph, London, 1956)

Ritter, Gerhard *The Sword and the Sceptre: the Problem of Militarism in Germany* Vol 2 (Allen Lane, London, 1972)

Rosinski, Herbert *The German Army* (Pall Mall, London 1966 edition)

Ruge, Friedrich *Rommel in Normandy* (Macdonald & Jane's, London, 1979)

Schall-Riancour, Heidemarie Gräfin *Aufstand und Gehrosam Offizierstum und Generalstab im Umbruch: Leben und Wirken von Generaloberst Franz Halder, Generalstabschef 1938–1942* (Wiesbaden, 1972)

Schlabrendorff, Fabian von *Revolt against Hitler* (Eyre & Spottiswoode, London, 1948)

Schweppenburg, Gen Baron Geyr von *The Critical Years* (Allan Wingate, London, 1952)

Seaton, Albert *The German Army 1933–45* (Weidenfeld & Nicolson, London, 1982)

Senger und Etterlin, F von *Neither Hope nor Fear* (Macdonald, London, 1963)

Shirer, William L *The Rise and Fall of the Third Reich* (Book Club Associates edition, 1971)

Shulman, Milton *Defeat in the West* (Secker & Warburg, London, 1986 edition)

Smith, Jean Edward ed *The Papers of General Lucius Clay: Germany 1945–1949* (Indiana Univ Press, 1974)

Speidel, Lt Gen Hans *We Defended Normandy* (Herbert Jenkins, London, 1951)

Stahlberg, Alexander *Bounden Duty: The Memoirs of a German Officer 1932–1945* (Brassey's, London, 1990)

Sullivan, Matthew Barry *Thresholds of Peace: Four Hundred Thousand German Prisoners and the People of Britain 1944–1948* (Hamish Hamilton, London, 1979)

Taylor, Telford *Sword and Swastika: the Wehrmacht in the Third Reich* (Gollancz, London, 1953)

Taylor, Telford *The March of Conquest: the German Victories in Western Europe, 1940* (Edward Hulton, London, 1959)

Taylor, Telford *The Breaking Wave: the German Defeat in the Summer of 1940* (Weidenfeld & Nicolson, London, 1967)

Tloke, Hilgegard von ed *Heeres Adjutant bei Hitler 1939–1943: Aufseichnunge des Majores Engel* (Stuttgart, 1974)

Trevor-Roper, H R ed *Hitler's War Directives 1939–1945* (Sidgwick & Jackson, London, 1964)

Tuchman, Barbara W *The Guns of August* (Constable, London, 1962)

Van Creveld, Martin *Supplying War: Logistics from Wallenstein to Patton* (Cambridge Univ Press, London, 1977)

Vogelsang, Thilo *Reichswehr, Staat und NSDAP: Beitrage zur deutschen Geschichte* (Stuttgart, 1962)

Warlimont, Walter *Inside Hitler's Headquarters 1939–1945* (Weidenfeld & Nicolson, London, 1964)

Watt, Richard M *The Kings Depart* (Weidenfeld & Nicolson, London, 1968)

Westphal, Gen Siegfried *The German Army in the West* (Collins, London, 1951)

Wheeler-Bennett, John W *The Nemesis of Power: the German Army in Politics 1918–1945* (Macmillan, London, 1953)

Whitcomb, Philip trans *France during the German Occupation 1940–1944: a Collection of 292 Statements on the Government of Maréchal Pétain and Pierre Laval* (Hoover Institute, Stanford Univ, 1958) 3 vols.

Wistrich, Robert *Who's Who in Nazi Germany* (Weidenfeld & Nicolson, London, 1982)

Zartner, Christian *Der Frankreich Feldzug 10 Mai 1940* (Berlin/Vienna 1980)

INDEX

Aa Canal 116
Aachen 22, 206, 207, 209, 210, 211, 213, 216
Abbeville 112, 180
Abetz, Otto 159, 285
Adam, Gen. Wilhelm 79, 80
Adams, Col. 295
Aire 115
Aisne, River 26, 31, 32, 110, 121
Albert 26
Albert Canal 205
Albrecht, Adm. 68
Alexandria 152
Alfieri, Dino 150
Altergrabow 51
Amiens 26, 27, 106, 126
Amos (von Rundstedt's batman) 228, 233
Anglo-German Naval Treaty (1935) 66
Anschluss 75, 251
Antonescu, Gen. Ion 136, 138, 148
Antwerp 32, 34, 37, 205, 209, 215
Arbeitstab von Rundstedt 82–3
Archangel 131
Ardennes counter-offensive 209–223
Arenberg 204
Armentiéres 113, 118
Army, British (–1918) – II Corps 25; 4 Inf. Div. 25
Army, British (1939–45) – 21st Army Gp. 204, 205, 209; Second Army 151, 191, 209, 210, 213, 225; Eighth Army 173; 3 Inf. Div. 186; 11 Armd. Div. 205; 1 Army Tk. Bde. 112; 1 SAS Regt. 256; Small Scale Raiding Force 164, 319
Army, Canadian (1939–45) – First Army 209; 2 Inf. Div. 162
Army, French (–1918) – Fourth Army 37; Fifth Army 25, 30, 31, 37; Sixth Army 26, 27, 29, 31; Seventh Army 30; Groupe d'Amade 26
Army, French (1939–45) – First Army 108, 213, 223, 226; Seventh Army 108; 4 Armd. Div. 110–11
Army, German (–1918) – First Army 21–32; Second Army 24–31; Third Army 31; Fourth Army 31; Fifth Army 31; Seventh Army 32; Nineteenth Army 37–8; *Südarmee* 36; Army Det. D. 36, 37; II Corps 21, 22, 26, 29, 30; III Corps 21, 22, 26; III Res. Corps 21; IV Corps 21, 22, 26; IV Res. Corps 21–32; IX Corps 22, 31; XI Corps 17, 21; XV Corps 18, 37, 39; XVIII Corps 16; XXV Res. Corps 36; LIII Corps 36; 7 Res. Div. 24, 25, 28; 22 Inf. Div. 4, 14, 21; 22 Res. Div. 21–32; 38 Inf. Div. 21; 86 Inf. Div. 32–3; 43 Res. Bde. 21, 22; 44 Res. Bde. 21; 5 Drag. Regt. 14; 13 Hussar Regt. 4; 11 Fd. Arty. Regt. 14; 27 Fd. Arty. Regt. 7; 80 Inf. Regt. 6; 83 Inf. Regt. 6, 9–11; 99 Inf. Regt. 18–19; 163 Inf. Regt. 6; 171 Inf. Regt. 17, 20
Army, German (1919–33) – 1 Cav. Div. 57; 2 Cav. Div. 49, 53, 57; 2 Inf. Div. 46; 3 Cav. Div. 44, 46; 3 Inf. Div. 53, 57; 9 Inf. Regt. 56; 18 Inf. Regt. 48, 52; 3 Prussian MT Bn. 52
Army, German (1933–45) – Army Gp. A 96–122; Army Gp. B 96, 97,

Army, German (1933–45) —
continued
98, 101, 113, 122, 128, 176, 179,
188, 203, 205–6, 221; Army Gp. C
96, 107, 120; Army Cp. D 133,
158–9, 160; Army Gp. G 174, 179,
205–7, 209, 214, 223, 226, 228;
Army Gp. H 211, 226; Army Gp.
Centre 131, 141, 149; Army Gp.
North 82, 83, 88, 89, 141; Army
Gp. South 83–94, 132, 133, 136,
139–57, 287; Army Gp. Upper
Rhine 223; First Army 160, 205,
223, 226; First Para. Army 205,
208, 226; First Pz. Army 152–5;
Second Army 78, 105, 107, 109,
121, 151; Third Army 84, 91;
Fourth Army 87, 105, 107, 109,
110, 113, 118; Fifth Pz. Army 205,
208, 210, 211, 213, 226; Sixth Army
125, 132, 139, 140, 153, 168, 186,
210, 211, 218–19; Seventh Army
160, 184, 188, 196, 205, 210, 226;
Eighth Army 83, 89, 92, 93; Ninth
Army 125, 126; Tenth Army 78,
83, 88, 89, 92, 93, 94; Eleventh
Army 132, 136, 141, 144, 150,
152, 153; Twelfth Army 78, 97,
107, 109, 121; Fourteenth Army
78, 83, 88, 89, 92, 93; Fifteenth
Army 160, 161, 188, 190, 192,
205, 210, 211, 213, 226; Sixteenth
Army 97, 107, 109, 121, 125, 126;
Seventeenth Army 132, 140, 151,
153, 154; Nineteenth Army 174,
198, 203, 205, 213, 226; Twenty-
Fifth Army 211; Pz. Gp. West
179, 188, 189, 205; 1st Pz. Gp.
141, 143; II Para Corps 226; III
Corps 154; XI Corps 89; XIV
Mot. Corps 104; XV Corps 107;
XVI Pz. Corps 110, 120; XIX Pz.
Corps 92, 100, 107, 110;
XXXVIII Corps 104; XLI Pz.
Corps 107, 116; XLVII Corps
195; LXXX Corps 256;
LXXXIV Corps 186; 1 Lt.
Div. 78; 1 Pz. Div. 111, 116; 2
Pz. Div. 112, 179–80, 188, 192; 4
Pz. Div. 88, 103; 5 Pz. Div. 112;
6 VG Div. 80; 7 Inf. Div. 87; 7
Pz. Div. 105, 111-12, 207; 9 Pz.
Div. 110; 10 Pz. Div 87, 162,
164, 170; 11 Pz. Div. 144, 228; 13

Pz. Div. 154; 14 Pz. Div. 154; 16
Pz. Div. 144; 18 Inf. Div. 75, 82,
84; 21 Pz. Div. 186, 188, 189, 192,
197; 27 Pz. Div. 162; 30 Inf. Div.
89; 91 Inf. Div. 192; 116 Pz. Div.
188; 352 Inf. Div. 192; 709 Inf.
Div. 192; 716 Inf. Div. 188, 189,
192; Pz. Lehr Div. 180, 185, 186,
189; 150 Pz. Bde. 218; 6 Para.
Regt. 192; 12 Arty. Regt. 76; 18
Inf. Regt. 80, 308
Army, Italian (1939–45) – Fourth
Army 167, 173; Celere Div. 167
Army, Polish – Poznan Army 88, 89
Army, Russian (–1918) – Tenth Army
33
Army, Soviet (1941)–Bryansk Front
151; South Front 143, 154; South-
West Front 143; Western Front
143; Kiev Mil. Dist. 139; Odessa
Mil. Dist. 140; Fifth Army 140,
141, 144, 145; Sixth Army 140,
141; Ninth Army 141; Eighteenth
Army 141; Twenty-Sixth Army
145
Army, US (1944–45) – 6th Army
Gp. 203, 225; 12th Army Gp.
209, 225, 233; First Army 205,
208, 209, 210, 226, 227; Third
Army 206, 226; Seventh Army
213, 223, 226, 227, 233; Ninth
Army 210, 225, 227; 5 Armd.
Div. 205; 29 Inf. Div. 309; 36
Inf. Div. 230
Arnhem 207
Arolsen 10
Arras 112, 114, 115
Aschersleben 3
Ascq 320
ASHCAN 233, 316
Atlantic Wall 159, 160, 170, 175, 177
Attlee, Clement 317
Augustdorf 308
Auxerre 125

Babi Yar 151
Baden Baden 213
Bad Kissingen 52
Bad Oeynhausen 275
Badoglio, Marshal Pietro 173
Bad Tölz 172, 199, 201, 230, 233
Bad Weissee 63
Bailleul 118

Balck, Gen. Hermann 205, 207–8, 209, 213, 223
BAOR (British Army of the Rhine) 273, 275, 289
Bassenge, Gen. Gerd 238
Bastogne 110, 221, 222, 223, 247
Bayerlein, Gen. Fritz 180
Bayeux 193
Bayreuth 230
Beck, Gen. Ludwig 66, 70–1, 75, 76, 78, 79, 82, 169, 182, 199, 316
Bedford, Conn. 309
Belaya Tserkov 144
Belfort 122, 210, 213
Bell, Bishop of Chichester 290, 291
Bellenger, Capt. Frederick 259, 264
Berchtesgaden (Obersalzberg) 84, 160, 173, 181, 193, 196, 198, 313
Berdichev 142, 145–6, 148, 149, 152, 248, 319
Beresina, River 141
Bergmann, Gen. Walter von 43
Bergues 118
Berlin 1, 21, 40, 43, 47, 52, 53, 55, 56, 63, 65, 66, 80, 82, 101, 126–7, 128, 132, 214, 223, 229, 230, 312
Bernd, Lt. Bernhard 238
Beseler, Gen. von 5, 34
Bethune 113, 115
Bevin, Ernest 259, 261, 264, 268, 273, 277-8, 280, 282, 290
Bialystok 141
Bilse, Lt. Oswald 17
Bismarck, Prince Otto von 7, 8
Bitburg 107
Bittrich, SS Obgpfr. Willi 64
Blaskowitz, Gen. Johannes 66, 83, 88, 89, 91, 93, 94, 161, 205, 223, 226, 268, 284
Bloem, Capt. Walter 25, 30
Blomberg, FM Werner von 44, 55, 60, 61, 62–3, 64, 65 67–8, 70, 71, 72, 252, 315
Blum, Dr 256
Blumentritt, Gen. Günther 54, 80, 82, 83, 99, 105, 117, 119, 122, 125, 126, 129, 132, 168, 171, 179, 186, 189, 194, 195, 197, 203–4, 237, 238, 247, 252, 253, 257, 304, 307, 310, 311
Bock, FM Fedor von 44, 57, 79, 82, 96, 97, 99, 105, 111, 115, 116, 117, 121, 125, 127, 128, 130, 132, 140, 141, 156, 241
Bordeaux 122, 165

Borgmann, Lt. Col. 198
Bormann, Martin 215, 222
Bothmer, Gen. Graf von 36, 37–8
Boulogne 124, 177, 178, 179, 183
Bradley, Gen. Omar 225
Brandenberger, Gen. Erich 205, 210, 226
Brauchitsch, FM Walther von 66, 73, 75, 76–7, 89, 91, 94, 96–106, 109, 110, 115, 116–17, 120, 123, 124, 126, 129, 131, 132, 134, 138, 143, 150, 153–4, 155, 156, 241, 246, 256, 257–8, 259, 260, 267, 270, 272–8, 282–3, 296, 313, 316, 319
Braun, Otto 56
Bredow, Gen. Ferdinand von 54
Bredow, Kurt von 63
Brennecke, Gen. Karl 118
Brenner Pass 130
Breslau 49, 66, 75, 133, 135, 136, 137
Brest-Litovsk, Treaty of (1918) 36, 37
Brighton 124
Britain, Battle of 126, 129
British Military Hospitals – No. 94 (Hamburg) 281, 292, 295; No. 99 (Stafford) 257, 267
Brody 143
Brozi, Lt. Col. 16
Brüning, Heinrich 53, 54, 56
Brusilov, Gen. 34, 36
Brussels 22, 24
Bryansk 153
Budenny, Marshal Semyon 143, 151, 241
Bülow, Gen. Karl von 24–32
Bug, River 33, 94, 140
Burgdorf, Gen. Wilhelm 200, 208
Burke, 2Lt. Joseph 230–1
Busch, FM Ernst 77, 97, 101, 103, 106, 121, 125, 126, 181, 234, 235
Bzura, Battle of 90, 92

Caen 160, 186, 188, 192, 193, 195, 197
Calais 113, 219
Calvacoressi, Peter 251–2
Cambrai 111
Canal Du Nord 112
Canaris, Adm. Wilhelm 78, 86, 92
Carentan 192
Casablanca 168
Cassel 118
Cassibile 173
Caumont 195
Chajn, Lean 288

Chamberlain, Neville 77, 79
Charles Edward Stuart (the Young
  Pretender) 1
Charles X of Sweden 2
Charles XII of Sweden 2
Charleville 115, 116, 121, 132
Chartres 186, 189
Chelm 93
Cherbourg 124, 189, 191, 193, 194,
  195, 197, 205
Christiansen, Gen. Friedrich 159, 160,
  211, 213
Churchill, Winston 79, 135, 164, 168,
  277, 286
Clay, Gen. Lucius 258, 262, 268, 281
Clements, Lt. Col. Charles 265–6, 271
Cleve 226
Colmar 17–20, 213, 226
Cologne 225, 227
Commando/Parachutist Orders 163–5,
  251, 257, 259, 279, 284, 287, 318–19
Commissar Order 134, 137–8, 249,
  259, 279, 318–19
Comyns Clark, Sir Arthur 299
Construction Bn 800 86
Convention of Tauroggen (1811) 311
Cort, David 221
Cracow 83, 88, 89
Crimea 149, 152
CROWCASS (Central Registry of War
  Crimes and Security Suspects)
  233, 252, 255
Cummings, A. J. 269
Cunningham, Adm. Viscount 318
Czestochowa 88

Dachau 248
Daladier, Edouard 77
Danube, River 85
Danzig 21
Dawes Plan 49
De Gaulle, Charles 111
De L'Isle and Dudley, Lord 279
De Luce, Daniel 305, 306
Delmer, Sefton 255
Dempsey, Gen. Sir Miles 209
Denazification 293–301
Devers, Gen. Jacob 225
Dieppe 126, 170, 183
Dieppe Raid 161–4
Dietrich, SS Obstgpfr. Sepp 154, 156,
  157, 162–3, 186, 189, 199, 210, 214,
  218–19, 222

Diez 5
Dinant 107
Dnieper, River 132, 137, 140, 145, 150,
  152, 153
Dniester, River 36, 143
Doenitz, Grand Adm. Karl 165, 196
Dollmann, Gen. Friedrich 123, 184,
  189, 196, 198
Donat, Gen. Hans von 286–7
Donets, River 153
Douglas, MRAF Sir Sholto (later
  Lord) 261–3, 264
Dover 124
Draper, Lt. Col. Gerald (later Col.
  Prof.) 286, 287, 288, 299
Dresden 43, 83
Dreux 162
Düsseldorf 210, 225, 227
Du Gard, Martin 166, 183
Dulles, Allen 182
Dunkirk 118–19, 126, 232
DUSTBIN 233
Dusterberg, Col. Theodor 53

Ebert, Friedrich 39, 40, 43
Edmonds, Brig. Gen. Sir James 5, 13
Eicke, SS Obgpfr. Theodor 91, 112
Eisenhower, Gen. Dwight 173, 184,
  206, 207, 218, 222
Elbe, River 230
Eliot, T. S. 278
Elwyn-Jones, Frederick (later
  Lord) 260, 262, 264, 269, 288, 295
Elzborn, Gen. 46
Engel, Maj. Gerhard 115, 118, 119,
  156, 169, 171, 314
Eperon, Arthur 305
Erfurt 230
Etzdorf, Hasso von 99
Exner, Dr 246

Falaise 203
Falkenhausen, Gen. Nikolaus von 159,
  182, 183, 249
Falley, Gen. Wilhelm 192
Feuchtinger, Gen. Edgar 186, 188, 192
Fichtenhain 210
Fismes 32
Fontainebleu 161
Foot, Michael 279
Förtsch, Gen. 226
Forbach 17
Forstner, Lt. Freiherr von 18–19

Franco, Gen. Francisco 84, 130
François-Poncet, André 65
Frank, Hans 94
Frankfurt-am-Main 4, 81
Frankfurt-am-Oder 57
Franks, Sir (later Lord) Oliver 279
Frederick I of Prussia 2
Frederick II (The Great) of Prussia 2, 15, 106, 310
Frederick III, Kaiser 4, 7
Frederick William, King of Prussia 311
Freikorps 40, 41, 43, 44
Freisler, Roland 201, 202
French Resistance 160, 165, 174, 178, 185, 195, 320
Frick, Wilhelm 59
Fritsch, Gen. Werner Freiherr von 61, 63, 65, 66, 68, 70–6, 82, 311, 314, 316
Fromm, Gen. Friedrich 199
Frontiers, Battle of 24
Funck, Gen. Hans von 195

Gallenkamp, Gen. Kurt 257
Gamelin, Marshal Maurice 109
Gehrden 298
Geilenkirchen 210
Gennevillers 161
George V, King of Britain 68, 109, 315
George VI, King of Britain 304
German–Soviet Non-Aggression Pact (1939) 85, 87
Gilbert, G. M. 247
Goebbels, Josef 154, 160, 169, 174, 199, 208, 228, 229, 312
Goerdeler, Dr Hans 78, 182
Goering, Hermann 59, 63, 66, 71, 73, 75, 115, 118, 119, 123, 126, 129, 159, 196
Goerlitz, Walter 311
Goisern 128
Gollancz, Victor 279, 284, 287
Gorki 131
Gotha 230
Gravelines 116, 117, 126
Gravell, Dean 271
Greiffenberg, von 115
Grimm, Dr Walter 285, 292, 296
Grizedale Hall (No. 1 PW Camp) 234, 238–43
Groener, Gen. Wilhelm 40, 41, 42, 50, 53

Gronau, Gen. von 29, 30
Grondona, Col. L. St Claire 235–6, 238
Groscurth, Helmut 169
Grosse Generalstab 14–16, 22, 40, 41
Grosse Lichterfelde 4–5
Guderian, Gen. Heinz 48, 50, 52, 69, 77, 92, 100–1, 106, 108, 109–12, 121–2, 150, 157, 200, 223, 286, 309
Guetler, Hans 255
Guise, Battle of 26
Gustavus Adolphus 2
Gyldenfeldt, von 113, 116

Hahnke, Gen. 7
Halder, Gen. Franz 73, 78, 79, 85, 91, 96, 97, 99, 101, 105, 108, 109, 110, 111, 113–15, 116–17, 118, 119, 120, 121, 122, 124, 126, 129, 131, 132, 133, 136, 138, 141, 144, 145, 149, 150, 153, 155, 168, 202, 237, 241, 248, 259
Halle 3
Hamburg 253, 281, 289, 299
Hammerstein-Equord, Gen. Kurt Freiherr von 44, 54, 55, 57, 61, 316
Hanke, Karl 137
Hannover 6, 266, 270, 293, 303, 306
'Hart, W. E.' 46, 48, 222, 242
Harz Mts 1, 3, 230
Hasler, Lt. Col. 'Blondie' 165
Hassell, Ulrich von 78, 80, 99, 137
Hastings 124
Hausser, SS Obgpfr. Paul 64, 162, 170, 194, 197, 226
Hays, Gen. George 293, 297, 298
Heinrici, Gen. Siegfried 242
Helldorf, Heinrich Graf von 71
Helmstedt 1
Hemmler, Col. von 38
Henderson, Lord 285, 291, 296
Hennigs, Col. von 11
Hentsch, Col. 29, 31
Heringen, Gen. von 12
Herrlingen 208
Hertz, Dr 233
Hess, Rudolf 62
Hesse, Prof. Dr Kurt 303
Hewel, Walther 145
Heydrich, Reinhard 63, 91, 146, 200
Heye, Gen. Wilhelm 49, 55
Hillgruber, Andreas 310

Himmler, Heinrich   63, 71, 72, 92, 151,
  159, 222, 319
Hindenburg, FM Paul von   33, 40, 42,
  49, 53, 56, 59, 63, 311, 315
Hitler, Adolf   47, 49, 53, 55, 57, 58, 59,
  60, 62, 62–80, 81, 83–6, 91, 93, 94,
  96, 97–107, 110, 111, 115 22, 123,
  124, 126, 127, 129–37, 143, 145,
  149–52, 153, 154–7, 159, 160, 162,
  163, 164–9, 173–6, 179, 181–2, 184,
  185–6, 188, 191, 192, 193–201, 202,
  205, 208–17, 221, 226, 228–9,
  245–6, 249, 255, 260, 305, 311, 315,
  316, 319
Höflich, Sgt.   18
Hoare, Sir Samuel   182
Hodges, Gen. Courtney   206, 208, 226
Hoepner, Gen. Erich   79, 110, 122, 201
Honour, Prussian Code of   8–9, 17, 72
Hore-Belisha, Leslie   240
Horrocks, Gen. Sir Brian   254
Horthy, Adm. Miklos   232
Hossbach, Col. Friedrich   71, 72
Hoth, Gen. Hermann   107, 109, 111–
  12, 118, 149
Hübner, SS Gpfr. Rudolf   228
Hürtgen Forest   208
Hutchinson, Joseph   240

Ilse, Col.   16
Iltenau   91
IMT (International Military Tribunal)
  233, 246–52, 256, 258, 260, 268,
  314, 316, 317
Inter-Allied Military Control
  Commission   43
International Red Cross   238, 267, 280,
  286
Irtel (von Rundstedt's driver)   228,
  233, 298
Island Farm, Bridgend (No 11 PW
  Camp)   243, 246, 247, 252–6, 257,
  265–6, 267, 271

Jablunka Pass   87
Jellicoe, Earl   266
Jena   230
Jeschonnek, Gen. Hans   118, 119
Jodl, Gen. Albert   115, 117, 131, 156,
  180, 189, 191, 192, 193, 194, 196,
  209–10, 214, 233, 245, 246
Joffre, Marshal Joseph   26
John, Otto   255, 281, 286, 287

Johnson, Nunnally   306
Jowitt, Viscount   262, 264–5, 273, 284,
  290
Jüterbog   77
July 1944 Bomb Plot   199–202, 237,
  255, 308, 312, 314

Kaltenbrunner, Ernst   200
Kampisch, Gen.   68
Kapp Putsch   43–4, 55, 251, 312
Kapp, Dr Walther   43–4
Kassel   6, 9, 17, 40, 48, 80, 96, 152,
  156, 164, 230, 249, 292
Katowice   88, 92
Keisel, Obstbnfhr. Dr Georg   202
Keitel, FM Wilhelm   63, 67, 71, 73, 74,
  82, 92, 98, 100, 111, 123, 126, 129,
  144, 156, 176, 184, 186, 191, 193,
  196, 197–8, 200, 202, 208, 233, 245,
  252, 313, 316
Kerensky, Alexander   36
Kesselring, FM Albert   176, 204,
  228–9, 260
Kharkov   152
Kiel   38, 42
Kiev   131, 140, 143–4, 145, 150, 151,
  248
Kingston, Capt. F. S.   241
Kirchheim, Gen. Heinrich   201
Kirkpatrick, Sir Ivone   282
Kirovograd   145
Kirponos, Gen. M. P.   140, 141, 151
Kleist, Col. von   37
Kleist, FM Ewald von   53, 66, 107–8,
  109–10, 113, 116, 118, 132, 135,
  136, 140, 141, 143, 145, 150, 151,
  152, 153, 154–5, 160, 181, 238, 241,
  247, 252
Kleist-Schmenzin, Maj. Ewald von
  78–9
Klotz, Dr Helmut   54
Kluck, Gen. Alexander von   21–32, 96
Kluge, FM Hans von   75, 97, 105, 114,
  115, 116, 117–18, 169, 176, 198,
  199, 203
Knobelsdorff, Gen. Otto von   205
Königsberg   66, 70
Koblenz   5, 27, 96, 100, 101, 104, 106,
  107, 162
Kock   94
Kolberg   41
Kopf, Heinrich   302
Krancke, Adm.   159

Krebs, Gen. Hans 209
Kressenstein, Gen. Kress von 75
Kretschmer, Cdr. Otto 238
Kriegsakademie, Berlin 10–14
Krosigk, Count Schwerin von 54
Kruse, Gen. Kurt 236
Krushchev, Nikita 151
Küchler, FM Georg von 75, 91, 181, 262
Küstrin 13, 57
Kursk 173
Kutno 90, 93, 116
Kutrzeba, Gen. 90

La Roche Guyon 194
Lammers, Dr Hans 157
Landrecies 25
Landsberg 286
Lanzerac, Gen. Charles 25, 26
Laternser, Dr Hans 246, 247, 250, 252, 287, 299
Lattre de Tassigny, Gen. Jean de 223
Laval, Pierre 167, 174
Law on the Provisional Reichswehr 41
Lawrence, Lord Justice 246
Le Cateau 25, 110
Le Havre 124
Le Touquet 126
Leeb, FM Wilhelm von 44, 47, 63, 75, 78, 81, 89, 96, 99, 120, 123, 132, 138, 151, 232, 241, 262, 284
Lees, Capt. Ted 247, 252, 257, 270
Leipzig 73, 83, 157
Lemberg 33
Leningrad 131, 137, 149, 151
Lens 113, 115
Lequis, Gen. Arnold von 39
Leverkühn, Dr 246
Ley, Dr Robert 127
Liddell Hart, Capt. (later Sir) Basil 46, 54, 55, 79, 121, 125, 202, 208, 229, 238, 240–4, 267, 271, 272, 274, 275, 276, 277, 280, 281, 283, 284, 285, 286, 288, 289, 296, 302–3, 304, 305–6, 308, 317, 319
Liege 210
Liegnitz 82, 86
Linde, Gen. 14
Lindemann, Gen. Georg 181
Linz 84
List, FM Siegmund 78, 83, 88, 97, 105, 108, 109, 121, 122, 130, 232
Lodz 83

Loire, River 160
Lokhvitsa 151
Louvain 22
Lübeck 292
Lüttwitz, Gen. Walter Freiherr von 43–4, 55
Lublin 88, 140
Ludendorff, Gen. Erich von 37
Luftwaffe – Luftflotte 2 102; Luftflotte 3 159
Lutze, Viktor 62
Lvov 92, 93, 140, 141
Lyme Bay 124, 128
Lyons 122

Maas, River 211, 213
Maastricht 210
Macaskie, Mr 258, 262
Mackensen, Gen. Eberhard von 154, 269
Maclean, Fitzroy 268
Madrid 182
Maginot Line 96
Maikop 153
Mainz 4
Maisel, Gen. Ernst 208
Malmédy 219, 249
Mannheim 225
Manstein, FM Erich von 75, 82, 84–5, 87, 88, 89, 90, 94, 97–104, 134, 152, 169, 181, 241, 244, 246, 256, 257, 258, 261, 262, 267, 268, 270, 272, 273–4, 276, 278, 281, 283, 284, 287, 288–92, 294, 295, 299, 300, 310, 312, 313, 320
Manteuffel, Gen. Hasso von 205, 214, 218, 219, 222, 223, 226, 237
Manteuffel, Gen. von 13
Marazzini, Gen. 167
March, Frederic 302
March-Phillipps, Maj. Gus 164
Marcks, Gen. Erich 130–1, 186
MARCO, Operation 284–91, 295, 299, 318
Mareuil 31
Margival Conference 193–4, 302
Marne, Battle of 27–31
Marsden-Smedley, Basil 271
Marseilles 122, 167
Maruipol 152
Marwitz, Gen. Georg von der 25, 26
Mason, James 302
Matter, Gen. Freiherr von 20

Mauberge 24, 32
Maunoury, Gen. Michel-Joseph 26,
30–1, 32
Mayen 105
Mayer, Col. von 9
McAuliffe, Gen. Anthony 221
Mechelen 102, 105
Mein Kampf 130
Meindl, Gen. Eugen 226
Mellenthin, Gen. Friedrich von 160,
207, 208, 214
Memel 81
Messe, Marshal Giovanni 136, 150,
234
Metz 17, 193, 209, 213
Meuse, River 104, 106, 107, 108, 218,
222
Mius, River 155
Mock, Dr 171–2
Model, FM Walter 181, 203, 205, 209–
10, 214, 219, 226, 228, 229, 241
Moltke, FM Helmuth von (The
Elder) 6, 159, 247, 250
Moltke, Gen. Helmuth von (The
Younger) 14–17, 22, 27, 29
Moltke, Helmuth von 182
Mondor Les Bains 232
Mons, Battle of 24–5
Montcornet 111
Montgomery, FM Viscount 151, 162,
173, 195, 205, 206, 207, 209, 221,
222, 225, 227, 230, 234, 245, 254
Monthermé 107
Mortain 203
Morton, Lt. Col. Ryn 238, 242
Moscow 131, 137, 140, 149, 151, 152,
156, 163, 181
Moselle, River 206, 207, 227
Mountbatten, Earl 162
Müller, Hermann 53
Müller, Klaus-Jürgen 85
Müller-Hillebrand, Gen. B. 237
Mulde, River 230
Mulhouse 17
Munich 21, 46, 49, 82, 84, 99
Munsterlager 273, 275–6, 278, 281,
282, 289
Murray, Prof. Gilbert 277, 281, 284
Mussolini, Benito 69, 84, 86, 87, 130,
135, 149, 173

Nancy 206
Narew, River 33

Navy, German (1939–45) – Group
West 159, 165
Nawrocky, Lt. Col. 303
Neave, Airey 252
Nedda, Krug von 166
Needham, J. 295, 298, 299, 300
Neisse 84, 86
Neubronn, Gen. Alexander Freiherr
von 167, 174, 182
Neuhammer 84, 149
Neurath, Konstantin Freiherr von 54,
68, 70
Newton, Lorna 274
Niedermann, Paul 281
Niemöller, Pastor 249
Night of the Long Knives 54, 63–4,
315
Nightingale, R. A. 275
Nijmegen 213, 225
Nikotow 88
Nordstadt Hospital 293, 295
Noske, Gustav 40, 42, 43–4
Noyon 32

O'Meara, Brig. F. J. 289
Oberg, Carl 159
Obersalzberg, see under Berchtesgaden
Obstfelder, Gen. Hans von 223
Oder River 57, 230
Odessa 150, 152
Odhams Publishing House 303
Office of Strategic Services (OSS) 182
Ohlendorff, SS Gpfr. Otto 286
Oise, River 26–7, 109
Olbricht, Gen. Friedrich 199–200
Operations, Allied –
AQUATINT 164;
BLACKCOCK 225;
BLOCKBUSTER 225, 227;
BULBASKET 256; DYNAMO
118–19; EPSOM 195, 197;
FRANKTON 165, 319;
GRENADE 225; VERITABLE
225, 226; MARKET-GARDEN
206–7, 209, 213; RUTTER (later
JUBILEE) 162–4; STARKEY
174; VERITABLE 225, 225
Operations, German – ANTON 166–
7; BARBAROSSA 132–3, 132–57;
Bodenplatte 223; Case Green
76–7; Case Red 115, 118, 119,
120–2; Case White 81–93; Case
Yellow 96–120, 124; CITADEL

173; FELIX 130; MARITA 135; *Nordwind* 222, 223; OTTO 131; SEALION 124–9; TYPHOON 152–3, 156; WATCH ON THE RHINE 215–25
Oppershausen 302, 303
Oradour 195, 238
Oranienberg 248
Oranienstein 5
Orne, River 186, 191
Ostend 113, 124, 126
Oster, Gen. Hans 78, 99
Ott, Lt.-Col. Eugen 312
Ourq, River 29–30
Overseas Reconstruction Committee (ORC) 270–1, 273, 277, 281

Paderborn 48
Paget, Reginald (later Lord) 282, 290, 296, 299
Pakenham, Lord (now Earl of Longford) 263–4, 266
Pantcheff, Maj. 'Bunny' 237
Papen, Franz von 53–7, 58, 60
Paris 26, 27, 40, 106, 120–1, 125, 158, 161, 182
Parmoor, Baron 278
Pas de Calais 177, 178, 179, 188
Patch, Gen. Alexander 223, 227, 230
Patton, Gen. George 206, 207, 209, 213, 221, 222, 226, 227, 318
Paul, Prince of Yugoslavia 135
Paulus, FM Friedrich 131, 149, 169, 181, 263–4
Pétain, Marshal Philippe 68, 124, 164, 166–7, 169, 174–5, 183, 312
Peace Pledge Union 290
Peiper, Obstfhr. Joachim 218–19
Peipus, Lake 36
Perré, Jean 166
Pervomaysk 145
Peter, King of Yugoslavia 135
Pilica, River 88
Plan D 108
Ploesti oilfield 136, 149
Poitiers 256
Polish Corridor 41, 83, 91
Poltava 153, 156
Poltava, Battle of 2
Portsmouth 124, 183
Potapov, Gen. M. I. 144, 145
Potsdam 43

Pozen 128
Pripet Marshes 131, 132, 139, 140, 143, 144, 146
Priss, M. L. 301
Proskurov 145
Przemysl 33, 89, 92

Radom 89
Raeder, Grand Adm. Erich 66, 124, 126, 159, 196
Rambouillet 183
Rapp, Walter 281
Rastenburg 137, 150, 158, 199, 209, 214
Ratzeburg 42, 292
Reading, Marquess of 284
Redgrave Hall (231 PW Hospital) 272–4
Reichenau, FM Walter von 61, 63, 67, 71, 73, 77, 83, 85, 88, 92, 97, 101, 125, 132, 136, 139, 140, 144, 145, 147–8, 153, 155, 157, 241, 251
Reichswald 225, 226
Reimann, Gen. von 30
Reims 32, 37, 121, 203
Reinhardt, Gen. Georg-Hans 88, 89, 107, 109, 111, 116
Reinhardt, Gen. Walther 41, 43, 48
Remagen 227–8
Remer, Maj. Otto 199, 312
Rennes 184, 192
Renthe-Fink, Cecil von 166
Reuter, Col. 19
Rhine, River 205, 206, 212, 213, 225, 226, 227
Rhineland 72
Rhineland, reoccupation of 67
Rhône, River 167
Richthofen, Gen. Freiherr von 36
Ridgway, Ernie 239
Riemann, Lt. Gen. von 21, 22
Robertson, Gen. Sir Brian 259, 262, 264, 266, 268, 269, 271, 276–7, 278, 281, 285, 295, 298, 299
Roermond 225
Rohde, SS Bdefr. Ernst 249
Rome 173
Rommel, FM Erwin 105, 112, 116, 168, 173, 176–83, 189, 190–1, 193–8, 204, 207, 208, 221, 247, 252, 302–3
Rommel, Gen. (Polish) 92
Roosevelt, Franklin D. 168

Roques, Gen. von 272
Rosenberg, Alfred 146
Rostov-on-Don 131, 154, 163
Rouen 188
RSHA (*Reichs Sicherheitshauptamt*) 146, 200, 202
Ruge, Adm. Friedrich 181, 208, 209
Rundstedt, Adelheid von (von Rundstedt's mother) 3, 42, 123
Rundstedt, Barbara von (von Rundstedt's grandchild – later Papanastassiou) 65, 256, 267, 306, 309
Rundstedt, Bila (Luise) von (von Rundstedt's wife) 12, 48, 52, 65, 96, 102, 127, 128, 133, 141, 143, 145, 148, 149, 150–1, 152, 153, 156, 158, 161, 162, 164, 168, 172–3, 199, 228, 229–31, 233, 249, 267, 270, 275, 281, 289, 292, 296, 299, 301, 304, 306
Rundstedt, Ditha (Editha) von (von Rundstedt's daughter-in-law) 65, 72, 84, 126, 128, 157, 161, 172, 208, 230, 256, 276, 279, 281, 297, 298, 302, 303, 304, 308
Rundstedt, Eberhard von (von Rundstedt's brother) 3–4, 6, 39, 42
Rundstedt, Eberhard von (von Rundstedt's grandson) 128, 255, 298
Rundstedt, Editha von (von Rundstedt's granddaughter – later Vogler) 161, 255
Rundstedt, FM Gerd von
  Acting ability 4, 5, 245
  Allied views of 148–9, 173, 177, 190, 204, 221–2, 232, 236–7, 238, 309
  Approach of WW2, attitude to 68–9, 85, 87
  Ardennes Counter-Offensive 213–23, 236, 247
  Artistic ability 3, 254
  Blumentritt's biography of 303, 304, 305
  Captivity, conduct in 231, 232, 235–7, 238–41, 253–4, 265–6, 271, 275–6, 316–17
  Chain of command, belief in 78, 101, 103, 177, 313
  Conviviality 309
  Coolness under fire 108

Courtesy 256, 309
Death of son, reactions to 267, 270
Decorations 9, 17, 32, 34, 36, 38, 94, 123, 198, 226, 229, 315
Defence of the West 170–1, 175–80, 188–9, 191–5, 204–9, 232
Denazification, problems of 293–301
Depression 34, 133, 149–50, 169, 171, 190–1, 270, 275, 287, 292, 296, 302, 309
Diligence 10, 11, 12, 16, 47
Diplomacy 109–10, 136, 167, 173, 237
Dismissals by Hitler 155–6, 197–9, 228–9, 233
Duty, concept of 158, 204, 314
Family relationships 12, 48, 51–2, 152, 158, 270, 304, 309
Fellow commanders, views on 60–1, 72, 74, 111, 123, 127, 210
Finances 10, 157, 294, 303–4, 306
Fritsch Affair 71–6
Halt orders, France 1940 109, 113–20
Health 32, 34, 48, 154, 171–2, 198, 230, 242, 256, 257, 268, 270, 289, 290, 297, 304, 309, 313–14
Hitler, relations with 55, 60, 67–8, 72–5, 150, 157–9, 173, 182, 191, 192, 193–5, 203–4, 205, 208–9, 210, 222, 228, 245, 247, 312, 313, 315–16
Honour, concept of 8–9, 17, 72, 76, 201–2, 312, 314
Horsemanship 10, 46, 47, 48–9
Humour 4, 34, 125, 241, 254, 305
Impatience 101, 150, 162, 183
IMT Nuremberg 246–52
Intellect 309
Irascibility 122, 171, 249, 250, 287
Lifestyle 46, 65, 102, 125, 128, 129, 151, 161, 213, 306
Modesty 11, 16, 308
Moral courage 310
Nazi race policy, attitude to 62
Pétain, relations with 164, 166–7, 169, 174–5, 183
Plots against Hitler, attitude to 60, 79, 99–100, 125, 137, 169, 171, 182, 191, 200–2, 221, 237, 241, 243, 303, 311, 312–14
Politics 44, 54, 57, 61, 72, 166, 190, 251, 312–13, 315–16
Popularity 10, 11, 34, 38, 47, 269

Publicity, shuns 127, 177, 302
Religious faith 308
Rommel, relations with 176–84,
190–1, 208
Rommel Desert Fox, and 302–6
Russia, campaign in, attitude
to 121, 132, 137, 138, 141, 143–4,
152, 153–4, 248–9
SEALION, and 125–9
Stoicism 235, 309
Tank warfare, views on 50, 69, 103,
250
Waffen-SS commanders, views
on 219, 254
War crimes, connection with 87, 90–
1, 97, 134, 137–8, 145–8, 151–2,
160–1, 163–5, 171, 178–9, 213, 219,
233, 238, 248–50, 251, 256–7, 258
passim, 317–20
Rundstedt, Gerd Arnold Konrad von
(von Rondstedt's father) 3, 5
Rundstedt, Gerd von (von Rundstedt's
grandson) 72, 249, 256, 281, 304,
320
Rundstedt, Hans Gerd von (von
Rundstedt's son) 12, 51, 54, 65,
106, 123, 127, 161, 172, 199, 204,
228, 230, 234, 237, 238, 247, 253,
255, 266–7, 270
Rundstedt, Joachim von (von
Rundstedt's brother) 3, 6, 39, 42,
225
Rundstedt, Udo von (von Rundstedt's
brother) 3, 4, 6, 39, 42, 292, 301

SA (*Sturmabteilungen*) 55, 61–2, 315
Saar, River 213, 227
Salerno 173
Salmuth, Gen. Hans von 189
Salviati, Capt. von 125, 137, 151, 171
Sambre, River 25
San, River 88, 89, 93, 94
Sargent, Sir Orme 264, 277
Sark, Isle of 164
Sauckel, Fritz 178, 213
Sauer, River 206
Saverne Gap 223
Schacht, Hjalmar 78
Scheldt, River 183, 205, 207, 209
Schiedemann, Philipp 49
Schlabrendorff, Fabian von 60
Schleicher, Gen. Kurt von 53–4, 55,
56, 58, 59, 63, 311, 312, 315

Schlemm, Gen. Alfred 184, 226, 227
Schlieffen, Count Alfred von 15–16,
22, 32
Schloss Ziegenberg 215, 228
Schmundt, Gen. Rudolf 115, 156, 157,
168, 181, 193, 198, 200, 263
Schobert, Gen. Ritter von 132, 136,
138, 141, 143, 152, 251
Schulenburg, Gen. Friedrich Graf
von 71
Schuschnigg, Kurt von 251
Schweppenburg, Gen. Geyr von 67,
159, 179, 195, 197, 198
Scotland, Lt. Col. A. P. 237
SD (*Sicherheitsdienst*) 91
Sedan 99, 100, 105, 106, 107, 108
Seeckt, Gen. Hans von 43, 44, 46, 49–
50, 51, 55, 85, 311
Seidel, Gen. Hans Georg von 265
Seine, River 26, 133, 188
Senger und Etterlin, Gen. Frido
von 204, 254, 255, 272
Serre, River 109
Severing, Karl 56
Seydlitz-Kurzbach, Gen. Walter
von 181, 263–4
Seyss-Inquart, Arthur 159
Shapcott, Brig. H. 236, 238, 271, 274,
285
Shawcross, Sir Hartley (now Lord)
258–9, 260, 262, 264, 270, 273, 282,
285
Shinwell, Emanuel (later Lord) 264,
267–8, 270, 272, 277, 278, 282, 289,
290
Shulman, Milton 119, 125, 137, 197,
244–6
Siebourg, Gen. 37
Sieg im Westen 127
Siegler, Dr Freiherr von 304
Silkin, Sam (later Lord) 299
Simpson, Gen. Sir Frank 299
Simpson, Gen. William 225, 227
Simpson, J. L. 298
Sitwell, Osbert 278
Skorzeny, Otto 218–19, 233
Sluch, River 146
Smith-Dorrien, Gen. Sir Horace 25
Smolensk 145
Sodenstern, Gen. Georg von 85, 105,
106, 109, 110, 115, 117, 121, 125,
132, 135, 155–6, 174, 198, 310
Soissons 31, 121, 203

Sokolovsky, Marshal   269
Soldatensender Calais   219
Solz   229, 275, 293, 296, 298, 299
Somme, River   25, 110, 121, 177, 178, 180
Sordet, Gen.   25
Southampton   183
Spa   232
Spartacists   40
Special Operations Executive (SOE)   163
Speer, Albert   159, 212
Speidel, Gen. Hans   183, 186, 189, 190, 194, 199, 202, 208, 209
Sperrle, FM Hugo   159, 178, 284
SS Einsatzgruppen   92, 95, 145–6, 148, 151, 248, 263, 264, 285, 287, 319
SS Totenkopfverbände   91
St Etienne   174
St Germain-en-Laye   125, 129, 137, 161, 169, 172, 198
St Laurent   164
St Nazaire   160
St Omer   113, 116, 117
St Quentin   110, 111
St Trond   22
St Vith   219
Stahlberg, Alexander   312
Stalin, Josef   130, 131, 139, 151
Stalingrad   153, 168, 169, 170, 181, 182
Stara Konstantinov   144, 145
Stauffenburg, Col. Claus von   199–200, 312
Stavelot   219
Steiner, SS Obgrpfr. Felix   64
Stendal   1
Stettin   21, 47–8, 66
Stewart, Michael (later Lord)   283
Stieff, Gen. Helmuth   201
Stokes, Richard   279, 282, 283, 284, 297
Strang, Sir William   261
Strasbourg   17, 18
Strasser, Dr Ernst   308
Strauss, Gen. Rudolf   125, 258, 261, 265, 270, 272, 273, 274, 278, 279, 281, 283, 284, 288–95
Stülpnagel, Gen. Joachim von   44
Stülpnagel, Gen. Karl-Heinrich von   132, 140, 159, 161
Stülpnagel, Gen. Otto von   71, 151, 152, 161, 182, 183, 200, 268

Student, Gen. Karl   205, 208, 211, 226, 253
Stuttgart   21, 42
Sudetenland   78–80
Sullivan, Matthew Barry   240

Taganrog   153
Tannenburg, Battle of   84
Tarnopol   146
Tarnow   141
Taylor, Prof. Telford   98, 256, 258, 260–1, 262, 264, 270, 274, 317
The Hague   161
Thoma, Freiherr von   10
Thoma, Gen. Wilhelm Ritter von   179, 234, 235, 238
Thomas, Elgiva   256
Thomas, Gen. Georg   99–100
Three Power Moscow Declaration (1943)   288
Timoshenko, Marshal Semyon   139, 151
Tirlemont   22
Todt, Fritz   159
Tomaszow   94
Tongres   22
Topham, Maj. Denis   244, 253, 271
Toulouse   174
Tresckow, Gen. Henning von   99
Trevelyan, John   238
Trier   206
Tripartite Pact (1940)   130
Trott, Adam von   182, 183, 229
Truppengeneralstab   14
Tuchachevsky, Marshal Mikhail   57
Tyulenev, Gen. I. V.   140, 141–2
20th Century Fox   302, 305

Ulm   208
Uman   145, 150
UNWCC (United Nations War Crimes Commission)   261, 266
US Military Academy West Point   321

Venlo   213
Vercellino, Gen. Mario   168, 173
Verdun   109
Versailles   218
Versailles, Treaty of   42, 47, 49, 51, 66, 91
Vesle, River   31
Victor Emmanuel, King of Italy   173
Vienna   83

Vienna Award (1940) 135
Vimy 118
Vinnitsa 140, 143, 145
Vire 191
Vishbek 266
Vistula, River 89, 92, 93, 215, 223, 225
Voronezh 153
Voroshilovgrad 155
Voss, Adm. Hans 253
Vyazma 153

Waal, River 213
Waffen-SS (formerly SS-VT) – I SS Pz.
  Corps 162, 186, 189, 195, 197,
  211, 219; II SS Pz. Corps 194,
  207, 211; XII SS Pz. Corps 204; 1
  SS Pz. Div. (Leibstandarte) 65,
  83, 88, 91, 110, 119, 154, 155, 162,
  163, 170, 186, 192, 195, 218–19; 2
  SS Pz. Div. (Das Reich) 162, 170,
  195, 238; 3 SS Pz. Div. (Totenkopf)
  112; 9 SS Pz. Div. (Hohenstaufen)
  170; 10 SS Pz. Div. (Frundsberg)
  170; 12 SS Pz. Gren. Div.
  (Hitlerjugend) 186, 189, 192; 17
  SS Pz. Gren. Div. (Götz von
  Berlichingen) 185, 230; SS-
  VTMot. Div. 110; SS
  Deutschland 91; SS
  Germania 91; SS Arty Regt. 91
Wagner, Gen. Eduard 90
Waldersee, Count von 15
Waldersee, Maj. Count von 169
Wall Street Crash 53
Wallendorf 206
Warlimont, Gen. Walter 131, 173
Warsaw 33, 34, 37, 83, 89, 92–3, 94,
  103, 288
Warthe, River 88
Wasnerin 173
WCIU (War Crimes Investigation
  Unit) 237, 275
Weichs, FM Maxmilian von 75, 77,
  105, 121, 151, 181, 241
Weimar 40, 41, 230

Werl 269, 299
Wernitz, Gen. von 34
Werra, Capt. Franz von 238
West Wall 85, 205, 206, 208, 225, 227
Westphal, Gen. Siegfried 204, 206,
  207, 209, 214–15, 223, 246, 247, 309
Weygand Line 121
Wheeler-Bennett, Sir John 259, 285
Wiesbaden 233
Wiese, Gen. Friedrich 203, 205
Wietersheim, Gen. Gustav von 104,
  107
Wilhelm II, Kaiser 7–8, 19, 38
Wilhelmina, Queen of Netherlands 10
Wilhelmshöhe 40
William of Orange 1
William, Crown Prince of Prussia 49
William, Prince of Prussia 125
Wilmot, Chester 305
Wilton Park (No. 11 PW Camp) 179,
  234–8
Witzleben, FM Erwin von 63, 66, 78,
  79, 82, 85, 123, 133, 158, 182, 201
Wöhler, Gen. Otto 272
Worthing 128
Worysch, Udo von 82
Wright, Lord 261
Wuppertal 256

Yorck, Gen. Johann von 311–12
Young, Desmond 302
Young, Judge John C. 274
Ypres 113

Zabern Affair 18–19
Zamosch 141
Zangen, Gen. Gustav von 205, 210,
  226
Zeebrugge 160
Zeitzler, Gen. Kurt 160, 164, 168, 200,
  310
Zhukov, Marshal Georgi 139, 143, 241
Zimmermann, Gen. Bodo 168, 172–3,
  176, 178, 189, 200, 203, 205, 219
Zossen 97